Living Wages Around the World

Living Wages Around the World

Manual for Measurement

Richard Anker

Senior Research Fellow, Political Economy Research Institute, University of Massachusetts, Amherst, USA, formerly of the International Labour Organization

Martha Anker

Independent Researcher, formerly of the World Health Organization and the School of Public Health and Health Sciences, University of Massachusetts, Amherst, USA

EE Edward Elgar PUBLISHING

Cheltenham, UK • Northampton, MA, USA

Published by
Edward Elgar Publishing Limited
The Lypiatts
15 Lansdown Road
Cheltenham
Glos GL50 2JA
UK

Edward Elgar Publishing, Inc.
William Pratt House
9 Dewey Court
Northampton
Massachusetts 01060
USA

A catalogue record for this book
is available from the British Library

Library of Congress Control Number: 2016949932

This book is available electronically in the **Elgar**online
Economics subject collection
DOI 10.4337/9781786431462

MIX
Paper from
responsible sources
FSC
www.fsc.org
FSC® C013056

ISBN 978 1 78643 145 5 (cased)
ISBN 978 1 78643 147 9 (paperback)
ISBN 978 1 78643 146 2 (eBook)

Typeset by Servis Filmsetting Ltd, Stockport, Cheshire
Printed and bound in Great Britain by TJ International Ltd, Padstow, Cornwall

Contents

Acknowledgments

There are many people and organizations to thank, because this manual is based on more than 10 years of work on measuring living wages. We would like to thank Tiffany and Company who we have worked with closely for close to 10 years and is committed to paying a living wage to workers in their diamond polishing factories in developing countries. They got us started on developing a methodology for estimating location-specific living wages.

We, of course, need to thank members of the Global Living Wage Coalition (GLWC) who we have worked closely with for the past three years on living wages (Fairtrade International, Forest Stewardship Council, GoodWeave International, Rainforest Alliance, Sustainable Agricultural Network, Social Accountability International, UTZ, and the ISEAL Alliance). These organizations had the vision and courage to include living wages in their standards and to work together on this. Their support has helped broaden and clarify our work on living wages and now to support an ever increasing number of living wage studies and estimates using our methodology. In particular, we would like to single out Wilbert Flinterman of Fairtrade International who first approached us to extend our methodology to products that Fairtrade certifies and to gain wider acceptance for this methodology. Our work on living wages and this manual have benefited greatly from his vision, advice, and support. We would also like to thank Michelle Bhattacharyya and Kristin Komives for their leadership of the GLWC, and members of the GLWC management group, which has included Oliver Bach, Rohini Barreto, Philip Chambers, Wilbert Flinterman, Mariecke van der Glas, Noura Hanna, Alex Katz, Zachary Kiarie, Biko Nagara, and Stephanie Wilson.

There are many people over the years whose insights and inputs we have benefited from and it is impossible to list them all. There are also the many excellent researchers from a score of countries from whom we continue to learn who have used or are currently using our methodology to estimate living wages for their country. We would like to thank Nicole Anker for her excellent work reviewing national laws on in kind benefits, and Philippe Hein who made insightful comments on an earlier draft of this manual.

Funding for this manual has come from the Dutch and German governments as well as from Fairtrade International, Forest Stewardship Council, Sustainable Agricultural Network, Rainforest Alliance, and UTZ.

Foreword

Does someone in your family have a job, and, if so, how much does it pay? For the overwhelming majority of the world's population, how one answers these two questions determines, more than anything else, what one's living standard will be. It follows that a fundamental determinant of human well-being in all countries throughout the world is whether the people who come to work every day, regardless of their occupation, are paid at least a living wage for their efforts. It also follows that creating an abundance of living wage jobs must be a centerpiece of any policy agenda that is genuinely committed to raising living standards for working people and the poor in all countries of the world.

But what exactly do we mean by the term 'living wage'? In his 1997 book *A Living Wage: American Workers and the Making of a Consumer Society*, the historian Lawrence Glickman writes that in the historical development of the living wage movement, supporters used the living wage concept to define a wage level that offers workers 'the ability to support families, to maintain self-respect, and to have both the means and the leisure to participate in the civic life of the nation.' (p. 66) This Glickman definition of a living wage bears a close correspondence with the ideas of the economist Amartya Sen on defining poverty relative to the achievement of what he calls 'capabilities' (for example, in his 2000 book *Development as Freedom*). These capabilities include such things as the ability to read and write, to lead a long and healthy life, to have freedom of movement, and to participate meaningfully in the civic life of the community.

Glickman and Sen provide us with important benchmarks. But they also still leave us with a formidable challenge: how can we translate their broad concepts into actual wage levels? What, in other words, is a wage level in, say, Nairobi, Kenya, or Veracruz, Mexico, that will enable workers in these places to support their families, to maintain self-respect, and to have the capability to participate meaningfully in the civic life of one's community?

Answering this question is the task that Richard Anker and Martha Anker have set for themselves in *Living Wages Around the World: Manual for Measurement*. My bottom-line assessment of their efforts is straightforward: they have been extremely successful. Their work can serve as a reliable and effective resource for establishing living wage standards in all countries and regions. Let me briefly convey some of the factors that have led me to this conclusion.

Anker and Anker begin their discussion by presenting a definition of living wages that does not fully encompass the broad vision conveyed by Glickman or Sen, but that nevertheless offers the major virtue of being workable. This definition, which has been adopted by the Global Living Wage Coalition, is as follows:

> Remuneration received for a standard work week by a worker in a particular place sufficient to afford a decent standard of living for the worker and her or his family. Elements of a decent standard of living include food, water, housing, education, health care, transport, clothing, and other essential needs, including provision for unexpected events. (Global Living Wage Coalition, 2016)

Working from this definition, they then develop a methodology that can measure what this level of remuneration needs to be. They show that their methodology can be applied in all country and regional settings. This holds even for situations, as will be common throughout the developing world, in which access to reliable statistics on costs of living and prevailing wage structures is limited. The first thing that makes their approach workable is that they use only three expenditure groups to estimate the costs of a basic but decent life style for a worker and her/his family: food, for a low-cost nutritious diet; housing, for basic healthy housing; and other essential expenses for a family, including education and health care. They then add a small margin for sustainability and emergencies. Within this simple framework, they then provide extensive detail on how to determine what constitutes decent consumption levels in each of these categories of necessities. Researchers can work within their framework to make effective use of large amounts of information on, for example, local food prices to generate an overall cost-of-living estimate. But their approach also enables researchers to produce reliable estimates even when only limited data are available. Having shown how to generate reliable regionally specific cost-of-living figures, Anker and Anker then guide readers through all the steps necessary to estimate a wage-rate figure that will constitute a living wage within any regional setting. They next explain how to measure prevailing wages in a region as well as the difference between the regional prevailing wage and their estimate of what should be the region's living wage standard. The last section offers suggestions on how to write a living wage report and to update their estimates over time.

Along the way, they tackle a wide range of important specific issues. These include: how to incorporate taxes and government support programs in establishing what the living wage standard should be; how to treat in kind payments as alternatives to wage payments; how to deal with the fact that jobs don't always offer people a standard 40-hour workweek; and how to incorporate agricultural work, in which payments are generally not provided in the form of hourly wages. They also walk readers through case studies based on their own projects over several years in Malawi, Kenya, the Dominican Republic and South Africa.

In short, *Living Wages Around the World* is detailed and rigorous while also being simple in its basics and eminently practical. As such, it is capable of effectively supporting wide-ranging efforts to bring higher living standards and greater justice to working people and their families in all regions and countries of the world.

Robert Pollin
Distinguished Professor of Economics and
Co-Director, Political Economy Research Institute (PERI)
University of Massachusetts-Amherst

1. Introduction

1 BACKGROUND

1.1 Living Wage is a Decent Wage

Decent work is not possible without decent wages.[1] Indeed, one of the first things, if not the first thing, workers want to know about a job is how much it pays – and with good reason since wages are the main determinant of the standard of living for the vast majority of people in paid employment in the world. It must never be forgotten that 'Necessitous men are not free men' (Roosevelt, 1944).

Living wage has become the accepted term in English for describing decent wages. Its translations in French ('*salaire decent*') and Spanish ('*salario digno*') according to Google Translate clearly express the fact that a living wage is a decent wage.

1.2 Recent Upsurge of Interest in and Acceptance of Living Wage

Living wage has captured the attention of workers, governments, employers, NGOs, international organizations and the body politic around the world in recent years. Minimum wage must equal '*salario digno*' in Ecuador because of its 2008 Constitution (Ecuador Ministry of Labor, 2015), and minimum wage in Vietnam must 'ensure minimal living needs of the employees and their families' because of the 2012 labor code (ILO, 2014a). The former Prime Minister of the United Kingdom David Cameron declared that a national living wage would become the law of the land for workers aged 25 and over, and more than 2,000 companies and organizations in the United Kingdom have become living wage companies (Living Wage Foundation, 2016). There are now well over 100 municipalities in the United States with living wage ordinances for government employees and contractors (Center on Wisconsin Strategy, 2013). Many corporations include living wage in their corporate codes of conduct for their worldwide supply chains. Many sustainability standard and certification organizations now include living wage in their codes of practice such as Fairtrade International (Fairtrade), Social Accountability International

(SAI), UTZ, Sustainable Agriculture Network (SAN), Rainforest Alliance (RA), Forestry Stewardship Council (FSC), and GoodWeave International (GoodWeave). Many trade unions call for payment of a living wage and use living wage as an organizing and public awareness tool such as IndustriALL and the International Textile, Garment and Leather Workers' Federation. Multi-stakeholder initiatives and government sponsored public-private partnership initiatives are underway on living wages such as the Ethical Trading Initiative (ETI), the Dutch Sustainable Trade Initiative (IDH), and the Ethical Tea Partnership (ETP).

1.3 Historical Background and Wide Acceptance of Idea of Living Wage

Living wage – the idea that workers should be paid a decent wage and not have to live in poverty – has such a long and distinguished history that it should be considered a mainstream idea, and in any case very far from a radical idea. Well-respected individuals, institutions and organizations have advocated payment of a living wage for hundreds of years. This includes Declarations of Human Rights; popes; presidents of countries; constitutions of countries; the International Labor Organization Constitution; academics famous for championing free market economics; industrialists; and codes of conduct of companies and certifying organizations. The following quotes give a flavor of the distinguished history of living wage. Many more quotes can be found in Anker (2011).

Adam Smith (1776):

> No society can surely be flourishing and happy, of which the far greater part of the members are poor and miserable. It is but equity, besides, that they who feed, clothe and lodge the whole body of the people should have such a share of the produce of their own labour as to be themselves tolerably well fed, clothed and lodged. . . . These necessaries and conveniences are: not only commodities which are indispensably necessary for the support of life, but whatever the custom of the country renders it indecent for creditable people, even of the lowest order, to be without. (Anker, 2011, p. 80)

Pope Leo XIII (1891):

> Remuneration must be enough to support the wage earner in reasonable and frugal comfort. If through necessity, or fear of a worse evil, the workman accepts harder conditions because an employer or contractor will give him no better, he is the victim of fraud and injustice. (Anker, 2011, p. 82)

ILO Constitution Preamble (1919):

> Whereas universal and lasting peace can be established only if it is based upon social justice; And whereas conditions of labour exist involving such injustice, hardship and privation to large numbers of people as to produce unrest so great that the peace and harmony of the world are imperilled; and an improvement of those conditions is urgently required; as, for example, by . . . the provision of an adequate living wage. (Anker, 2011, p. 69)

And ILO Philadelphia Declaration Annex to ILO Constitution (1944):

> Policies in regard to wages and earnings, hours and other conditions of work calculated to ensure a just share of the fruits of progress to all, and a minimum living wage to all employed and in need of protection. (Anker, 2011, p. 69)

John D. Rockefeller, twentieth-century industrialist cum robber baron (1921):

> The purpose of industry is quite as much to advance social well-being as material progress. . . . Every man is entitled to an opportunity to earn a living, to fair wage, to reasonable hours of work and proper working conditions, to decent home, to opportunity to play, to learn, to worship, and to love, as well as to toil, and that responsibility rests as heavily upon industry as upon government or society, to see that these conditions and opportunities prevail. (Anker, 2011, p. 80)

United Nations' Universal Declaration of Human Rights (1948):

> Everyone who works has the right to just and favorable remuneration ensuring for himself and his family an existence worthy of human dignity. (Anker, 2011, p. 67)

1.4 Need for Methodology and Manual to Measure Living Wages

Developing a methodology for measuring credible living wages/decent wages, especially for locations in developing countries, has motivated our work now for over a decade. See the next section for an indication of some of this work. We have dubbed the methodology we have developed the Anker methodology.

In doing this work, it became apparent that a manual was needed on how to measure credible living wages especially for developing countries and to write informative living wage reports that could lead to action on wages. We came to realize that our work on living wages was sufficiently innovative and useful that we needed to put our ideas and approaches down on paper so that others could use them. Although technical notes exist that describe other living wage methodologies, they are not comprehensive manuals. They are generally cryptic, provide weak justification for their methodology, and do not consider how to measure prevailing wages and so determine if workers receive a living wage. Hence this book.

There are, of course, other methodologies that have been used to measure living wage. Indeed, we reviewed and critically analyzed 26 living wage methodologies for ILO in 2011 (Anker, 2011). One conclusion of this review was that there was as yet no standard methodology for measuring living wage that could be recommended.

In our review, we found that methodologies for developing countries fell into three main types according to the type of data used. The most common methodology for developing countries uses country-specific data on household expenditures to measure living costs for two expense groups (food and all other costs) in the same way that national poverty lines are estimated by the World Bank (Ravaillon, 1998).[2] The use of only two expense groups and reliance on household expenditure survey data creates a number of serious problems for measuring a living wage. It means that: (i) transparency is lost because most living costs are included in an opaque black box (since the food share of household expenditure is usually less than 50% in developing countries and often well below 50% in urban areas); (ii) living cost estimates are often insufficient for decency in many developing countries (since they are based on current living conditions according to household survey data and these are less than decent in many developing countries); and (iii) it is very difficult to estimate separate credible living wages for rural and urban areas or different cities within countries (because housing costs are the important reason for differences in living costs within countries and they are subsumed within the very large non-food black box). Our living wage methodology improves on other common methodologies by estimating housing costs separately from other non-food costs. This allows us to ensure that workers can afford decent housing on a living wage as well as to estimate credible living wages for different areas and cities within countries. Common living wage methodologies for developing countries almost always assume that there are either one or two workers per family. Since neither assumption is realistic, our methodology estimates the number of workers per couple in a country and location that is appropriate for that country and location based on local male and female labor force participation rates, unemployment rates, and part-time employment rates of men and women.

Our 2011 ILO review found that living wage methodologies for developed countries are quite different, and generally better, than those for developing countries. Developed country methodologies tend to be better documented and more transparent regarding the living standard that could be afforded on a living wage. They use more expense groups (typically five or six), which is a big improvement over the two expense groups typically used in developing country methodologies. Costs of different expenses (e.g. model diet, two- or three-bedroom house, second-hand car, institutional child care, and health care) by city and state are generally taken from published data series.[3] A major problem with this approach for developing countries is that representative data series of different living expenses are not available for developing countries.[4] Our conclusion is that high income country living wage methodologies cannot be easily transported to developing countries. Credible living wage estimates for developing countries, we feel, require collection of primary data on prices and living costs in areas where workers live. It is for this reason that our methodology requires that new data be collected on local food prices, housing costs, health care costs, and education costs.

Our methodology was designed to correct for many of the problems of other living wage methodologies while keeping in mind data availability on living costs in developing countries. It was also designed so that living wage studies and estimates would be transparent and sufficiently descriptive to form the basis for stakeholder dialogue and action on wages. New and innovative aspects of our methodology are described in greater detail in Chapter 2. Some key principles of our methodology include:

- **Transparency**
  Our methodology clearly sets out its principles and assumptions and strongly recommends that these are indicated in living wage reports. This transparency enables stakeholders and others to understand, and have the possibility to question, the local standards and methods used to estimate the living wage and so what workers and their families could and could not afford if they earned a living wage.
- **Normative basis**
  Our methodology estimates living wage based on normative standards for nutritious food, healthy housing, adequate health care, and education of children through secondary school. Other methodologies for developing countries typically calculate a living wage based on cost of a model diet that only ensures sufficient calories and do not consider whether other aspects of proper nutrition are met nor do they consider whether workers can afford healthy housing, adequate health care, and education for their children.
- **Time and place-specific estimates**
  Our methodology calls for separate living wage estimates for rural and urban areas in all countries and for separate living wage estimates in major cities and regions in large countries. And living wages increase with economic development and rising incomes,

which makes them time and place-sensitive. This contrasts with other common methodologies for developing countries that typically estimate one living wage for each country.[5]

- **International comparability**
  Our living wage estimates are comparable between countries, because they are based on the same principles everywhere.
- **Practical and modest cost**
  Our methodology uses a judicious mix of secondary data analysis and primary data collection and analysis. This is because some relevant secondary data on living costs of workers in developing countries are not available. This approach is both practical and has modest cost while remaining sufficiently rigorous. Methods based exclusively on published data do not yield credible estimates for developing countries.
- **Prevailing wages and determining if workers receive a living wage**
  Our methodology develops principles and guidelines for measuring prevailing wages so that it is possible to compare them with a living wage and determine gaps between prevailing wages and a living wage. All forms of remuneration including in kind benefits and cash allowances are considered.
- **Living wage reports more than only a number**
  Living wage reports that use our methodology are expected to be much more than simply a number – the living wage estimate. They are expected to paint a picture of what it means to live on less than a living wage as well as how basic the living standard would be for workers who would earn a living wage. This type of report is important in our experience to starting and facilitating effective stakeholder dialogue and value chain dialogue and so to getting action on raising wages. Other typical living wage methodologies for developing countries are not clear about what it means to live on less than a living wage.

1.5 Extensive Acceptance and Experience with Anker Methodology

There is a good deal of experience in using our methodology in a wide range of locations. It was first developed to help a multinational corporation, Tiffany, with factories in urban areas in developing countries set wages, since it has a policy of paying its workers a living wage. This resulted in living wage estimates for nine countries. This work built on in particular the work we had done on estimating national living wages for countries using data from international databases (Anker, 2005) and our 30 years of experience in measuring poverty (e.g. Van der Hoeven and Anker, 1994;

Bilsborrow et al., 1998) and socio-economic, demographic and health phenomena (e.g. Anker and Anker, 1989; Anker, 1991). Our methodology was further extended and improved through work for members of the Global Living Wage Coalition (GLWC) who needed living wage estimates to audit their living wage standards (see Section 1.13). This meant that our methodology needed to be extended to rural areas since a number of GLWC members certify agricultural products, and that we needed to develop principles for measuring prevailing wages so that gaps between prevailing wages and a living wage could be measured.

To begin with, we undertook four living wage studies in agricultural areas of four developing countries (Dominican Republic, Kenya, Malawi, and South Africa) (see Anker and Anker, 2013a, 2013b, 2014 and 2014a).[6] The study that focused on the tea growing area of rural southern Malawi became a catalyst, following earlier work by Ethical Tea Partnership (ETP) and Oxfam (2013), for a large multi-stakeholder project whose aim is 'to achieve a competitive, profitable Malawi tea industry where workers earn a living wage and small holders are thriving by 2020' (ETP, 2015). This project brings together major multinational corporations (such as Unilever, Tata, Twinings, and Marks and Spencer), Tea Association of Malawi (TAML) and local tea estates, NGOs (such as Oxfam, ETP, Fairtrade International, Rainforest Alliance, and UTZ), and IDH public-private partnership sustainability trade initiative. We are on the wages committee for this project with the task of measuring and monitoring progress on wages. Currently, our methodology is being used by other researchers under our supervision for the GLWC to estimate living wages in 20 locations in 13 countries in Africa (Ethiopia, Tanzania), Asia (Bangladesh, China – six cities, India – rural Uttar Pradesh and urban Tamil Nadu, Pakistan, Sri Lanka, Vietnam – rural and urban), and Latin America (Brazil, Ecuador, Guatemala, Nicaragua, Mexico). Funders of these studies include GLWC members, major multinational corporations in garments, outdoor wear, supermarkets, seafood, and electronics (including EILEEN FISHER, Lidl, Superunie, Foppen, and a number of others that want to keep their names confidential) and the Dutch and German governments. Living wage estimates from these studies will be used by members of the GLWC to help implement their living wage standard and multinational corporations to evaluate wages in their supply chain. All of these studies will be made publically available in the hope that studies will lead to improvement of wages. It is with the above backdrop that we have written this manual, so that other researchers and the GLWC will be able to use our methodology to undertake living wage studies and estimate living wages for their country and location.

1.6 Consensus on the Definition of a Living Wage

Our 2011 ILO review of living wage descriptions, definitions and methodologies (Anker 2011) found a consensus about what constitutes a living wage. This review concluded that there is general agreement that a living wage: (i) is a right according to the international community; (ii) needs to be sufficient to support a basic but decent standard of living that is appropriate for a particular time and place and that improves with economic development; (iii) needs to be sufficient to support a family; (iv) needs to be increased to take into consideration payroll and income taxes to ensure sufficient take home pay and so sufficient disposable income; and (v) needs to be earned in normal working time and not require overtime.

This consensus is reflected in the definition of a living wage agreed to by the GLWC and is the definition used in this manual.

> Remuneration received for a standard work week by a worker in a particular place sufficient to afford a decent standard of living for the worker and her or his family. Elements of a decent standard of living include food, water, housing, education, health care, transport, clothing, and other essential needs including provision for unexpected events. (Global Living Wage Coalition, 2016)

It is worth noting that there has been a change in the four years since our 2011 review of living wage methodologies in the extent of agreement on the definition of a living wage. In 2011 despite the fact we found that there was a consensus of what is a living wage based on the more than 60 descriptions of living wages that we looked at, we also found many examples of companies that said that they would not consider doing anything about raising wages because there was no agreed definition of a living wage. Now, several years later, one does not hear this excuse for inaction on living wages very often, and there now appears to be a broad consensus on the definition of a living wage.

1.7 Living Wage and Subjectivity/Judgment

One oft-mentioned criticism of living wage estimates is that they require judgment (i.e. are partly subjective) and therefore cannot be definitively measured, since reasonable people can differ about what living standard they think a living wage should be able to support. While it is important to recognize that measurement of a living wage does require judgment and that a living wage cannot be measured with precision down to the dollar or peso, we believe that living wages can be measured with sufficient precision to be useful. This view was expressed well more than 100 years ago in a book entitled *A Living Wage* (Ryan, 1906, quoted in Anker, 2011, pp. 11–12) (bold added for emphasis):

> The question naturally arises, what precisely does this [living wage] imply in terms of goods and money? Unless an attempt is made to answer it, the whole discussion of wage-rights and obligations remains too abstract, too vague to be of practical value. . . . **Evidently the question before us cannot be answered with absolute precision. . . . There remains the supreme difficulty of translating 'reasonable comfort' into more concrete terms**. In all probability the individual estimates of no body of men no matter how competent and well-meaning, would be in entire agreement. And no prudent person would assert that a slight deduction from the amount that he regards as certainly sufficient for a decent livelihood would render the remainder certainly insufficient. . . . Nevertheless, the question **[what is a living wage] can be answered with sufficient definiteness to safeguard the human dignity of the laborer and his family, and that is all that anyone cares to know**. We can distinguish twilight from darkness, although we cannot identify the precise moment when one merges into the other. Though we cannot say just when artificial light becomes more effective than that of the waning day, we usually call it into service before the approaching darkness proves inconvenient. Thus it is with the living wage. Some rates of remuneration we know to be certainly adequate and others to be no less certainly inadequate. While we may not be able to put our finger on the precise point of the descending scale at which the rate ceases to be sufficient, we can approximate it in such a way that the resulting inaccuracy will not produce notable inconvenience.

Subjectivity is not an obstacle to acceptance of economic concepts. Many widely accepted and useful economic concepts are based in part on subjectivity including Gross Domestic Product (GDP), unemployment, and poverty. GDP per capita is a widely accepted measure of economic wellbeing of a country. GDP is the sum of the value of all goods and services produced by 'economic activity' in a country. Yet the definition of economic activity is subjective (Anker and Anker, 1989). Unpaid work on a family farm is included, but unpaid housework, child care, care for the elderly and voluntary work are excluded. It has been estimated that unpaid household work is worth close to one-half of measured GDP (Goldschmidt-Clermont, 1982 and 1987). This definition of economic activity, and so GDP and GDP per capita, clearly represents a male-oriented view of work. Also, GDP does not distinguish between 'good' outputs and 'bad' outputs, so that in a strange twist, GDP per capita is increased by pollution even though it reduces welfare.

Unemployment rate is also partly subjective. It is based on responses to survey questions about economic activity, availability for work, and whether actively looking for work in the past week. The definition of economic activity is subjective (see above), and someone without work who would like to work but stopped actively looking for work because the job market is very poor would not be considered to be unemployed. S/he would be considered a so-called discouraged worker who had exited the labor force. Despite substantial subjectivity, changes in unemployment rates move financial markets and topple governments.

The above discussion demonstrates that subjectivity and judgment are not insurmountable obstacles to acceptance of economic concepts and their measurement. At the same time, it is also clear that for economic concepts to be widely accepted and used, clear rules and transparency are required. This manual is intended to help provide clear standards, rules and transparency for measuring a living wage.

1.8 Minimum Wage and Living Wage are Not the Same

Minimum wage and living wage have similar objectives – ensure that full-time workers do not live in poverty. Therefore, it is not surprising that many people think of minimum wage and living wage as similar or the same thing. This confusion is reinforced when governments use the term living wage to describe their minimum wage such as the United Kingdom, and the ILO in its Philadelphia Declaration Annex to the ILO Constitution uses both 'minimum' and 'living' when it states that workers should receive 'a minimum living wage.'

Minimum wages and living wages are, however, quite different in practice. First of all, minimum wage is a legal construct with the force of law. Employers must pay at least the minimum wage or be subject to fines and other legal enforcement measures. Living wage, in contrast, is almost always voluntary. Employers are not forced to pay a living wage by government excepting in the few countries and cities where the distinction between minimum wage and living wage has become blurred.[7] Second, minimum wage and living wage are set or estimated in different ways. Minimum wage is set by government that balances two competing objectives – a desire to reduce poverty and provide for the needs of workers and their families through work (aka living wage) and a desire to stimulate employment and economic growth. As indicated in Article 3 of ILO Convention 131 (Minimum Wage Fixing) (1970), two factors should 'be taken into consideration in determining the level of minimum wages' (although the ILO Committee of Experts for the International Labour Conference in 1992 stated that 'the fundamental and ultimate objective is to ensure to workers a minimum wage that will provide a satisfactory standard of living for them and their families' (ILO, 1992, p. 162)):

> (a) the needs of workers and their families, taking into account the general level of wages in the country, the cost of living, social security benefits, and the relative living standards of other social groups; and
>
> (b) economic factors, including the requirements of economic development, levels of productivity and the desirability of attaining and maintaining a high level of employment.

This means that a minimum wage is set in a political process and so can be set at any level with the relative power of employers and workers playing an important role.[8] A minimum wage could be set at so low a level that minimum wage workers live in poverty. Or, a minimum wage could be set at such a high level that many employers evade the law and consequently many workers have no choice but to work in the informal sector. We do not address how high countries should set their minimum wage, or whether minimum wages should equal a living wage.

Living wage, in contrast, is typically estimated based on research to estimate the cost of a basic acceptable living standard. Since this living standard should be normative-based, it is theoretically insulated from political considerations and the relative power of workers and employers. Living wage is only concerned with worker needs, that is, only with part (a) of the ILO minimum wage convention.

One objective of this manual is help ensure that governments, stakeholders, and the public have credible living wage estimates available so that discussions and the ultimate decision on where to set a minimum wage take into consideration element (a) in the ILO Minimum Wage Convention.

1.9 Manual Goes Beyond Estimating Living Wage to Developing Principles for Estimating Prevailing Wages and Determining Gaps between Prevailing Wages and a Living Wage

Living wages need to be looked at in context relative to prevailing wages to understand what raising current wages to a living wage might mean for workers and employers. The situation is obviously not the same when a living wage is 10% higher than prevailing wages compared with when it is 100% higher. It is also important to know whether prevailing wages have increased or decreased in the past decade taking inflation into account and so if workers are under increasing pressure to make ends meet. The situation for workers is quite different when workers' real wages have been falling compared with when they have been increasing. To address these issues, this manual develops principles and guidelines for measuring prevailing wages so that they can be compared to a living wage. This includes guidelines on how to treat and value all forms of remuneration (e.g. in kind benefits, cash allowances, and overtime pay). The intention is for researchers to use these guidelines to determine typical prevailing wages in an industry and therefore gaps to a living wage in order to inform discussions with companies, workers, and the value chain and develop action plans to raise wages in the industry. Auditors can also use these guidelines to compare wages in specific establishments to a living wage.

1.10 Manual is More than Only a How to Do It Document

This manual is a comprehensive document. It covers all aspects of estimating a living wage, determining prevailing wages and gaps to a living wage, and writing of a living wage report. It also provides background information and provides documentation on national and international standards, and justifies why a particular approach is used. How to estimate each component of a living wage is explained. This is followed by illustrative examples of how to do this. In short, this manual is more than simply a how to do it document.

1.11 Living Wage Reports should be More than Simply a Number

We believe that it is important for living wage reports to be more than simply a detailed description and reporting of a number – the living wage estimate. Our feeling is that living wage reports should tell a story and paint a picture of what it means for workers and their families to live on less than a living wage as well as how basic is the standard of living afforded by a living wage. This includes embedding photos of local housing and local markets as they are quite effective in illustrating what the situation is in a location, especially for international readers without much knowledge of the local situation. Although the main reason for this manual and purpose of living wage studies and reports is to estimate credible living wages and indicate gaps from prevailing wages, we feel that it is important for living wage reports to bring readers on a journey of understanding of workers' lives and their possible need for higher wages. In this way, it is more likely that employers, governments and others will be convinced of the need for higher wages and perhaps earning of at least a living wage.

1.12 Multinational Companies need Widely Accepted and Credible Living Wage Methodology and Estimates

Many multinational companies are interested in the wages and living conditions of workers in their global supply chain. This includes multinationals with their own factories, farms or offices; multinationals that subcontract from factories, farms or offices where they influence how products are made; and multinationals that procure products and services without being involved in their production.[9] To implement a living wage policy or a policy of increasing wages in their supply chain, such companies need credible living wage estimates so that they have an idea of the dimensions of possible wage problems and so financial implications of committing to payment of a living wage. This is how the world works today – numeric targets are needed. This means that a credible methodology and credible living wage estimates are important for progress to be made with the involvement of multinationals.

1.13 Commitment to Living Wage of Eight Organizations Involved with Certification and Standard Setting for Corporate Social Responsibility

Work on living wage was significantly moved forward when eight organizations involved with certification and standard setting for corporate responsibility came together in 2013 to work on living wage (Fairtrade International, Forest Stewardship Council, GoodWeave International, ISEAL Alliance, Sustainable Agriculture Network, Rainforest Alliance, Social Accountability International, and UTZ). We have been closely collaborating with this group since its inception. 'The long term goal and shared mission of our organizations is to seek improvements in workers' conditions, including wage levels, in the farms, factories and supply chains participating in our respective certification systems and beyond' (Global Living Wage Coalition, 2016). The group is now known as the Global Living Wage Coalition (GLWC). This collaboration enabled these organizations to agree to include a living wage clause in their codes of practice with a common living wage definition (see above); to use the Anker living wage methodology described in this manual to measure living wage; and to jointly sponsor living wage studies in many countries.

1.14 Living Wage and Living Income

There is a growing interest in livelihoods of small farmers and so in the measurement of living income of small holder households. This interest is similar in many ways to the interest in living wage. Both are concerned with living standards of workers and whether earnings from work are sufficient for workers and their families to be able to afford a decent standard of living – in one case for small farmers and small business owners (living income) and in the other case for employees (living wage). This means that measurement of living income and living wage have in common the need to know the cost of a basic but acceptable living standard for a family. Since this cost is the same for all families in a location regardless of employment status, living wage studies based on our methodology can be used by living income studies to measure the cost of a decent living standard for families. This is currently being done for a living income study in Malawi. Indeed, partly for this reason, this manual has been structured so that a living wage study (Section I of this manual) can be used for a living income study and estimate.

1.15 Many Other Uses of a Living Wage Manual and Credible Living Wage Estimates

This manual is intended for researchers to enable them to estimate a credible living wage for their country and write an informative report about the life and living conditions of typical workers. There are many uses for credible living wage estimates and this manual in addition to those discussed above such as for multinational companies and standard setting organizations.

- Governments interested in setting appropriate minimum wages; estimating realistic poverty lines; formulating policies for reducing poverty, income inequality, and improving livelihoods of small producers and businesses; and improving labor clauses in international trade agreements.
- Trade unions interested in improved wage negotiations and collective bargaining agreements; and public awareness raising campaigns on wages and needs of workers.
- International organizations such as United Nations, UNDP, ILO, FAO, UNICEF, and the World Bank interested in improving advice to governments, trade unions, employers, NGOs, and the public; improving measurement of decent work to better monitor Millennium Development Goals; improving measurement of poverty; and improving setting of minimum wages and programs for poverty alleviation, trade union development, and livelihoods.
- Third World factories, offices and farms interested in attracting business from multinational companies; increasing productivity and reducing production cost by reducing labor turnover, recruiting better quality workers, reducing rejection rates, and increasing worker commitment and effort; and reducing number of strikes, work slowdowns, and labor unrest.
- Researchers, NGOs, and others interested in issues related to wages, livelihoods, poverty, labor markets, inequality, and trade unions and worker rights.

- The public interested in information on differences in living costs of different cities and areas.

1.16 Manual Outline

This manual is presented in four sections. Section I describes how to estimate the cost of a basic but acceptable living standard for a worker and his or her family in a particular location. Section II describes how to estimate a living wage once cost of a basic but decent living standard is known. Section III describes how to estimate prevailing wages and gaps to a living wage. Section IV provides suggestions on how to write a living wage report and update a living wage estimate in the future.

We have developed various tools to assist researchers in estimating a living wage. This includes an Excel program to determine required number of calories, and an Excel program to develop an appropriate model diet for a location. These are described in this manual and are available at https://www.e-elgar.com/living-wages-around-the-world-companion-site. The manual also contains data collection forms and dummy tables.

NOTES

1. 'Decent work for all' became the organizing framework and principal objective of the ILO in 1999. In 2008, decent work became part of the United Nations Millennium Development Goal Target 1B. In 2015, decent work and the four pillars of the Decent Work Agenda became integral elements of the 2030 Agenda for Sustainable Development of the United Nations.
2. One other type of methodology for developing countries estimates living wage using information on the spending and demographics of workers in specific factories. This type of methodology is not acceptable because there cannot be a different living wage for every factory and have that depend on the spending and demographic composition of employees in the factory, since this could lead to discrimination based on age, sex, marital status, family size, and work participation of spouses. This could set in motion a race to the bottom as regards wages. An additional problem of this type of methodology is that its living wage estimates would replicate current living conditions of factory workers, which are very often very poor at present. Another type of methodology for developing countries estimates a living wage for one country and uses this estimate to extrapolate to living wage estimates for all countries. This type of methodology is not acceptable, because living conditions, prices, spending patterns, labor markets, and demographics differ greatly across countries.
3. Accuracy of these data sets is not questioned. When a secondary data series does not exist for a variable, methodologies such as EPI and MIT living wage calculators for the United States use the same value for every city and area in the United States. For example, both assume that food costs are identical in every city and area in the United States.
4. Wage Indicator Foundation tries to get around this problem by generating its own data series of living expenses for each country and city by asking visitors to their website to fill in an online questionnaire about the cost of food, housing, transport, etc. But since visitors to their website are typically higher income persons (and not often typical workers),

the prices and living cost data collected are generally too high and not representative for typical workers in these countries.

5. The Asian Floor Wage goes further and uses one living wage for all of Asia in terms of purchasing power.
6. This has also included background papers that looked at Engel's Law for 207 countries (Anker, 2011a) and at in kind benefits as partial payment of living wages in national laws for 162 countries (Anker and Anker, 2015).
7. For example, the United Kingdom is expected to call its minimum wage a living wage even though it is not really a living wage. Many municipal living wage ordinances in the United States were set in a political process. (Luce, 2004).
8. Arbitrariness of minimum wages is illustrated by the fact that the ratio of minimum wage to average wage in Asia ranged from 23% in India to 91% in Philippines and in Latin America this ratio ranged from 27% in Mexico and Nicaragua to 97% in Paraguay according to ILO (2008a). In Bangladesh, the minimum wage for garment workers nearly doubled overnight in 2010 going from Taka1,662 to Taka3,000 (BBC News, 2010).
9. There are, in addition, many others (such as governments, airlines, universities) that procure products without getting involved in how products are produced.

2. Overview of the Anker living wage methodology

PART I. BACKGROUND

This manual describes how to estimate a living wage using the Anker methodology. There are many new aspects to this methodology. The current chapter provides a brief description of the methodology, and what is new and different about it compared with other common methodologies for developing countries. Table 2A.1 in Appendix 2.1 provides a summary of the primary and secondary data needed to estimate a living wage using this methodology.

Some key features of the methodology that make it practical, realistic, and an improvement on other methodologies for developing countries include the following (see Anker, 2011 for a review of other living wage methodologies).

- Greater use is made of normative standards than other typical living wage methodologies for developing countries.
- Transparency is emphasized with assumptions and calculations clearly indicated in a living wage report so that it is more than simply a number.
- Judicious mix is made of rapid assessment methods and secondary data to make it possible to estimate credible, location-specific living wages in a practical way.
- Low-cost nutritious model diet is developed that is consistent with local food habits and WHO/FAO nutrition guidelines to ensure that there are sufficient calories and acceptable amounts of proteins, fats, carbohydrates, and fruits and vegetables. This is done using Excel programs developed for this purpose.
- Cost of the model diet is estimated using local food prices collected through a new survey of local food markets that mimics the way that cost-conscious workers buy food.
- Housing costs are estimated separately using a local healthy housing standard that is established based on international minimum standards and local housing conditions with the cost of such housing determined based on visits to local housing.

- Secondary data are used to estimate the cost of all other essential needs, and are carefully scrutinized and adjusted as necessary. This result is checked against new primary data on local health care and education costs collected using rapid assessment methods to help ensure that the living wage includes sufficient funds for these human rights.
- Family size and number of workers per family used to estimate a living wage are location-specific as they are determined based on secondary data for the location.
- Separate living wages are estimated for rural and urban areas rather than using one living wage for an entire country. In larger countries, separate estimates are made for different regions and major cities.
- Provision of social goods by the state is allowed to reduce the living wage. For example, when free meals are provided at school, the cost of the living wage model diet is reduced because fewer meals need to be prepared at home. The post checks on health care and education are affected by the cost, quality and availability of public services.
- Mandatory payroll deductions and income tax are taken into consideration to ensure that workers have sufficient take home pay to be able to afford a basic but decent standard of living.
- Guidelines are provided on how to measure prevailing wages so that they can be compared with a living wage and so learn if workers receive a living wage and employers pay a living wage. This includes detailed guidelines on how to value in kind benefits and cash allowances.

PART II. DESCRIPTION OF LIVING WAGE METHODOLOGY

2.1 How a Living Wage is Estimated

2.1.1 Estimating cost of a basic but decent living standard for a reference size family

Estimating a living wage begins by estimating the cost of a basic but decent life style for a worker and his/her family. This involves adding up the cost of three expenditure groups: food (for a low-cost nutritious diet), housing (for basic healthy housing), and other essential expenses for a family, and then adding a small margin for sustainability and emergencies. This is illustrated in Figure 2.1.

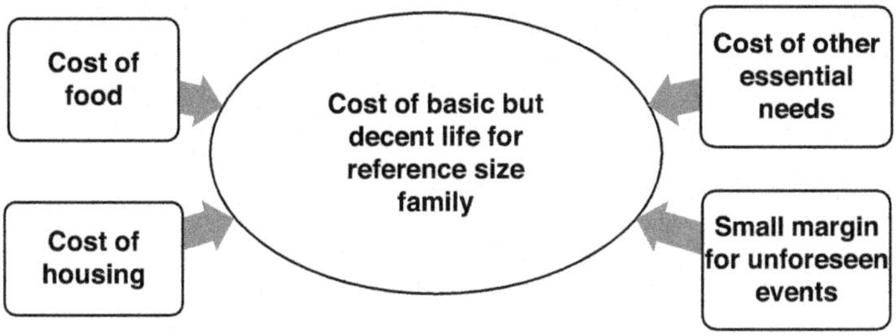

Figure 2.1 Cost of a basic but decent life for a family

Figure 2.2 From cost of basic but decent life to net living wage

Figure 2.3 From net living wage to gross living wage

2.1.2 Going from cost of a basic but decent life to a net living wage

The next step defrays the cost of a basic but decent life for the reference size family over the number of workers per reference size family (Figure 2.2), which is always between one and two full-time workers per couple, and which depends on local conditions as regards labor force participation rates, unemployment rates, and part-time employment rates.

2.1.3 Going from net living wage to gross living wage

The gross pay required for workers to have sufficient take home pay is calculated by adding statutory payroll deductions and income tax that would be assessed on a living wage (Figure 2.3). Workers need to end up with sufficient take home pay to afford a basic but decent standard of living.

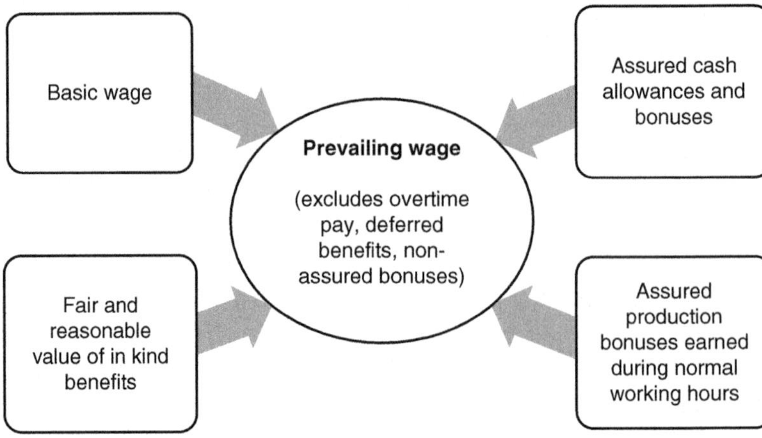

Figure 2.4 Determining prevailing wage in an establishment or industry and so if workers are paid a living wage

2.1.4 Determining prevailing wages and whether workers are paid a living wage

Estimating a living wage provides one side of an equation for comparing current wages with a living wage and determining if workers earn a living wage. The other side of the equation is prevailing wages earned during normal working hours (Figure 2.4).

Determining prevailing wages is not as simple as it may seem at first glance because remuneration comes in many different forms. Prevailing wages are determined by adding up the value of all forms of remuneration using guidelines described in this manual regarding which forms of remuneration should be included and how each of these should be valued for comparison with a living wage. Some forms of remuneration such as overtime and deferred benefits are excluded. Special rules are provided for how to value in kind benefits because of their controversial nature.

2.2 Use of Three Main Costs – a Practical but Rigorous Approach

As illustrated in Figure 2.1, the cost of a basic but decent life is estimated using three expense components – food, housing, and other essential needs. A small margin is added for sustainability and unforeseen events. The use of three cost components to estimate a living wage is a practical compromise between listing and pricing the cost of each and every family need, as was common 100 years ago, and the use of two cost components (food and other essential needs) as is common in most other living wage and poverty line estimates today for developing countries. The main disadvantages of the first approach are that it is very time consuming to create such a list and virtually impossible to obtain agreement on the necessity and quality of each and every item. The main disadvantage of the second approach is that the 'other essential needs' category has no normative basis despite the fact that it almost always represents well over one-half of all expenditures and this makes it impossible to understand what standard of living is implied by a living wage or whether it is even close to being decent.

Our methodology, which estimates housing costs separately, is a compromise between the two approaches noted above. It has several important advantages. First, directly estimating the cost of housing based on a housing standard, significantly increases the normative basis of the living wage estimate. It ensures that workers can afford decent housing. Second, it greatly decreases the size of the opaque 'other essential needs' category. This helps stakeholders and others to understand the basic but decent standard of living that the living wage is based on. Our methodology also uses post checks with adjustments when necessary to ensure that decent education and medical care can be afforded on a living wage.

2.2.1 Estimating food cost using a low-cost nutritious diet and local food prices

Food is almost always the largest expense in developing countries for a worker and his/her family. For this reason, a good deal of attention is paid in our methodology to developing an appropriate model diet and estimating its cost. Food costs are based on the cost of a low-cost nutritious model diet that is in keeping with local food preferences. Key features of our methodology for estimating food costs include:

1. The model diet must meet FAO and WHO nutritional guidelines as regards calories, macronutrients, and fruits and vegetables. Almost all other living wage and poverty line methodologies for developing countries use a model diet that only ensures sufficient calories.
2. Two Excel spreadsheets were developed (and are available on the Edward Elgar website) to assist researchers in creating an appropriate model diet that is nutritious, consistent with local food preferences, and relatively inexpensive for a nutritious diet.
3. The cost of the model diet is estimated using local food prices that workers typically pay. These food prices are determined based on a new survey of local markets where workers typically shop.

2.2.2 Estimating housing costs using international healthy housing standards, local housing conditions, and local housing costs

Housing is usually the second largest expense for a worker and family in developing countries. Housing costs are estimated separately. This is in contrast to most other living wage and poverty line methodologies for developing countries that estimate all non-food costs (including housing) in one go. In our methodology, a local standard for healthy housing is set based on international and national standards, and local housing conditions. The cost of renting a dwelling that meets this basic standard is then estimated based on visits to a range of acceptable and unacceptable rental homes in the location.[1]

There are many advantages to this approach including:

1. Ensuring that workers can afford decent housing on a living wage (in contrast other typical methods for developing countries usually replicate the current poor housing conditions many workers now have). This also makes it much easier to estimate different living wages within countries, because housing is almost always the main reason for differences in living costs across locations within countries.
2. Increasing transparency, since a living wage is based on normative standards for food and housing which are the two largest expenditure groups in developing countries and almost always well over half of all expenditures.

2.2.3 Estimating other essential expenses using secondary data

While the estimate of both food and housing costs (usually the two largest household expenses in developing countries) are based on normative standards, it would be too difficult and time consuming to estimate the cost of all other expenses using normative standards, because this would require listing and obtaining agreement on each and every item needed by a family as regards quantities and qualities. Nor would this be practical. Therefore, our methodology relies primarily on secondary data from a recent household expenditure survey to estimate the cost of other essential expenses.

The cost of other essential expenses is estimated by multiplying the ratio of non-food and non-housing expenditures to food expenditures from a recent household expenditure survey by the cost of the living wage model diet. This is a simple, quick and practical way to estimate the cost of other essential expenses and is similar to the typical approach used by other living wage and poverty line methodologies for developing countries to estimate all non-food costs. However, there are some major differences.

1. First, and most importantly, the 'other essential expenses' component in our methodology is much smaller than in most other typical methodologies for developing countries, because ours does not include housing. This increases the extent to which our living wage estimate is based on normative standards. This also increases cross-country comparability because national statistical offices differ in how they measure housing expenditure, with somewhat less than half the countries totally ignoring the cost or value of owner-occupied housing.
2. Second, our methodology closely scrutinizes how the household expenditure data used to estimate 'other essential needs' are classified and measured and makes adjustments whenever necessary. This is important because there are differences in how countries measure and classify household expenditure data, and these can affect the non-food/ non-housing to food ratio used to estimate other essential needs.
3. Third, amounts for health care and education included in a preliminary estimate of the cost of other essential needs are checked against information on the cost of decent education and health care collected in new fieldwork, with amounts for these increased when necessary.

2.2.3.1 Post checks for health care and education Health care and education are considered as human rights around the world. For this reason, they are given special attention in our methodology to make sure that sufficient amounts are included in the living wage estimate for decent education of children and health care. This has the advantage of further increasing the normative basis of a living wage estimate as well as its transparency. There are two main steps to these post checks:

1. First, information is collected in new fieldwork on the local cost of acceptable education and health care.
2. Second, costs of decent education and health care according to this new fieldwork are compared with amounts included for them in the preliminary estimate of non-food and non-housing costs with amounts for these increased when necessary.

2.3 Adding Small Margin for Sustainability and Unforeseen Events

A small margin is added to the cost of food, housing and other essential needs to allow for unforeseen events. This small margin is included in our methodology to ensure that workers earning a living wage are not easily plunged into poverty from which they may never be able to get out by unforeseen events such as accident or illness.

2.4 Reference Family Size

Determining the reference family size to be supported by a living wage is very important because a living wage is a family wage. Our methodology allows reference family size to vary by country and location depending on average household size and total fertility rate and child mortality rate in the location, with different reference family sizes for rural and urban areas common.

2.5 Number of Workers per Family

Most other living wage methodologies for developing countries assume either one or two workers per family (Anker, 2011). Neither assumption is realistic in the twenty-first century. First, many women are in the labor force all over the world, so the assumption of one (usually male) bread-winner per family is not realistic. Second, not all adult family members work full-time – some are unable to find work, some need or want to stay home for various reasons, and some work part-time. This means that an assumption of two full-time workers per family is not realistic. Therefore, the number of workers per family in our methodology is always between one and two. Our methodology allows the number of workers per family to vary by country and location based on labor force participation rates, unemployment rates, and part-time employment rates.

2.6 Statutory Deductions from Pay: Gross Pay and Net Pay

Up to this point, a living wage estimate was concerned with the income that a family needs for a basic but decent life. This is the disposable income or take home pay required. Yet, workers in most countries (even workers with low pay) have statutory payroll deductions (e.g. social security taxes, contributions to national health systems, union fees) and sometimes income taxes to pay. Therefore, in order for workers to have enough net pay (after deductions), statutory deductions that would be assessed to workers earning a living wage need to be added to the net living wage estimate to get a gross living wage estimate. Other living wage methodologies for developing countries do not always address this issue. Our experience indicates that it is important to explicitly take into consideration statutory deductions from pay – otherwise they are too easily forgotten.

2.7 Need for More than One Living Wage per Country

Cost of a basic but decent life style is different for rural and urban areas in almost all countries. Housing costs are often very different, as are the patterns of expenses. Therefore, it is not reasonable to have one living wage estimate applied to an entire country. There should be at a minimum separate living wages for rural and urban areas. Larger countries require separate living wage estimates for different regions and for different major cities.

2.8 Estimating Prevailing Wages and Gaps to a Living Wage

Determining the gap between prevailing wages and a living wage is often the most important reason for doing a living wage study. Companies, standard setting organizations, governments, trade unions, international organizations, NGOs and the public are interested in knowing this gap.

Our living wage methodology separates the task of estimating a living wage from the task of determining prevailing wages and so whether a living wage is paid in an industry or by an employer and the size of the gap between prevailing wages and a living wage. Guidelines are provided on how to measure prevailing wages for comparison to a living wage. This is not as straightforward as it might seem, because remuneration has many components (e.g. basic wage, cash allowances and bonuses, productivity bonuses, overtime, fringe benefits, and in kind benefits). Some forms of remuneration are excluded such as overtime (because one aspect of the definition of a living wage is that it should be earned in normal working time) and deferred benefits (because they are not available to pay for on-going living expenses). Special rules are provided for how to value in kind benefits because of their controversial nature. Information on wages disaggregated by form of remuneration is often obtainable from a CBA or from cooperating establishments. Information on average wages is almost always available from secondary sources for industries and occupations. Although average wages are rarely exactly comparable to a living wage, they are nevertheless useful to put the living wage in context.

2.9 Selecting Study Location(s) for a Living Wage Estimate Balancing Need for Place-specific Living Wage and Advantages of Generalizable Living Wage

Because living wage study budgets are limited, it is necessary to select areas for primary data collection judiciously. The decision on where to collect primary data on food prices and housing costs needs to balance the need for (i) a living wage to be place-specific, (ii) advantages of being able to generalize a living wage estimate to larger areas, and (iii) limited budgets for fieldwork. It is neither practical nor desirable to have a different living wage for every small area or neighborhood, partly because workers can commute to work and partly because of implication for study costs. In addition, secondary data are usually only available for large areas such as all rural areas or all urban areas. It should always be kept in mind that a living wage is the same for all workers in a geographic area and it is not situational and does not vary by establishment.

To decide on where to collect local area primary data, researchers should start by drawing a map of the study area or city and indicate on it where factories or farms are concentrated, along with number of factories and number of workers in each location. Such information can be obtained from local key informants, establishment registers, standard setting organizations, and sponsors of a living wage study. Based on this information, discussions with sponsoring agencies and key informants and possibly a scoping visit, the researcher should select the geographic area or areas for primary data collection that best reflect and represent living costs for typical workers. Once a geographic area or areas are selected, specific locations to collect primary data on food prices and housing costs should be purposefully selected.

2.9.1 Selecting study locations for industries that produce agricultural commodities

Agricultural commodities such as tea, coffee, cocoa, etc. are generally grown over very large geographic regions. Primary data should be collected in regions that are typical of the larger geographical area in which the commodity is produced, so that the living wage estimate is representative of the area as a whole. In Malawi, we collected primary data in two large districts in Southern Malawi where most tea plantations are located. In Kenya, we collected primary data in the area around Lake Naivasha where most flower farms are located. In South Africa where the wine grape growing area covers several hundred kilometers, we selected a single typical area that was considered by local key informants as having typical prices and living costs for the wine grape growing region.

2.9.2 Selecting study locations for factories and industries

Export-oriented factories in developing countries are generally concentrated in particular areas of cities, often in industrial zones located in the city outskirts where costs are lower. This means that living costs for factory workers are usually lower than living costs for the city as a whole and especially for the city center.

A living wage for factory workers should be based on local food and housing costs for areas that are representative of where factory workers live with two provisos. Locations should be within reasonable commuting distance, and slums should be excluded because they are not decent places to live. For example, many garment factories in Dhaka, Bangladesh, are concentrated in the Mirpur district of Dhaka and in separate satellite cities in the greater metropolitan area. Electronics factories in Shanghai are located in the outskirts of the city. Factories in Santo Domingo, Phnom Penh, Nagpur, and a second tier city in Vietnam where we have estimated living wages are concentrated in industrial zones just outside each of these cities with workers generally commuting short distances. In Johannesburg, we found that factory workers commuted from separate townships such as Soweto that are themselves separate cities as Soweto has more than 1 million persons. These examples illustrate that there is considerable variation across countries and cities in where factories are located and factory workers live.

NOTE

1. In locations where rental markets are not well developed, such as in many rural areas, the user cost of owner-occupied housing is used to estimate local housing costs.

APPENDIX 2.1

Table 2A.1 Use of primary and secondary data for estimating a living wage

Cost	Use of primary and secondary data
Food costs	
1. Required number of calories	Secondary data Excel living wage calorie calculator program is used (based on WHO equations). Inputs are needed on average adult height (secondary data), reference family size (see below), and assumptions of physical activity levels of adults and children.
2. Model diet	Primary and secondary data Excel living wage model diet program is used. Primary data Local market survey (see below) to determine food prices and identify common low-cost foods to represent each food group in model diet. Secondary data Other model diets and/or reported food consumption (e.g. from poverty line, nutritionists, household surveys, FAOSTAT); nutritional content and percentage inedible of each food; percentage distribution of food expenditure from another source used only as a check on the model diet.
3. Local food prices	Primary and secondary data Primary data Local food market survey. Secondary data Monthly food price data from another source and research articles to determine possible seasonality of food prices.
Housing costs	
1. Local housing standard	Primary and secondary data Secondary data International minimum standards, local housing conditions from household surveys and registers, and local housing standards from governments and NGOs. Primary data Discussions with workers and key informants to possibly modify local housing standard.
2. Cost of acceptable local housing	
a. Rent	Primary data Rent for acceptable local housing or user cost of owner-occupied housing in locations with small rental market.

Table 2A.1 (continued)

Cost	Use of primary and secondary data
b. Utilities	Primary and secondary data Secondary data Percentage of household expenditure for utilities from household expenditure survey. Primary data Local housing survey.
c. Maintenance and minor repairs	Primary data Local housing survey and discussions with workers and key informants.
d. Taxes and fees	Secondary data Applicable property and other taxes, user fees, and other fees.
Non-food non-housing (NFNH) costs	
1. Preliminary estimate of NFNH	Secondary data Household expenditure data for expenditure groups by income quintile or decile, by location.
a. Education post check	Primary data Typical local cost for education of children until the end of secondary school through discussions with workers, school personnel, and other key informants.
b. Health care post check	Primary and secondary data Secondary data Average number of visits per person per year to different types of health care providers (public clinics, private doctors, pharmacists, etc.). Primary data Typical cost per visit for each type of provider collected from clinics, pharmacies and discussions with workers and key informants.
Additional funds	
1. For sustainability	5% by assumption.
2. For parents and relatives	Usually 0. Otherwise by assumption usually equal to around 5% or one day of living wage.
Number of workers per family	Secondary data Labor force participation rates, unemployment rates, and part-time employment rates by age, sex and location.
Reference family size	Secondary data Average household size, distribution of households by number of members, total fertility rate, and under 5 mortality rate.

Table 2A.1 (continued)

Cost	Use of primary and secondary data
Statutory deductions from pay	Secondary data Information on income tax, social security taxes, union fees, and other deductions from pay.
Wages	
1. Prevailing wages that are comparable to a living wage	Primary data Payroll data from individual establishments. Information on the types of in kind benefits provided by employer. Cost of each common in kind benefit to employer, market value, replacement cost to workers. Collective bargaining agreements (CBAs).
2. Other wages	Secondary data Average prevailing wages for relevant occupations and industries. Minimum wages. Poverty line wages. Other living wage estimates from unions, NGOs, government.

SECTION I

Cost of a basic but decent life for worker and family

3. Model diet for a living wage

PART I. BACKGROUND

In low income countries, on average, around 48% of all expenditures are for food, and in lower middle income countries, on average, around 37% of all expenditures are for food (Anker, 2011a). Therefore, estimating food costs is necessarily a very important part of estimating a living wage. The estimate of food costs for a living wage should be sufficient for workers and their families to afford a nutritious, palatable diet.

The approach used in our methodology to estimate food costs is to first create a model diet that meets WHO recommendations on nutrition, is consistent with local food preferences, and is relatively low in cost for a nutritious diet. The cost of the model diet is then estimated using local food prices determined through a local market survey that mimics the ways in which cost-conscious workers shop for food.

Developing a new approach was necessary for estimating food costs because suitable model diets for a living wage are not available in most countries. Although model diets exist for many countries, they have usually been developed for other purposes and generally are not appropriate for estimating food costs for a living wage. Model diets used to estimate national poverty lines are based on observed food consumption of households that consume the required number of calories, so they include sufficient calories by design. However, they do not concern themselves with other nutritional needs and therefore do not usually have sufficient macronutrients and micronutrients. Model diets developed by nutritionists generally do not fully consider food costs and as a result are not low in cost. What all of this means is that it was necessary to develop a new approach to creating a model diet for estimating a living wage. We have developed two Excel model diet programs to help create a model diet for a living wage.

3.1 Key Features of the Approach Used to Create a Living Wage Model Diet and Estimate its Cost

Key features of the approach we developed for creating a model diet include:

- WHO recommendations for calories, proteins, fats, carbohydrates and fruits and vegetables are used.
- We created an Excel calorie requirement program to calculate the number of calories required per person per day for a reference size family based on WHO (2004) recommendations.
- We created an Excel model diet program to develop an appropriate model diet for a living wage.
- The Excel model diet program uses a practical iterative process. First, a preliminary model diet is created based on a model diet from nutritionists, or a model diet used to estimate a poverty line, or food consumption reported in a household survey. This starting diet is, then, adjusted to ensure that WHO nutritional recommendations are met, the diet is consistent with local food preferences, and the diet is relatively low in cost for a nutritious diet by taking relative food prices into consideration.
- The model diet purposely includes a limited number of relatively inexpensive foods (around 20 foods) for simplicity. The cost of this model diet is then increased by a small percent to allow for the purchase of a greater variety of foods. This is in contrast to the 35–60 food items usually included in poverty line and other model diets. The advantage of our method is that it is simpler, yet accomplishes the same thing of ensuring variety.
- The Excel model diet program takes into account the difference between amount of food purchased and amount edible. This avoids a common mistake of other living wage estimates – which is to calculate the number of calories based on purchased weight of foods without deducting the weight of inedible parts such as skin of banana, shell of egg, and bone in meat.
- The Excel model diet program is flexible. It can be used to modify a model diet created by nutritionists to ensure that it is relatively low in cost, or to modify a model diet based on reported local food consumption so that it satisfies various nutritional standards.

The remainder of this chapter is divided into three parts. Part II indicates general characteristics of an appropriate low-cost nutritious model diet for estimating living wage. Part III discusses nutritional requirements in depth. Part IV is concerned with how to create an appropriate model diet. It describes three approaches typically used to develop model diets, as well as our new approach and provides an example.

PART II. PRINCIPLES OF MODEL DIET FOR ESTIMATING A LIVING WAGE

Model diets created for estimating a living wage should ideally be nutritious, relatively low in cost, consistent with local food preferences, consistent with a country's development level, and expressed as far as possible in number of portions per week or per day so that it is easy to understand by the public. Each of these characteristics is discussed below:

3.2 Characteristics of a Model Diet

3.2.1 Model diet should be nutritious

The following guidance is used to ensure that the model diet created for a living wage study follows WHO recommendations on nutrition:

- Number of calories in the model diet needs to be sufficient according to WHO (2004) recommendations. We created an Excel calorie requirement program for this calculation.
- At least 10% of calories must come from proteins as recommended by WHO/FAO (2003). Also, in accordance with these recommendations, proteins need to come from a variety of sources including some 'higher quality' sources of proteins such as foods of animal-origin and legumes.
- Some dairy (which is rich in calcium and high quality protein) should be included in the diet, especially for children (FAO, 2014a).
- 15–30% of calories must come from fats as recommended by WHO/FAO (2003).
- 55–75% of calories must come from carbohydrates as recommended by WHO/FAO (2003).
- At least 300 grams[1] of vegetables and fruits per day (including legumes) must be included in the model diet to help provide micronutrients and minerals.

3.2.2 Foods in a model diet should be consistent with local preferences

A model diet should reflect local food preferences so that it is palatable to the local population. This means that the diet should include the types of foods preferred in the location. For example, the preferred cereal in a country might be rice, wheat, or maize; the preferred root and tuber might be potato or cassava; the preferred legume might be dhal, or beans; and the preferred meat might be chicken, pork, or beef.

3.2.3 Model diet should be relatively low in cost for a nutritious diet

A model diet should include less expensive meats, cereals, fruits, vegetables, etc. in order to keep food costs down while maintaining nutrition. Section 4.9.3 discusses how lower cost food items to include in a model diet are chosen.

3.2.4 Model diet should be consistent with development level of location

Consumption of foods that are relatively expensive per calorie (e.g. meats, fruits, and vegetables) is known to increase with economic development and per capita income, because people have a preference for these foods when they can afford them. An increasing percentage of calories from proteins usually goes hand in hand with economic development. For this reason, quantities of more expensive foods should increase in a living wage model diet along with economic development.

3.2.5 Model diet should be expressed as far as possible in numbers of servings so it is easy to understand

Quantities of each food in a model diet should be stated, to the extent possible, in a way that is understandable to the public. This increases transparency and the ability to convey the type of basic life style that a living wage is able to support. For example, the model diet we used to estimate a living wage in the Dominican Republic included one roll of bread per day, one cup of milk per day for children, three eggs per week, six meat meals per week, three tablespoons of cooking oil per day, and seven teaspoons of sugar per day.

PART III. NUTRITIONAL RECOMMENDATIONS USED TO CREATE A MODEL DIET FOR A LIVING WAGE

As mentioned above, our Excel model diet program uses WHO/FAO recommendations on calories and nutrients to ensure that the model diet is nutritious. This section begins with a description of how calorie requirements are calculated and describes how to use the Excel calorie requirements program. Next, protein requirements are discussed in detail, because foods that are high in protein tend to be relatively expensive and therefore the amount of protein in a diet is an important determinant of its cost. Third, details are presented about the number of edible grams of each of the major food groups to include in the model diet, such as amounts of fruits and vegetables, milk and dairy, sugar, oils and fats.

3.3 How to Determine Calories Needed for a Family

Since ensuring that a model diet has sufficient calories is essential, we created an Excel calorie requirement program to calculate the number of calories required per person per day for different family sizes.

Calculation of the number of calories in the model diet is based on WHO (2004) guidelines on the average number of calories people need per day. Calorie requirements are calculated separately for adults and children. The average number of calories required per person for a family depends on the reference family size. Equations to calculate the average number of calories per person needed (known as the Schofield equations) are based on:

- age
- sex
- body size
- physical activity level

3.3.1 Calories needed for adults

Adults require energy for: (1) basic bodily functions and (2) physical activity. Adults no longer require energy for growth.

3.3.1.1 Calories needed for basic bodily functions (adults) BMR (basic metabolic rate) is the number of calories needed for basic body functions essential for life, such as 'cell function and replacement; the synthesis, secretion and metabolism of enzymes and hormones . . .; maintenance of body temperature; the uninterrupted work of cardiac and respiratory muscles; and brain function' (WHO, 2004, p. 7). BMR is related to body size, age and sex, and it represents 45–70% of an adult's daily energy expenditure. For our living wage model diet, we use average values for males and females ages 30–60. The Schofield equations for males and females ages 30–60 are as follows (WHO, 2004):

1. BMR per day for males ages 30–60 = 873.1 + 11.472 × kg
2. BMR per day for females ages 30–60 = 845.6 + 8.126 × kg

WHO (2004) suggests using the weight that corresponds to the average attained adult height and a body mass index (BMI)[2] of 21 as the basis for estimating calorie requirements rather than average body weight. Average attained height of a population is a stable indicator of nutritional needs, as it varies little during adulthood. We follow this recommendation.

3.3.1.2 Calories needed for physical activity (adults) Calories needed for physical activity vary greatly from activity to activity. These differences are expressed by the physical activity ratio (PAR), which when multiplied by BMR indicates calories required for a particular activity. The PAR for sleep, for example, is 1, while the PAR for dressing and showering is 3.3, and the PAR for non-mechanized agricultural work is 4.1.[3] Since a person does a variety of activities during a day, in order to get an estimate of the overall physical activity ratio for a day, PAR values are weighted by the length of time of each activity and summed.

PAR for a typical day has been categorized into three overall physical activity levels (PAL) – namely light activity (sedentary), moderate activity, and vigorous activity with PAL values of 1.4–1.69, 1.7–1.99, and 2.0–2.4 respectively. For example, a light activity day might consist of 8 hours of sleep (PAR 1), 8 hours of office work (PAR 1.5), 2 hours of light leisure activities such as chatting or watching TV (PAR 1.4), and 1 hour each of personal care (PAR 2.3), eating (PAR 1.5), cooking (PAR 2.1), general housework (PAR 2.8), driving a car to and from work (PAR 2.0) and walking without a load (PAR 3.2). The weighted average of these activities during the day in this example is a PAL of 1.53, which is in the light activity range.

If 8 hours of office work (PAR 1.5) is replaced by 8 hours of non-mechanized agricultural work (PAR 4.1), 1 hour of general household work (PAR 2.8) by 1 hour collecting water/wood (PAR 4.4), and 1 hour of driving a car to and from work (PAR 2.0) by 1 hour of non-mechanized domestic chores (PAR 2.3), the overall PAL is 2.25, which is in the vigorous activity range.

The average number of calories required at each activity level equals PAL × BMR. We use the mid-point of each PAL range to estimate calorie needs for the living wage model diet as this is customary (Table 3.1).

Table 3.1 PAL multipliers for sedentary, moderate, and vigorous life styles

Physical activity level (PAL)	Range of PAL values	Mid-point of range
Light	1.41–1.69	1.55
Moderate	1.70–1.99	1.85
Vigorous	2.00–2.40	2.20

Source: WHO (2004).

3.3.2 Calories needed for children and adolescents

Children and adolescents require energy for growth as well as for basic body functions and physical activity. We use values from WHO (2004)[4] to estimate calorie needs of children for our model diet. These values are based on Schofield equations and represent energy requirements for a reference population with moderate activity level for a broad spectrum of countries. The average number of calories required per day for children ages 0–17 with moderate activity level is 1892.[5] If children engage in vigorous activities such as walking or biking long distances to school and doing several hours of energy-demanding chores every day, or practice energy-demanding sports for several hours a day, the average number of calories required per day per child would be 2221, whereas if children have a sedentary life style (e.g. use motorized vehicles to get to school, and spend almost all of their leisure time in sedentary activities such as reading, watching television, or playing with very little body displacement) and do not engage in any sports, average daily calorie requirements would be 1663.

It is customary to assume that children have moderate activity levels, since they should spend much of their time in school. Calorie requirements for light activity level or a vigorous activity level can be used when there is a good reason to believe that these represent local conditions.

3.3.3 Calories needed for a reference size family

We recommend using the following assumptions for physical activity levels to calculate calorie needs:

- Vigorous activity level for adults engaging in non-mechanized farm work
- Moderate activity level for other adults
- Moderate activity level for children

These are typical assumptions but are relatively conservative assumptions for rural areas where physical activity is generally more intense than in urban areas. In rural areas, for example, all adults might have vigorous activity levels. Some judgment is needed here. In the rural area of Malawi, for example, where there is no electricity and water and firewood for cooking have to be collected by family members, all adults have vigorous activity. In contrast, in rural Dominican Republic where there is generally piped water and electricity and cooking is generally done with LPG gas, we considered that only one adult (the worker on a farm/plantation) had vigorous activity.

3.3.4 Additional calories needed during pregnancy and lactation

3.3.4.1 Pregnancy According to WHO (Clugston, n.d.) a woman needs on average 285 additional calories per day during pregnancy. (More calories are needed in the last trimester, and fewer additional calories are needed during the first trimester.) While it is extremely important that pregnant women have additional calories, pregnancy does not add many extra calories on average per person in the family, since additional calories are only needed for nine months per full-term pregnancy, only for years in which the mother is pregnant, and only for one family member. In populations where women have two children on average, the additional 285 calories per day needed for each pregnancy when averaged over all childbearing years implies an additional 12 extra calories per day for the woman, and so only three additional calories per day per family member for a family of four. Even in a country with extremely high fertility, additional calories required for pregnancy are small when averaged over all years for the entire family. The Excel calorie requirements program makes a small addition for calorie needs during pregnancy.

3.3.4.2 Lactation Our Excel calorie requirement program does not adjust average calorie requirements for lactation partly because additional calories needed for lactation vary enormously with feeding practices (such as length and exclusivity of breastfeeding) which vary widely from country to country (WHO, 2004). In addition, production of human milk has been estimated to be 80–85% efficient (Butte and King, 2002), so that most of the calories needed to produce human milk ultimately go to the breastfed child. While adding a small number of additional calories per person for lactation in some high fertility countries may be reasonable, the adjustment would be small when averaged over the entire family and over many years.[6]

3.3.5 National databases for calorie requirements

Some countries have national nutritional standards based on international standards and local conditions. For example, the Government of India, National Institute of Nutrition (2010) has nutritional standards for India. They estimated their own PARs (physical activity ratios) and PALs (physical activity levels) based on typical activities and life styles in India.[7] They also have standards for proteins and other micronutrients based on foods found in the Indian diet. Similarly, the Government of Vietnam, National Institute of Nutrition (2014) have their own equations for calorie requirements and physical activity levels. Such national standards could be used when they are available and based on high quality research.

3.3.6 Excel program for calculating calories needed

We created an Excel program to calculate the number of calories needed by a reference size family. The Excel calorie requirement program has four worksheets. It is available on the Edward Elgar website.

3.3.6.1 Calorie requirements worksheet 1 The first worksheet entitled '1. Adults' calculates calorie requirements for adult males and females with sedentary, moderate and vigorous activity levels. To use this worksheet, input the average attained height of adult males and females in cells E14 and E15. The worksheet automatically calculates the healthy weight of the population using a BMI of 21 (in cells G14 and G15).[8] The program also calculates the calorie requirements based on this weight with sedentary, moderate and vigorous activity levels (cells F30 through H40).

The attained height of adult males and females can often be found from nutritional studies or from a table in Wikipedia (2014) called 'average height around the world.' This table not only lists heights, but importantly also provides references. The Demographic and Health Survey (DHS) is another source of information on attained height – but only for the height of women. If DHS is used for adult women, a reasonable assumption for adult males would be to multiply women's height by 1.08.[9] Note that if it is not possible to find average adult height, weight can be used as the input into the spreadsheet (although it is preferable to use height).

3.3.6.2 Calorie requirements worksheet 2 The second worksheet entitled '2. Calories per family member' calculates the average number of calories per person for the reference family size. For this worksheet, it is necessary to input the reference family size plus assumptions about activity levels. A small addition to this is added for pregnancy based on the number of children in the reference size family.

3.3.6.3 Calorie requirements worksheet 3 The third worksheet entitled '3. Calories per child' consists of tables with calorie needs for children and for infants. Calorie needs for children and infants are assumed to be the same worldwide. This worksheet is included for reference purposes only. It is used in Worksheet 4 as a basis for determining the replacement cost of meals provided at school or work. No input is required for Worksheet 3.

3.3.6.4 Calorie requirements worksheet 4 The fourth worksheet entitled '4. Estimated cost of meals' calculates the replacement cost of meals eaten away from home by children and adults. It is used to calculate how much money is saved when children are provided free meals in school or adults are provided meals by their employer. Worksheet 4 uses information from Worksheets 1, 2, and 3.

VALUE OF MEALS PREPARED AT HOME FOR ADULTS AND REPLACEMENT COST OF MEALS IN THE WORKPLACE Assumptions about the proportion of daily calories consumed in each meal – breakfast, lunch and dinner – should be entered in cells F13–F15 of Worksheet 4. Check to see that the sum of these proportions is 1 (cell F16). Then enter cost of the model diet per person per day in cell F21. Worksheet 4 calculates the replacement cost of breakfast, lunch and dinner for adults provided with meals at work based on the cost of the model diet and the worker's activity level.

VALUE OF CHILDREN'S MEALS PREPARED AT HOME AND REPLACEMENT VALUE OF FREE LUNCH AT SCHOOL When children eat free meals at school, the cost of food for the family should be reduced by the amount it would have cost to prepare the school meal at home. This can be calculated from the Excel calorie requirements program.

The cost of lunch for children of different ages is calculated in cells E38 to E55. The following equation can be used to calculate the average replacement value of a free lunch provided at school. The equation takes into account that the lunch is provided only for children of certain ages, and only on school days:

> *Replacement value of free lunch provided in school* = (*# years of school during which free lunch is provided* ÷ *18 years as a child*) × (*number of school days in year* ÷ 365) × (*average value of free lunch for relevant age groups from Excel program*)

The replacement value of free lunches at school should be deducted from the cost of the living wage model diet since free school lunches reduce the need for families to provide lunch for their children.

3.4 Proteins

Food costs are sensitive to the amount and quality of proteins in a diet, because high quality proteins are relatively expensive per calorie (see Anker, 2006 and 2006a). Healthy diets should have at least 10–15% of calories from proteins according to WHO/FAO (2003) and proteins should come from a variety of sources with a substantial proportion of high quality proteins such as from meat, fish, chicken, egg, and dairy (WHO/FAO/UNU, 2007). We suggest that all model diets contain some high quality proteins daily, and this amount should increase with economic development.

3.4.1 What are proteins and how many are needed?

Proteins are large complex molecules made up of 20 different smaller molecules called amino acids combined in long chains. Amino acids are required to maintain good health, especially to build, maintain and replace body tissues and organs. Eight amino acids are considered to be 'essential amino acids' (that adults cannot synthesize themselves and so must be obtained from food). There are 10 essential amino acids for children.

Determining how much protein is required for health is difficult, because proteins differ in their amino acid composition and in how easily they can be digested (Millward, 2013). Consequently, recommendations on required amounts and types of proteins are complex and controversial. Nonetheless, WHO/FAO (2003) and WHO/FAO/UNU (2007) recommend that a minimum of 10% of calories should come from proteins. CDC (2013a) also suggests that at least 10% of daily calories come from proteins. We follow this recommendation. We suggest that around 10–11% of calories should come from proteins for low income countries, with this percentage rising with development level and per capita income such as to 11–12% for lower middle income countries, 12–14% for upper middle income countries, and 15+% for high income countries.

Some of the proteins in the living wage model diet should be high quality proteins in keeping with the most recent revision of WHO/FAO/UNU (2007) guidelines on protein and amino acid requirements. This is especially critical in countries with considerable malnutrition. A recent review of protein quality and malnutrition in Africa highlighted the need for adequate amounts of protein and for high quality protein – 'the amount of protein consumed is insufficient in comparison with requirements . . . The low intake of good-quality protein remains a threat to livelihoods' (Schoenfeldt and Hall, 2012, S69). Since high quality proteins, especially animal-based foods, are relatively expensive per calorie, large amounts would make the model diet too expensive, but at least 20 grams of high quality proteins should usually be included in model diets.

3.5 Suggested Number of Grams to Include in Living Wage Model Diet for Each Food Group

WHO and FAO recommend amounts of foods to consume daily from each food group to ensure sufficient macronutrients and micronutrients.

3.5.1 Fruits and vegetables

Fruits and vegetables are important for good nutrition as they contain many micronutrients not found elsewhere. According to WHO (n.d.), 'benefit of fruits and vegetables cannot be ascribed to a single or mix of nutrients and bioactive substances. Therefore, this category was included rather than the nutrients themselves.' Our model diet follows the same strategy – of not listing every micronutrient and bioactive substance of importance, but assuming that eating sufficient amounts of a variety of fruits and vegetables will provide necessary micronutrients.

WHO/FAO (2003) recommends that people eat at least 400 grams of fruits and vegetables per person per day – not including roots and tubers (such as potatoes and cassava) but including legumes such as beans and pulses. This is equivalent to at least five servings of fruits and vegetables per day (using a standard serving size of approximately 80 grams).

However, a low percentage of people in the world actually consume 400+ grams of fruits and vegetables per day. According to WHO (n.d.) 'only a small and negligible minority of the world's population consumes the generally recommended high average intake of fruits and vegetables.' This is especially true for developing countries. A review of fruit and vegetable consumption in 10 Sub-Saharan African countries (Ruel et al., 2005) indicated that average consumption of fruits and vegetables was well below 200 grams per person in all 10 countries, with fruit and vegetable consumption lowest in the poorest quintile in each country. An analysis of the 2002–2003 World Health Survey from 52 mainly low and middle income countries (Hall et al., 2009) indicated that 78% of respondents 'consumed less than the minimum recommended 5 servings of fruits and vegetables.' Low consumption of fruits and vegetables in lower income countries is not surprising because they are expensive per calorie (e.g. studies for Rwanda and Cambodia cited in Ruel et al. (2005) found that tomatoes were 12 times more expensive per calorie than starches in Rwanda; and vegetables in Cambodia were 10 to 40 times more expensive per calorie than rice).

In view of the fact that the WHO recommendation is not reached by even close to a majority of people in even high income countries,[10] we feel that it would be both unrealistic and unnecessary to include 400 grams per day of fruits, vegetables, and legumes in a living wage model diet. Instead, we include a minimum of 300 grams of fruits, vegetables, and legumes in living wage model diets for low income countries, and increase this by 25 grams with each development level (low income to lower middle income, lower middle income to upper middle income, and upper middle income to high income income). The lower limit of 300 grams is similar to the approximately 3–5 portions of vegetables and fruits per day recommended in the University of Stellenbosch model diet for South Africa (NICUS, 2007), and not very different from actual consumption levels of fruits and vegetables in high income countries. Note that 2–4 vegetables should be included in a living wage model diet with at least one green leafy vegetable, as well as 1–2 fruits and 1–2 legumes in order to ensure a range of micronutrients (with additional variety of fruits and vegetables allowed for by funds for additional variety that are added to the cost of the model diet).

3.5.2 Milk and dairy

Living wage model diets should generally include at least 1 cup of milk per day for children and some milk for adults to add to coffee and tea, such as quarter of a cup, or possibly some yogurt or cheese. This recommendation is far from a hard and fast rule and some judgment is required especially in areas where people do not drink much milk out of choice.

Dairy is generally an important component of a diet. According to FAO (2014a), milk is 'a major source of dietary energy, high-quality protein and fat. . . . Bioavailability of some nutrients in milk, for example calcium, is high compared with that in other foods in the diet.' The consumption of milk and dairy products is particularly important for calcium. 'The mineral profiles in milk and bones have much in common. With the exception of small fish that are eaten whole, including the bones, few foods naturally contain as much calcium as milk' (Muehlhoff et al., 2013, p. 125).

Despite the recognized need for milk, 'there are no global recommendations for milk or dairy consumption' (FAO, 2014a). Not surprisingly, countries vary widely in their recommendations for milk and dairy. A recent FAO review of national guidelines on milk and dairy consumption for 42 countries, including 14 developing countries, found that national recommendations differed widely (Muehlhoff et al., 2013). Of the 14 developing countries in this study, 11 recommended at least one and sometimes two cups of milk or dairy equivalent per day for both adults and children (exceptions being Oman and El Salvador, which recommended around half a cup of milk per day, and Guatemala, which recommended milk at least twice a week). It is worth noting that India (which has many vegetarians) and Chile among developing countries recommended the most milk or dairy (at least three servings per day). Most, but not all, developed countries recommended at least two servings of milk or dairy per day for adults and children.

There are also wide differences between countries in the consumption of dairy. The proportion of calories derived from dairy products in developing countries ranges from slightly less than 2% in East and South-East Asia and 3% in Sub-Saharan Africa to around 7% in South Asia, Latin America and the Caribbean (Muehlhoff et al., 2013). Part of the reason for the low percentage in East and South-East Asia, may be widespread lactose intolerance among adults.

In light of the above, it is difficult to be dogmatic about the need to include large amounts of milk in model diets. The suggested minimum amount of milk for a living wage model diet stated above of one cup for children and a quarter of a cup for adults is on the low side relative to recommendations of nutritionists and national guidelines. Note that the amount of milk included in a living wage model diet sometimes needs to be limited because of its cost. The cost of milk in a model diet should not generally exceed somewhere around 10–15% of food expenditure except in countries such as India with many vegetarians who do not consume meats, fish, and egg.

3.5.3 Meats, fish and eggs

Meats, fish and eggs are relatively expensive per calorie. Despite this, they are included in model diets in part because they are important sources of high quality proteins, and in part because there is a strong preference for them in most countries. The quantity of meats, fish and eggs in living wage model diets depends on level of development and local preferences. The distribution of quantities between meats, milk, fish and eggs should depend to a significant extent on their relative prices. A living wage model diet needs to balance local preferences and relative prices to achieve a healthy but relatively inexpensive diet. For example, in Malawi, small dried fish were an important part of the local diet, and they were less expensive per protein and per calorie than either meat or chicken. Therefore, in Malawi, small dried fish was included in our model diet, but meat and chicken were not. In Kenya, fish was not included in our model diet because meat was preferred by most Kenyans, and was less expensive.

3.5.4 Sugar

Living wage model diets should generally include at most 30 grams of sugar per day (equivalent to around six to seven teaspoons of sugar per person per day), and less in countries with little sugar consumption. This recommendation is based on WHO (2015, p. 4):

> WHO recommends reducing the intake of free sugars to less than 10% of total energy intake . . . and suggests a further reduction of the intake of free sugars to below 5% . . . For countries with a low intake of free sugars, levels should not be increased. Higher intakes of free sugars threaten the nutrient quality of diets by providing significant energy without specific nutrients.

Thirty grams of sugar a day is approximately 5% of energy intake in a 2400 calorie diet. This amount can be increased somewhat in locations where it would not be palatable to have only 30 grams of sugar per person per day.

3.5.5 Oils and fats

WHO recommends that 15–30% of calories should come from fats. Our living wage model diet typically includes 30–34 grams of oil per person per day (approximately equivalent to two tablespoons). Thirty grams of oil contains approximately 265 calories and 34 grams contains approximately 300 calories, which represent around 12–14% of calories for a diet with 2200 calories per day. Note that other items in the diet, such as animal products, also contain fats.

3.5.6 Roots and tubers and starchy plantains

The quantity of roots and tubers consumed varies greatly from country to country. For this reason, we suggest relying mainly on national data on local food consumption as a guide to determining the amount of roots and tubers to include in a living wage model diet. We also suggest relying on data on local food consumption to determine the amount of starchy plantains in a model diet. Starchy plantains should only be included in model diets in countries in which they are important. Although starchy plantains are a staple food in some countries, they are so unimportant in many other countries that they should not be included in the living wage model diet for many countries.

3.5.7 Cereals

Cereals are the most important source of calories in diets around the world. Cereals come in prepared forms (e.g., bread and noodles) and unprepared forms (e.g., rice and wheat flour). From one to four different cereals should be included in living wage model diets depending on consumption habits in the area. The amount of bread in a model diet should be set in terms of number of slices of bread or number of rolls. Note that in our Excel model diet program, the number of grams of unprepared cereals is determined after the number of calories from all the other foods has been calculated, to ensure that the model diet provides exactly the required number of calories.

3.5.8 Beans, soy, pulses, legumes and nuts

Nutritionists typically recommend eating legumes or soy often, because they are a good source of protein and other nutrients. However, there is high variation across countries in the extent to which diets include legumes and soy. Living wage model diets should generally contain between 28 and 56 grams (one to two servings) of beans, soy, pulses, legumes or nuts in light of their nutritional value (especially proteins) with number of grams dependent on local preferences. An upper limit is needed to keep a model diet palatable.

3.5.9 Coffee and tea

Coffee and tea are drunk around the world. Living wage model diets should include one of these depending on local preferences. The amount should be determined using an assumption on the number of cups for adults per day. Soft drinks should not be included in a living wage model diet.

PART IV. CREATING A LIVING WAGE MODEL DIET

Part IV describes how a model diet for estimating a living wage should be developed. It begins by discussing three typical approaches for developing model diets. It goes on to describe the approach used in our living wage methodology and explains why this approach is used and its advantages over the other approaches. How to create a living wage model diet, and how to use the model diet Excel program are explained.

3.6 Typical Approaches Used to Create Model Diets

This section describes three typical approaches that have been used to create a model diet. One approach relies on recommendations of nutritionists who are interested in advising the public on healthy eating. A second approach relies on actual food consumption as observed on household expenditure surveys. This approach is often used to estimate poverty lines. A third hybrid approach relies on mathematical optimization processes using information on nutritional requirements, actual food consumption, and relative food prices. This approach is used by more sophisticated government departments and universities.

3.6.1 Typical approach 1: Recommendation of nutritionists

One typical approach has nutritionists creating a model diet that meets minimum nutritional standards and is consistent with national food preferences. Government ministries, nutrition institutes, and universities often create this type of model diet to provide advice and information to the public on healthy eating. These model diets are generally based on WHO/FAO recommendations.

The major advantage of this type of model diet for estimating a living wage is that the diet is nutritious. Other advantages are that such diets usually exclude foods like cookies, cakes, soft drinks, and alcohol that are not necessary for health, and that they almost always take into consideration national food preferences. Their main disadvantage is that they do not generally give very much consideration to food costs. Their main purpose is to inform the public about healthy eating. As a result, model diets created by nutritionists tend to be more expensive than we feel is warranted for estimating a living wage.

In summary, while model diets prepared by nutritionists are very useful to help to set a model diet for a living wage, they should not be used for estimating a living wage without adjustment because they tend to be unnecessarily expensive for a living wage. They are, however, a useful basis for starting to construct an appropriate diet for estimating a living wage.

3.6.2 Typical approach 2: Reported food consumption

A second common approach determines a model diet based on reported food consumption from a household expenditure survey. Such model diets are commonly used by the World Bank and governments to estimate food costs for poverty lines (Ravaillon, 1998). Based on household survey data, the average number of calories per person per day is calculated for each household. The household income decile or quintile where the required number of calories per person is achieved is identified – and the reported food consumption of this household income decile or quintile becomes the model diet used to estimate a poverty line.[11] There are usually around 35–60 food items included in such model diets because only common food items are included.

This approach has several advantages for estimating a living wage. It ensures that the model diet has a sufficient number of calories. It ensures that the model diet is consistent with local food preferences and the qualities and quantities of foods that people purchase. This approach also has several disadvantages. It does not ensure that the model diet is nutritious beyond having a sufficient number of calories. As it happens, the poorer a country the more likely it is that a model diet based exclusively on reported food consumption will be unacceptable nutritionally and/or culturally. This is because many poor people in poor countries do not have enough income to eat well. Another disadvantage is that reported food consumption data are often problematic because of numerous technical difficulties in collecting such data from households. In Vietnam, for example, 31% of food expenditure was for foods with unknown numbers of calories such as meals eaten away from home and 'other vegetables' (Vietnam National Wage Council, 2014). It is difficult to understand from these data exactly what foods and how many calories households in Vietnam actually consume. A further complication is that many countries include alcohol, tobacco, narcotics, and food eaten away from home in restaurants and street markets as part of food expenditures (Anker, 2011a).

In summary, while model diets based on actual food consumption have important advantages, they should not be used to estimate a living wage without adjustments. They can, however, provide a useful basis to start to construct an appropriate model diet for estimating a living wage.

3.6.3 Typical approach 3: Mathematical optimization model

A third approach uses a mathematical optimization model. It, in essence, melds the two approaches described above while also taking food prices into consideration. A model diet is set using a mathematical optimization model that takes into consideration nutritional standards (e.g. calories, macronutrients, micronutrients), food habits and preferences (e.g. actual food consumption), and food prices and costs. The food baskets[12] developed by the United States Department of Agriculture (USDA) provide good examples of this approach[13] – although it is worth noting that USDA (2007) uses common sense when necessary, because blind use of its mathematical optimization model often leads to nonsensical results.[14,15]

There are several advantages to this approach. It takes into account nutritional requirements, food preferences, and food prices in such a way as to minimize costs while maintaining nutrition and food preferences. The main disadvantages of this approach are its complexity, high skill level required to use it, and need for considerable judgment to ensure reasonable results. These disadvantages mean that this approach is not practical to use on a widespread basis.

3.7 Our Approach to Creating a Living Wage Model Diet: A Practical Optimization Process

We use a simplified version of the third approach described above to create a living wage model diet. For this purpose we developed an Excel model diet program that uses an iterative process. First, initial quantities and specific foods in the diet are specified based on actual food consumption or on nutritional guidelines for the location or country. Then adjustments are made to this initial diet to ensure nutritional quality, acceptability to local workers, and relatively low-cost.

Section 3.7.1 explains the general structure of our living wage model diet and how to select specific foods from each major food group. Section 3.7.2 discusses cost of salt, spices, and condiments. Section 3.7.3 discusses the need for a varied diet and its extra cost, while Section 3.7.4 discusses the cost of food spoilage and wastage. Inedible portions of foods and the nutritional content of foods are discussed in Sections 3.7.5 and 3.7.6. The Living Wage Excel model diet program is discussed in Section 3.8.

3.7.1 General structure of a living wage model diet: 11 food groups

A living wage model diet should generally include 11 food groups with around 20 food items. Table 3.2 indicates typical food groups and typical food items included in a living wage model diet. There are two groups of cereals, unprepared cereals or grains (such as rice, wheat, maize, etc.) and prepared cereals (such as bread and noodles). Prepared cereals are optional and should only be included when they are an integral part of the local diet. Roots and tubers and starchy fruits and vegetables are also divided into two groups. Starchy fruits and vegetables such as plantains should only be included in a model diet when they are an important part of the diet in a location. Vegetables are also divided into two groups, green leafy vegetables and other vegetables. This is because diets should contain a variety of vegetables. The cost of a model diet is then increased by a small percentage to allow for salt, spices and condiments; minimal spoilage; and some additional variety.

3.7.2 Salt, spices, sauces and condiments

Salt, spices, sauces and condiments are required for food to be palatable. For simplicity, living wage model diets increase food costs by a small percentage to allow for salt, spices, and condiments rather than specifying many different items in the model diet. An appropriate percentage to use depends on the complexity of local cuisine.[16] A useful source for determining what percentage to add to food costs for salt, spices, sauces and condiments are household expenditure survey data or CPI expenditure weights. In the absence of national data on household expenditure for salt, spices and condiments, 1–3% should be used (although this percentage can be higher as it was above 5% in study areas in Bangladesh, India and Sri Lanka according to household income and expenditure surveys).

3.7.3 Importance of variety in a diet

Variety is important for a nutritious diet. No one can be expected to eat exactly the same foods every day as this would not be palatable – nor would this be nutritious as variety is important to ensure a range of micronutrients, macronutrients, and minerals. Model diets typically account for this by including 35–60 food items. For practical reasons, a living wage model diet includes fewer foods (usually around 20 food items) – and then increases the total cost of the model diet by a certain percentage to allow for additional variety. This is a much simpler way to accomplish the same goal of providing for needed variety.

We recommend adding between 10% and 15% to the cost of a living wage model diet for variety. What percentage to use should depend on the number of food items included in a living wage diet (the more food items included the lower the additional percentage needed for variety), extent

Table 3.2 Typical food groups, examples of specific foods, and amounts typically included in a living wage model diet

Food groups included in model diet	Examples of specific food items	Amount (number of grams)	Comments
1A. Cereals and grains	Rice Wheat Maize	Number of grams of most important cereal set by Excel program.	Include 1–3 common cereals with the most important cereal in the first row. Use minimum acceptable quality.
1B. Prepared cereals (optional)	Bread Pasta	Base amount on number of grams in typical unit (e.g. in slice or roll of bread).	Include when common. More expensive per calorie than unprepared cereals. Often excluded in low income countries. Exclude cakes.
2A. Roots and tubers	Potato Cassava Sweet potato	Base amount on typical consumption in country/location.	Include 2 items when one type is not dominant.
2B. Starchy fruits and vegetables (optional)	Plantains Green banana	Base amount on typical consumption in country/location.	Include only when important part of local diet. Include 1–2 items.
3. Legumes and nuts	Beans Pulses Peas Lentils Soy and tofu Nuts	Base amount on typical consumption in country/location and need for low-cost high quality proteins.	Include 1–2 lower cost acceptable varieties.
4. Dairy	Milk Cheese Yoghurt	Usually at least 1 cup of milk for children and ¼+ cup for adults.	Convert powdered milk into equivalent cups of liquid milk. Amount of dairy included in diet increases with development.
5. Eggs	Chicken egg Duck egg	Base amount on number of grams in medium size eggs.	Use most common and least expensive egg. Usually chicken egg. Amount increases with development. When weight is not marked on

Table 3.2 (continued)

Food groups included in model diet	Examples of specific food items	Amount (number of grams)	Comments
			package – need to weigh eggs to determine their average weight.
6. Meats and fish	Beef Chicken Pork Fish (fresh/ dried) Sausage Offal Liver	Base amount on acceptable number of meals per week (using 85 edible grams per serving). Amount increases with development.	Use 1–4 lowest cost meats/fish per protein considering waste. Can include offal and liver or sausage sometimes to reduce cost. Note dried meat and fish have more calories and proteins per edible gram than fresh meat or fish.
7A. Green leafy vegetables (GLV)	Spinach Kale Cabbage Greens Pumpkin leaf	Total amount of fruits and vegetables should be at least 300 edible grams including legumes and nuts. Amount increases with development.	Include 1–2 lowest cost widely available GLV per edible gram.
7B. Other vegetables (at least one other vegetable should not be a green leafy vegetable)	Carrot Tomato Pumpkin Squash Eggplant Onion	For simplicity, amount of each vegetable and amount of each fruit should be equal, with 25% or 33% of total fruits and vegetables for fruits.	Include at least 2 low cost widely available other vegetables. In countries where tomato and onion are used like spices and included in almost every meal, small amounts of these should be included in the model diet.
8. Fruits	Banana Orange Apple Mango Papaya		Include 1–2 lowest cost widely available fruit(s) per edible gram. Will often include seasonal fruit.

Table 3.2 (continued)

Food groups included in model diet	Examples of specific food items	Amount (number of grams)	Comments
9. Oils and fats	Sunflower oil Corn oil Animal fat	30–34 grams (2–2.5 tablespoons) usually.	Include lowest cost acceptable oil/fat per liter.
10. Sugar	Brown sugar White sugar	24–30 grams (6–7 teaspoons) usually.	Include lower cost sugar per kilo. Exclude confectionaries.
11. Non-alcoholic beverages	Tea Coffee	2–3 cups per adult of either coffee or tea (usually 2 grams per cup of tea, 7 grams per cup of coffee).	Include lower cost acceptable quality coffee or tea. Exclude soft drinks. Exclude alcohol and wine.
12. Other (Optional)	Coconut Fish sauce		Include in countries where a food is used in almost all meals and is not accounted for in the above food groups (e.g. coconut in Sri Lanka and fish sauce in Vietnam).
(Additional to model diet) Spices, salt, sauces and condiments	Salt Spices Sauces Condiments Soup cubes	% of cost of model diet. Base on typical % of household food expenditure according to household expenditure data.	Typically 1–3% of all food costs. Exclude snacks.

to which one or two food items is dominant in food groups, and development level as additional variety becomes increasingly expected with greater economic development (e.g. United States Thrifty Food Plan includes 7 cereals, 10 dairy, 19 vegetables, 11 fruits, 4 oils, and 4 sugars).

3.7.4 Food wastage and spoilage

Even under the best of circumstances, some food is wasted. People are not perfect housekeepers, and there is always some spoilage and food loss due to mold, insects, rodents, etc. In addition, some food is discarded or burnt. Spoilage is particularly important in poorer environments where there is restricted food storage capacity and lack of refrigeration, while discarded food is particularly important in more developed countries. We recommend adding 3–5% to the cost of a model diet for wastage and spoilage. This percentage increases with development. This assumption is very conservative. In the United States, for example, the government Thrifty Food Plan recommended for low income persons assumes 10% waste and the liberal Food Plan assumes 20% waste (USDA, 2007).

3.7.5 Inedible parts of food

Parts of many foods are not consumed because they are inedible. For example, people do not eat the skin of a banana, or the pit of a mango, or the shell of an egg. Since model diets are expressed in edible grams and food prices often include inedible parts, it is necessary to know the proportion of each food that is edible. Values for proportion inedible for a wide variety of foods are available from a USDA NAL nutrient online database (see Appendix 3.1).

3.7.5.1 Country-specific values for proportion inedible It often makes sense to adjust USDA NAL values for percentage inedible to be more realistic for a country or to use country-specific databases. There are several reasons why this is often a good idea, especially for vegetables. The FAO/INFOODS (International Network of Food Data Systems) website lists country- and region-specific food composition databases.

1. Not all foods are included in the USDA NAL database. It is not unusual to come across foods in developing countries that are not included in the USDA NAL database. For example, in Malawi many varieties of fish are found only in Lake Malawi. There are different varieties of mangos around the world, some with large pits and some with small pits, and different varieties of oranges, tangerines, and bananas with thicker or thinner skins.
2. Foods are often prepared for sale differently in other countries than in the United States and this affects the proportion inedible. For example in Vietnam, vegetables sold in local markets include roots and stems (that are usually cut off before sale in the United States). In India, wheat is typically sold in its husk, and this is separated from

the grain and discarded during milling. Meats are sold with differing amounts of bones and fat around the world, which affects the proportion edible. In short, the percentage edible of foods often differs across countries because of how they are prepared for sale.

3. People in developing countries often throw away fewer parts of foods than people in the United States, especially in low income countries. In Kenya, for example, people eat the mango skin whereas people throw the mango skin away in most of the world. In Malawi, people eat small dried fish from Lake Malawi in their entirety – bones, head and skin. They also discard a much smaller proportion of green leafy vegetables than is typical in the United States. In Vietnam, the heads of fish are boiled for soup broth and eaten when they are soft, whereas in the United States fish heads are thrown away. In China 5% of potato is considered inedible (China CDC, 2009) compared with 25% in the United States (USDA NAL, 2014).

The above discussion means that it is not unusual to need to adjust proportion inedible indicated in the USDA NAL nutrient database, especially for meats, fish, vegetables and fruits and sometimes for cereals. It therefore makes sense to consult the FAO/INFOODS database to see if a national or regional database is available, and to discuss this issue with workers and key informants.

It is relatively easy for researchers to estimate the proportion edible themselves to see if USDA NAL or FAO/INFOODS databases provide a good benchmark for proportion edible, by purchasing food from a local market, weighing the food, and having a local person prepare the food for eating or cooking. Then separately weigh the edible and discarded portions and calculate percentage edible.[17] This provides a rough check on edible portions.

3.7.6 Nutritional content of foods (calories, protein, fats, and carbohydrates)

In order to determine whether a model diet meets nutritional requirements, it is necessary to know the nutritional content of foods and to include this information in the Excel living wage model diet program. The USDA NAL online database is an excellent source on nutritional content for a wide variety of foods. Appendix 3.1 lists the nutritional content for common foods drawn from this database. For convenience average values for different types of rice, fruits and vegetables, beans, etc. are calculated. The FAO/INFOODS database (discussed above) lists national and regional databases with nutritional information that are sometimes better to use than USDA NAL. For example, the number of calories in milk depends on fat content of milk, which varies across countries depending on the types of cows and milk animals. This means that it is preferable to use data from a national food composition database if it is available rather than the USDA NAL database for the nutritional content of milk. Indeed, researchers have used country-specific food composition databases for creating model diets for living wage studies in Bangladesh, China and India.

3.8 Excel Living Wage Model Diet Program

We created an Excel model diet program to help researchers create a model diet for estimating a living wage that is nutritious, consistent with local food preferences, and relatively low in cost for a nutritious diet. The Excel program includes four worksheets – to be used in order. The remainder of this section describes each worksheet – its primary aim, required inputs, and resulting outputs. This program is available on the Edward Elgar website.

3.8.1 Excel model diet program: Worksheet 1 (data entry and creation of a preliminary diet with sufficient calories)

There are two aims of this worksheet: (i) to input all data needed for the program and (ii) to develop an initial diet with the required number of calories per person.

3.8.1.1 Required number of calories per person The number of calories required per person is entered at the top of Worksheet 1. This value is taken from the Excel calorie requirements program.

3.8.1.2 Starting diet The starting diet should be based on another source. This can be either a model diet for the country/location or a diet based on food consumption from a recent household expenditure survey.[18] Using a country- or location-specific starting diet is important because such a diet usually contains quantities of foods commonly consumed in the study location.

3.8.1.3 Enter whether starting diet is in purchased grams or edible grams Quantities for each food in the starting diet can be inputted either in purchased grams or edible grams. Diets from household expenditure surveys are often stated in purchased grams, whereas diets from nutritionists are almost always stated in edible grams. When purchased grams are entered, the Excel program automatically calculates the number of edible grams. When edible grams are entered, the Excel program automatically calculates the number of purchased grams.

3.8.1.4 Select a small number of food items to represent each major food group group Instructions in the Excel model diet program indicate the number of food items to include in each major group. When the data source for the starting diet has more food items in a major food group than the living wage model diet, the total number of grams in the major food group should be distributed equally over the food items included in the Excel model diet program. For example, if the data source includes 20 grams for each of 5 different fruits, the two common fruits selected for the model diet should have 50 grams each to begin with.

3.8.1.5 Additional inputs

- Nutritional composition of each food item (number of calories, proteins, fats and carbohydrates per 100 grams)
- Proportion edible for each food item (1 is used when no inedible parts)
- Percentage to add to cost for salt, spices, sauces, and condiments
- Percentage to add to cost for some additional variety
- Percentage to add to cost for minimal wastage and spoilage
- Cost per kilo of each food item based on a local market survey
- Percentage distribution of food costs from another source such as household survey or another model diet

3.8.1.6 Adjustment made in Worksheet 1 to ensure required number of calories Worksheet 1 automatically adjusts initial quantities in the starting diet so that this diet includes the required number of calories. For example, if a starting diet contains 2000 calories and calorie requirements call for 2200 calories, the quantity for each food item in the input diet would be increased by 10% (i.e. increased by 2200 required calories divided by 2000 calories found in the diet before adjustment). It is worth noting that the most common methodology for estimating food costs for poverty lines and living wages stops right here.

3.8.2 Excel model diet program: Worksheet 2 (adjustments to make the diet nutritious in more than only calories)

The main purpose of Worksheet 2 is to adjust the model diet from Worksheet 1 so that it is nutritious in terms of macronutrients (acceptable percentages of calories from proteins, fats, and carbohydrates) and micronutrients (minimum number of grams of vegetables and fruits) and has reasonable and healthy amounts of sugar, oils and fats, dairy, and coffee/tea. Worksheet 2 begins with the model diet with required number of calories carried over from Worksheet 1. The diet at this point is rarely nutritious unless the starting diet was a model diet from nutritionists.

3.8.2.1 Useful nutritional indicators calculated on Worksheet 2 There are a number of useful indicators calculated in Worksheet 2 to help researchers evaluate whether the diet meets nutritional recommendations. These include:

- Number of grams of proteins, fats and carbohydrates from each food item and in total
- Percentage of calories from proteins, fats and carbohydrates in the model diet
- Total number of grams of fruits, vegetables, and legumes

3.8.2.2 Iterative process to develop a model diet that meets nutritional requirement and is palatable The iterative process involves the analyst changing quantities of edible grams of food items included in the model diet, so that nutritional requirements are met while keeping the diet palatable. Suggestions for quantities of each food group to include are provided in the Excel sheet, but these are general suggestions partly based on experience, and are not hard and fast rules. Each time a change is made, the analyst can check how that change affected the percentage of calories coming from proteins, fats and carbohydrates in the model diet.

- To begin with, the analyst should change numbers of edible grams in such a way that amounts of sugar, oils, fruits and vegetables, coffee/tea and milk are reasonable and healthy. Often, the amount of sugar decreases and amounts of fruits and vegetables and milk increase.
- Next, amounts of protein-rich foods should be adjusted so that percentage of calories from proteins, fats and carbohydrates all fall within desired ranges.

Note that none of the above changes will affect the total number of calories in the model diet because the Excel model diet program automatically adjusts the amount of cereals to keep total calories constant.

3.8.3 Excel model diet program: Worksheet 3 (adjustments for relative prices and distribution of food costs)

The purpose of Worksheet 3 is to ensure that the final model diet is relatively inexpensive for a nutritious diet. Worksheet 3 begins with the model diet carried over from Worksheet 2 that is palatable and nutritious in terms of calories, macronutrients and fruits and vegetables. Worksheet 3 includes indicators of relative food prices and costs, which are useful for helping to decide how to reduce the cost of the model diet while maintaining its nutritional value. These indicators include:

- Cost per protein of each food
- Cost per calorie of each food
- Percentage of the cost of the model diet for each food
- Percentage distribution of food costs by food group from another source
- Total cost of the model diet

In Worksheet 3, the diet is change in an iterative way to reduce costs while keeping similar nutritional values. This process has four steps:

STEP 1: Substitute less expensive protein-rich foods for more expensive protein-rich foods.

Protein-rich foods are almost always among the most expensive foods in a model diet, and there are often large differences between costs of different protein-rich foods. Step 1 begins with an examination of the cost per protein for protein-rich foods (pulses/beans/tofu, meats/fish, eggs, and dairy). Based on relative costs per protein of protein-rich foods, quantities of these foods should be adjusted (with possibility of dropping an especially expensive protein-rich food), so that there are greater quantities of less expensive protein-rich foods and smaller quantities of more expensive ones, while keeping a similar percentage of calories from proteins. In this way the cost of the model diet can be reduced without affecting the amount of protein. Some animal-based foods, including milk for children, should remain in the diet even when they are relatively expensive. However, it is important to keep local preferences in mind when making these adjustments, so that, for example, not all meat should be replaced by eggs even when eggs are the less expensive. For the same reason, it is important to limit amounts of legumes. Percentages of calories from proteins, fats, and carbohydrates from Worksheet 2 are shown on Worksheet 3 so that the effects of changes in the nutritional content of the model diet in Worksheet 3 can be easily seen. Step 1 sometimes results in a sizable reduction in the cost of the model diet.

STEP 2: Substitute other less expensive foods for more expensive foods.

A further reduction in the cost of the model diet while maintaining its nutritious nature can often be achieved by:

- Adjusting the distribution of the amounts of prepared cereals, roots and tubers, and starchy plantains (foods high in carbohydrates) depending on their relative cost per calorie. Prepared cereals such as bread and pasta are more expensive than unprepared cereals. However, local norms need to be kept in mind about whether people typically prepare pasta and bread from scratch or buy them, and how much of these they eat.

- Increasing the amount of oil if the percentage of calories from fats in the model diet is low (below 20%) and the cost per calorie of oil is lower than the cost per calorie of the main cereal.

STEP 3: Limit the percentage of total food costs spent for each food or food group.

The percentage of the cost of a model diet for each food and food group can be a very useful indicator for assessing the reasonableness of a model diet. If this percentage is too high for any food or food group, it is usually advisable to reduce the amount for that food item or food group in the model diet. For example, if the cost of animal-based foods is greater than 45–50% of the cost of the model diet, the amount of animal-based foods should usually be reduced.

STEP 4: Compare the percentage distribution of food costs in the model diet with the percentage distribution of food costs from another source.

This serves as a further check on how reasonable the model diet is. Large differences between the percentage distribution of food costs by food groups in the model diet compared with the percentage distribution from another source (entered in Worksheet 1) should be explainable or lead to adjustments in the living wage model diet.

3.8.4 Excel model diet program: Worksheet 4 (final diet)

Worksheet 4 displays the final model diet, the cost of each food item, and the total cost of the model diet with and without additional costs for salt, spices and condiments, waste and spoilage, and additional variety.

3.9 Hypothetical Example: Creating a Living Wage Model Diet

This example is roughly based on the model diet developed in the Kenya living wage study for the Lake Naivasha area. Prices of foods and amounts in the initial starting diet have been changed for illustrative purposes.

3.9.1 Worksheet 1. Entering required information and setting initial diet

3.9.1.1 Initial diet and assumptions The starting diet we used was the poverty line diet for urban Kenya (KNBS, 2007), which was based on food consumption of urban households according to a household expenditure survey. This diet included 34 foods, which we aggregated into 11 major food groups. The foods we selected to represent each food group were acceptable foods with the lowest cost per edible gram for the food group found from a local food market survey carried out as part of a living wage study. We included only beef in the meat/fish group, because people did not eat much fish in the part of the Kenya we focused on.

The 2288 calories per person entered at the top of Worksheet 1 (not shown in Table 3.3) was calculated in the Excel calorie requirement program. Percentages for miscellaneous food costs entered at the bottom of Worksheet 1 were 11% for variety, 3% for waste/spoilage, and 1% for salt/spices/condiments (as found in a recent household expenditure survey). Nutritional content and proportion edible were taken from the USDA NAL online database. Cost per kilo of each food item was based on our local market survey of food prices. Since this is a hypothetical example, prices were changed to better illustrate use of the Excel model diet program.

3.9.1.2 Adjusting number of edible grams to ensure total calories required The starting diet contained 2095 calories, which was less than the 2288 calories required (calculated by the calorie requirement Excel program). This meant that the number of grams of each food in the initial diet was automatically increased by a factor of 2288/2095 on Worksheet 1. Table 3.3 is taken from Worksheet 1, which displays both the original number of edible grams and the number of edible grams in the adjusted diet.

3.9.2 Worksheet 2. Adjusting initial model diet to ensure acceptable nutrition in addition to required calories

Worksheet 2 begins with the adjusted initial diet from Worksheet 1 that contains the required number of calories. Nutritional adjustments were made on Worksheet 2, which resulted in a new model diet that meets nutritional requirements, is consistent with Kenya's development level and food preferences, and keeps the total number of calories the same. Worksheet 2 is displayed in Table 3.4. The main differences between the diet from Worksheet 1 and the diet developed in Worksheet 2 were: (1) decreases in amounts of sugar, tea, egg, and meats and (2) increases in amounts of milk, maize meal, fruits and vegetables. The decrease in sugar was because a living wage model diet generally limits sugar to 30 grams per person per day, which is less than people in urban Kenya currently consume. The decrease in tea was because we assumed 2 cups of tea per day for adults. Decreases in quantities of egg and meats came about to keep the percentage of calories from proteins reasonable for a low income country. Milk was increased to allow children 1 cup of milk per day and adults ¼ cup per day for tea. Note that it is not uncommon to see an increase in milk in living wage model diets, because the nutritional standard for milk is often higher than the amount consumed in low income countries. Fruits and vegetables were increased to a total of 325 grams per day including legumes to ensure sufficient micronutrients. The increase in the quantity of maize meal occurs because the Excel program automatically adjusts the value of the main cereal to maintain the required number of calories. As a

Table 3.3 Worksheet 1. Data input

Food group	Food item	Edible grams	Proportion edible	Purchased grams	Calories/100g	Protein/100g	Fats / 100g	Carbs/ 100g	Cost per kilo	# calories in original diet	# calories adjusted to total calories required	# Edible grams adjusted to total calories required	% Distribution of food expenditure from another source
1.A Cereals and grains (e.g. rice, wheat, maize)	Maize	270	1	270	361	10.3	3.9	76.9	36.5	975	1064	295	23.5%
1.B Prepared cereals (e.g. bread and noodles)	Bread	72	1	72	265	8.9	3.3	49.4	124.0	191	208	79	7.3%
2.A Roots and tubers (e.g. potato, cassava)	Potato	100	0.75	133	77	2.0	0.1	17.5	24.0	77	84	109	5.0%
2.B Starchy fruit or vegetable (e.g. plaintains)													
3. Pulses, legumes, beans and nuts	Beans	24	1	24	343	21.2	1.8	62.3	75.0	82	90	26	4.9%
4. Dairy (e.g. milk, sour milk, curd)	Milk	130	1	130	61	3.2	3.3	4.8	60.0	79	87	142	17.9%

Table 3.3 (continued)

Food group	Food item	Edible grams	Proportion edible	Purchased grams	Calories/100g	Protein/100g	Fats / 100g	Carbs/ 100g	Cost per kilo	# calories in original diet	# calories adjusted to total calories required	# Edible grams adjusted to total calories required	% Distribution of food expenditure from another source
5. Eggs	Eggs	8	0.88	9	143	12.6	9.5	0.7	120.0	11	12	9	2.7%
6. Meats & Fish (max of 3 meats and 2 fish)	Beef	52	0.85	61	249	19.1	18.8	0.0	330.0	129	141	57	12.3%
7.A Green leafy vegetables	Kale	40	0.61	66	49	4.3	0.9	8.8	17.3	20	21	44	9.9%
	Cabbage	40	0.80	50	25	1.3	0.1	5.6	11.5	10	11	44	
7.B Other vegetables	Carrot	40	0.89	45	41	1.2	0.3	12.3	29.6	16	18	44	
8. Fruits (max 2 fruits)	Banana	30	0.64	47	89	1.1	0.3	22.8	39.8	27	29	33	6.2%
	Mango	30	0.62	48	60	0.8	0.4	15.0	35.2	18	20	33	
9. Oils & fats	Oil	27	1	27	884	0.0	100.0	0.0	138.0	239	261	29	5.3%
10. Sugar	Sugar	57	1	57	387	0.0	0.0	100.0	83.0	221	241	62	4.1%

11. Nonalcoholic beverages	Tea	2	1	2	1	0	0	0.3	450.0	0	0	2.6	9.0%
12. Other													
TOTAL										2095	2288		
Additional costs													
Percentage added for salt, spices, sauces, and condiments	Usually 1% to 3%. Base on household expenditure survey data when possible.												**1%**
Percentage added for spoilage and waste	Add 3% to 5% for wastage and spoilage for developing countries. % increases with development. This assumption is very conservative.												**3%**
Percentage added for variety	Between 10% and 15% added for developing countries to allow for variety. % increases with development.												**11%**

Table 3.4 Worksheet 2. Nutrition adjustments

Food group	Food item	# Grams edible adjusted to total calories required (output from calorie adjustment worksheet)	Grams edible with adjust-ments for % P, %F, %C, & judgement	Suggestions on quantities to use	Expla-nation of adjust-ments made	Calories/ 100g	Calories in work-sheet 1 diet
1.A Cereals and grains (for example: rice, wheat, maize)	Maize	295	324	No changes allowed for main cereal		361	1064
1.B Prepared cereals (for example: bread and noodles)	Bread	79	79	Use appropriate number of slices or rolls		265	208
2.A Roots and tubers (for example: potato, cassava)	Potato	109	109	Amount depends on food habits (see worksheet 1)		77	84
2.B Starchy fruit or vegetable (for example: plaintains)				Amount depends on food habits (see worksheet 1)			
3. Pulses, legumes, beans (for example: legumes, beans, nuts)	Beans	26	26	Usually between 1 and 2 servings (28-56 grams)		343	90
4. Dairy (for example: milk, sour milk, curd)	Milk	142	171	Usually at least 1 cup pd for children and some milk for adults for coffee/tea	1 cup to age 16 & 1/4 cup for adults to use in tea	61	87
5. Eggs	Eggs	9	6	Usually in terms of number of eggs pw. Medium egg usually around 50 grams	1 per week	143	12
6. Meats & Fish (maximum of 3 meats and 2 fish)	Beef	57	36	Usually in terms of number of servings per week (a serving is usually 85 edible grams). Quantity of meat increases with development	3 meals per week	249	141

Calories in diet	% Calories in diet	Protiens/ 100g	Grams protiens in work-sheet 1 diet	Grams proteins in diet	Fats/ 100g	Grams fat in worksheet 1 diet	Grams fat in diet	Carbs/ 100g	Grams carbs in worksheet 1 diet	Grams carbs in diet
1170	51.1	10.3	30.4	33.4	3.9	11.5	12.6	76.9	226.8	249
208	9.1	8.9	7.0	7.0	3.3	2.6	2.6	49.4	38.8	39
84	3.7	2.0	2.2	2.2	0.1	0.1	0.1	17.5	19.1	19
90	3.9	21.2	5.6	5.6	1.8	0.5	0.5	62.3	16.3	16
104	4.6	3.2	4.5	5.5	3.3	4.7	5.6	4.8	6.8	8
9	0.4	12.6	1.1	0.8	9.5	0.8	0.6	0.7	0.1	0
91	4.0	19.1	10.8	7.0	18.8	10.7	6.8	0.0	0.0	0

Table 3.4 (continued)

Food group	Food item	# Grams edible adjusted to total calories required (output from calorie adjustment worksheet)	Grams edible with adjust-ments for %P, %F, %C, & judgement	Suggestions on quantities to use	Expla-nation of adjust-ments made	Calories/ 100g	Calories in work-sheet 1 diet
7.A Green leafy vegetables	Kale	44	66	At least 1 GLV and 1 fruit.	Increased all fruits	49	21
	Cabbage	44	66	Minimum 300	and	25	11
7.B Other vegetables	Carrot	44	66	grams of fruits plus vegetables plus legumes	vegetables by 15.4 to ensure	41	18
8. Fruits	Banana	33	50	Increase by 25	325	89	29
	Mango	33	50	grams for each development level	grams of legumes, fruits and vegetables	60	20
9. Oils & fats	Oil	29	30	Usually 30-34 grams. It can be lower if >15% fats in diet	30 usual	884	261
10. Sugar	Sugar	62	30	Usually between 24 and 30 grams	30 is usual maximum	387	241
11. Nonalcoholic beverages	Tea	2.6	2.6	No soft drinks. Tea 2 grams and coffee 7 grams per cup. Usually 2 cups pd for adults	2 cups per adult per day	1	0
12. Other				No cakes or confection			
TOTAL		Fruits + vegetables + legumes	325				2288

result of these changes, the new diet in Worksheet 2 had 11.7% of calories from proteins, which was not too far from our 11–12% target; 23.6% of calories came from fats and 64.7% of from carbohydrates, all of which were within required ranges.

3.9.3 Worksheet 3. Taking relative food prices into account

The purpose of Worksheet 3 is to: (i) change the mix of foods to make the diet less expensive, while maintaining nutritional standards, and (ii) check that the percentage distribution of food expenditures in the model

Calories in diet	% Calories in diet	Protiens/ 100g	Grams protiens in work-sheet 1 diet	Grams proteins in diet	Fats/ 100g	Grams fat in worksheet 1 diet	Grams fat in diet	Carbs /100g	Grams carbs in worksheet 1 diet	Grams carbs in diet
33	1.4	4.3	1.9	2.9	0.9	0.4	0.6	8.8	3.8	6
17	0.7	1.3	0.6	0.9	0.1	0.0	0.1	5.6	2.4	4
27	1.2	1.2	0.5	0.8	0.3	0.1	0.2	12.3	5.4	8
44	1.9	1.1	0.4	0.5	0.3	0.1	0.1	22.8	7.5	11
30	1.3	0.8	0.3	0.4	0.4	0.1	0.2	15.0	4.9	7
265	11.6	0.0	0.0	0.0	100.0	29.5	30.0	0.0	0.0	0
116	5.1	0.0	0.0	0.0	0.0	0.0	0.0	100.0	62.3	30
0	0.0	0.0	0.0	0.0	0.0	0.0	0.0	0.3	0.0	0
2288			65.2	67.0		61.2	60.1		394.2	398
			11.4%	11.7%		24.1%	23.6%		64.5%	64.7%

diet is not very different than the distribution from another source, unless there is a good explanation and justification for the differences. Worksheet 3 is shown in Table 3.5. In the first step we reduced the cost of protein-rich foods. The cost per protein of beans was around one-sixth the cost per protein of meat, and the cost per protein of eggs was about half the cost per protein of meat. Therefore we increased the amount of beans to one and a half portions per day and eggs to two per week, and reduced meat to two portions per week. Note that despite these changes, the percentage of calories from proteins remained unchanged. The only

Table 3.5 Worksheet 3. Taking prices into account

Food Groups	Food item	# Edible grams from work-sheet 2 diet	Final grams edible with adjustments for %P, quality %P, %F, %C & relative food prices	Explanation of final adjustments	# Grams purchased	Calories/ 100g	Calories in final diet	% Calories final diet
1.A Cereals and grains (for example: rice, wheat, maize)	Maize	324	344		344	361	1242	54.3
1.B Prepared cereals (for example: bread and noodles)	Bread	79	42	Reduced to 2 slices per day	42	265	111	4.9
2.A Roots and tubers (for example: potato, cassava)	Potato	109	109		146	77	84	3.7
2.B Starchy fruit or vegetable (for example: plaintains)								
3. Pulses, legumes, beans (for example: legumes, beans, nuts)	Beans	26	42	Increased to 1.5 portions per day as inexpensive protein	42	343	144	6.3
4. Dairy (for example: milk, sour milk, curd)	Milk	171	171		171	61	104	4.6
5. Eggs	Eggs	6	13	Increased to 2 eggs per week	15	143	19	0.8
6. Meats & Fish (maximum of 3 meats and 2 fish)	Beef	36	24	Reduced to 2 portions per week	28	249	60	2.6
7.A Green leafy vegetables	Kale	66	63		103	49	31	1.3
7.B Other vegetables	Cabbage	66	63		79	25	16	0.7
	Carrot	66	63		71	41	26	1.1
8. Fruits	Banana	50	47		74	89	42	1.8
	Mango	50	47		76	60	28	1.2

Protein/ 100g	Grams proteins final diet	Fats/ 100g	Grams fat final diet	Carbs/ 100g	Grams carbs final diet	Cost per kilo	% Distribution of food expenditure from another source	% Distribution of costs in model diet	Cost per protien final model diet	Cost per calorie final model diet
10.3	35.4	3.9	13.4	76.9	265	37	23.5%	19.8%	0.35	0.010
8.9	3.7	3.3	1.4	49.4	21	124	7.3%	8.2%	1.39	0.047
2.0	2.2	0.1	0.1	17.5	19	24	5.0%	5.5%	1.60	0.042
21.19	8.9	1.8	0.8	62.3	26	75	4.9%	5.0%	0.35	0.022
3.2	5.5	3.3	5.6	4.8	8	60	17.9%	16.1%	1.88	0.098
12.6	1.6	9.5	1.2	0.7	0	120	2.7%	2.8%	1.08	0.095
19.1	4.6	18.8	4.5	0.0	0	330	12.3%	14.7%	2.03	0.156
4.3	2.7	0.9	0.6	8.8	6	17	9.9%	2.8%	0.66	0.058
1.3	0.8	0.1	0.1	5.6	4	12	0.0%	1.4%	1.11	0.058
1.2	0.8	0.3	0.2	12.3	8	30	0.0%	3.3%	2.77	0.081
1.1	0.5	0.3	0.1	22.8	11	40	6.2%	4.6%	5.65	0.070
0.8	0.4	0.4	0.2	15	7	35	0.0%	4.2%	7.10	0.095

Table 3.5 (continued)

Food Groups	Food item	# Edible grams from work-sheet 2 diet	Final grams edible with adjustments for %P, quality %P, %F, %C & relative food prices	Expla-nation of final adjust-ments	# Grams pur-chased	Calories/ 100g	Calories in final diet	% Calories final diet
9. Oils & fats	Oil	30	30		30	884	265	11.6
10. Sugar	Sugar	30	30		30	387	116	5.1
11. Nonalcoholic beverages	Tea	2	2		2	1	0	0.0
12. Other								
TOTAL		Fruits + vegetables + legumes	325				2288	

other change in Worksheet 3 was to reduce the amount of bread to two slices a day per person, because bread is expensive relative to maize and discussions with workers indicated that two slices of bread per day was considered decent.

Next, we compared the percentage distribution of costs by major food group for the model diet with the percentage distribution from a household expenditure survey. They were fairly similar – the main difference being that Kenyans spend 9% of their food budget on non-alcoholic beverages, while only around 1% is spent on tea in our model diet, most likely due to the consumption of soft drinks, which are not included in our model diet.

Worksheet 3 reduced the cost of the model diet by 10% (from around KSh81 to KSh73) without substantially changing its nutritional value.

3.9.4 Worksheet 4. Final diet

Cost of the model diet is calculated in Worksheet 4 based on the prices entered into Worksheet 1. This cost was increased by 15% in this example to allow for some variety, salt, spices, sauces and condiments, and for minimal spoilage and wastage using percentages entered in worksheet 1. Table 3.6 presents Worksheet 4.

3.9.4.1 Conclusions The model diet is consistent with local food preferences, level of development, and relative prices in Kenya.

Protein/-100g	Grams proteins final diet	Fats/ 100g	Grams fat final diet	Carbs/ 100g	Grams carbs final diet	Cost per kilo	% Distribution of food expenditure from another source	% Distribution of costs in model diet	Cost per protien final model diet	Cost per calorie final model diet
0	0.0	100	30.0	0	0	138	5.3%	6.5%	–	0.016
0	0.0	0	0.0	100	30	83	4.1%	3.9%	–	0.021
0	0.0	0	0.0	0.3	0	450	9.0%	1.1%	–	45.000
	67		58.2		404					
	11.7%		22.9%		65.4%					

- Maize meal is central to the model diet. It is an inexpensive source of calories, and it provides 55% of all calories in the model diet.
- There was relatively little meat (beef) in the model diet in order to keep the diet relatively low in cost.
- Considerable amount of beans (42 grams) is included in the model diet. This helps ensure there is a sufficient number of quality proteins at relatively low-cost because beans are much less expensive per protein compared to beef. Beans are a central part of the Kenyan diet.
- A reasonably large amount of potato is included in the model diet because it is the lowest cost, and most commonly eaten, root and tuber in Kenya.
- Vegetables are represented by carrots, cabbage, and kale. They are plentiful and inexpensive in local markets which helps reduce food costs. It also helps increase calcium and iron as green leafy vegetables, such as kale, are relatively high in these. Note that the 11% for variety enables workers to purchase a greater variety of vegetables to help ensure a range of micronutrients.
- Quantity of milk is 1 cup per day for children, and a quarter cup per day for adults to add to tea.

Table 3.6 Worksheet 4. Final model diet and food cost per person per day

	Food item	Edible grams	Purchased grams	Cost per kilo	Cost
1.A Cereals and grains	Maize	344	344	36.5	12.56
(for example: rice, wheat, maize)					
1.B Prepared cereals	Bread	42	42	124.0	5.21
(for example: bread and noodles)					
2.A Roots and tubers	Potato	109	146	24.0	3.49
(for example: potato, cassava)					
2.B Starchy fruit or vegetable					
(for example: plaintains)					
3. Pulses, legumes, beans	Beans	42	42	75.0	3.15
(for example: legumes, beans, nuts)					
4. Dairy	Milk	171	171	60.0	10.25
(for example: milk, sour milk, curd)					
5. Eggs	Eggs	13	15	120.0	1.77
6. Meats & Fish	Beef	24	28	330.0	9.32
(maximum of 3 meats and 2 fish)					

7.A Green leafy vegetables	Kale	63	103	17.3	1.78
	Cabbage	63	79	11.5	0.90
7.B Other vegetables	Carrot	63	71	29.6	2.09
8. Fruits	Banana	47	74	39.8	2.93
	Mango	47	76	35.0	2.68
9. Oils & fats	Oil	30	30	138.0	4.14
10. Sugar	Sugar	30	30	83.0	2.49
11. Nonalcoholic beverages	Tea	2	2	450.0	0.72
12. Other					
Total cost of model diet excluding additional costs indicated below					63.49
Total cost of model diet including additional costs indicated below					73.01
Percentage added for salt, spices, sauces, and condiments	Usually 1% to 3%. Base on household expenditure survey data when possible.				1%
Percentage added for spoilage and waste	The living wage model diet typically adds 3% to 5% for wastage and spoilage for devloping countries. % increases with development. This assumption is very conservative.				3%
Percentage added for variety	Typically between 10% and 15% additional cost for developing countries should be added to cost of a living wage model diets to allow for variety. What % to use should depend on the number of food items included in a living wage diet (the more food items included the lower the additional percentage needed for variety), extent to which one or two food items is dominant in each food group, and development level as additional variety is increasingly needed for palatability.				11%

NOTES

1. WHO/FAO (2003) recommend 400 grams of fruits and vegetables per person per day including legumes – but since this target is not even met in most developed countries, we decided on a minimum of 300 grams (see Section 3.5.1).
2. The body mass indicator (BMI) is equal to weight (in kilos) divided by height squared (in meters). A healthy weight is generally indicated by BMI of 18.5–24.9.
3. See WHO (2004) Table 5.1 for PAR values for a variety of daily activities.
4. Table 3.2 from WHO (2004) is used for energy requirements during first year of life; Table 4.5 is used for energy requirements for boys ages 1–17; and Table 4.6 is used for energy requirements for girls ages 1–17.
5. This estimate of 1892 calories per child was made using an equal weighting of all ages. This is very similar to the 1875 calories required per child for one child age 6 and one child age 11 with moderate activity.
6. According to WHO (Clugston, n.d.), a breastfeeding mother requires an additional 500 calories per day. Assuming 80% efficiency in production of breastmilk – 400 of the additional calories go to the child and therefore only 100 extra calories per day are required for the family. For a family with 2 children, this amounts to 2.9 additional calories per family member per day over the reproductive years, and 4.3 additional calories for a family with 6 children.
7. Government of India (2010) also has its own equations for BMR, which result in slightly lower energy requirements than those of WHO (2004).
8. It is possible to change BMI in the Excel program when there is a good reason.
9. 1.08 was the median and modal value for 130 locations in Wikipedia (2014). This ratio was between 1.07 and 1.09 for roughly two-thirds of the locations.
10. The EUFIC (2012) review of fruit and vegetable consumption in 19 Western European countries found only 4 countries with average consumption of over 400 grams per day of fruits and vegetables, 7 countries with average consumption of 300–400 grams, and 8 countries with average consumption less than 300 grams per day. In the United States, median intake of fruits and vegetables in 2011 was 2.6 portions per day for adults and 2.3 portions per day for adolescents, which is around one-half of the recommended 5 portions per day (CDC, 2013).
11. This approach implicitly assumes that: (i) reported number of calories consumed per person increases monotonically with household income (otherwise it might not be possible to unambiguously identify the household income decile or quintile where required number of calories is attained); (ii) reported number of calories consumed per person in the lowest household income decile is less than the required number of calories per person (otherwise lowest income decile or quintile would be the income decile or quintile identified and this would be unfortunate as it would mean that food consumption of very poor persons would be used to set a model diet); and (iii) calorie requirements (which are partly determined by body size and activity level) do not systematically vary by income.
12. There are 'four official USDA food plans. The Thrifty Food Plan serves as a national standard for a nutritious diet at a minimal cost and is used as the basis for maximum food stamp allotments. The Low-Cost, Moderate-Cost, and Liberal Food Plans are used for various purposes: bankruptcy courts often use the Low-Cost Food Plan to determine the portion of a bankrupt person's income to allocate to necessary food expenses. The Department of Defense uses the value of the Liberal Food Plan to determine the Basic Allowance for Subsistence rates for all service members. Many divorce courts use the values of the USDA Food Plans to set alimony payments' (Carlson et al., 2007, p. ES-1).
13. In technical language, 'the model is a constrained nonlinear optimization, with linear constraints and a nonlinear objective function. The model is programmed in the General Algebraic Modeling System and solved sequentially with both the Minos and Conopt solvers' (Carlson et al., 2007, p. A2-1).

14. An example of how blind use of a linear programming optimization model can lead to senseless results is provided by Chastre et al. (2007, p. 45). They reported that 'in Ethiopia the diet requires enormous quantities of black pepper . . . [29 and 27 grams per day in each season for children less than 24 months and 351 and 321 grams in each season for a family of 5 persons] which are unlikely to be consumable in particular for young children.'
15. For example, USDA (Carlson et al., 2007, p. A2-1) relaxed two nutrition requirements ('it is not possible for most baskets to meet RDA [required daily allowance] for vitamin E nor the AI [adequate intake] for potassium). Hence these dietary constraints were relaxed in the models'). In another example where common sense was used, 'consumption constraints are placed on all food groups to prevent the solution from containing an unreasonable amount of food from a single group. These constraints also force a more varied diet than the model would otherwise contain.'
16. In some countries, specific condiments, sauces or spices are important enough to include as a separate food item in the model diet. For example fish sauce in Vietnam and coconut in Sri Lanka are such integral parts of cooking that they were included under 'other' foods in living wage model diets for these countries.
17. For example in Kenya, we estimated what percentage of a mango is edible by weighing several local mangos with and without the pit. In Vietnam and Mauritius, we purchased a variety of vegetables and fish and weighed them before and after workers prepared them for cooking.
18. When relevant data are unavailable, FAOSTAT food balance supply data can be used, but this is a less desirable starting diet because it is based on food availability rather than household consumption.

APPENDIX 3.1

Table 3A.1 Nutritional content and percent inedible of common foods

Food group/ Food item	No. calories per 100 grams	No. proteins per 100 grams	No. fats per 100 grams	No. carbo-hydrates per 100 grams	% inedible (blank when no waste)
Cereals/grains					
Rice, white short	358	6.5	0.5	79.2	
Rice, white medium	360	6.6	0.6	79.3	
Rice, white long	365	7.1	0.7	80.0	
Rice, brown medium	362	7.5	2.7	76.2	
Rice, brown long	370	7.9	2.9	77.2	
RICE, WHITE AVERAGE (3)	361	6.7	0.6	79.5	
RICE, BROWN AVERAGE (2)	366	7.7	2.8	76.7	
Wheat flour, white all purpose	364	10.3	1.0	76.3	
Wheat flour, whole grain	340	13.2	2.5	72.0	
Wheat soft	340	10.7	2.0	75.4	
Wheat hard	342	11.3	1.7	75.9	
Wheat durum	339	13.7	2.5	71.1	
WHEAT AVERAGE (3)	340	11.9	2.1	74.1	
Corn flour whole grain	361	6.9	3.9	76.9	
Corn whole grain yellow	365	9.4	4.7	74.3	
Sorghum grain	329	10.6	3.5	72.9	
Sorghum flour whole grain	359	8.4	3.3	76.6	
Millet	378	11.0	4.2	72.9	

Prepared cereals/grains					
Bread, white	266	8.9	3.3	49.4	
Bread, whole wheat	267	10.7	3.2	48.7	
Naan, commercial	291	9.6	5.7	50.4	
Naan, whole wheat	286	10.2	6.7	46.2	
Pita, white	275	9.1	1.2	55.7	
Pita, whole wheat	266	9.8	2.6	55.0	
Pasta, fresh	288	11.3	1.3	54.7	
Macaroni, spaghetti, dry	371	13.0	1.5	74.7	
Macaroni, spaghetti, dry, whole wheat	348	14.6	1.4	75.0	
Rice noodles, dry	364	6.0	0.6	80.2	
Fruits					
Apple	52	0.3	0.2	13.8	10% (core, stem)
Apricot	48	1.4	0.4	11.1	7% (pit)
Banana	89	1.1	0.3	22.8	36% (skin)
Guava	68	2.6	1.0	14.3	22% (skin)
Mandarin	53	0.8	0.3	13.3	26% (peel, seeds)
Mango	60	0.8	0.4	15.0	29% (seed, skin)
Orange	47	0.9	0.1	11.8	27% (peel, seeds)
Papaya	43	0.5	0.3	10.8	38% (skin, stems)
Passion fruit	97	2.2	0.7	23.4	48% (shell)
Peach	39	0.9	0.3	9.5	4% (pit)
Pear	57	0.4	0.1	15.2	10% (stem, core, seed)

Table 3A.1 (continued)

Food group/ Food item	No. calories per 100 grams	No. proteins per 100 grams	No. fats per 100 grams	No. carbo-hydrates per 100 grams	% inedible (blank when no waste)
Pineapple	50	0.5	0.1	13.1	49% (8% core, 18% crown, 28% parings)
Watermelon	30	0.6	0.2	7.6	48% (rind, seeds)
AVERAGE FRUIT (13 excluding avocado)	56	1.0	0.3	14.0	25% (considerable variation)
Avocado	160	2.0	14.7	8.5	26% (skin, seeds)
Coconut	354	3.3	33.5	15.2	48% (shell, skin, water)
Plantains					
Plantains	122	1.3	0.4	31.9	35% (skin, stems)
Vegetables					
Kale	49	4.3	0.9	8.8	39% (stem ends, tough stems & midrib parts)
Pak choy	13	1.5	0.2	2.2	12% (base, damaged leaves)
Spinach	23	2.9	0.4	3.6	28% (large stems & roots)
Sweet potato leaves	42	2.5	0.5	8.8	6% (tough stems & bruised leaves)
Cabbage	25	1.3	0.1	5.6	20% (outer leaves & core)
GLV VEGETABLE AVERAGE (5)	30	2.5	0.4	5.8	21% (considerable variation)
Pumpkin	26	1.0	0.1	6.5	30% (seeds, rind, stems)

Tomato	18	0.9	0.2	3.9	9% (core, stems)
Carrot	52	1.2	0.3	12.3	11% (crown top & scrapings)
Onion	40	1.1	0.1	9.3	10% (stem ends, sprouts, defects)
Squash, summer (e.g. zucchini)	16	1.2	0.2	3.4	5% (ends)
Squash, winter (e.g. butternut, acorn)	34	1.0	0.1	8.6	29% (seeds, rind, stems)
Eggplant	25	1.0	0.2	5.9	19% (ends, parings, trimmings)
Cauliflower	25	1.9	0.3	5.0	61% (leaf, stalks, core, trimmings)
Broccoli	34	2.8	0.4	6.6	39% (leaves, tough stalks, trimmings)
Cucumber	15	0.7	0.1	3.6	3% (ends)
Radish	16	0.7	0.1	3.4	10% (stem ends, rootlets, trimmings)
NON-GLV VEGETABLE AVERAGE (11)	27	1.2	0.2	6.2	21% (considerable variation)
Roots and tubers					
Cassava	160	1.4	0.3	38.1	16% (skin)
Potato	77	2.0	0.1	17.5	25% (parings, trimmings)
Sweet potato	86	1.6	0.1	27.9	28% (parings, trimmings)
Yam	118	1.5	0.2	20.1	14% (skin)
Eggs					
Chicken egg	143	12.6	9.5	0.7	12% (shell)
Duck eggs	185	12.8	13.8	1.5	12% (shell)

Table 3A.1 (continued)

Food group/ Food item	No. calories per 100 grams	No. proteins per 100 grams	No. fats per 100 grams	No. carbo-hydrates per 100 grams	% inedible (blank when no waste)
Meats					
Chuck blade roast w/bone 1/8” fat	248	17.2	19.4	0.0	19% (bone)
Bottom round 1/8” fat	187	20.7	10.9	0.0	3% (connective tissue)
Salami, dry or hard pork	407	22.6	39.8	1.6	
Salami, beef & pork	336	21.9	25.9	2.4	
Ham, regular sliced (11% fat)	178	22.6	9.0	0.0	
Chicken broiler or fryer meat & skin raw (no giblets or neck)	215	18.6	15.1	0.0	32% (bone)
Chicken giblets	124	17.9	4.5	1.8	
Chicken liver	119	16.9	4.8	0.7	
Pork, fresh shoulder	186	17.4	12.4	0.0	24% (9% bone, 15% connective tissue)
Pork, cured bacon	417	12.6	39.7	1.3	
Lamb, shoulder blade, lean only	151	19.3	7.6	0.0	
Lamb, rib 1/4 inch fat	372	14.5	34.4	0.0	27% (bone)
Goat, lean only	109	20.6	2.3	0.0	
Fish					
Anchovy	131	20.4	4.8	0.0	
Catfish	95	16.4	2.8	0.0	
Carp	127	17.4	5.6	0.0	
Herring	158	18.0	9.0	0.0	

Whiting	90	18.3	1.3	0.0	
Sea bass	97	18.4	2.0	0.0	
Snapper	100	20.5	1.3	0.0	
Salmon	208	20.4	13.4	0.0	
Whitefish	134	19.1	5.9	0.0	
Cod	82	17.8	0.7	0.0	
Tilapia	96	20.1	1.7	0.0	
Rook fish, Pacific	90	18.4	1.3	0.0	
Mackerel, Atlantic	205	18.6	13.9	0.0	
Mackerel, Spanish	139	19.3	6.3	0.0	
FISH AVERAGE (14)	125	18.9	1.9	0.0	Between 25% and 50% for whole fish depending on size and type of fish; 40% is typical based on our experience
FISH, WHITE (9)	101	18.5	2.5	0.0	
OILY FISH (5)	168	19.3	9.5	0.0	
Oils					
Oil (soybean, peanut, palm, canola, etc.)	884	0.0	100.0	0.0	
Sugar					
White	387	0.0	0.0	100.0	
Brown	380	0.1	0.0	98.1	
Dairy					
Milk (cow)	61	3.2	3.3	4.8	
Milk, dry	496	26.3	26.7	38.4	
Milk, evaporated	134	6.8	7.6	10.0	
Yoghurt	61	3.5	3.3	4.7	

Table 3A.1 (continued)

Food group/ Food item	No. calories per 100 grams	No. proteins per 100 grams	No. fats per 100 grams	No. carbo-hydrates per 100 grams	% inedible (blank when no waste)
Non-alcoholic beverages					
Coffee	1	0.0	0.0	0.3	
Tea	1	0.0	0.0	0.3	
Pulses, beans, nuts					
Peanuts	567	25.8	49.2	16.1	
Tofu, regular	76	8.1	4.8	1.9	
Tofu, firm	145	15.8	8.7	4.3	
Beans sprouts	122	13.1	6.7	9.6	
Lentils	352	24.6	1.1	63.4	
Beans, red kidney	347	23.9	1.2	62.6	
Beans, mung	337	22.5	1.1	61.3	
Beans, navy	337	22.3	1.5	60.8	
Beans, pinto	347	21.4	1.2	62.6	
Beans, white	336	21.1	1.2	62.6	
Beans, chick peas	378	20.5	6.0	63.0	
Beans, lima	338	21.5	0.7	63.4	
AVERAGE BEANS (7)	346	21.9	1.8	62.3	

Note: GLV means green leafy vegetable. Percentage inedible for fish taken from Bangladesh National Nutrition Council (2013).

Source: USDA NAL online database.

APPENDIX 3.2

Table 3A.2 Typical sizes of common food items (in purchased grams)

Food item	Small	Medium/typical	Large
Banana	158	184	213
Apple	166	202	248
Orange	107	179	252
Mandarin	84	119	162
Papaya	174	–	1260
Avocado	–	272	–
Coconut	–	763	–
Eggplant	–	677	–
Cauliflower	294	1508	2154
Broccoli	–	997	–
Cucumber	–	310	–
Radish	2	5	10
Onion	78	122	167
Tomato	69	135	200
Carrot	56	69	81
Chicken egg	42	50	57
Duck egg	–	70	–
Bread	–	29 per slice	–
Pita	–	60	–
Naan	–	106	–
Cooking oil	–	13.6 per tablespoon	–
Sugar	–	4.2 per teaspoon	–
Milk	–	244 per cup	–

Source: USDA NAL online database.

4. Local food prices

PART I. BACKGROUND AND OVERVIEW

4.1 Introduction

Food is the most important expense for workers in almost all developing countries. For this reason, ascertaining local food prices is a major part of the primary data collection for a living wage study in our methodology. This chapter describes how to determine food prices to use to estimate the cost of a living wage model diet (described in Chapter 3).

4.1.1 Why collect local food prices

There are several reasons why living wage studies collect local food prices. First, relevant, reliable, and recent prices for a wide variety of foods are rarely available from other sources. Second, even when food prices are reported on a regular basis, they are usually only reported for a restricted number of foods and often only for the capital city. Third, we have found that prices reported by government and NGOs are typically higher than workers actually pay, since workers often buy food from different locations and in different qualities and quantities. In our living wage methodology a special effort is made to ascertain food prices for a basic acceptable quality level that reflect how cost-conscious workers typically shop for food. This is not done in government statistics that are mainly concerned with tracking changes in food prices for CPI and so usually follow prices of easily identifiable foods (e.g. 125 gram Kraft cheese box; one kilo of Maharajah brand rice; Uha brand soybean oil sold in a prepackaged plastic one liter bottle).

4.1.2 Collecting local food prices that mimic the way that cost-conscious workers buy food

Our living wage methodology collects local food prices in a cost-effective way. At the same time, our methodology attempts to make sure that these prices are unbiased and representative of prices paid by workers. Prices are collected for a variety of qualities and quantities for each food from the types of venues where workers typically shop. In the analysis stage, the lowest priced foods of acceptable quality for each major food group are identified and subsequently used to calculate the cost of the living wage model diet. The idea of the methodology is to mimic the way in which cost-conscious workers who earn a living wage would shop for food. This includes buying foods that are on sale, in season, and of basic acceptable quality.

4.1.3 Steps in a local food price survey

Below is an overview of the steps in a local food price survey. Each step is explained in detail in the remainder of this chapter.

- Decide on which food items to price and adapt data collection forms. Examples of food price forms based on previous living wage studies are presented in Appendix 4.1. Different forms are provided for shops and supermarkets and for multi-vendor venues such as open air markets. These examples always need to be modified to be relevant for a location. Sometimes they need to be translated into the local language.
- Identify, hire and train local investigators to help in the collection of local food prices.
- Determine places that workers typically shop and make a schedule of venues to visit as part of the food price survey. Include one to two days of field testing and training in the schedule.
- Visit some venues where workers typically shop together with one or two local workers and decide on quantities and qualities of each food item to price.
- Modify data collection forms accordingly.
- Pretest data collection forms and procedures, and make necessary changes. Results from a pretest can often be used in final analysis.
- Collect food price data from local venues.
- Enter food prices into an Excel spreadsheet each evening during the food price survey. The least expensive food items to represent each food group will be identified during analysis.
- As food price collection continues, the supervisor can decide to stop collecting prices of more expensive items in each food group when this becomes clear.
- Check to see that investigators are collecting sufficient price points for each food item. This is especially important for foods with high price variability and foods that form a high proportion of food expenditure in the living wage model diet.
- Analyze food prices collected and determine price per kilo for each food item, and based on this, identify the least expensive food(s) per edible gram in each major food group to include in the model diet.

4.2 Selecting Specific Food Items on Which to Collect Prices

Model diets (Chapter 3) are always comprised of major food groups. They do not usually indicate specific food items. For example, model diets include vegetables, but do not specify which vegetables. Model diets include dairy, but do not usually indicate whether this is fresh milk, powdered milk, UHT milk, or cheese or yogurt. Guidance is provided below on how to decide on specific foods for which to collect prices. In general, the specific foods selected for pricing should be relatively inexpensive, commonly consumed and available, and culturally acceptable. At a later stage, the least expensive acceptable foods in each food group would be selected to include in the living wage model diet.

4.2.1 Fruits and vegetables

There is almost always a wide variety of fruits and vegetables to choose from. To begin with, prices should be collected for many fruits and vegetables (except especially expensive ones). Analysis of the prices collected will enable selection of the least expensive fruits and vegetables to include in the model diet.

It is worth noting that since fruits and vegetables vary greatly in proportion edible, there may be a difference between the least expensive fruits and vegetables per purchased gram and the least expensive per edible gram. This means that the proportion edible needs to be considered when selecting the least expensive fruits and vegetables to include in a model diet.

It is also worth noting that in some countries, including India, Bangladesh, and Pakistan, tomato and onion are used like spices and eaten in almost every meal. Therefore, small amounts of tomato and onion should be included in the model diet even if they are not the least expensive.

4.2.2 Beans and pulses

Beans and pulses are inexpensive sources of proteins, and so usually an important part of low-cost nutritious diets. The beans or pulses included in a model diet should be relatively inexpensive for this food group and commonly eaten by workers. When beans or pulses are an important part of the diet, it is appropriate to include two types of beans or pulses in a model diet. For example, in the Dominican Republic we used equal quantities of black beans and pinto beans; in Kenya, where many different beans are sold, we used equal quantities of red kidney beans (which were found in all markets) and the least expensive other bean found in each shop.

4.2.3 Oils and fats

Normally only one oil is included in a model diet. It is usually an inexpensive vegetable oil that is of acceptable quality to workers. The type of oil included varies across countries. In Malawi, we used cooking oil sold in open air markets from a large container. In Kenya, we used solid cooking oil sold in chunks in shops. In the Dominican Republic, we used soybean oil sold in a 128 ounce prepackaged plastic bottle. In Mauritius, we used vegetable oil sold in a one liter prepackaged plastic bottle.

4.2.4 Meats, chicken, and fish

It is necessary to identify early in the fieldwork the cuts and types of meats that are relatively inexpensive, and commonly eaten by workers and acceptable to them, so that prices can be collected for these. Note that prices should be collected only for animal products that are culturally acceptable. Beef is not acceptable in most of India. Pork is not acceptable in Muslim countries.

In Malawi, small dried fish that are eaten whole turned out to be the most commonly eaten inexpensive animal product. These small dried fish had the added advantage of providing needed calcium, since milk was imported and very expensive in Malawi. In countries where freezers are common, frozen chicken or frozen fish might be less expensive than fresh chicken and fresh fish, as we found in living wage studies in South Africa and the Dominican Republic.

4.2.5 Eggs

When different types of eggs are sold, such as chicken eggs, duck eggs, organic eggs, and 'industrial' eggs, the least expensive widely eaten type should be selected. In countries where the weight of eggs is not listed on a package, eggs should be weighed during fieldwork to determine average number of grams per egg and therefore cost per kilo.

4.2.6 Milk

Milk is almost always used to represent dairy products. Milk can be powdered, fresh, evaporated, or UHT. Use the type of milk that is least expensive per liter, provided that it is widely available and commonly used. For powdered milk, the quantity of powdered milk that makes one liter of milk when water is added should be noted. This is usually indicated on the package. In some countries yogurt and/or cheese are also included in model diets.

4.2.7 Grains

The main grain eaten in a country is usually common knowledge. Researchers need to be careful in countries where there are regional differences in diets. For example, while rice is the most important grain in China, there are regions where wheat is more important. Also, in some countries, people typically eat more than one grain daily. In India, rice and wheat (for chapatti and nan, flat breads made from wheat flour) are both important – and therefore both rice and wheat should be included in a model diet for most of India.

The quality and consequently the cost per kilo of grains such as rice and wheat can be quite different. This means that prices need to be collected for several acceptable and relatively inexpensive varieties. In this, it is useful to ask vendors and workers about which widely available varieties of rice and wheat are felt to be decent.

In locations where grains need to be milled, the cost of milling needs to be ascertained. We found, for example, that workers in Malawi bought maize that needed to be milled and workers in India bought wheat that needed to be milled.

4.2.8 Sugar

Both brown sugar and white sugar are usually available. Prices should be collected for both of these until it becomes clear which is less expensive.

4.2.9 Summary

Table 4.1 summarizes the above discussion. Suggestions are provided on the number of food items to include in a living wage model diet for each major food group together with examples and comments.

PART II. COLLECTING LOCAL FOOD PRICES

4.3 Selecting Venues Where Workers Buy Food

4.3.1 Types of venues where workers buy food

Workers buy food in a variety of settings. In some parts of the world, workers buy food mainly in open air markets. In other parts of the world, workers buy food mainly from street vendors, or from small neighborhood stores, and in other parts of the world, workers buy mainly from supermarkets.

Different types of foods are typically sold in several different types of venues. For example, workers might buy meats from small local butchers, fruits and vegetables from green grocers or open air markets, and staples

Table 4.1 Summary regarding food items on which to collect local food prices

Food group	Number food items in typical living wage model diet	Comments	Examples
Main grain (ground or whole)	1–3 main cereals	If ground after purchase, grinding cost should be included in cost. Choose acceptable but inexpensive qualities on which to collect prices.	Wheat and maize are sometimes ground into flour after purchase. Rice sometimes needs to be husked and cleaned after purchase.
Prepared grain	0–2	Depends on food habits and development level. Often not included at low development level.	Bread, noodles
Legumes, beans, pulses and nuts	1–2	Cheap source of quality protein. Choose 1 or 2 inexpensive but common varieties.	Beans, pulses, nuts
Roots and tubers	1–2	Amount consumed varies greatly across countries.	Potato, cassava, sweet potato
Starchy fruit or vegetable	0–2	Optional. Important in some countries only.	Plantains
Oils and fats	1	Choose inexpensive, common cooking oil of acceptable quality.	Soybean oil, corn oil, peanut oil
Sugar	1	Choose least expensive, common sugar. Ignore confectionaries.	Brown sugar or white sugar
Vegetables	3–4	Choose at least 1 green leafy and 1 non-green leafy vegetable. Choose least expensive vegetables per edible gram.	Green leafy vegetables: spinach, kale, cabbage. Non-green leafy vegetables: eggplant, tomato, onion.

Table 4.1 (continued)

Food group	Number food items in typical living wage model diet	Comments	Examples
		In some countries, tomatoes and onions are used like spices – in the sense that they are included in almost every meal. Small amounts of these should be included in the model diet in such countries.	
Fruits	1–2	Choose least expensive per edible gram. Often seasonal and banana.	Banana (year round), mango, apple, orange
Meats and fish	1–3	Choose least expensive types of meats and/or fish (considering waste) of acceptable quality.	Dried fish and dried meat have more calories and nutrients than fresh fish or meat – so can be more economical even when more expensive per gram. Small fish not always considered palatable/ acceptable.
Egg	1	Inexpensive variety, usually chicken egg.	Chicken egg, duck egg
Milk and dairy	1–2	Usually milk. Whether fresh, powdered, evaporated, or UHT milk depends on local conditions and relative prices. Other dairy is sometimes also included.	Milk, sour milk, yoghurt
Coffee/tea	1	Choose least expensive acceptable brand of tea or coffee. Ignore sodas.	Coffee, tea

such as cereals, cooking oil, coffee and sugar from supermarkets. In urban India, for example, while workers typically buy most of their food in open air markets, they also often buy seasonal fruits and vegetables from itinerant street vendors, milk from a dairy, and vegetable oil and sugar from a small shop. In rural Malawi while workers typically buy most of their food in large weekly or biweekly open air markets, fruits and vegetables and staples that they run out of before the next market day are bought from small local open air markets and small shops. In Mauritius, workers mostly buy staples (powdered milk, rice, flour, breakfast cereals, pulses, sugar, oil and tea) from supermarkets; potatoes, vegetables and fruits from biweekly open air markets; meats and fish from butchers, cold storage shops and supermarkets; eggs from open air markets and supermarkets; and bread from local shops. Where workers buy different foods depends on factors such as price, convenience/proximity, availability of credit, and storage possibilities at home that depend in turn on climate, housing, and ownership of a refrigerator.

4.3.2 Selecting venues to visit to collect local food prices

Differences in food shopping patterns around the world mean that it is not possible to specify a universal approach of where to collect local food price data. It is necessary to determine where and how frequently workers typically shop for each major food group. It is common in many countries to buy staples such as cereals, sugar and cooking oil (foods that store well) in larger quantities from supermarkets or shops where they are less expensive and to buy foods that do not store well and are eaten throughout the week such as fruits, vegetables, meats, and fresh milk from places near home such as from local shops, local markets and street vendors.

Names, locations and opening hours of supermarkets, neighborhood shops, and open air markets, where workers shop are needed to develop a schedule of venues to visit. Discussions with key informants and workers are the best way to determine where and how frequently workers shop for each type of food. Female workers are generally (but not always) better informants than male workers since women generally have greater responsibility for shopping and cooking.

Based on discussions with workers and key informants, researchers should have a good idea of the following information (see Table 4.2 for an example for the Dominican Republic):

1. Where workers shop for *each* of the following: cereals, bread, noodles, roots and tubers, legumes, meats, fish, milk, egg, vegetables, fruits, sugar, oil, and coffee/tea.

Table 4.2 Example of types of venues where workers buy different foods, rural Dominican Republic ('✓' indicates yes)

Food group	Specific foods	Supermarket	Small grocery store	Street vendors	Fresh air market
Cereals	Rice/ Maize	✓	✓		
Bread	Bread	✓	✓		
Roots and tubers	Potato/ Cassava	✓	✓	✓	
Starchy fruits & vegetables	Green plantains	✓	✓	✓	✓
Pulses	Beans	✓	✓		✓
Dairy	Milk	✓	✓		
Eggs	Egg	✓	✓	✓	
Meats	Chicken Salami	✓	✓	✓	
Fruits and vegetables	Many	✓	✓	✓	✓
Sugar		✓	✓		
Oil		✓	✓		
Beer		✓	✓		
Coffee/tea		✓	✓		
Comment on food shopping pattern		Supermarket in city was far from banana plantations so workers shopped at super-market once a month.	Workers bought mostly from neighborhood groceries close to home. These groceries gave credit, which was important.	There were some street vendors – but they were often not available.	Fresh air market in city – far from banana plantations so workers did not often shop there.

2. How often and in what quantities workers typically buy each type of food from each type of vendor.
3. Names, locations and opening times of venues where workers shop.

It is assumed that it is easy to find street vendors, small neighborhood shops and small tuck shops since there are many of them, and so it is not necessary to collect names and addresses for these in advance. Nor is it necessary to identify in advance names of individual sellers in open air markets since vendors can be easily found when visiting such markets.

4.4 Maximum Amounts of Each Food Item Purchased at a Time

The unit price of food is affected by the quantity purchased. Unit food prices are generally lower when larger quantities are purchased. This means that it is often necessary to collect information for a range of quantities, at least at first, to find the lowest per kilo price. This information on size or quantity should be recorded in the data collection forms used when collecting local food prices.

We typically use some simple rules of thumb to help determine the maximum quantity to use to collect food price data. These are based on the quantity of each food item in the model diet and the length of time each food item keeps without spoiling.

1. For staple foods that keep for weeks or months without spoiling (e.g. cereals, cooking oil, sugar, coffee/tea), the quantity purchased should not exceed the amount needed by the reference family for about four weeks in the living wage model diet. Our feeling is that it is generally reasonable to assume that workers earning a living wage would have enough money and storage capacity to purchase a one month's supply of staple foods that store well.
2. For foods such as fruits, vegetables, meats and fish that spoil quickly, the maximum amount purchased should depend on how long an item can keep without spoiling. For example, meat and fish need to be eaten the same day when workers do not own a refrigerator (although dried fish and dried meat can be kept for several days without refrigeration).
3. We have found that workers in poor areas often purchase foods in tiny quantities and this is expensive per kilo. Often, this occurs at the end of the pay period when workers do not have enough money left to purchase larger quantities even though larger quantities are less expensive per kilo. We do not recommend collecting prices for tiny quantities, because workers earning a living wage would have enough money left at the end of the month to be able to buy larger quantities which are less expensive per kilo.

The above suggestions are meant to help in setting maximum quantities for collecting food price data. Obviously, some judgment is needed. Prices need to be collected for a range of quantities for each food in order to find the lowest per kilo for each food. Observing the amount of shelf space in supermarkets and shops devoted to different quantities can be very useful. In Mauritius, for example, we found that most rice in supermarkets was sold in 5 kilo bags – and we used this as the maximum quantity to price for rice.

4.5 Quality of Foods to Collect Prices for

Food prices obviously vary by quality. Filet mignon costs more than chuck, and boneless chuck costs more than untrimmed chuck with bone. Big fish cost more than little fish. The quality of food selected for a living wage model diet should be the lowest quality that is considered acceptable/decent to workers. For example, an acceptable quality rice should be selected rather than the highest quality rice; inexpensive vegetable oil should be selected rather than expensive olive oil; and frozen chicken rather than fresh chicken should be selected when frozen chicken is less expensive and workers have refrigerators. Note that food that is rotten or of dubious origin and so a possible threat to health should never be considered acceptable quality. Selecting the quantities and qualities of foods on which to collect prices is normally done in the initial days of pretesting. It is useful to have local workers accompany researchers to show them what they typically purchase.

4.6 Fieldwork Logistics

This section explains the basic steps in preparing for and carrying out a survey of food prices in local markets.

4.6.1 Modify food price data collection forms

The first step, before the fieldwork begins, is to modify the data collection forms provided at the end of this chapter for local conditions and if necessary translate them into the local language. Note that even after preliminary modifications, the data collection forms are likely to need further modification after field testing to include more precise quantities and qualities.

4.6.2 Identify and train field investigators

It is necessary to identify and train local field investigators to help in the collection of local food prices. Our experience shows that it is best to have two investigators working together to collect food prices. Having trained local investigators is also important so that they could be asked to collect additional food prices if this becomes apparent as being necessary during data analysis.

Field investigators should be:

- Familiar with where and how workers shop for food
- Able to speak the local language
- Able to talk to key informants, workers, and vendors about food prices, food preferences and shopping habits of workers
- Able to enter food prices collected into an Excel spreadsheet

4.6.3 Identify local workers to assist in collection of food prices

We have found it extremely useful for local workers to accompany the researchers, especially during the first days of collecting food price data. Local workers can take researchers to the places they themselves buy food, and help obtain cooperation of local shopkeepers. An additional benefit of having workers involved in the collection of food prices is that their involvement increases the likelihood of workers and employers accepting the results of the study when it is finished, because they know how the data were collected.

4.6.4 Select sales venues to visit

Venues visited should reflect where workers typically shop for food. Section 4.3 describes how to determine where workers shop for food. Several venues for each type of market should be visited. It is not necessary to take a random sample of all possible venues. In fact, even for estimating CPI, 'many countries nevertheless continue to rely heavily on purposeful selection of outlets and products because random sampling may be too difficult and costly' (ILO et al., 2004, p. 24). The aim is to visit a variety of venues to reflect as far as possible the places that workers typically shop – so that the prices collected are reasonably representative of prices that workers pay for food.

4.6.5 Number of venues, number of sellers, and number of price points for each food item

There are no hard and fast rules to indicate how many venues of each type of market to go to. We recommend at least five different venues for each type. For markets with many different sellers, such as open air markets or street vendors, prices of each food should be collected from several sellers in each market, because prices vary by seller. In this way, the average or typical price for each food item in each market/venue visited can be determined. We recommend collecting prices for each food item from two (or three) vendors in each multiple-vendor market. These vendors should not be adjacent to each other.

We recommend that a minimum of around 10 price points be collected for each common and relatively inexpensive food item (i.e. for foods that are good candidates to be included in a living wage model diet) in order to have a sufficient number of price points so that it is possible to exclude outliers and still be able to calculate representative food prices. There cannot be, however, a hard and fast rule on the number of price points to collect. The number of price points depends in part on the variability in food prices. A situation where very similar or exactly the same prices are found in markets for a particular food (say for milk, oil, sugar) is quite different than a situation where prices of particular foods (e.g. tomatoes, mangos, fish) vary considerably across markets. Collecting additional prices for foods with low price variability is unlikely to be very important. In contrast, it is important to collect additional prices for foods with high price variability. Also, it is worth noting that in some locations the number of possible price points is limited by the small number of different sales venues (such as supermarkets and open air markets) in the location.

4.6.6 Pretest of local market survey

One or two days should be set aside for a pretest. The purpose of a pretest is to identify the quality and quantities of food items to price, train investigators, test data collection forms and finalize procedures. As discussed above, it is very useful for workers to accompany researchers to shopping venues to help decide on types of foods and appropriate quantities and qualities of each food item to price. Problems encountered during the pretest should be discussed and resolved. Results from the pretest can often be used in final analyses.

4.6.7 Times to avoid collecting food prices

Food prices, especially for fresh products such as fruits and vegetables, can be volatile. For example, prices often spike around holidays and storms. In places where prices differ by time of day and/or day of the week, it is important to take this variability into consideration since the goal is to determine food prices that are representative of the prices workers typically pay.

4.6.7.1 Day of week Food prices are often higher on weekends than on weekdays (ILO et al., 2004). Although this might imply that food price data collection should not be done on weekends, this is not necessarily the case. Whether or not weekends should be avoided depends on when workers buy their food, since we are interested in determining food prices that workers pay. This means that food prices should be collected on the days of the week that workers typically buy their food, including weekends if this is when workers shop, even if prices are higher on weekends.

4.6.7.2 Time of day Food prices often vary by time of day (ILO et al., 2004). They might be, for example, higher in the morning, before new shipments arrive and lower at the end of the day for perishables. For the most part, prices should be collected at the time of day that workers typically shop for their food. Note that differences in food prices during the day are not generally important for staples and nonperishables.

4.6.7.3 Days near holidays and storms Food prices are typically higher on days approaching holiday periods (ILO et al., 2004). Food prices should not be collected on these days. Food prices are also affected by major storms, being higher just before, during, and just after major storms. For this reason, food price data should not be collected on such days.

4.6.8 Supervising and monitoring collection of food prices

Data collection forms should be checked over by the supervisor or another investigator as soon as they are completed in order to identify and resolve any problems with the completed forms, such as unclear handwriting or columns left blank. It is important that corrections are done soon after forms are completed, while details are still clear in the mind of investigators. Data should be entered into the Excel spreadsheet every evening after fieldwork. Notes should be added for a particular food price when there is an explanation why a particular food price is unusually high or unusually low. It is also important to keep track of the number of prices collected and entered in the Excel worksheet for each food so as to identify common and relatively inexpensive foods with very few price points, so that future data collection can pay particular attention to these food items. For example, after two days of data collection in Kenya, we realized that very few prices for tomatoes and milk had been collected. Therefore, on subsequent days, price collectors particularly looked for these items in the markets they visited.

It is reasonable to stop collecting prices of especially expensive items, since they would not be selected to include in the model diet. This helps increase the speed of the fieldwork, because data would be collected on fewer items as fieldwork goes along.

4.7 Other Considerations for Collecting Food Prices

4.7.1 Need to weigh foods when not sold by weight

Some foods are sold by the piece, bunch, heap, or bag and not sold by weight. Since model diets are expressed in grams, it is important to weigh foods sold in this way, to ascertain their cost per kilo. Price collectors need a small kitchen scale and a bowl to weigh these items. Normally, at least three pieces should be weighed to determine the average weight and therefore cost per kilo. For example, when tomatoes are sold by the piece, the price collector/investigator should weigh at least three typically sized tomatoes and record both the price per tomato and the average weight per tomato for each seller. The same should be done for food sold by bunch such as spinach. Three average size bunches should be weighed, and the price per bunch and average weight per bunch should be recorded.

4.7.2 Need for small budget to buy food

Often it is necessary to purchase some food from vendors to find out food prices. This is especially likely to be necessary when vendors are busy. The need to buy from vendors differs by country. In some countries, vendors are willing to provide accurate information on food prices without any purchases (e.g. we found this to be the case in Kenya and Mauritius), while in other countries vendors are not willing to indicate prices unless something is purchased (e.g. we found this to be the case in Vietnam). In other countries prices per kilo are almost always posted (e.g. China). A small budget should be provided so that investigators can purchase some foods from vendors when this is necessary.

4.7.3 Possible need to engage in bargaining

In some places bargaining is an integral part of purchasing food. This is especially important in Africa and in the Middle East:

> The principle is that [in places where price bargaining is common], price collection should be carried out in conditions that simulate as closely as possible situations in which real transactions actually take place. Price collectors should behave like regular purchasers by actually purchasing items to be priced and spread their purchases over the day to ensure representativeness. (ILO et al., 2004)

One approach that some national statistical offices in the Middle East use is to give field investigators a certain amount of money and ask them to purchase a list of food items, with the incentive that investigators can keep whatever they do not end up spending (ILO et al., 2004).

4.7.4 Possible need to find milling charges for cereals

In some countries, it is common for workers to purchase maize or wheat and have it milled after purchase. In such countries price collectors need to find the cost of milling.

PART III. COLLECTION AND ANALYSIS OF LOCAL FOOD PRICES

4.8 Description of Data Collection Forms

4.8.1 Information collected

Data collection forms have been developed for collecting local food prices. There are different forms for different types of market/venue in order to make data collection easier. Appendix 4.1 provides examples of data collection forms for: (i) supermarkets and grocery shops that sell foods from many different food groups, and specialized shops that mainly sell one or a few different food groups (for example, butcheries, milk depots, green groceries, grain shops, etc.), (ii) open air markets with multiple vendors and street vendors.

4.8.2 Forms for different types of markets

4.8.2.1 Supermarket food price collection forms For supermarkets – which sell a wide variety of foods – data collection forms should cover all foods. Brand name should be indicated because price per kilo differs by brand. Prices should be collected for at least two or three inexpensive brands for each food in each supermarket. Supermarket chains will often have their own relatively inexpensive brand, which should be included on the form. Price collectors should note on the form when an item is not available – so that it is clear that the investigator did not accidently forget to record this price. Supermarkets often run promotions that are attractive to workers, often at the end of the month. When a particular food item is on promotion/sale this should be noted on the form because this helps explain when a price is unusually low.

4.8.2.2 Small/medium size grocery store food price collection forms Data collection forms for small grocery stores are similar to those for supermarkets, even though such stores sell fewer items. When it is clear that certain items are not sold in small grocery stores in a locality, these items can be dropped from the forms. For example, frozen food was not sold in small grocery stores in the Dominican Republic, and so frozen food items were dropped from these forms.

4.8.2.3 Specialty store food price collection forms Separate forms for different types of specialty stores are useful. For example, there could be a form for butcheries, a different data collection form for green grocers, and a third data collection form for tuck shops – with different foods included in each form for each type of shop. These forms will be shorter than the forms for supermarkets or grocery stores because only food items sold in the particular type of specialty shop would be included.

4.8.2.4 Open air market food price collection forms Open air markets usually have many small vendors for each food item. For example, 10 or more vendors might be selling tomatoes. It is necessary to collect price information from two or three different sellers for each item, partly because prices differ across sellers and partly because price per kilo for food sold by the piece or bunch will differ even when price per piece or bunch is the same for all sellers, because each piece or bunch has a different weight. The sellers selected should not be adjacent to one another.

4.8.2.5 Street seller food price collection forms Price collection forms for street sellers should be similar to those for open air markets. Usually, information can be collected on one form for several street sellers selling the same item.

4.9 Analysis of Local Food Prices

There are two aims of the analysis of food prices: (i) to identify the least expensive foods in each major food group to include in the model diet, and (ii) to estimate cost per kilo for each food. In order to do this, it is necessary to determine the average/typical price that workers pay for each food item. This is done in several steps. Details for each step are discussed in the remainder of this section.

4.9.1 Cleaning the data

Data should be carefully scrutinized before analysis to look for possible 'outliers' that should be excluded from analysis, since these values are likely to be errors. An error could be due to incorrect units or kilos (e.g. price for 500 grams of rice might have been recorded as the price for one kilo of rice), or due to reporting error (e.g. shopkeeper provided poor information possibly out of misunderstanding), or due to transcription error (e.g. data was entered incorrectly on food price form or in Excel). It is not possible to set hard and fast rules on how to identify outliers. But values that are 30% or more above or below average deserve further scrutiny to make sure that they are not errors. Sometimes, explanations for outliers can be found. For example, prices of products 'on promotion' are usually lower than products not on promotion. Prices of food sold by the bunch or piece have considerable variation because of differing weights. If no explanation can be found for a price that is far outside the usual range, the outlier price should be deleted from further analysis.

4.9.2 Determining representative price for each food item

Determining the representative price for each food item is done in two steps. First, a representative price for each venue is calculated in a way that mimics the way that price-conscious shoppers buy food. Second, these representative prices are averaged over all markets, possibly taking into consideration the relative importance of each type of market.

4.9.2.1 Representative prices for venues with one 'seller' For venues with one 'seller' (such as supermarkets, specialty shops and grocery stores) the representative price for each food item should be the price of the least expensive acceptable brand/variety and quantity. For example, supermarkets always sell several brands of rice. Each brand often has several types of rice (e.g. long grain, short grain, jasmine, or basmati), and each of these is often sold in different quantities (e.g. 1 kg, 5 kg and 10 kg). So, there may be many prices of rice in each supermarket. We assume that cost-conscious shoppers would normally purchase the least expensive acceptable quality rice. Therefore, to represent the price per kilo that a cost-conscious worker would likely pay for rice, the researcher should select the least expensive acceptable quality rice for the least expensive quantity provided the quantity is not more than the maximums suggested in Section 4.4.

4.9.2.2 Representative prices for multi-vendor markets and street sellers Multi-vendor venues such as open air markets or street sellers may sell different varieties of the same food item. For example, open air markets and specialty stores may sell several different varieties of rice from large gunny sacks. A two-step process is used to determine the representative price of each food item sold in a multi-vendor market.

1. First, for each vendor in open air market A, select the least expensive acceptable variety/brand of each food item as the representative price of that food item for that vendor. For example, if vendor A sells rice, the price per kilo of the least expensive acceptable rice s/he sells should be selected as the 'representative' price of rice for vendor A. Similar calculations should be done for each vendor for each food item.
2. Second, to get the price for each food item for open air market A, calculate the 'representative' (mean or median) price per kilo for that food item over all vendors from whom prices were collected in the market A.[1]

4.9.2.3 Determining typical price of each food item across all venues Once a representative price for each food item for each venue has been determined, the next step is to aggregate these data over all venues. We recommend using the trimmed mean (whereby the average price is calculated after removing a percentage of the highest and the lowest prices) or the median. In this way, food prices are determined in a way that is not unduly influenced by unusually high or unusually low prices. There is a trimmean command in Excel.

4.9.3 Selecting specific foods to include in each food group in model diet

The least expensive food item or items per edible gram in each major group should be selected to represent each major food group in the living wage model diet. This might be kidney beans for legumes, potatoes for roots and tubers, and banana and oranges for fruits.

4.10 Examples: Selecting Foods to Include in the Model Diet

4.10.1 Single-vendor market example for rice

Table 4.3 provides a hypothetical example of how to select the representative price of rice for one supermarket and two minimarkets. Many varieties of rice are sold in each venue both in bulk and in packages, which is not unusual for a staple food such as rice. Rice is sold in different quantities in these markets, with larger quantities less costly per kilo. This is typical in most locations.

The quality of one variety of rice sold in bulk in this example (i.e. quality 3) is not acceptable and it is therefore excluded. The lowest price for acceptable quality rice in this example is 70 in Supermarket A, 85 in Minimarket B, and 80 in Minimarket C.

4.10.2 Multiple-vendor market for rice

Table 4.4 provides a hypothetical example of an open air market (venue D) with multiple sellers of rice. Rice prices of three vendors are shown. Two varieties of rice (Malwa and broken rice) are excluded from analysis because they are not acceptable to workers. The lowest price of acceptable rice is 70 from vendor 1, 75 from vendor 2, and 80 from vendor 3. The average lowest price across these three vendors in venue D is 75.

Table 4.5 provides a hypothetical example of how to determine the price of rice based on prices for 13 venues. The trimmed mean of the lowest price per kilo from each venue is 73.9. This should be used as the cost of a kilo of rice in the living wage model diet.

4.10.3 Selecting vegetables to include in the model diet

Table 4.6 provides a hypothetical example of how to determine prices per kilo for vegetables. In this example information is provided for 11 venues. Notice that vegetables sold in only a few venues (pumpkin, spinach and eggplant) were excluded from analysis because it is not appropriate to include foods in a model diet that are not widely available. The trimmed

Table 4.3 Hypothetical example: Determining price of the least expensive acceptable variety of rice in three shops

Type/brand/quality of rice		Supermarket A	Mini market B	Mini market C
Rice sold in bulk	Quantity	Price per kg	Price per kg	Price per kg
Rice quality 1 (Sindano)	1 kg	120	NA	NA
Rice quality 2 (Pakistan)	1 kg	110	NA	NA
Rice quality 2 (Indian)	1 kg	70	NA	NA
Rice quality 2 (5 star)	1 kg	80	85	NA
Rice quality 2 (Moshi)	1 kg	80	NA	80
Rice quality 3 (Broken – not considered acceptable by workers)	1 kg	NA	60	55
Packaged rice				
Rice quality 1 (Pearl)	1 kg	190	NA	NA
Rice quality 1 (Pearl)	5 kg	179	NA	NA
Rice quality 1 (Pishori Cil)	2 kg	180	190	NA
Rice quality 1 (Dawaat)	1 kg	120	NA	130
Rice quality 1 (Dawaat)	2 kg	100	135	NA
Rice quality 1 (Pishori Mwea)	1 kg	125	NA	120
Rice quality 1 (Pishori Mwea)	2 kg	140	155	NA
Rice quality 1 (Pishori Mwea)	5 kg	NA	145	160
Price of least expensive acceptable quality rice in each shop		**70**	**85**	**80**

Note: NA indicates not available.

mean of the least expensive price of each vegetable across venues is considered the representative price for each vegetable. It is divided by the proportion edible to get a representative price per edible kilo. In this example, the least expensive green leafy vegetable is cabbage (17.8 per edible kilo), and the least expensive non-green leafy vegetable is tomato (78.9 per edible kilo). The next least expensive vegetable is kale (41.0 per edible kilo). These three vegetables would be selected to include in the model diet.

4.11 Possible Adjustment of Local Food Prices for Seasonality

Although food prices collected are intended to be representative of typical prices during the year, they are collected over a relatively short period of

Table 4.4 Hypothetical example of determining the cost of the least expensive acceptable variety of rice in a venue with three vendors in venue D

Type/brand/quantity of rice		Vendor 1	Vendor 2	Vendor 3
	Quantity	Price per kg	Price per kg	Price per kg
Rice quality 1	1 kg	120	125	130
Rice quality 2 (Indian)	1 kg	70	75	NA
Rice quality 2 (5 star)	1 kg	85	85	NA
Rice quality 2 (Moshi)	1 kg	80	NA	80
Rice quality 3 (Malwa – not considered acceptable by workers)	1 kg	60	NA	65
Rice quality 3 (broken – not considered acceptable by workers)	3 kg	50	55	60
Price of least expensive acceptable rice for each vendor		70	75	80
Representative price of rice Venue D		75		

Note: NA indicates not available.

Table 4.5 Hypothetical example: Determining the price of rice per kilo to include in model diet in a location with 13 venues using 20% trimmed mean

Venue	A	B	C	D	E	F	G	H	I	J	K	L	M
Representative price for each venue	70	85	80	75	70	72	85	80	65	68	72	70	71
Trimmed mean (20%) over all venues							73.9						

time (usually 5 to 10 days), and so some consideration of possible seasonal variation of food prices is required. One way in which our methodology reduces the effect of seasonal variation of food prices is that less expensive food items at the time of the food price survey are included in the model diet. This means that foods that are out of season (and so relatively expensive) are generally excluded from the model diet.

Table 4.6 Hypothetical example: Determining prices of vegetables from 11 venues

Food item	Lowest price in each venue													
	A	B	C	D	E	F	G	H	I	J	K	20%Trimmed mean	Proportion edible	Price per edible kilo
Tomato	80	63	70	75	77	68	75	67			71	71.8	0.91	78.9
Carrot	80	112	90		95		85	110	118		95	97.8	0.89	109.9
Pumpkin	80						66							
Kale	25	19	23	41	35	22	32	20	24	18		25.0	0.61	41.0
Spinach	25			21			50							
Eggplant	80													
Cabbage	15	13	11	12	12	14	23		14	16	18	14.3	0.80	17.8
Onion	105		68	72	133	65	49	75		80	63	75.4	0.90	83.8

SUMMARY – Vegetables and prices to include in model diet

Least expensive green leafy vegetable (GLV)	Price per kg	Least expensive non-GLV	Price per kg	Next least expensive vegetable	Price per kg
Cabbage	17.8	Tomato	78.9	Kale	41.0

Use of seasonal foods does not, however, necessarily account for all price variations over the year. The price of some foods purchased throughout the year such as maize, rice and fish can vary over the year in some countries. Prices of vegetables and fruits can be higher on average in some seasons even when using seasonal items. This means that an analysis of food prices by season should be done using secondary data sources, to see if prices for different foods collected in a local market survey are typical, relatively high or relatively low for the year. Adjustments should be made to food prices for food items with large seasonal variations – in order to arrive at more average/typical prices throughout the year.

Ascertaining seasonality in food prices can be best done using monthly food prices for several years – when such data are available which is not unusual. We found such prices for Kenya and Mauritius on government websites, and for Malawi on an NGO website. In China average monthly food prices for 50 cities are reported by the national statistical office. Analyzing monthly prices for a food item over several years is a good way to determine if there is a seasonal pattern as well as to see if the same seasonal pattern is found consistently every year. The ratio of the price in the study month to the average price of a particular food item over a calendar year of over a 12 month period (starting 6 months before the month of data collection in order to reduce the effect of any trend over time in food prices because of inflation) provides a good indication of the extent to which prices collected are representative of prices throughout the year and so if an adjustment is needed for seasonality. This ratio should be calculated for several years – to be sure that the ratio reflects consistent seasonal differences.

It is important to keep in mind that even when there is a strong seasonal price variation for a particular food, the price of this food at the time of a food price survey may be average for the year. For example, the price of onions in Kenya has a strong consistent seasonal pattern related to harvest times, but the price of onion in March, the month of the local food price survey for our living wage study, was average for the year (see example below).

One possible problem that researchers should be aware of is that governments sometimes sell foods at subsidized prices. This often affects market prices and therefore seasonality in prices for these foods in years when this is done. For example, in Malawi the government was selling large quantities of maize at a reduced price at the time of our local food price survey and this had the effect of negating the high price for maize usually found at this time of year.

As a supplement to analyzing food price data by month, key informants should be asked about seasonal patterns in food prices, because this is often common knowledge. In addition, published articles can also be useful as we found in Kenya (see example below).

4.11.1 Example 1: Adjusting local food prices for seasonality: Kenya

We collected food prices in the Lake Naivasha area of Kenya in March 2014 for a living wage study. Two sources were used to help determine if these March food prices were reasonably representative of prices throughout the year:

1. Monthly food prices were reported by Kenya National Bureau of Statistics (KNBS, 2015) on its website for 2012–2013. These food prices are used to estimate urban CPI.
2. Academic journal article that analyzed seasonality of wholesale fruit and vegetable prices in Nairobi, Mombasa and Kisumu for 1994–2003 (Mathenge and Tschirley, 2006).

We calculated the ratio of the March price to average price for the year (September to September bracketing March) for each food item in the KNBS data. This ratio indicated that March prices were similar to average price throughout the year for beef, offal, milk, maize flour, sugar, tomato, and cabbage. There were too few months of data to draw conclusions for mango, carrot, spinach, and kale. The price of potato was slightly higher in March than its average price for the year (by about 5%), although it was difficult to draw conclusions on this because potato prices were not reported for October–January for either 2012 or 2013.

Partly because of the incomplete nature of KNBS data, we also relied on Mathenge and Tschirley (2006) who analyzed food price data for seven foods (banana, orange, kale, tomato, onion, cabbage, and potato) for 10 years from three cities (Nairobi, Mombasa, and Kisumu). They found consistent seasonality in prices for potato and vegetables but not for either fruit.

Based on our analysis of seasonality in food prices, we decided to reduce the prices we collected in March by one-third for kale/spinach and by 5% for potato. We did not reduce the price we collected for cabbage despite its generally higher price in March, because the price of cabbage observed in our local market survey was very low at only KSh11.5 per kilo, about $0.06 per pound.

4.11.2 Example 2: Adjusting of local food prices for seasonality: Malawi

We collected food prices in the areas surrounding tea estates in Southern Malawi in January 2014. To determine whether January prices were reasonably representative of prices throughout the year, we used monthly food price data collected by the Center for Social Concern (CfSC) for Blantyre city (closest location to tea estate area in these data) from January 2008 (earliest available date) to December 2013 (latest available date). We calculated the ratio of the January price relative to the average price for the July to June period that bracketed January. We found that the January price was reasonably similar to the average price throughout the year for fish, sugar, milk, cooking oil, and tea. The January price was on average around 10% higher than the average price for the year for maize, beans and cassava and around 30% higher for rape, but these percentages varied greatly from year to year. In light of these results, we decreased January prices for beans and cassava by 10% and left unchanged all other January prices. We did not change the green leafy vegetable prices because we used the lowest price for all types of green leafy vegetables to cost our model diet regardless of whether this was pumpkin leaves, okra leaves, mustard leaves, rape, etc.

We looked more carefully at seasonality in the price of maize, partly because maize is a large expense for families in Malawi as it is the main staple food, and partly because there is a common belief in Malawi that the price of maize increases in the months before a new harvest and falls during and right after a new harvest. We did indeed find this pattern in CfSC data – but this pattern was more complicated than the simple pattern we heard about. We found that maize prices tended to spike in February and March. We also found that prices tended to fall sharply for two or three months after a new harvest. But the seasonal pattern described did not occur every year. For example, maize price did not increase sharply before the new harvests in 2010, 2011 or 2012 and it did not decrease sharply around the time of the new harvest in 2010 or 2012. Part of the reason for these surprising years may be traceable to government intervention as the Agricultural Development and Marketing Corporation (ADMARC) releases maize on to the market from time to time to reduce the market price. We found ADMARC was doing this in January 2014 at the time of our local food price survey. All of this meant that it was not possible to know if the January 2014 maize prices we observed were or were not typical for January, and for this reason we decided not to adjust the price of maize we observed.

NOTE

1. The reason why the least expensive vendor in a multi-vendor market is not selected is that shoppers cannot easily compare prices per kilo in such markets. This is especially true for foods sold by the bunch or piece.

APPENDIX 4.1 DATA COLLECTION FORMS FOR LOCAL FOOD PRICES

Table 4A.1 Example of multi-vendor form to collect food price data for cereals

Modify to include main cereals for local area							
Cereals (rice, wheat, maize, bread, noodles)							
Market name							
Market location							
Seller's address/location (if fixed location)							
Investigator's name							
Date completed							
Seller's address (if fixed)		Seller 1			Seller 2		
	Quality and name (only for acceptable quality)	Quantity	Price	Price per kg	Quantity	Price	Price per kg
Rice							
Wheat flour							
Maize							
Maize milling charge							
Noodles (indicate type)							
Bread (indicate if white or brown)		Weight of loaf in grams and number of slices per loaf	Price per loaf	Price per kg	Weight of loaf in grams and number of slices per loaf	Price per loaf	Price per kg
Buns (indicate type)		Weight of bun	Price per bun	Price per kg	Weight of bun	Price per bun	Price per kg

Table 4A.2 Example of data collection form to collect cereal prices for shops and supermarkets

Similar forms can be used to collect prices of other food items

Modify to include main cereals for local area					
CEREALS (e.g. rice, maize, wheat, sorghum, bread, noodles)					
Market place			Investigator		
Seller name			Date completed		
Seller address			Time completed		
Rice brand & quality	Size in kg	Price	Price per kg		On sale? (indicate if yes)
Wheat brand & quality					
Maize brand & quality					
Noodle brand & quality					
Bread brand & quality	Weight of loaf in grams	Price of loaf	Price per kg	Number of slices	On sale? (indicate if yes)
Buns (indicate type)	Weight of bun	Price per bun	Price per kg		On sale? (indicate if yes)

5. Local housing standard for a living wage

PART I. BACKGROUND AND CONCEPTUAL FRAMEWORK

Housing is almost always the second biggest expense for workers in developing countries (after food) and the biggest expense for workers in developed countries. Adequate housing is considered to be a right by the international community. For these reasons it is important to ensure that a living wage is high enough for workers to be able to afford decent housing. With this in mind, our living wage methodology estimates housing costs separately based on a normative standard of decent, healthy housing. Two steps are used to estimate housing costs.

The first step creates a normative standard for decent housing for a family in a given location based on international principles and local conditions. The second step estimates the cost of local housing that meets the local decent housing standard. This cost is estimated primarily through a local housing market survey that includes visits to homes in neighborhoods where workers live.

5.1 Advantages of Approach Used to Estimate Housing Costs

In contrast to our methodology, the most common methodologies for estimating living wages and poverty lines for developing countries do not ensure that workers earning a living wage would be able to afford decent housing, because these common methodologies estimate all non-food expenses (including housing) in one go based in large part on secondary household expenditure survey data. For example, if food expenditure is 50% of all expenditures according to a household survey, non-food costs would be assumed to be equal to food cost. If food expenditure is 33% of all expenditures, non-food costs would be assumed to be twice the cost of food. In these common methodologies, housing costs are subsumed within non-food costs. Problems with this common approach include:

- No attention is given to ensuring that funds for non-food needs are sufficient to meet minimum standards. This includes housing.
- Funds will not be sufficient for decent housing for a family when many people currently live in substandard housing which is reflected in household expenditure statistics.
- National statistical offices differ in how they measure housing expenditures. Nearly half of countries in the world assume that owner-occupied housing has no cost or user value. This means that expenditure for housing according to household expenditure statistics is much too low in close to half of all countries. Thus, it is not possible to get a good estimate of housing costs by relying on national statistics alone, especially in countries that do not include the value or user cost of owner-occupied housing in their statistics.

Our approach has several advantages compared to the common methodology discussed above.

- Our approach ensures that sufficient funds are available for workers to be able to afford decent housing for their family and so avoids the possibility of replicating the substandard housing found in many developing countries today.
- Our approach avoids the problem of relying on household expenditure data, which is especially important in the many countries where national statistical offices do not measure the value or cost of owner-occupied housing.
- By measuring local housing costs separately, our approach allows separate estimates of living wages for different areas within a country, because housing costs are the most important reason for differences in living costs between rural and urban areas and between big and small cities.

PART II. PRINCIPLES AND CHARACTERISTICS OF DECENT HOUSING FOR A LIVING WAGE

The normative standard for decent housing is established based on:

- Principles of minimum standards for housing from international conventions, international organizations, and standard setting organizations
- Housing standards set by government
- Housing conditions in a location

International principles provide broad guidelines, indicating, for example, that acceptable housing needs to have a durable structure, adequate sanitation, and safe water. They provide the principles and general characteristics of decent housing. Information on local housing conditions (e.g. percentage of dwellings made from various building materials and percentage of dwellings with various types of toilets, and housing standards of government authorities) identify what would be acceptable for decency in a location for each housing principle and characteristic. For example, while international principles indicate that safe water is required, information on local housing conditions would help determine whether for decency safe water needs to be piped indoors, piped nearby the house, or drawn from a nearby well. While international principles require adequate sanitary facilities, information on local housing conditions help determine whether the toilet needs to be a flush toilet or a pit latrine, as well as whether toilet facilities can be shared and still be considered decent. However, not having access to safe water near the house or not having access to decent sanitary facilities – which might be typical in some locations – would violate international principles of healthy housing and therefore could never be considered acceptable.

5.2 Review of International Housing Standards

We begin discussion of appropriate standards for decent and healthy housing with a review of international housing conventions, standards, and recommendations. This includes the right to adequate housing (Section 5.2.1) and principles for adequate housing included in international conventions and recommendations (Section 5.2.2).

5.2.1 Right to adequate housing

Adequate housing is considered a right according to the international community (italics added for emphasis).[1]

- Article 25 of the 1948 Universal Declaration of Human Rights states that: 'Everyone has the right to a standard of living adequate for health and well-being for himself and for his family, including food, clothing, *housing* and medical care and necessary social services.'
- Article 11(1) of the 1966 International Covenant on Economic, Social, and Cultural Rights 'recognize the right of everyone to an adequate standard of living for himself and his family, including adequate food, clothing and *housing*.'
- The 1944 Declaration of Philadelphia of the International Labour Organization (ILO), which is an annex to its constitution, 'recognizes

> the solemn obligation of the International Labour Organization to further among the nations of the world programs which will achieve: . . . III (i) the provision of adequate nutrition, *housing* and facilities for recreation and culture.'

Many countries include housing rights in their constitutions and laws which are often modeled after international standards and principles (Thiele, 2002).

5.2.2 Principles for adequate housing in international conventions and recommendations and according to international organizations

International organizations have developed principles of adequate, decent and healthy housing. This includes the International Covenant on Economic, Social and Cultural Rights (United Nations, 1966), ILO Recommendation No. 115 Concerning Workers' Housing (1961), World Health Organization Principles of Healthy Housing (1989), and UN-Habitat (2009, 2013). For detailed descriptions of the definitions and principles of these, see Appendix 5.1. Table 5.1 summarizes this.

Although these definitions and principles emphasize different aspects of decency, there is a great deal of overlap. Acceptable/adequate housing needs to have the following attributes:

- Durable structure
- Sufficient living space
- Access to safe water
- Access to sanitary toilet and washing facilities
- Adequate lighting
- Adequate ventilation
- Adequate food storage
- Separation from animal quarters
- Protection from cold, damp, heat, rain, wind or other threats to health, structural hazards, and disease vectors

Acceptable housing cannot be located in:

- Slum[2]
- Unsafe area
- Hazardous area
- Area without refuse disposal
- Area without site drainage
- Area lacking emergency services

Table 5.1 Housing standards in international conventions and recommendations[a]

Standard	International Covenant on Economic, Social and Cultural Rights	ILO Recommendation No. 115 Concerning Workers' Housing	WHO healthy housing
Safe water[b]	✓	✓	✓
Sanitation/toilet & sewage disposal[b]	✓	✓	✓
Sufficient living space[b]	✓	Persons per room and/or floor area	Persons per room
Durable structure (protection against elements)[b]	✓	✓	✓
Good condition & state of repair[b]	✓[e]	✓[f]	✓
Physical safety	✓		✓
Adequate ventilation		✓	✓
Adequate lighting	✓	✓	✓
Safe food storage		✓	✓
Washing facilities	✓	✓	✓
Separation from animals		✓	✓
Electricity			
No site hazards[b, c]	Drainage Polluted	Earthquake	Many[d]
Refuse/solid waste disposal	✓	✓	✓
Emergency services	✓		✓
Protection from elements	✓[e]	✓[f]	✓

Notes:

[a] UN-Habitat urban slum housing definition is not included in this table, because it includes only five elements: 'inadequate access to safe water; inadequate access to sanitation and other infrastructure; poor structural quality of housing; overcrowding; insecure residential status' in addition to security of tenure.

[b] Element included in UN-Habitat definition of urban slum housing.

[c] According to UN-Habitat the following locations should be considered as hazardous 'housing in geologically hazardous zones (landslide/earthquake and flood areas); housing on or under garbage mountains; housing around high-industrial pollution areas; housing around other unprotected high-risk zones (e.g. railroads, airports, energy transmission lines)' (UN-Habitat, 2003, p. 12).

[d] WHO indicates the following site hazards: earthquakes, hurricanes, wind, noise, pollution, floods, and landslides.

Table 5.1 (continued)

[e] Implied by 'protection from cold, damp, heat, rain, wind or other threats to health, structural hazards, and disease vectors' (International Covenant on Economic, Social, and Cultural Rights, 1966).
[f] Implied by 'protection against heat, cold, damp' (ILO Recommendation No. 155).

Sources: International Covenant on Economic, Social and Cultural Rights (1966), ILO Recommendation No. 115 Concerning Workers' Housing (1961), WHO (1989), UN-Habitat (2003).

5.2.3 Rural and urban differences

Although distinctions between rural and urban areas are not explicitly mentioned in the above principles, it is clear that some housing standards can be relaxed in rural areas while maintaining the principles of healthy housing. Population density in urban areas means that community services (e.g. refuse collection, street lighting, and public safety) are more important in urban areas than in rural areas.

5.3 Housing Standards of Certifying and Standard Setting Organizations

Standard setting organizations have codes of practice that companies need to meet to be certified. These codes of practice include housing standards. The Sustainable Agricultural Network/Rainforest Alliance (2005) standard is an example:

> Housing provided by the farm for permanent or temporary workers living there must be well-designed, built and maintained to foster good hygienic, health and safety conditions. Living quarters must be separated from production areas. In absence of applicable laws the following elements and characteristics apply:
>
> - Dormitories must be constructed with wooden floors above the ground or floors made from asphalt or concrete, roofs in good condition without leaks, and with appropriate ventilation and lighting.
> - Ceiling must not be lower than 2.5 meters at any point.
> - Five square meters of space per person in sleeping areas.
> - Heating for cold climates.
> - One toilet for every 15 persons; one urinal for every 25 men.
> - One shower per ten persons, separated by gender.

There is some consensus across the GLWC members as regards elements of acceptable housing. At the same time, these standards are less comprehensive in scope than those of international organizations, probably because some GLWC members are concerned with farm dormitory accommodation. Elements of acceptable housing that appear in the codes of practice of at least half of GLWC members are:

- Good condition/clean
- Potable/safe water
- Sanitary facilities
- Security/safety
- Appropriate ventilation
- Bathing/shower facilities

5.4 Housing Conditions in Europe and United States over Past 75 Years

It is useful to be aware that housing conditions in Europe and the United States 75–100 years ago when they were much poorer, were similar to housing conditions in many developing countries today. In the United States in the 1930s, for example, housing conditions were poor indeed in some parts of the South. Less than 1% of houses had a private flush toilet or running water among Knott County, Kentucky, farms; 49% of houses in Charleston, South Carolina, and 21% of houses in Atlanta, Georgia did not have an indoor private toilet; 50% of houses in Charleston, and 29% of houses in Atlanta did not have electricity (Williams et al., 1937).

5.5 Measurement of Adequate Living Space

Two approaches are used to measure whether a dwelling has adequate living space. One approach uses number of square meters or square feet of living space. The other approach uses number of rooms or bedrooms.[3] We feel that for a living wage, the preferred approach for measuring adequate living space is the number of square meters or square feet of living space. The International Comparison Program (ICP) of the World Bank reached the same conclusion: 'The best quality measure [of housing] is the total surface space of dwellings' (Blades, 2010), and 'The ICP manual and other documents of the 2005 ICP sought square meters of internal living space as the preferred indicator' (Heston, 2013, p. 325).

On the other hand, because of its simplicity, number of rooms or number of persons per room is the easier of the two approaches to use and it was used to measure overcrowded housing roughly 100 years ago. 'The most widely adopted [measure of crowding] because it is at once simple and significant, is based on the number of persons living in one and the same dwelling: the number of persons per room' (ILO, 1928). Roughly at the same time, an ILO Committee of Statistical Experts Resolution (1935) recognized that 'Rents distinguished only according to number of rooms do not form a sufficient basis for comparison. The Committee accordingly recommends that particulars for the rent of each category of dwellings should be accompanied by an indication of total floor space . . . showing the levels of rent expressed (a) per room and (b) per square meter of total floor space' (ILO, 1935, p. 113).

A major problem with a number of rooms or persons per room definition for measuring local housing costs for a living wage is that room sizes are quite variable around the world. For example, government low income housing in India includes very small rooms of 9–11 square meters (Uttar Pradesh Housing and Development Board, 2014). In contrast, floor plans for affordable housing in South Africa include one large room of 30–45 square meters (Moolla et al., 2011) – with occupants frequently dividing this large room into smaller spaces for privacy using high dressers, curtains, etc. Another problem with the number of rooms definition is that rent is related more to amount of floor space than to number of rooms. A third disadvantage is that the number of rooms measure is so discrete in nature that it cannot be changed smoothly as a country develops and incomes increase. This is attested to by the fact that the definition of overcrowding established by the United Kingdom in 1935 continues to be law in the United Kingdom today (House of Commons Library, 2011). In contrast, the amount of living space for acceptable housing can be increased less abruptly with economic development. Malaysia and China provide good examples of this. Minimum floor space for public housing in Malaysia (Hadi, 2014) increased from 37.1 square meters (1956–1981) to 49.2 square meters (1982–1996), 52 square meters (1997–1998), and 60.3 square meters (1999–present). In Shenzhen, China, gross floor space for low rent housing went from 45 square meters in 2008 to 50 square meters for 2–3 person households and 65 square meters for 4+ person households in 2014 (Wang et al., 2016). An added advantage of using a square meters of living space standard is that in locations where it is difficult to find acceptable housing with the required amenities and somewhere around the number of square meters required, it is possible to estimate rent for acceptable housing with the required number of square meters by regressing rent per square meter on number of square meters of floor space. We used this approach for a living wage study in Vietnam (Anker and Anker, 2015) and Wang et al. (2016) used this approach for a living wage study for Shenzhen, China.

These two approaches for measuring adequate living space for a living wage are discussed below. Both are legitimate approaches. Although we prefer the number of square meters or feet approach, the number of rooms approach is also worth using in many situations.

Table 5.2 Definition of overcrowding in housing used in Europe 100 years ago

Location	Definition of overcrowding (persons per room)
Finland 1919	≥3 per room
Prague 1921	>2 per heated room
France 1901–1911	>2 per room
Copenhagen 1921	>2 per room
Fredericksburg 1921	>2 per room
Norway 1920	>2 per room
Warsaw 1919	>2 per room

Source: ILO (1928).

5.5.1 Number of persons per room (or per bedroom)

In the 1920s when ILO, governments and researchers became interested in comparing living conditions across countries 'overcrowding' was the most common concept used for measuring housing quality. The typical definition of overcrowding at that time in Europe was more than two persons per room (Table 5.2). This is a more stringent definition than the more than three persons per room definition currently used by UN-Habitat for urban areas in developing countries. UN-Habitat changed to this definition of overcrowding not because it was preferable from a conceptual point of view, but because a more than two persons per room definition yielded what were felt to be uncomfortably high percentages of overcrowding. 'After observing the statistical distribution of more than two persons per room throughout the world, UN-Habitat revised its definition to three persons per room' (UN-Habitat, 2006, p. 70).

The United Kingdom still defines overcrowding as more than two persons per room.This means that at least two rooms that can potentially be used for sleeping purposes (e.g. bedroom, dining room, and living room) are required for a family of four, and three such rooms are required for a family of five.[4] Other developed countries define overcrowding based on number of persons per bedroom to better reflect improved housing conditions in developed countries over the last 80 years. This includes Ireland, Canada and Australia (Ireland, Office of the Attorney General, 1966; Australian Bureau of Statistics. 2011).[5]

5.5.2 Floor space

5.5.2.1 Amount of floor space around the world The United Nations (2000) indicates average (median) floor space per person by development level, region and country based on information for 188 cities. It was 11.9 square meters for the world, 7.3 for least developed countries, 8.6 for Africa, 10.2 for Asia and Oceania (excluding Australia, New Zealand and Japan), 11.0 for Latin America and Caribbean and 21.3 for more developed regions. These data imply around the following number of square meters of floor space for a family of 4 persons: 29 (least developed countries), 35 (Africa), 41 (Asia and Oceania), 44 (Latin America and Caribbean), 48 (World), and 85 (more developed regions). According to EUROSTAT (2014), average (mean) space per dwelling was around 53 square meters (ranging from 34 to 69) for 11 former socialist countries in East and Central Europe and around 78 square meters (ranging from 63 to 100) for 18 other European Union countries. Floor space is higher still in the United States where households at the 20th percentile of the household income distribution had 28.8 square meters per person in 1985 and 33.5 square meters per person in 2005, implying around 115 and 134 square meters respectively for a lower income household of 4 persons (United States Department of Housing and Urban Development, 2007). The amount of floor space found in different regions and at different development levels implies somewhere around 35 square meters of floor space for low income countries (using median value for Africa as a proxy) and around 80+ square meters for high income countries (using European countries as a proxy).

5.5.2.2 Amount of floor space for government supported low income and affordable housing[6] National, state, and city governments typically have housing departments and authorities that provide or subsidize affordable and/or low income housing. These programs are called by different names such as 'low rent housing,' 'low-cost housing,' 'affordable housing,' 'social housing,' and 'public housing,' but they all have the same purpose – to provide or encourage the building of low-cost housing. Guidelines are often provided along with floor plans. These represent what government feels is minimum acceptable housing. As Habitat for Humanity International (2008) put it: 'Each country has its own understanding of adequate housing, which may also vary within national boundaries.' Countries sometimes also have laws that specify minimum living space allowed for newly constructed flats and houses.

It is important to keep in mind that there is a difference between covered floor space (sometimes referred to as gross floor space or plinth area) and living space (sometimes referred to as carpet area or usable floor space).

Floor area is 'the area contained within the outer surface of external walls of a building measured at each floor level' (Republic of Kenya, National Building and Planning Authority, 2009, p. A-23) while living space is 'the floor area of the usable rooms' (Bureau of India Standards, 2002, p. 1). Countries differ in what they include in covered area and living space. India, for example, includes in covered space 100% of the area of balconies and verandah protected by a roof and 50% of those not protected by a roof. India excludes from living space (called carpet area in India): verandahs, balconies, entrance halls or porches, bathrooms and WCs, and kitchens and pantries (Bureau of Indian Standards, 2002). Many other countries include kitchens and WCs and treatment of balconies and verandahs depends on climate and whether enclosed. In China, common areas such as elevators and stairwells are apportioned and counted as part of each apartment's living space. All of this means that the size of the difference between living space and covered space differs across countries. At a minimum, around 10% of space is lost to thickness of internal and external walls.[7] How much more than 10% is lost depends on the floor plan, number of internal walls, and which areas are included or excluded when calculating living space. As a rule of thumb, we have found a 12% difference is generally a reasonable approximation, although we found this difference to be as high as 20% for Sri Lanka tea estate houses.

To get an idea of national standards for living space for countries at different development levels, we put together information on this for 16 countries (Table 5.3). Some of these are discussed below.

SOUTH AFRICA South Africa has laws and regulations concerned with adequate living space. South African Basic Conditions of Employment Act No. 75 for Farm Worker Section (Republic of South Africa, 1997, p. 8) indicates that it is acceptable to deduct the value of free accommodation from wages only when 'the house is not less than 30 square meters in size'. South Africa Housing Consumer Protection Measures Act of 1998 indicates that 'houses must be at least 30 square meters in size' (ETU, 2014). The South Africa government's Reconstruction and Development Programme (RDP) for 'low-cost' housing builds small houses consisting of one large room (Thale, 2001; Cox, 2008) that has 30–45 square meters of living space (Pottie, 2003) with typical RDP houses around 36 square meters (Moolla et al., 2011).

INDIA National and state governments in India have departments, authorities, and schemes concerned with provision of affordable housing. They set standards for living space to carry out their mandates. This includes federal Government of India Ministry of Housing and Urban Poverty Alleviation

(JNNURM) (2013) and each state such as Maharashtra (Maharashtra Housing and Area Development Authority (MHADHA), 2014) and Uttar Pradesh (Uttar Pradesh Housing and Development Board (UPAVP), 2014), the two largest states in India. Amount of living space allowed is specified as a function of family income to ensure affordability with repayment of home loan not exceeding 30–40% of monthly income. Four income groups are used: (1) EWS (economically weaker section), (2) LIG (low income group), (3) MIG (middle income group), and (4) HIG (high income group). The living space standard used by these three Indian government authorities is similar. Living space for EWS housing is up to around 28 square meters (300 square feet). Living space for LIG housing – that we feel is relevant for a living wage estimate for urban workers in India since the living wage we estimated for Nagpur in 2013 fell within the LIG low income group (Anker and Anker, 2013) – ranged from around 28 square meters to around 48 square meters (around 36 square meters on average).[8] Living space for the middle income group ranged from around 48–80 square meters and living space for the high income group was 80+ square meters.

KENYA Republic of Kenya Ministry of Housing (2004, p. 9) considers urban 'low-cost housing' as 'comprising a minimum of two habitable rooms, cooking area and sanitary facilities, covering a minimum gross floor area of 40 square meters for each household.' It considers that 'urban middle-cost housing is covering a minimum gross floor area of 60 square meters.' This implies a minimum of around 36 square meters of living space for low-cost housing and a minimum of around 53 square meters of floor space for middle-cost housing (assuming inner and outer walls occupy 12% of the gross floor space).

VIETNAM Article 47(2) of the 2015 Housing Law in Vietnam sets a minimum of 30 square meters and a maximum of 59 square meters for urban 'social housing.' Decree 99/2015 Article 6(2) states that new flats cannot be smaller than 30 square meters.

CHINA Government supported 'low rent' housing in Shenzhen, China, a major elite city in what is now an upper middle income country, included a maximum of 45 square meters of gross living space (around 40 square meters of living space) in 2008. This standard increased to 50 square meters (around 44 square meters of living space) in 2014 for 2–3 person households and 65 square meters (around 57 square meters of living space) for households with 4 or more persons (Wang et al., 2016). This is an example of how minimum living space standard increases with economic development and rising incomes.

MALAYSIA Minimum requirement for 'public housing' in Kuala Lumpur (capital city of an upper middle income country) is currently 3 bedrooms and 60 square meters of floor space. This minimum requirement has increased over time along with Malaysia's economic development. It was 1 bedroom and 37 square meters from 1956 to 1981, 2 bedrooms and 52 square meters from 1982 to 1996, and 2 bedrooms and 52 square meters from 1997 to 1998 (Hadi, 2014).

HABITAT FOR HUMANITY Habitat for Humanity builds basic low-cost housing around the world that meets minimum international standards for healthy housing while using local materials and being consistent with local norms and conditions. This means that Habitat for Humanity floor plans can be a valuable source for determining minimum living space requirements for a living wage. We used the Habitat for Humanity floor plan for rural Malawi of 30 square meters to help determine the cost of decent housing for a living wage for this very poor country (Anker and Anker, 2013).

OTHER EXAMPLES A minimum of 30 square meters is used for government 'affordable housing for low income households' in Nigeria (lower middle income country). Around 40 square meters is used for government housing for 'low income households' in tea estate housing in Sri Lanka (lower middle income country). Around 50 square meters is the standard for 'low income housing' in Tunisia, 'affordable housing' in Mexico (upper middle income countries) and 'social housing' in Morocco (lower middle income country). Around 60 square meters is the minimum size allowed in Brazil (Sao Paulo). Around 70 square meters of living space is used for 'social housing' in United Kingdom and Ireland, and 90 square meters is used for 'public housing' in New York City.

SUMMARY AND GUIDELINES FOR AMOUNT OF FLOOR SPACE Based on government living space guidelines for lower income households, we suggest the following guidelines for floor space in lieu of a local government standard. However, since such guidelines are common, it is always best to make the effort to find a local standard.

- 30–36 square meters of living space for low income countries.
  This standard is consistent with multiple examples in Table 5.3. This includes housing for farm workers and low income households in South Africa, low income households in urban India, social housing in Vietnam, and affordable housing for low income households in Nigeria. Furthermore, around 30 square meters for a family of 4 and 37 square meters for a family of 5 is implied by median floor area

Table 5.3 Living space guidelines for lower income households, 16 countries

Country	Development level	Gross National Income (GNI) per capita in PPP, 2014	Income group in country	Living space (square meters)
Malawi (rural)	Low income	790	Low income households	30
Kenya (urban)	Lower middle	2,940	Low income households	35
			Middle income households	53
Vietnam	Lower middle	5,350	Social housing (low income)	30
India (urban)	Lower middle	5,630	Low income households	28–48
			Middle income households	48–80
			High income households	80+
India (Maharashtra)			Low income households	28–45
India (Uttar Pradesh)			Low income households	29–50
Nigeria	Lower middle	5,710	Affordable housing (low income)	30
Morocco	Lower middle	7,290	Social housing (low income, less than twice the minimum wage)	50
Sri Lanka (tea estates)	Lower middle	10,300	Tea estates workers	40
Tunisia	Upper middle	11,020	Low income households (1–2 minimum wage)	50
South Africa (farm workers)	Upper middle	12,700	Farm workers	30
South Africa (urban)			Low income households	30–45 (36 average)
China (Shenzhen)	Upper middle	13,170	Low rent housing	44 (for 2–3 persons); 57 (for 4+ persons)
Brazil (Sao Paulo)	Upper middle	15,570	Minimum size allowed	60
Mexico (urban)	Upper middle	16,840	Affordable housing	50

Table 5.3 (continued)

Country	Development level	Gross National Income (GNI) per capita in PPP, 2014	Income group in country	Living space (square meters)
Malaysia (Kuala Lumpur)	Upper middle	24,770	Minimum size allowed	60
United Kingdom	High income	39,500	Social housing for 4 persons (low income)	70
Ireland	High income	42,830	Social housing for 4 persons (low income)	73
USA (New York City)	High income	55,900	Public housing (low income)	90

Notes: Values for Kenya and China assume that gross floor space is 12% more than living space. Value for Sri Lanka was reduced by roughly 20% based on our calculations from a floor plan.

Sources: Woetzel, Ram, Mishke, Garemo, Sankhe (2014), Anker and Anker (2014a), Republic of Kenya (2004), Government of India (2012), Maharashtra Housing and Area Development Authority (2014), Uttar Pradesh Housing and Development Board (2014), Vietnam Government (2005), Hadi (2014), Centre for affordable housing finance in Africa (2015), CABE (2010), Republic of South Africa (1997), Pottie (2003), Moolla, Kotz and Block (2011), Wang (2016), Thibbotuwawa (2016). GNI per capita from World Bank Development Indicators.

per person in cities in least developed countries according to United Nations (2000). 30–36 square meters is also consistent with living space in the Sustainable Agricultural Network/Rainforest Alliance standard (2005, p. 22) that requires '5 square meters of space per person in sleeping areas' for dormitory accommodation considering the need for more than sleeping areas for families.

- 36–60 square meters for middle income countries.
  This range is consistent with many examples from Table 5.3. It is also consistent with median floor space found in Asia, Latin America and Caribbean and former socialist countries in East and Central Europe. This broad range allows leeway for researchers, although lower middle income countries would be usually in the 36–48 square meter range and upper middle income countries would usually be in the 48–60 square meter range.

- 70+ square meters for high income countries.
  This is the standard used for social housing in the United Kingdom and Ireland. It is also consistent with median floor space in the European Union. This standard will be low, however, for some high income countries since 90 square meters is used for New York City public housing.

5.6 Principles of Housing Standards for Estimating a Living Wage

Table 5.4 presents international minimum acceptable housing standards (based mainly on housing principles in international conventions, covenants and recommendations) and indicates how housing standards are likely to differ between rural and urban areas in a country as well as how they are likely to change with economic development. These minimum standards need to be met by a local housing standard used to estimate a living wage.

Table 5.5 provides a template that researchers should use to determine and document an acceptable local housing standard for estimating a living wage. Column 1 lists characteristics of a housing standard, column 2 provides international minimum standards, and column 3 provides comments and examples of local standards. The local housing standard decided on should be entered in column 4. The local housing standard can be higher than the minimum international standard if local conditions are higher than the international minimum standards – but it should not be lower even if local conditions are worse.

PART III. DEVELOPING A LOCAL HOUSING STANDARD

The local standard for acceptable housing needs to meet both international minimal standards as well as local norms. Depending on data availability and study focus, this standard could be set for a city, region, rural areas, or urban areas in a country. For example, while an improved pit toilet close to the house is acceptable in rural Kenya, it is not acceptable in urban Vietnam where almost all houses have an indoor flush toilet. International housing standards call for adequate lighting, but do not require electricity because it is not always available. This means that electricity would not be required in locations where relatively few households have electricity. In contrast, a house without electricity would not be acceptable or decent in locations where most houses have electricity.

Table 5.4 Principles of acceptable housing, minimum acceptable standard, likely rural-urban differences, and likely improvements with economic development

Principle	Minimum acceptable standard	Likely rural & urban differences	Improvement with development	Examples of acceptable standard
Durable structure (protection against elements)	Permanent floor above ground Permanent walls Permanent roof without leaks			Cement/stone/tile/wood floor Brick/cement/well-joined walls Permanent foundation & floor Zinc or iron sheet/ cement/tile roof
Safe water	Safe water in or near house	May need to be inside house in urban	Piped Piped in house	Piped Pump Protected well
Safe sanitation (toilet & sewage disposal)	Safe toilet in or near house, shared by few families	Flush toilet may be needed in urban	Private toilet Flush toilet in house	Flush toilet Pit latrine with slab VIP toilet
Refuse/solid waste disposal	Minimal garbage in street	More important in urban		
Adequate space	30 sq m Ceiling ≥2 meters		Living space increases with development	30–36 sq m low income countries 36–60 sq m middle income countries 70+ sq m high income countries
Good condition & state of repair	Based on observation			Good foundation Good state of repair
Adequate ventilation	≥1 window per room		>1 window per room	
Comfortable ambient temperature	Extreme temperatures not acceptable		Indoor heat in cold climate & cooling in hot climate	Indoor heating Air conditioning

Table 5.4 (continued)

Principle	Minimum acceptable standard	Likely rural & urban differences	Improvement with development	Examples of acceptable standard
Adequate lighting	≥1 window per room or another light source		Electricity More lights	Electricity Kerosene Dry cells
Safe food storage	Separate area		Refrigerator	Refrigerator Cupboard Bins
Ventilation for cooking areas	Minimal indoor air pollution from cooking	Often cook outdoors in rural	Chimney for evacuating smoke	Adequate evacuation of fumes if cook indoors
Electricity	Depends on electric grid and cost	May not be available in rural	Becomes standard	
Site hazards	Should be absent			Surface water drainage problem Industrial pollution Landslides Flood zone
Physical safety	Required	Street lights often needed for urban		Slums not acceptable
Separation from production	Required	Often important in rural		Animals in or near house not acceptable

Table 5.5 Template to determine and describe local housing standard

Housing characteristics	International minimum standards	Comments and examples of possible local standards	Local standard (common in location & meets international standard)
Materials			
Walls	Durable material providing protection from elements	Cement, stone, baked bricks (can't be mud, sticks, or iron sheets)	
Roof	Durable material without leaks	Corrugated iron Tile Cement	
Floor	Durable material	Cement (can't be mud or dung)	
Amenities			
Toilet	At least pit latrine with slab	Pit latrine with slab, VIP toilet, flush toilet (can't be pit latrine without slab)	
Water	Safe water not far from home	Piped into dwelling or yard, public tap, borehole/tube well, protected well (can't be unprotected well)	
Electricity	Not required	Requirement in many locations	
Ventilation & lighting			
Ventilation quality	Good ventilation – especially important when cook indoors	Generally need chimney when cook indoors	
Lighting	Adequate		
Number of windows	Sufficient for adequate lighting and ventilation		
Living space			
Number of square meters of living space	≥30 sq m	Increases with development Might differ in rural and urban areas	
Number of rooms	≤ 2 persons per room excluding kitchen and toilet or bath	Number of bedrooms standard used in higher income countries	

Table 5.5 (continued)

Housing characteristics	International minimum standards	Comments and examples of possible local standards	Local standard (common in location & meets international standard)
Kitchen location	If kitchen is inside house, adequate ventilation for cooking needed	May be in separate building in some locations	
Condition	In good state of repair	In good state of repair	In good state of repair
Environment	Not a slum No site hazards such as: surface water drainage, industrial pollution, danger of landslides, flood zone		

Note that the local housing standard needs to be developed before local housing costs are collected in a local housing market survey (see Chapter 6), because this standard indicates the types of houses that need to be visited and costed during fieldwork.

5.7 Secondary Data on Local Housing Conditions

5.7.1 Data from surveys and censuses

Our methodology relies on secondary data to indicate local housing conditions. A variety of sources are usually available such as housing surveys, socio-economic household surveys, Demographic and Health Surveys (DHS), and population censuses. This also includes international databases such as World Bank World Development Indicators, CIA Factsheets, UNICEF, and UN-Habitat.

Table 5.6 provides a data collection form that can be used to record information on housing commonly found in secondary sources. This form should be adapted to reflect housing conditions in a study location. It provides a good starting point for developing a local housing standard. Information on housing characteristics should be recorded separately for rural and urban areas and location of interest whenever possible.

Table 5.6 Example of form to record secondary data on local housing characteristics (adapt to local data available)

Source and year: ______________________________

Characteristics	Urban %	Rural %	Location of interest (when possible) %	Comments and decisions on local acceptable standard for each bolded characteristic
Structure				
Permanent				
Semi-permanent (wall or roof not permanent)				
Temporary (e.g. mud or stick walls)				
Roof				
Corrugated iron				
Concrete/tile				
Thatch				
Other (specify)				
Floor				
Cement/tile				
Earth/dung				
Wood				
Other (specify)				
Walls				
Cement/stone/ brick				
Wood				
Mud/mud with stone or stick				
Iron sheet				
Bamboo				
Other (specify)				

Table 5.6 (continued)

Source and year: ______________________________

Characteristics	Urban %	Rural %	Location of interest (when possible) %	Comments and decisions on local acceptable standard for each bolded characteristic
Electricity				
Lighting source				
Paraffin/kerosene				
Firewood				
Other (specify)				
Cooking fuel				
Wood				
Charcoal				
Kerosene				
LPG				
Electricity				
Straw/grass				
Other (specify)				
Water source				
Piped into house				
Piped into dwelling or yard				
Public tap				
Borehole/tube well				
Protected well				
Unprotected well				
Unprotected spring/river/lake				
Rainwater				
Other (specify)				
Toilet facility				
Pit latrine with slab				

Table 5.6 (continued)

Source and year: ____________________

Characteristics	Urban %	Rural %	Location of interest (when possible) %	Comments and decisions on local acceptable standard for each bolded characteristic
Pit latrine without slab/open pit				
VIP toilet				
Flush toilet				
No facility, bush				
Other (specify)				
Number of rooms (or number of bedrooms)				
1				
2				
3				
4+				
Average number of square meters per dwelling (and/or per person). Indicate if covered space or living space.				

5.7.2 Information from governments, local housing authorities, and local NGOs such as Habitat for Humanity

As indicated above, national, state and local governments set building codes and pass laws that include minimum housing standards. Also, government housing departments and authorities often build or subsidize low-cost and affordable housing. Some NGOs, such as Habitat for Humanity, build basic housing for lower income families.

An effort should be made to find floor plans and housing standards used by governments and NGOs for low-cost and affordable housing. The local Rainforest Alliance office is also worth contacting, since it often has a locally adapted housing standard for accommodation on plantations and large farms.

5.8 Setting Local Housing Standard Using International Housing Standards and Local Housing Conditions and Norms

The local housing standard for decent housing needs to meet minimum international standards as well as local housing conditions and norms. This means that while local housing standards can never be below international minimum standards they can and often are above.

The local housing standard should specify the following characteristics:

1. Acceptable construction materials for walls, roof and floor.
2. Acceptable amenities such as toilet, water, and electricity.
3. Acceptable living space (in terms of square meters or number of rooms).
4. Acceptable ventilation and lighting.
5. Acceptable environment (e.g. not located in a slum or hazardous area).

5.8.1 Example: how to decide on acceptable construction materials for walls and floor

Generally speaking, common construction materials used in a location that meet the international standards for durability should be used as the local housing standard for walls, floor, and roof. For example, suppose the distribution of construction material for walls in a location was 30% brick, 60% mud, and 10% cement; and construction material for floors was 70% mud and 30% cement or tiles. While mud is the most common material for walls and floor, it does not meet international minimum standards. Brick should be selected for walls and cement or tiles selected for the floor because they are common and durable (and although cement would also be acceptable for walls, it is usually more expensive). Consequently, the local housing market survey would need to concentrate on houses with brick (or cement) walls and cement (or tile) floor.

5.9 Examples of Setting Local Living Wage Housing Standards

This section uses information from household surveys on housing conditions for the Dominican Republic and Malawi to illustrate how secondary housing data can be used to help set a local housing standard. These examples illustrate how very different housing conditions can be in rural and urban areas in developing countries.

Table 5.7 Dominican Republic housing conditions in urban and rural areas according to household survey data and what should be local acceptable housing standards

Characteristics	Urban	Rural	Comments about acceptable standard
Roof			
Zinc/corrugated iron	52.0%	82.1%	Either corrugated iron or cement/tile
Concrete/tile	47.2	16.0	acceptable standard in U & R if does not leak.
Floor			
Cement/tile	97.9%	91.2%	Cement/tile acceptable standard
Earth/dung	1.5	7.5	in U & R if not badly broken.
Wood	1.9	0.6	
Other	0.5	0.5	
Walls			
Cement/stone/brick	78.4%	49.5%	Cement/stone/brick acceptable in U.
Wood planks	17.2	38.1	Cement/stone/brick acceptable
Palm	1.4	8.2	in R throughout country.
Iron sheet	10.1	3.3	Wood acceptable if it is well joined
Bamboo/wood & mud	8.8	48.7	and not in hurricane zone.
Other	4.7	10.2	
Lighting source			
Electricity	99.5%	89.8%	Use electricity and kerosene as standard for lighting in U. Use kerosene or battery for R.
Cooking fuel			
LPG	92.1%	69.4%	LPG acceptable standard in U & R.
Firewood		18.2	
Charcoal		5.7	
No cooking facility	4.6	6.3	Not acceptable.
Water source			
Piped into dwelling	58.9%	28.2%	Piped into dwelling acceptable
Piped into yard	33.0	45.1	standard in U.
Well	2.1	10.0	Piped into house or yard
Truck delivery	4.2	2.9	acceptable standard for R.
Spring/river/creek		8.8	
Rainwater		3.9	
Drinking water source			
Bottled water	66.8%	34.6%	Bottled water used in U & R because
Tap inside	17.5	8.8	water in the Dominican Republic
Tap, public	see above	22.0	generally not safe to drink. Include
Well/spring		10.0	cost of bottled water in housing cost.

Table 5.7 (continued)

Characteristics	Urban	Rural	Comments about acceptable standard
Rain		17.5	
Truck	11.8	6.6	
Toilet facility			
Indoor flush	72.5%	30.4%	Indoor private flush toilet
Indoor flush, shared	5.7	1.8	acceptable in U.
Pit latrine with seat	17.6	53.7	Flush toilet or pit latrine with seat
Pit latrine without seat	1.7	5.7	acceptable standard in R if clean &
			with decent drainage and depth.
Consumer durables			
Refrigerator	78.3%	53.1%	Refrigerator norm in U & R.
Washing machine	75.6%	54.7%	Washing machine norm in U & R.

Source: Centro de Estudios Sociales y Deomgráficos (CESDEM), 2008.

5.9.1 Example of urban and rural housing conditions that generally meet international standards at least on paper: Dominican Republic

Housing conditions in the Dominican Republic meet or exceed minimum international housing standards according to household survey data. This is true for both rural and urban areas (Table 5.7). A majority of houses in both rural and urban Dominican Republic have a cement or corrugated iron roof; cement or tile floor; cement, brick or wood walls; electricity; water pipe in house or yard; flush toilet or pit toilet with seat; and refrigerator and washing machine. Despite this, we found when visiting housing in rural areas that many homes were not actually acceptable for decency. First, wood walls, which are common in rural Dominican Republic, are often so poorly joined that wind, rain and light easily pass through. Second, wood walls are not acceptable in the south of the country, because this is a hurricane zone and poorly constructed wood houses cannot withstand hurricane force winds. Third, cement foundations and cement floors of many houses we visited were in a deteriorated state. Fourth, we found that most pit toilets were in very poor condition with very poor drainage. This example illustrates why it is necessary to visit local housing to determine if houses are acceptable and so the cost of acceptable local housing.

Table 5.8 Malawi housing conditions in rural and urban areas according to household survey data and what should be acceptable housing standards

Characteristics	Urban (U)	Rural (R)	Acceptable standard
Structure			
Permanent (concrete/brick/zinc)	56.7%	23.5%	Use international standard of permanent structure for U & R
Semi-permanent (either wall or roof not permanent)	27.9	24.1	
Temporary (thatch roof & sundried bricks)	15.4	52.4	
Roof	Not reported		
Corrugated iron			Use corrugated iron without leaks in R & U
Concrete/tile			
Thatch		common	
Floor			
Cement/tile	65.9%	14.1%	Use cement for R & U
Earth/dung	32.8	85.5	
Wall	Not reported		
Cement/stone/brick			Use international standard of permanent walls in R & U
Wood planks			
Stone & mud			
Electricity	34.7%	3.5%	Electricity could be standard in U. Electricity not standard in R.
Lighting source			
Electricity	32.6%	2.9%	Possibly use electricity as standard for lighting in U. Not in R.
Paraffin/kerosene	42.5	53.5	Use kerosene or battery for R depending on cost and availability
Firewood	0.7	8.9	
Battery	8.8	30.8	
Candle	15.2	2.7	
Cooking fuel			
Firewood	58.2%	94.1%	Use firewood as standard in R. Use either charcoal or firewood in U as standard depending on availability and cost.
Charcoal	36.7	3.7	
Electricity	9.2	0.2	
Other	0.9	1.9	

Table 5.8 (continued)

Characteristics	Urban (U)	Rural (R)	Acceptable standard
Water source			
Piped into dwelling or yard	31.0%	1.8%	Use piped into dwelling or yard as standard for U or possibly public tap if close by.
Public tap	45.3	10.1	
Borehole/tube well	12.8	58.8	Use any water source that is safe and within reasonable distance to house as standard for R.
Protected well	3.4	6.0	
Unprotected well	6.2	17.1	
Unprotected spring	0.8	2.3	
Toilet facility			
Pit latrine with slab	8.3%	4.0%	Use pit latrine with slab or VIP toilet as standard in R & U if clean and with acceptable drainage and depth.
Pit latrine without slab/open pit	61.9	77.5	
VIP toilet	1.5	1.6	
Flush toilet	1.6	0.4	
No facility, bush	2.4	12.5	
Consumer durables			
Refrigerator	15.7%	1.3%	Refrigerator not norm in U or R.

Source: Demographic and Health Survey, National Statistical Office, Zomba, Malawi and ICF Macro (2010).

5.9.2 Example of poor local housing conditions and so need to base acceptable housing standards mainly on international minimum standards: Rural Malawi

Data from the Malawi 2010 Demographic and Health Survey indicate that housing conditions are very poor in rural Malawi (Table 5.8). Only 14% of rural houses in Malawi have a cement floor; only 24% have a corrugated iron roof and cement or brick walls; only 7% have an improved toilet; and only 3% have electricity. Housing standards in rural Malawi are so poor that a local housing standard for a rural living wage needs to be based mainly on international minimum standards.

NOTES

1. Even the United Nations' Standard Minimum Rules for the Treatment of Prisoners (1957) includes standards for prisoner accommodations: 'Cells and prison dormitories shall provide adequate space, ventilation, lighting and sanitary facilities and are to be kept clean at all times.'

2. UN-Habitat (2003) found that 21 of 30 cities they studied had an official definition of a slum, and 28 of 30 cities had a widely used unofficial definition.
3. 'A room is defined as a space in a housing unit or other living quarters enclosed by walls reaching from the floor to the ceiling or roof covering, or to a height of at least 2 meters, or an area large enough to hold a bed for an adult that is at least 4 square meters' (OECD, Glossary of statistical terms. Available at https://stats.oecd.org/glossary/detail.asp?ID=2363. Accessed 8 July 2016).
4. Acceptable number of rooms is not affected by age and sex of family members, since UK law assumes that children above age 10 can sleep with their same sex parent (United Kingdom Housing Act, 1985).
5. Ireland defines overcrowding as: 'number of persons sleeping in the house and the number of rooms therein – are such that any two of those persons, being persons of ten years of age or more of opposite sexes and not being persons living together as husband and wife, must sleep in the same room' (Ireland, Office of the Attorney General, 1966).
6. The most common measure of affordable housing, that no more than 30% of household income can be for housing, can be traced back to US National Housing Act of 1937 (Schwartz and Wilson, undated; Woetzel et al., 2014).
7. The following example demonstrates that a minimum of around 10% of covered space is lost to internal and external walls. Take a simple 10 meter by 10 meter house (100 square meters covered space) with 2 internal walls that divide this house into 4 equal size rooms. If internal walls are 10 centimeters (4 inches) thick and external walls are 20 centimeters thick (8 inches), which are common thicknesses, around 10% of the covered space would consist of internal and external walls (2 meters of internal wall area and 8 meters of external wall area).
8. Typical LIG houses in India include a small living/sitting room, small kitchen, small toilet room, small bathing area, and 1 or 2 bedrooms.
9. Point 8 is concerned with 'housing accommodation for single workers or workers separated from their families [when this] is collective' (ILO Recommendation No. 115).

APPENDIX 5.1 SUMMARY OF DEFINITIONS AND PRINCIPLES OF ADEQUATE HOUSING OF INTERNATIONAL ORGANIZATIONS

1. International Covenant on Economic, Social and Cultural Rights

General Comment 4 on the Right to Adequate Housing in Article 11(1) of The International Covenant on Economic, Social and Cultural Rights (Office of the High Commissioner for Human Rights, 1991) is specific about what is meant by adequate housing:

> While adequacy is determined in part by social, economic, cultural, climatic, ecological and other factors, the Committee believes that it is nevertheless possible to identify certain aspects of right that must be taken into account for this purpose in any particular context. They include the following:
>
> (a) Legal security of tenure . . . legal protection against forced eviction, harassment and other threats . . .
> (b) Availability of services, materials, facilities and infrastructure . . . access to natural and common resources, safe drinking water, energy for cooking, heating and lighting, sanitation and washing facilities, means of food storage, refuse disposal, site drainage and emergency services . . .
> (c) Affordability . . . should be at a level that the attainment and satisfaction of other basic needs are not threatened or compromised . . .
> (d) Habitability . . . adequate space and protection from cold, damp, heat, rain, wind or other threats to health, structural hazards, and disease vectors. The physical safety of occupants must also be guaranteed. . .
> (e) Accessibility . . . must be accessible to those entitled to it . . . such as disadvantaged groups . . .
> (f) Location . . . allows access to employment options, health care services, schools, child care centers, and other social facilities . . . housing should not be built on polluted sites nor in immediate proximity to pollution sources . . .
> (g) Cultural adequacy . . . enable the expression of cultural identity and diversity of housing.

2. UN-Habitat

UN-Habitat developed a set of indicators to measure and monitor the state of the world's cities and in the progress of countries in reducing the number of people living in urban slums as part of the monitoring of poverty and Millennium Development Goals. Slums were defined by UN-Habitat (2013) as households that lacked either improved water, improved sanitation, sufficient living area (more than three persons per room), or durable housing. In 2012, 32.7% of urban households in developing regions lived in a slum according to UN-Habitat. This ranged from 13.3% in Northern Africa to 35.0% in South Asia and 61.7% in Sub-Sahara Africa.

The following definitions were used by UN-Habitat (2009) for the four elements included in its definition of a slum in addition to secure tenure.

- *Access to safe water* needs to be affordable (less than 10% of household income), available in sufficient quantity (at least 20 liters per person per day), and available without excessive physical efforts and time (less than 1 hour per day for minimum sufficient quantity). The following types of supply for drinking water in urban areas are considered acceptable: 'piped water into dwelling, plot or yard; public tap/standpipe; borehole/tube well; protected dug well; protected spring; rainwater collection and bottled water . . . where there is a secondary source of improved water for other uses such as personal hygiene and cooking' (p. 15).
- *Access to improved sanitation facilities* requires a toilet facility to be correctly constructed and maintained; shared by maximum of two households; and with septic system with sufficient capacity not to be clogged. The following toilet facilities are considered acceptable in urban areas: 'flush/pour-flush toilets or latrines connected to a sewer, septic tank or pit; ventilated improved pit latrine; pit latrine with slab or platform of any material which covers the pit entirely except for drop hole; and compositing toilets/latrines provided they are not public' (p. 16).
- *Overcrowding and sufficient living area* defined as more than three persons per room with 'a room defined as a space in a housing unit or other living quarters . . . of an area large enough to hold a bed for an adult, that is at least four square meters. The total number of types of rooms therefore includes bedrooms, dining rooms, living rooms, studies, habitable attics, servants' room, kitchen and other separate spaces intended for dwelling purposes' (p. 9).
- *Durable housing* is defined as 'a housing unit built on a non-hazardous location and has a structure permanent and adequate enough to protect its inhabitants from the extreme of climatic conditions such as rain, heat, cold, humidity. The following locations are considered hazardous: housing settled in geologically hazardous zones (landslides/earthquake and flood areas); garbage mountains; high industrial pollution areas; other high risk zones (e.g. railroads, airports, energy transmission lines). The following durability factors are considered when categorizing housing units: quality of construction (e.g. materials used for wall, floor and roof); compliance with local building codes, standards and by-laws' (p. 8).

3. International Labour Organization Recommendation No. 115 (1961) Concerning Workers' Housing

International Labour Organization passed a Recommendation Concerning Workers' Housing in 1961 that specifies housing standards. 'As a general principle', housing should have 'structural safety and reasonable levels of decency, hygiene and comfort'. This Recommendation includes 'Suggestions Concerning Methods of Application' (underlining added for emphasis):

> General Principles [of housing standards] should relate in particular to –
> 7(a) the minimum space per person or per family as expressed in terms of one or more of the following, due regard being had to the need for rooms of reasonable dimensions and proportions:
>
> (i) floor area;
> (ii) cubic volume; or
> (iii) size and number of rooms;
>
> 7(b) the supply of safe water in the workers' dwelling in such ample quantities as to provide for all personal and household uses;
> 7(c) adequate sewage and garbage disposal systems;
> 7(d) appropriate protection against heat, cold, damp, noise, fire, and disease-carrying animals, and, in particular, insects;
> 7(e) adequate sanitary and washing facilities, ventilation, cooking and storage facilities and natural and artificial lighting;
> 7(f) a minimum degree of privacy both –
>
> (i) as between individual persons within the household; and
> (ii) for the members of the household against undue disturbance by external factors; and
>
> 7(g) suitable separation of rooms devoted to living purposes from quarters for animals. . . .
> 8.[9] Workers' housing standards should be revised from time to time to take account of social, economic and technical development and increases of real income per head.
> 9. In general, and in localities where employment opportunities are not of a temporary character, workers' housing and related community facilities should be of durable construction.
> 10. The aim should be to construct workers' housing and related community facilities in the most suitable materials available, having regard to local conditions, such as liability to earthquakes.

4. World Health Organization Principles of Healthy Housing

WHO has six principles for health aspects of adequate housing (WHO, 1989). The following describes the first three principles which are particularly relevant for living wage.

1. **Protection against communicable diseases**
The following conditions are necessary to ensure protection against communicable diseases in WHO's Health Principles of Housing (WHO, 1989).

- **Safe and adequate water supply**

  The water supply should be either inside or relatively close to the dwelling. 'An adequate supply of safe and potable water assists in preventing the spread of gastrointestinal diseases, supports domestic and personal hygiene and provides and improved standard of living' (pp. 2–3). And 'having to carry water from a distance almost always means that there will be inadequate quantities in the home and an added risk of contamination' (p. 3).

- **Sanitary disposal of excreta and adequate toilets**

  'Sanitary disposal of excreta [which] reduces the faecal-oral transmission of disease and the breeding of insect vectors' (p. 4) is required. Note that 'Contamination may occur near houses, as when people defecate on the ground or in areas where food is grown, or when latrines are improperly located in relation to wells, set in soil lacking satisfactory drainage, or inadequately maintained . . . These hazards are worse in conditions of overcrowding, whether in slums, peri-urban settlements or temporary camps, where facilities for excreta disposal are absent, insufficient or badly maintained' (p. 4)

- **Disposal of solid wastes**

  'Adequate and safe disposal of solid domestic wastes reduces health risks and helps to provide a more pleasant living environment; appropriate methods of storage and disposal discourage insect and rodent vectors of disease and protect people against poisonous substances and objects likely to cause accidental injury' (p. 5). According to WHO (1989), hazards associated with inadequate and unsafe disposal of solid waste 'increase with urbanization and economic development, as consumption becomes more varied' (p. 5).

- **Drainage of surface water**

  'Efficient drainage of surface waters helps to control communicable diseases, safety hazards, and damage to homes and property' (p. 6). Breeding sites for vectors such as mosquitoes need to be prevented. Special attention is required as regards drainage near wells, latrines and kitchens. 'Inadequate drainage of surface waters – including domestic wastewater – results in pools or muddy and marshy areas that provide breeding places for mosquitos, flies and other insect vectors of disease. Standing waters near wells, latrines and kitchens are of special concern, as they are important loci of biological contamination' (p. 6).

- **Personal and domestic hygiene**

  'Adequate housing includes facilities for personal and domestic hygiene' (p. 6). Stables for animal husbandry should be at a reasonable distance from the house. 'Rural families engaged in animal husbandry are exposed to special hazards. The faeces and urine of animals kept inside dwellings may harbour pathogens and increase the difficulty of maintaining cleanliness, thus increasing exposure to insect and animal disease vectors. Stabling must be at a distance from dwellings and pets must be kept pest-free in order to reduce the transmission of disease, especially to children' (p. 7).

- **Safe food preparation and storage**

  'Healthy dwellings provide facilities for the safe preparation and storage of food, so that householders can employ sanitary food handling practices' (p. 7).

- **Structural safeguards against disease transmission**

  'Adequate housing provides structural safeguards against transmission of disease, including enough space to avoid overcrowding. Dirt floors not only make domestic hygiene difficult, but may harbor helminths. . . . Overcrowding, particularly in conjunction with poverty and inadequate facilities, have been shown to increase the transmission rates of such communicable diseases as tuberculosis, pneumonia, bronchitis and gastrointestinal infections' (p. 8).

2. **Protection against injuries, poisonings, and chronic disease**

- **Structural features and furnishing**

  'The proper sitting, structure and furnishing of dwellings protects health, promotes safety and reduces hazards' (p. 9). WHO emphasizes the importance of durable structures that provide 'safe, dry, comfortable abode that shelters residents against vermin, extremes of temperature and recurring hazards of nature' (p. 9).

- **Indoor air pollution**

  'Adequately designed, constructed and ventilated dwellings, free of toxic and irritating substances, reduce the risks of chronic respiratory diseases and malignancies' (p. 11). WHO recognizes that 'by far the most common problems arise from fuel combustion inside dwellings, whether from inadequate venting of heating and cooking devices or from the burning of biomass fuels (firewood, charcoal, crop residues, animal dung) in open fires' (p. 11).

- **Chemical safety**

  'Sensible precautions in the household reduce exposure to hazardous chemicals' (p. 12).

- **Use of home as a workplace**

  'Where a dwelling is also used as a workplace, those who live in it should be protected against hazards and contamination' (p. 12).

- **Adequate separation of stabling and working premises from living areas**

3. **Reducing psychological and social stresses to a minimum**
   This principle emphasizes the concept of the home as a refuge and the psychological and social stress that come from '*overcrowding in dwellings*, uncertainty of tenure, excessive noise, the struggle for survival, fear of crime and other threats to physical security' (p. 14). WHO notes that 'such stresses are all the greater for those . . . who are making the transition from rural to urban life' (p. 14).

6. Local cost of decent housing for a living wage

Chapter 5 was concerned with how to establish a standard for acceptable housing for a location. The current chapter is concerned with how to estimate the cost of local housing that meets the local standard.

Estimating the cost of acceptable housing focuses on rent, because it is much easier to collect rental prices than to estimate the cost of home ownership. Many national statistical offices (including the United States) use rent rather than the cost of owner-occupied housing to estimate housing cost when they estimate CPI. Section 6.1 describes how to carry out a local rental cost survey. Section 6.2 indicates how to analyze this information. Section 6.3 discusses the possibility of asking workers about how much they think it would cost to rent acceptable housing in the study location. Sections 6.4–6.5 discuss how to estimate utility costs, fees and routine maintenance and repair costs. In locations where almost all housing is owned rather than rented, finding representative rental costs is difficult. In this case, the user cost of owner-occupied housing is estimated and used as a proxy for rental cost (Section 6.6).

6.1 Local Rental Cost Survey

6.1.1 Locations to visit

Collection of information on rents should focus on areas where workers typically live. To help locate suitable areas to visit, it is very useful to have a map of the study area that indicates where factories or farms are concentrated as well as where workers typically live. One could start with a published map, or a map downloaded from the web, or a freehand drawn map. Based on discussions with knowledgeable persons, locations of interest such as farms and factories should be marked on the map along with notable roads, towns, landmarks, and markets. In urban areas, key characteristics of neighborhoods should be indicated such as whether they are expensive or unsafe or a slum since slums and unsafe neighborhoods are not acceptable for decent housing and housing in expensive neighborhoods is too costly.[1] It is also best to avoid neighborhoods that are far away from workplaces and so require an inordinately long commute. Figure 6.1

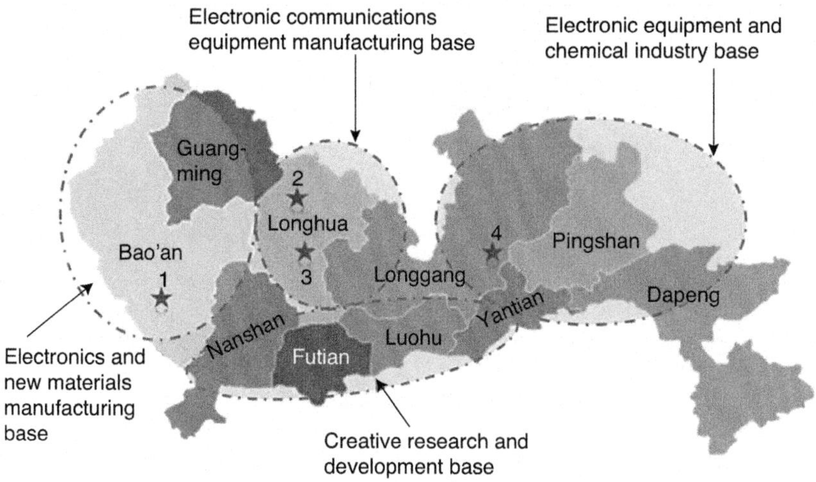

Notes: Stars indicate areas with a concentration of electronics factories. Star 1 represents an area with small electronics factories. Star 2 represents Guanlan Science and Technology Park (in Guanlan town). Star 3 represents Longhua Science and Technology Park (in Longhua Town). Star 4 represents LED lighting and electronic application factories located in Shangrong Science and Technology Industrial Park in Longgang District.

Source: Wang et al. (2016), base map from Wikimedia Commons (https://commons.wikimedia.org/wiki/File:Administrative_Divisions_of_Shenzhen_City.svg).

Figure 6.1 Districts, industrial bases, and study sites, Shenzhen, China

provides an example of a map of areas in Shenzhen, China that was used for a living wage study that focused on electronics factories in Shenzhen. Notice that factories and the areas where workers live were concentrated in the outskirts of Shenzhen where costs were lower than in the center of the city.

Maps showing the locations of factories sometimes already exist. For example, an interactive map indicating the number of registered and unregistered garment factories in many areas in the greater Dhaka area of Bangladesh is available from the Stern School of Business (Labowitz and Bauman-Pauly, 2015). This map was used to help select areas to collect information on food prices and housing costs for a living wage study that focused on garment factories in Dhaka.

The map used to select locations does not need to be sophisticated. For the Lake Naivasha area of Kenya where a living wage study focused on fresh cut flower farms, we used a hand-drawn map that indicated the main flower farms and the main communities where workers live (Figure 6.2). In other countries, we have asked local key informants to indicate locations

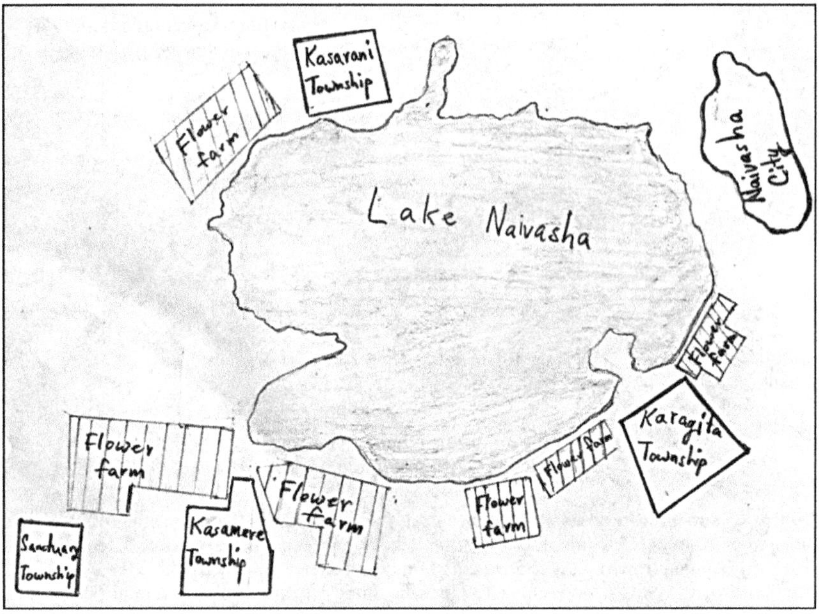

Figure 6.2 Flower farms and townships surrounding Lake Naivasha, Kenya

with the highest concentrations of workers on a road map that we purchased. For agricultural products/industries, we have used a map downloaded from the web of areas in a country where the product of focus is grown that we overlaid with locations of farms to help identify and choose representative study locations.

6.1.2 Number of neighborhoods to visit

There is no golden rule as to the number of neighborhoods to visit. This depends partly on time available, heterogeneity of living costs across neighborhoods where workers live, and size of the area covered. For estimating living wages in larger cities, at least three or four different areas should be covered with food and housing costs collected from at least two neighborhoods within each area.

6.1.3 Finding rental units to visit that meet the local living wage housing standard

It is often difficult to find basic acceptable rental units to visit, especially when prevailing wages are far below a living wage. In many locations in developing countries, workers' housing tends to be substandard because this is all that most workers can afford at present. At the same time, there is usually also a market for housing catering to higher income families that is well above the basic but decent housing standard for a living wage. The market for basic rental units that just meets a living wage housing standard is often relatively small when relatively few workers earn a living wage. This means that efficiency in identifying acceptable rental units to visit is required. Otherwise, an inordinate amount of time would be spent visiting housing below (and often well below) the local living wage housing standard.

We have found that the following approaches increase efficiency:

1. Ask workers about their current housing to identify acceptable housing worth visiting. This can be done individually or in focused group discussions. Workers who live in rented housing that is similar to the living wage local housing standard could be asked if it is OK to visit their homes. We have found it very useful to go with workers to their homes (usually after work, or during work when an employer is willing to excuse workers without reducing their pay). Workers are usually welcoming and other people in the neighborhood are much more willing to let an investigator visit their home when the investigator is accompanied by someone who is known to them. When possible, it is best to arrange to visit houses of several workers who live in a location on the same day to increase efficiency.
2. Visit rented homes of better paid workers such as supervisors and junior management. They are often more likely to be earning a living wage than production workers and so more likely to be able to afford decent housing. It is always necessary to keep in mind that we are interested in the cost of basic but decent housing, no matter who the renter is.
3. When visiting neighborhoods, ask people if they know of other rented homes that have the characteristics of the local living wage housing standard. We have found this to be an effective way of identifying acceptable rental housing.
4. Ask local merchants, such as neighborhood grocery store owners, if they know of rental housing in the location that meets the local housing standard. They are often quite knowledgeable and helpful.
5. Speak to local authorities concerned with affordable rental housing about housing costs. Note that if this information is to be used, such housing must be available to most workers. We found, for example, that low-cost municipal housing in South Africa had a waiting list that was sometimes decades long.

6. Whether visiting local real estate agents or consulting advertisements in the newspaper is of value depends on the location. In most locations in developing countries, real estate agents and newspapers do not deal with housing of the quality we are interested in. On the other hand, real estate agents were found to be useful in urban China where there is a large rental market for factory workers who share accommodations.
7. On several occasions, we have been able to augment our local market housing survey with data collected by others. In Kenya, we were provided with information from a survey of rental units carried out by the welfare committee of a large farm to help facilitate the transfer of workers from another location.
8. Data on rental costs are sometimes collected and reported by national statistical offices.
9. We have found it useful to ask workers in very co-operative establishments to fill in a questionnaire on the cost (rent, rental value if owned, utilities, fees, taxes) and characteristics of their homes (materials of roof, walls, floor, number of rooms, number of square meters, etc.). This helps identify rental units that meet the local living wage housing standard as well as provides useful information on housing costs. But this type of enquiry is not often possible.

6.1.4 Usefulness of visiting range of housing above and below local housing standard

Although we are interested in the cost of renting an acceptable house for a family, it is important to visit a range of dwellings that includes dwellings above and below the local housing standard. This provides a check on the estimated rental cost of acceptable housing, since rent for better and worse housing units bracket rent for acceptable housing units. This is also useful information for explaining to readers the type and the quality of housing workers currently live in.

6.1.5 Rural-urban differences

There are usually large differences between rural and urban housing markets and costs. There is often a far greater choice of rentals in urban areas than in rural areas. Indeed, often there is not much of a rental market in rural areas. In addition, acceptable housing standards often differ between rural and urban areas in part because of the higher population density in urban areas.

6.1.6 Data collection form for rental units

Table 6.1 is an example of a data collection form that can be used to collect local housing information. Data collected are used in several ways:

Table 6.1 Example of data collection form for rental units

Neighborhood	
Town/city/place	
Approximate distance and time from workplace	
Travel method and cost of one-way transport to workplace	
Is neighborhood a slum?	
Safety of neighborhood? (very safe, somewhat safe, unsafe?)	
Indicate environmental problems (e.g. street lights, drainage, sewage, garbage, etc.)	
Name of person/family (optional)	
Address	
Indicate if OWNED, RENTED or PROVIDED FREE	
Type of dwelling: flat, independent house, single room, etc.	
Total number of residents in dwelling	
Number of adults	
Number of children	
Material of dwelling	
Walls	
Roof	
Floor	
Condition of walls, floor roof, foundation (e.g. roof leaks, mold, etc.)	
Condition of walls	
Condition of roof	
Condition of floor	
Indicate if height of ceiling is less than 2 meters	
# Windows in dwelling	
Ventilation quality of dwelling (poor, fair, good, very good)	
Size of dwelling	
Total approximate number of square meters of living space	
Total # rooms	
# separate bedrooms	
# separate living/dining rooms	

Table 6.1 (continued)

If separate kitchen room inside? (yes or no)	
If proper ventilation of smoke from cooking? (yes or no)	
Is cooking done outside house? (yes or no)	
Amenities	
Electricity? (hours per day)	
Source of water	
Separate source of drinking water? If so specify	
Piped indoor water? (yes or no)	
If no indoor water: distance to water	
Number days per week water available	
How water stored (e.g. open or closed vessel, tank, jerry can, etc.)	
Toilet: pit, flush, or _____? (indicate)	
Toilet: inside or outside? (indicate)	
Condition of toilet (very good, good, fair, poor)	
If toilet fair or poor: Explain e.g. smell, drainage, building condition, etc.	
General condition of dwelling (very good, good, fair, poor)	
If condition fair or poor: Explain	
Consumer durables (yes or no)	
Refrigerator	
Motorbike	
Cost per month (indicate total cost of dwelling even if cost is shared with others)	
Rent per month	
Electricity cost per month (0 if included in rent)	
Water cost per month (0 if included in rent)	
Cooking fuel cost per month (0 if included in rent)	
Heating fuel: Number of months needed (0 if included in rent)	
(When used) Cost of heating fuel per month	
Other costs per month including fees and taxes (indicate type & amount)	
Investigator's opinion: Does house meet acceptable standards for location? (yes or no)	
If no: Indicate reasons why not acceptable	

(1) to determine whether or not a dwelling visited meets the local housing standard; (2) to estimate the cost of acceptable housing; and (3) to estimate the cost of utilities such as electricity, water, and cooking fuel, as well as other costs associated with renting a dwelling such as fees and taxes. As with all forms provided in this manual, this form should be adapted to local conditions.

6.2 Analysis and Presentation of Local Rental Cost Information

6.2.1 Table with local rental cost data

The easiest and most effective way to analyze and present data collected in a local housing survey is to create a table with each housing unit listed in a separate row in ascending order of their rent (see Table 6.2). Variables to describe each housing unit include: (i) whether visited; (ii) whether acceptable and meets or exceeds the local housing standard; (iii) rent per month; (iv) utility costs, fees, and other costs per month; (v) key characteristics such as walls, floor and roof; (vi) size in square meters and number and types of rooms; and (vii) comments. The comments column should indicate reasons why the dwelling was found to be unacceptable or acceptable and what the housing unit was like. Why rent may have been unusually high or unusually low might also be indicated (e.g. landlord was a relative, or rent had not changed in a long time). In this way, the type of housing available at different rents is clearly displayed and it is possible to see what rents are for dwellings below the housing standard, similar to the housing standard, and above the standard.

6.2.2 Photos of local housing

We have found it very effective and informative to include photos of local housing in living wage reports – photos of both unacceptable housing and basic acceptable housing. Photos provide a visual perspective and are easy to understand and especially useful for international readers who have little or no familiarity with local conditions. Photos can be especially effective in communicating when many workers currently live in poor housing and the basic nature of the local housing standard.

6.2.3 Example: Table presenting local rental costs for rural Dominican Republic

Table 6.2 lists rent from 14 rental units we visited in rural Dominican Republic. We concluded that acceptable housing rented for around RD$2,000 per month (although one of the lessons we learned from this pilot study is that we should have included more time for fieldwork). Although two acceptable units rented for RD$1,500, each of these had

Table 6.2 Cost of rented housing units visited, rural Dominican Republic

Acceptable standard?	Rent in local currency	Size & rooms	Comments
No	650	293 sq ft LR, 2 BR, K	Unsafe neighborhood. Poor condition, holes in walls and roof. Poor latrine with wooden platform and seat.
No	800	224 sq ft 1 Room	Only 1 room. No latrine nearby. Had to use neighbor's latrine. Poor ventilation as only 1 window.
No	1,000	446 sq ft LR, 2 BR, K	Unsafe neighborhood. Outside latrine in very poor condition despite indoor water. Steals electricity.
No	1,000	224 sq ft 1 Room	Only 1 room in poor condition with cracked cement walls, broken cement floor, and leaky zinc roof. No latrine nearby (uses neighbor's latrine). In sugar batey (i.e. bateyes are shantytowns with houses and shops close to sugar cane fields originally built by sugar plantations to house sugarcane cutters).
No	1,200	150 sq ft LR, 2 BR	Tiny rooms. 14 sq m. No kitchen – cooks outside with charcoal. Shares pit toilet in very poor condition. No electricity.
No	1,300	256 sq ft LR, 3 BR, K	Cement base in poor condition. Latrine in poor condition. Kitchen roof in poor condition. Small size as only 256 sq ft living space.
No	1,500 (same for 8 years)	391 sq ft LR, 2BR, K	Latrine in terrible condition. Damaged roof. Broken cement floor. Rent unchanged for eight years. In Mao city.
No	1,500	420 sq ft LR, 3 BR, K	Roof leaks. Broken cement base and floor. Water two days per week.
No	1,500	410 sq ft LR, 2 BR, K	Part of house had thatched roof. Roof leaked. Poor latrine. Wood walls in poor condition.
Yes	1,500 (same rent for 4 years. Increase expected soon)	365 sq ft (34 sq m.) LR, 2 BR, K	House in fair to good condition. Inside flush toilet. Rent unchanged for four years, and is expected to increase soon.
Yes	1,500 (same rent for 5 years. Daughter's godmother owns house)	372 sq ft LR, 2 BR, K	Cement house in good condition. Outside latrine in good condition. Outside water nearby. Rent unchanged for five years. Landlord is daughter's godmother.

Table 6.2 (continued)

Acceptable standard?	Rent in local currency	Size & rooms	Comments
No	2,000	299 sq ft LR, 2 BR, K, Bath	Impassible road & open culvert/sewer in front of house. Latrine 30 feet from house, in poor condition & shared with four families. Garbage behind house.
Yes	3,000	437 sq ft LR, 2 BR, K	Very good condition. Indoor water and toilet. Wood walls, cement base, zinc roof.
Yes	4,000 (newly rented)	370 sq ft LR, 2 BR, K	Very good condition. Indoor water and toilet. Wood walls, cement base, zinc roof. Recently rented.

Notes: LR indicates living room. BR indicates bedroom. K indicates kitchen.

a reason for exceptionally low rent (one was rented from a relative; rent for the other was expected to increase soon). Otherwise, we did not find other acceptable units except ones that were much more expensive. Based on this information, we concluded that rent for acceptable housing was above RD$1,500. At the same time, it was clear that RD$3,000 per month was too high, since dwellings well above the local housing standard rented for this amount. In this case, we decided to set rent for basic acceptable housing at a conservative RD$2,000 per month. This was on the lower side between the RD$1,500 which was known to be too low, and the RD$3,000 which was known to be too high. This rent was cross-checked with information from banana plantations on the cost of building and maintaining basic acceptable housing for families. It was noted in our living wage report that RD$2,000 per month was approximately two to three times the rent for one small room.

6.2.4 Estimating rent for an acceptable dwelling using rent per square meter

Since rent is related to dwelling size, it is possible to estimate rent for an acceptable dwelling from the rent of dwellings of various sizes using observed rent per square meter. Regressing rent (dependent variable) on number of square meters of floor space (independent variable) will indicate whether this relationship is linear or non-linear (such as log linear or quadratic).

Our experience is that the relationship between rent and amount of living space is more or less linear (i.e. cost per square meter is similar regardless of size of dwelling, and so twice as much space costs twice as much money) in places where workers rent one bare room without indoor amenities such as piped water, toilet, or kitchen with chimney (see Kenya example below), and non-linear (i.e. cost per square meter falls with size) when even small dwelling units include such amenities because the cost of these amenities is in a sense defrayed over a larger floor space (see Vietnam example below).

This method can provide useful information especially in locations where there are not many rental properties that just meet the local housing standard, but there are many rental properties with required amenities that are too small or too large. Regression results should not be used as a substitute for reported rents in locations where rental properties that are similar to the local housing standard can be found.

6.2.4.1 Example: Using rent per square meter in rental cost estimate for a second tier city in Vietnam Figure 6.3 provides an example of a non-linear relationship between rent per square meter and house size for houses in a second tier city in Vietnam where most housing has basic amenities of piped water, toilet, and separate kitchen. A log function reasonably represents the relationship between monthly rent (y axis) and size of housing unit in square meters (x axis), with rent per square meter decreasing with house size. Based on this relationship, rent for a housing unit with 36 square meters would cost VND939,637 (VND26,101 per square meter derived from regression multiplied by 36 square meters). Note that if one

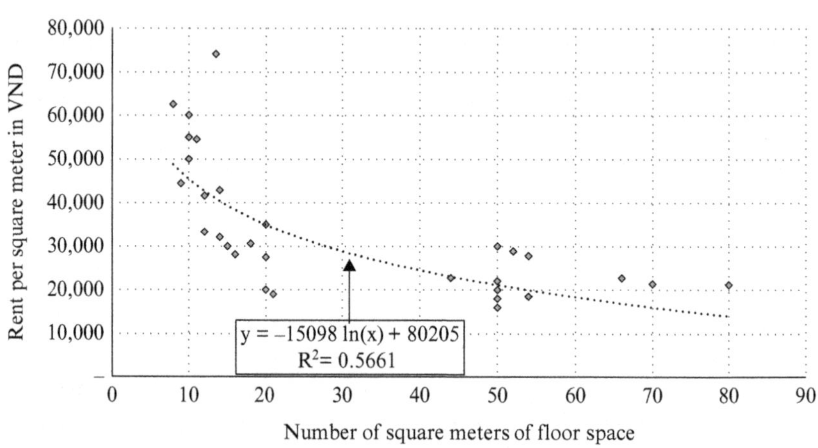

Figure 6.3 Rent per square meter as function of number of square meters for housing that meets all other characteristics of acceptable housing, tier two city in Vietnam

were interested in rent for units with 50 square meters, there would be no need for regression analysis, because a number of units with 50 square meters were observed.

6.2.5 Example: Estimate of rental cost in non-metropolitan urban Kenya

Table 6.3 includes results from our living wage local housing market survey for Lake Naivasha supplemented by a recent survey of available housing done by the workers' welfare committee from a large flower farm. Housing units for most workers consisted of one bare room without kitchen facilities, indoor water, or indoor toilet that was rented by a migrant worker living without his or her family. It was clear that the cost of acceptable housing was more than KSh4,000 per month, since none of the housing units visited with a rent below KSh4,000 were acceptable. At the same time, housing units visited with rent of KSh8,000 or above were more than acceptable. Therefore, rent for basic acceptable housing appeared to be between KSh4,000 and KSh8,000 per month.

To help determine where in the KSh4,000–8,000 range the cost of acceptable basic housing might be, we estimated that rent for the minimum 30–36 square meters required for decency in this location for a family to be around KSh5,400 by extrapolation. KSh5,400 was roughly three times the rent for a 10 feet by 10 feet room (i.e. 3 × KSh1,800) and around 1.5 times rent for two rooms with around 20 square meters of living space (i.e. 1.5 × KSh3,000–4,000). KSh5,400 was felt to be a very conservative estimate of rent for acceptable housing, since while this amount would be enough to rent housing with sufficient space, this space would not include a separate kitchen area with a chimney.

6.3 Asking Workers How Much They Think Rent is for Housing Similar to the Local Housing Standard

Statistical offices and researchers sometimes ask people how much they think it would cost to rent housing with particular characteristics. This includes asking home owners how much their house would rent for if it were rented out. In our case, people could be asked how much rent would be for housing that meets the local housing standard. This is a controversial approach to estimating rental costs, because the extent to which people provide reasonable answers varies greatly by country and location, and how questions are asked. Our experience in a number of countries is that this is not a good approach in locations where there is a small rental market for housing that just meets the local living wage housing standard. We have been struck by how variable and often inaccurate people's perceptions of rental costs are in different countries. Statistics South Africa (2008), also

Table 6.3 Cost of rented housing units visited, Lake Naivasha Kenya

Acceptable standard?	Source	No. rooms	Size in sq m	Rent per month	Comments[a]
No	Visited	1	9	400	Small. Mud walls. Leaky roof. No electricity. Poor ventilation.
No	WWC (24 separate single rooms)[b]	1		Median 1,050 Range (300–1,500)	Single room. 1 room only. No electricity. Usually 10 feet by 10 feet (9 square meters) in size. For previous year.
No	Visited	1	14	1,400	Small. Mud walls. Leaky roof. Poor ventilation.
No	Visited	1	9	1,500	Small in modern building.
No	Visited	1	9	1,500	Small, one room only.
No	Visited	1	9	1,600	Small. Electricity included in rent, but not allowed to use electric iron.
No	WWC (36 separate single rooms)[b]	1		Median 1,800 Range (1,000–2,200)	Small, one room only. Usually 10 feet by 10 feet (9 square meters) in size. With electricity. Rents for previous year.
No	Visited	1	11	2,000	Small, one room only.
No	Visited	2	16	2,500	Small, two rooms only. In nearby city.
No	Visited	2	21	2,500	Mud walls. Poor ventilation. No electricity.
No	Visited	3	29	3,000	No ventilation. Roof leaked. In nearby city.
No	Visited	2	19	3,500	18 people use one toilet. ½ hour walk to bus – dangerous at night to walk to home. Poor ventilation for cooking. In nearby city.
No	Visited	2.5	21	4,000	Poor ventilation for cooking. Too small.
No	WWC (13 two-room units)[b]	2		Median 4,000 Range (1,800–8,000)	10 units were KSh4,000; others were KSh4,500 and KSh8,000. 12 of 13 were in city. One unit in township near flower farms was KSh1,800. Rents for previous year.

Table 6.3 (continued)

Acceptable standard?	Source	No. rooms	Size in sq m	Rent per month	Comments[a]
No	Visited	2	19	4,000	Rooms not connected. To get to children's room needed to go through street. Poor ventilation for cooking.
Yes	Visited	4	46	8,000	In nearby city. Separate kitchen with chimney. Very nice.
	WWC (1 unit)[b]	3 bed rooms		12,500	In nearby city. Very nice. Rents for previous year.
Yes	Visited	4	96	15,000	In nearby city. Separate kitchen with chimney. Very nice.

Notes:

[a] Unless otherwise indicated, dwellings: (i) were located in urban townships near large flower farms; (ii) did not have indoor water; (iii) water needed to be boiled for drinking; (iv) cooking was done indoors without a chimney using small charcoal stove; and (v) shared pit toilet with concrete slab was of acceptable quality outside house.

[b] WWC indicates Workers' Welfare Committee of a large farm that looked at available housing in the area in the previous year for management.

found that persons owning a dwelling had 'difficulty' in providing 'a reliable estimate of the market value of their property.' On the other hand, recent living wage studies for cities in Brazil and China, where rental markets are well developed found it useful to ask workers about likely rent for basic acceptable housing (Barbosa et al., 2016, Wang et al., 2016). In short, while this approach can be used, this should be done cautiously and in any case restricted to locations with a well-developed housing market for basic acceptable housing.

6.4 Utility and Other Housing Costs

Utility costs and other housing costs such as taxes and user fees are an important part of housing costs. Utility costs include water, electricity, cooking fuel, heat, and lighting.

6.4.1 Collecting data on utility costs in local housing survey

To calculate utility costs, it is best to collect information on these costs from several sources in addition to the information collected on a local housing survey, since a local housing survey usually covers a relatively small number of houses. In this way, it is possible to estimate utility costs by triangulating between estimates from several sources.

Some utility costs such as water and cooking fuel, increase with family size. To estimate cost per family for water based on data from a local housing survey, it is best to calculate cost per person and multiply this by the reference family size for a living wage. Cost of other utilities, such as heat, electricity, and lighting, which are not as dependent on family size, should be used as reported for the family. Note that when using data on utility costs from a local housing survey, it is necessary to consider the possibility that utility costs indicated by a local housing survey are too low for decency. For example, low wage workers in poor countries might be able to afford only one or two light bulbs and few if any electrical items and for this reason spend very little for electricity; or their landlord might restrict their use of electrical items such as irons that consume a lot of electricity. In these situations, electricity consumption will be below what it would be if a living wage was earned.

6.4.2 Secondary data on household expenditure for utilities

Secondary data on the share of household expenditure for utilities from a recent household expenditure survey (or CPI expenditure weights) is a useful source of information. The ratio of the share of household expenditures for utilities to the share of household expenditures for food can be used to estimate utility costs for a living wage by multiplying this ratio by the cost of a living wage model diet. The advantage of these data is that they are based on a large number of households.

6.4.3 Additional sources of information on utility costs

1. Discussions with key informants, focus groups discussions with workers, and a questionnaire on housing and utility costs filled out by workers can provide useful information on utility costs.
2. Tax laws can be a potentially useful source when they indicate specific amounts that can be deducted for utilities for income tax purposes. For example, Kenya allows a deduction for electricity of KSh900 for agricultural workers and Ksh1,500 for urban areas (Kenya Revenue Authority, 2009).
3. When water is purchased, the cost for a minimum number of liters of water per person per day required according to WHO (2013) can be used. According to the standards used for emergencies, 20 liters per capita per day is required for drinking and cooking. Minimum water needs increase to 30 liters per day when personal washing is considered and to 40 liters per day when washing clothes is considered. Water for a flush toilet is considerable and in addition.

4. Drinking water is sometimes purchased separately from water used for other purposes. We have found that even poor households in all of the Dominican Republic and in urban Vietnam purchase bottled drinking water. Drinking water is usually purchased in large plastic jugs. The SPHERE international guidelines for emergencies call for a minimum of 2.5–3 liters of drinking water per person per day depending on climate, physical activity and physiology, and the Institute of Medicine of the National Academies (2004) for the United States indicates that a family of 4 persons (parents and 2 children) needs on average 8.4 liters of drinking water per day (3.0 liters for father, 2.2 liters for mother, and 1.6 liters per child).

6.4.4 Drawing together different information on utility costs

Estimates of utility costs from secondary data, a local housing survey, and other sources should be compared. Differences should be examined with reasons for differences considered as the basis for estimating utility costs.

6.5 Maintenance and Routine Repair Costs

Every dwelling has expenses for routine maintenance and repairs. How large this cost is for renters depends on responsibilities of renters and landlords for repairs and maintenance, condition of the dwelling, and climate. The cost of improvements should be excluded. Generally, we include nothing or a small amount for renters for repairs and maintenance.

6.6 User Cost of Owner-occupied Housing as a Proxy for Rental Cost in Locations, such as Rural Areas, Where There is Little or No Rental Market

Rent for acceptable local housing should be used to estimate housing costs whenever possible based on a local housing survey. This approach is followed because it is difficult and controversial to estimate the cost of housing to home owners and indeed for this reason many national statistical offices use rent to estimate housing costs when estimating CPI.

Unfortunately, this approach may not make sense in locations where not many dwellings are rented. This situation is common in rural areas in developing countries. In such situations, housing cost should be estimated, using what is called the user cost approach.

6.6.1 How to estimate user cost per month for local housing

Three approaches (user cost, payment outlays, and acquisition cost) are used by national statistical offices to estimate the cost of owner-occupied housing for estimating CPI (ILO et al., 2004). We use the user cost approach to estimate the rental equivalent value of acceptable owner-occupied housing when there is little or no rental market, as does the International Comparison Program (ICP) of the World Bank to determine parity purchasing parity values (PPP) for countries that lack rental market surveys (Heston, 2013).

The following information is needed to estimate the user cost of owner-occupied housing. It is best to obtain this information from several sources as a way of cross-checking the information.

- Cost of constructing a house (or housing unit) that meets the local housing standard.
- Expected service life of a newly constructed house or building. The better the construction and materials, the longer is the expected service life and therefore the lower is annual depreciation cost.
- Cost per year for routine maintenance and repairs. There is a trade-off between construction cost and annual maintenance costs. The better the construction, the lower are annual maintenance costs.
- Annual taxes, levies, fees, and house insurance.

The following equation is used to calculate the approximate annual user cost of an acceptable owner-occupied dwelling:[2]

> *Annual user cost of owner-occupied dwelling = Construction cost of new house excluding land cost ÷ Expected service life of house*[3]
> *+ Annual cost for routine maintenance and repairs*[4]
> *+ Annual taxes, fees, levies, and house insurance*[5]

It is important to note that the above equation does not include the opportunity cost of money tied up in a house (that could earn income through investments elsewhere) or the capital gains from appreciation of housing prices that are often included in the user cost approach (ILO et al., 2004). This is a controversial aspect of the user cost approach (ILO et al., 2004) and is often excluded in practice (Australian Bureau of Statistics, 2010). There are several reasons why we do not include opportunity cost and capital appreciation of owner-occupied housing to estimate the user cost of owner-occupied housing. First, in locations with little or no rental market (the situation in many rural areas in developing countries), where there are 'limited opportunities for substitution between owner-occupation and renting, it might be argued that the consumption element [of home ownership] dominates' (ILO et al., 2004, p. 184). Second, the opportunity cost of money tied up in a house and capital gain in the value of a house are counterbalancing (ILO et al., 2004). Third, houses in rural areas in developing countries are often built with considerable free family labor and the value of this labor cannot be easily put into alternative investments. Fourth, including opportunity cost and capital appreciation in an estimate of user cost would mean that this estimate would be very sensitive to uncertain assumptions (especially in areas without well-functioning housing and capital markets) about interest rates and capital appreciation rates, and this is not a good attribute of an estimation method (ILO et al., 2004).

It is also important to note that the above equation does not include interest costs of a possible mortgage (i.e. total cost of the mortgage minus the principal which is paid back). For example, a $100,000 mortgage for 25 years at 6.7% would consist of around $200,000 in total payments, and so around $100,000 in interest payments. Ignoring mortgage payments makes sense in locations where most home owners do not take out a bank mortgage to buy or construct their home – which includes most rural areas in developing countries. On the other hand, taking mortgage interest payments into consideration would make sense in locations where there is a well-functioning home loan system and most people buy or build houses using a mortgage from a bank. To get an idea of how important mortgage interest payments might be, we looked at this for Mauritius as part of a living wage study because over 90% of households in Mauritius own their home (Statistics Mauritius, 2012 Household Budget Survey). We found that approximately 50% of a home loan consists of interest payments (State Bank of Mauritius home loan calculator, 2016). This increased the user cost of housing by around 40%. Of course, each situation is different, since the importance of mortgage interest payments is significantly affected by the interest rate and number of years of the mortgage, which were 6.69% and 25 years in this Mauritius example.

6.6.2 Construction cost of new house or housing unit

We have obtained information in living wage studies from different sources on the cost of constructing and maintaining low-cost acceptable housing.

1. National, provincial and municipal authorities and officials are often valuable sources, especially departments responsible for increasing the supply of affordable housing. They frequently build and/or financially support housing that meets minimum housing standards. This cost can provide a ball-park figure. We used such information for living wage studies in the Dominican Republic and India.
2. NGOs that build low-cost housing are often a valuable source. This includes prominently Habitat for Humanity that uses local materials to build houses that meet international housing standards. We used

information on building costs from a local Habitat for Humanity office for living wage studies for Malawi and Kenya.

3. Employers that provide housing for workers are often a good source of information on the cost of constructing and maintaining housing. Such information was used for living wage studies for the Dominican Republic, Malawi, and Sri Lanka. Note that even when housing being built is above a local living wage housing standard, this information can be useful to help provide an upper bound on building costs.
4. Architects and building companies are often able to provide useful information on construction costs. They often use a simple rule of thumb on construction cost per square meter for houses with amenities. We have used this type of information in a number of countries. When discussing housing costs with architects, it is important to remind them of the basic nature of a typical local housing standard for a living wage, because architects are often concerned with higher quality construction.

6.6.3 Service life of a house

The expected service life of a house varies across countries and locations depending on materials used, construction quality, climate, and degree of maintenance and repair. 'European countries have generally used service lives of between 50 and 90 years. In the absence of any reliable information, an average service life of 70 years can be used' (OECD and Statistics Norway, 2010, p. 9). Western Balkan countries typically use around 70 years (OECD and Statistics Norway, 2010), and Iceland uses 66.7 years (Diewert, 2010). Habitat for Humanity in Malawi thought that the service life of houses they build was only around 30 years because of the prevalence of termites, high rainfall, and poor construction quality especially for the foundation. Sri Lanka tea estates felt that 50 years was reasonable. We feel that in lieu of other information, an assumption of 50 years of service life is reasonable for basic housing in most developing countries (and up to 70 years of service life in locations where housing quality is similar to housing quality in Europe and the United States).

6.6.4 Maintenance and repair costs for owner-occupied housing

We suggest using 2% for annual cost of maintenance and repairs in lieu of information on this for a study location. Greater or less than 2% could be used when this is felt to be appropriate for a study location. Data for the United States indicates that around 2% is a reasonable assumption as American households spend annually around 1.7% of the value of their house (including land) for maintenance and repairs (Gyourko and Tracy, 2005), and so over 2% of the value of the building itself considering that around one-third of the value of a house is usually for land. Beals (2012) suggests that households in the United States should spend between 1% and 4% of the value of a house (and so around 1.5% to 6% of the value of the building) on maintenance and repairs.

6.6.5 Taxes, fees, and levies

In locations where owners are required to pay taxes, fees, or levies on their home, these should be included in the user cost of owner-occupied dwellings.

6.6.6 Utility costs

The monthly cost of utilities such as electricity, lighting, water, gas, etc. is part of housing costs and should be added to the user cost of owner-occupied housing just as it is for rented housing.

6.6.7 Example of determining user cost of acceptable owner-occupied house: Rural Malawi

We were not able to find many rental units for our living wage study of rural Malawi. This reflected the setting where only 4% of rural households rented their homes according to 2010/11 Malawi IHS3 (Republic of Malawi, 2012). For this reason, we followed the user cost approach to estimate local housing costs. We estimated the cost of building a basic acceptable house and used assumptions on service life and maintenance costs.

We obtained information on the cost of building a basic acceptable house from Habitat for Humanity as well as from tea estates that had recently built houses for workers. A local Habitat for Humanity office indicated that a basic house cost K713,000 to construct in 2010. We increased this by the inflation rate since then to get a cost for 2014 of around K1,200,000. Habitat for Humanity houses had four small rooms with a total of 30 square meters of floor space, zinc roof, cement floor, and burnt brick walls. Windows had wooden frames that did not exactly fit and a tree trunk with multiple curves for the cross beam. These houses were in keeping with Habitat for Humanity principles of building with local materials and ensuring a decent standard considered appropriate for local conditions. Houses being built by tea estates were bigger, more expensive, and better constructed. One tea estate reported K3,209,000 as the cost for a new two unit building (or K1,605,000 per unit). Another tea estate reported K2,300,000 as the cost of a new house. We decided to use the cost of the Habitat for Humanity house as the basis of our estimate of housing costs.

To estimate the user cost of a Habitat for Humanity house, we talked to a Habitat for Humanity engineer and two tea plantation engineers.

They indicated that the likely service life of a Habitat for Humanity house was around 30 years. This meant that the depreciation cost was K4,333 per month on a straight-line basis (1,200,000/30/12). Estimated monthly maintenance costs would be K1,846 using 1.5% annual maintenance cost, which was slightly below our recommended baseline assumption of 2% in recognition of the short service life assumption used (1,200,000 ×.015/12). Taken together, the estimated user cost was K4,718. Note that this was a very conservative estimate because it was for such a basic house.

NOTES

1. Many cities have definitions of slums. UN-Habitat (2003a) found that 21 of 30 cities that they looked at had an official definition of slums and 28 of 30 had an unofficial definition.
2. It is not possible to determine rental value directly from a house's value. Data from the United States illustrate how variable this relationship is. The ratio of annual rent to house value for a $100,000 house ranged from 0.058 for the Caribbean (Puerto Rico and the US Virgin Islands), to 0.064 for Hawaii and Pacific, 0.082 for Washington DC, and 0.120 for Alaska (Diewert, 2010). Furthermore, this ratio falls with house value, for example going from 0.10 for a $100,000 house to 0.033 for a $900,000 house in 2004–06 in the United States (Diewert, 2010).
3. This represents depreciation of the housing asset. The cost of the land is ignored, because 'land remains at constant quality for all time' (ILO et al., 2004, p. 184). Land is around one-third of the value of a house in the United States, higher than one-third in Western Europe, and lower than one-third in less densely populated areas of Europe (OECD and Statistics Norway, 2010).
4. 'Expenditures on maintenance and repair are expenditure on repairing parts of a dwelling that are broken or dilapidated; repairing the roof, replacing window frames, painting the outside of a building are examples. Maintenance and repair expenditures do not extend the service life of a building beyond their previously expected lifetimes and do not involve enlarging the dwelling' (OECD and Statistics Norway, 2010, p. 6).
5. The cost of house insurance should be included in locations where it is common, and ignored in locations – most developing countries – where it is not common for workers. The cost of insuring the contents of a house should be subtracted to determine the net house insurance cost. The net cost of home insurance is generally less than 1% of house value in high income countries (OECD and Statistics Norway, 2010).

7. Non-food and non-housing costs

PART I. BACKGROUND

7.1 Introduction and Use of Secondary Data with Primary Data Post Checks

This chapter describes how to estimate the cost of all essential needs for decency besides food and housing. In our methodology, a preliminary estimate of non-food and non-housing (NFNH) costs is made using recent household expenditure survey data by multiplying the NFNH to Food expenditure ratio in these data by the cost of the living wage model diet. This yields a preliminary estimate of NFNH costs. Subsequently, post checks of the preliminary estimate of NFNH costs are done using primary data collected in the study location to help ensure that a living wage estimate is more normatively based and there are sufficient funds for health care and education which are considered human rights around the world.[1] Our approach is a practical compromise between the impractical approach of identifying and estimating the cost of each and every NFNH need of workers and families, and the conceptually problematic approach of most other living wage and poverty line methodologies for developing countries that uncritically use the current spending of households indicated by a recent household expenditure survey to measure all non-food needs. The latter approach is especially problematic in poor countries where many households at present have little left over to spend on NFNH needs.

7.2 What are NFNH Costs?

Countries differ in how they measure and classify NFNH expenditure. It is important for researchers to examine the national classification of household expenditures, and to adjust secondary household expenditure data to make them consistent with how food, housing, and NFNH are measured in our living wage methodology. This also increases cross-national comparability of living wage estimates.

Most, but far from all, countries use the internationally accepted classification for household expenditures COICOP (Classification of Individual

Consumption According to Purpose) or a similar classification for household expenditures collected from household budget or expenditure surveys. First-level expenditure groups in COICOP are listed below with an indication in brackets as to which of our three expenditure groups they belong: food, housing, NFNH. See Appendix 7.1 for a more detailed listing of COICOP, and Appendix II in ILO et al. (2004) for a highly detailed listing and description.

- Food and non-alcoholic beverages (Food)
- Alcoholic beverages, tobacco and narcotics (alcohol in NFNH; tobacco and narcotics excluded)
- Clothing and footwear (NFNH)
- Housing, water, electricity, gas and other fuels (Housing)
- Furnishings, household equipment and routine household maintenance (NFNH)
- Health (NFNH with post check)
- Transport (NFNH with possible post check)
- Communication (NFNH)
- Recreation and culture (NFNH)
- Education (NFNH with post check)
- Restaurants and hotels (part in Food and part in NFNH)
- Miscellaneous goods and services (NFNH)

7.3 Variability in How Countries Measure and Classify Food, Housing, and NFNH in Household Expenditure Statistics

Although COICOP forms the basis for most national classifications of household expenditures, many countries do not use COICOP. Many countries use an earlier version of COICOP, and many other countries that use the latest COICOP structure make adjustments.[2] It is therefore important for researchers to look closely at how national household expenditures are measured and classified, and then adjust reported household expenditure data to be consistent with our living wage methodology. Some common differences between classifications used by countries and the latest COICOP particularly relevant for our living wage methodology include the following. These are discussed in greater detail in Part II of this chapter.

- Alcohol and tobacco are often included in the food group in national household expenditure classifications because this is where they were included in previous versions of COICOP.[3] The food expenditure share in such data needs to be reduced, because alcohol and tobacco are not included in a living wage model diet in our methodology. In our methodology alcohol is included in NFNH expenditures and tobacco is excluded from expenditures altogether.

- Food eaten away from home is often included in the food group in national classifications even though food eaten away from home is treated as a separate expenditure group in COICOP.[4] This happens more frequently in countries where eating out is common such as in South-East Asia, East Asia, the United States, and parts of Latin America and Europe. When eating away from home is included in the food expenditure group, the percentage for food found in national statistics needs to be reduced by the portion of the cost of meals away from home for services and profit (e.g. food preparation, cooking, serving, and cleaning), and NFNH increased accordingly.
- When food eaten away from home is included in its own separate expenditure group as in COICOP, percentage for food needs to be increased by that portion of the cost of meals away from home for the food in these meals, with NFNH decreased accordingly.
- Anomalies are common in how countries classify household expenditure. Some anomalies affect NFNH estimates in our methodology. For example, Vietnam includes cooking fuel in the food expenditure group. This inflates the size of the food expenditure group, and therefore requires an adjustment in our methodology. Kenya includes only medicines in the health care expenditure group. This means that how much Kenyan households actually spend on health care is understated in Kenyan expenditure statistics. Existence of such anomalies in national statistics is one reason why post checks are done for health care, education, and sometimes transport in our methodology.
- There is considerable variation in how national statistical offices treat owner-occupied housing. Many (e.g. close to half of European countries) ignore owner-occupied housing, giving it zero cost in their household expenditure statistics. India ignores the cost of owner-occupied housing in rural areas only. Although in our methodology there is no need to make adjustments when owner-occupied housing is ignored in national statistics because we estimate housing costs separately based on a local market survey, this variability has a major effect on the estimate of non-food costs in other common living wage and poverty line methodologies for developing countries that estimate non-food costs in one go. For example, non-food costs would be underestimated by other methodologies in Vietnam where the cost and user value of owner-occupied housing are ignored in household expenditure statistics as only 4.7% of rural household expenditure and 7.4% of urban household expenditure is reported

to be for housing (for utilities) according to household expenditure data (Table 7.4). In Shanghai, a very expensive city, only 8% of household spending is reported to be for housing excluding utilities according to household expenditure data.

PART II. ESTIMATING NFNH COSTS FOR A LIVING WAGE: CONCEPTUAL AND EMPIRICAL ISSUES

Part II discusses conceptual and empirical issues that affect how non-food and non-housing (NFNH) costs are estimated in our methodology.

7.4 Different Approach Used to Estimate NFNH Costs than Used to Estimate Food and Housing Costs

NFNH costs are estimated by multiplying the NFNH to Food ratio based on secondary data by the cost of the model diet and possibly adjusting this preliminary NFNH estimate by post checks based on primary and secondary data:

NFNH = (*NFNH/Food ratio from secondary data* × *living wage model diet cost*) + *possible post checks adjustments for health care and education and transport*

This approach is conceptually different from the way that food and housing costs are estimated in our methodology.

1. Food and housing cost are estimated based on normative standards (nutritious diet and healthy housing standard). NFNH costs are based to a large extent on household expenditure survey data that reflect current spending. This approach is used for practical reasons because it would be too time-consuming and difficult to agree on quantity and quality standards for the wide range of NFNH needs. Note that use of an 'other expenses' group is common to almost all poverty line and living wage methodologies,[5] and that the 'other' expense group (NFNH) in our methodology is much smaller than the 'other' expense group (non-food) in other methodologies used in developing countries.
2. Post checks to the preliminary estimate of NFNH costs are done for health care and education to make sure that a living wage includes sufficient funds for these to increase the normative basis for NFNH because health care and education are considered human rights around the world. A post check is recommended for transport in

locations where this is an important expense, and food, housing, health care and education expenditures taken together are less than around 60–70% of all spending. This helps ensure that the size of the non-normatively based NFNH is not too large.

7.5 NFNH Costs and NFNH to Food Ratio Increase with Household Income and Economic Development

The NFNH to Food ratio increases with household income and economic development. This is because the income elasticity[6] of food expenditure is well below 1.0 as predicted by Engel's law[7] (Anker, 2011a) and the income elasticity of housing expenditure is only slightly above 1.0 (around 1.2 according to Seale and Regmi, 2006).[8] This means both that the food share of household expenditure should decrease with household income and the NFNH to Food ratio should increase with household income. This also means that the NFNH to Food ratio should usually be higher in urban areas compared to rural areas within countries, because urban areas tend to have higher income.

7.5.1 Food share falls with economic development

Table 7.1 and Figure 7.1 indicate the relationship between food share of household expenditure and income per capita for 207 countries and territories. Food share falls on average from 48% in low income countries to 15% in high income countries with the non-food to food ratio increasing on average from 1.08 to 5.67 (Table 7.1). Figure 7.1 shows that this relationship is non-linear. It is clear that Engel's Law, formulated in 1857, is still relevant in the twenty-first century (Anker, 2011a). At the same

Table 7.1 Average percentage food and non-food to food ratio by development level

Development level[a]	Percentage food[b]	Non-food to food ratio
Low income	48	1.08
Lower middle income	37	1.70
Upper middle income	29	2.45
High income	15	5.67

Notes:
[a] Countries were equally divided into four groups based on income per capita in PPP.
[b] Values based on a regression with per capita income percentage urban, income inequality, whether country was transition economy country, and if country was island state.

Source: Anker (2011a).

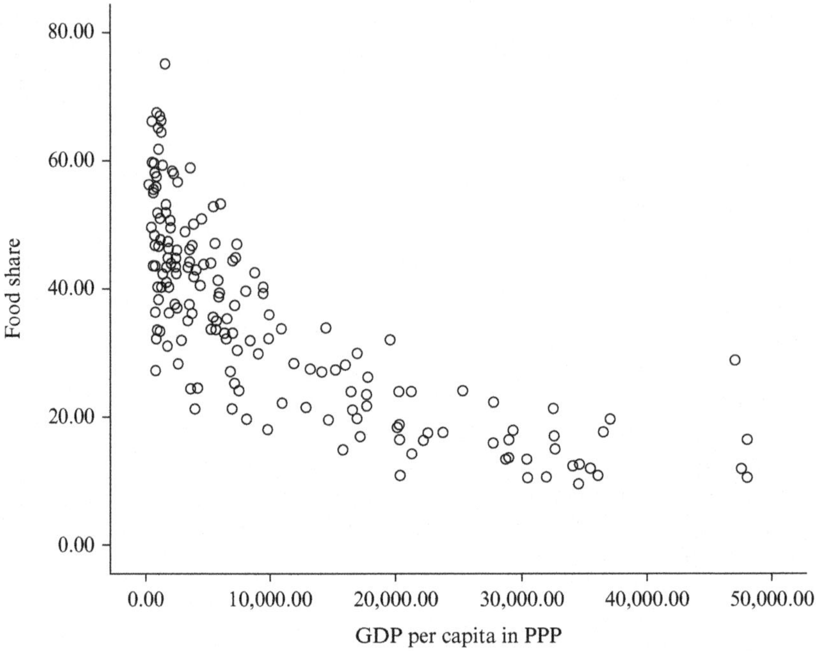

Source: Anker, 2011.

Figure 7.1 Food share of household expenditure as a function of income per capita in PPP (purchasing power parity), 207 countries or territories

time, since there are substantial differences in food shares for countries at similar per capita incomes, it is also clear that one needs to be cautious about using food share as the sole basis for estimating non-food costs as is done in other common methodologies for developing countries. Part of the reason for so much variability between food shares for countries with similar per capita incomes is measurement differences (e.g. data are sometimes only for urban areas; alcohol, tobacco, and eating away from home are sometimes included in the food expenditure group; cost or value of owner-occupied housing is ignored in some countries). Food share is also systematically different in certain types of countries (transition economy countries and island states have different food shares ceteris paribus) as well as significantly affected by household income inequality in a country (Anker, 2011a).

Figure 7.2 illustrates that the negative relationship between food share and per capita income found in the cross-national analysis in Figure 7.1

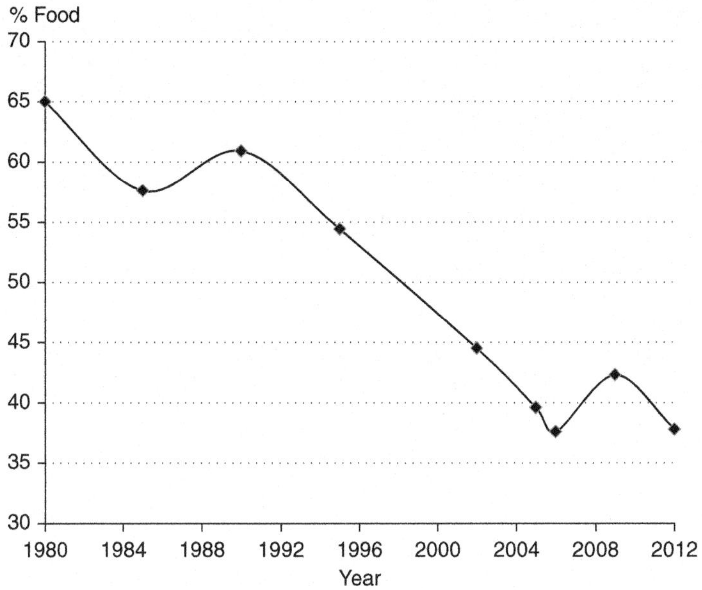

Notes: Real GDP per capita was 3.5 times higher in 2012 than in 1980.

Source: Government of Sri Lanka, 2015 (Table H1).

Figure 7.2 Falling food share of household expenditures in Sri Lanka, 1980–2012

is also found over time in countries such as Sri Lanka with increasing per capita income. Notice, however, that food share does not continuously fall every year probably due to short-term spikes in food prices in some years.

7.5.2 Food share falls and NFNH to food ratio increases with household income within countries

Table 7.2 provides information for five developing countries on how expenditure shares for food, housing, and NFNH and the NFNH to Food ratio differ with household income. The NFNH share and the NFNH to Food ratio both increase with income in all five countries and they are higher based on average (mean) expenditure (which is greatly influenced by spending of richer households) than for the median household. This means that:

- NFNH to Food ratio is affected by which part of the income distribution is used to measure it.

Table 7.2 *NFNH to Food ratio, food share, housing share, and NFNH share of household expenditures by household income decile, 5 developing countries where we adjusted data to be consistent with our methodology*

Expenditure group	Dominican Republic (national)				South Africa (primary urban)			
	30th %	40th %	Median household	Mean expenditure	30th %	40th %	Median household	Mean expenditure
% food adjusted	42.2	38.5	39.5	29.4	39.5	38.3	37.2	18.2
% housing	9.4	10.9	10.2	11.6	14.6	15.2	15.8	11.9
% NFNH adjusted	48.4	50.6	53.9	59.1	46.0	46.5	47.0	70.0
NFNH to Food ratio	1.15	1.31	1.50	2.01	1.16	1.21	1.26	3.85

Expenditure group	Vietnam (national)				Cambodia (Phnom Penh)			
	30th %	40th %	Median household	Mean expenditure	30th %	40th %	Median household	Mean expenditure
% food adjusted	49.5	48.3	47.1	44.3	53.3	50.0	47.3	46.8
% housing adjusted	8.2	8.1	8.0	8.4	25.9	28.0	29.3	29.5
% NFNH	42.4	43.6	45.0	47.1	20.8	22.0	23.4	23.7
NFNH to Food ratio	0.86	0.90	0.95	1.07	0.39	0.44	0.49	0.51

Expenditure group	India (urban Maharashtra)				India (rural Maharashtra)			
	30th %	40th %	Median household	Mean expenditure [d]	30th %	40th %	Median household	Mean expenditure
% food	40.6	38.9	36.1	32.1	55.7	54.2	53.3	50.5
% housing	26.6	27.1	28.4	28.9	11.6	12.6	12.4	12.1
% NFNH	32.9	34.1	35.5	39.0	32.7	33.2	34.3	37.4
NFNH to Food ratio	0.81	0.88	0.98	1.21	0.58	0.60	0.64	0.74

Notes: Reported food expenditure was adjusted, when necessary, to exclude cooking fuel, alcohol, tobacco, and part of food eaten away from home. Reported housing expenditure was adjusted to include cooking fuel when cooking fuel was included in food group. Reported NFNH expenditure was adjusted as necessary to include alcohol and part of food eaten away from home. Data are per household except for Cambodia, which is per person.

Sources: Cambodia National Institute of Statistics, 2009 for Cambodia (special tabulation); Oficina Nacional de Estadistica, 2007 for Dominican Republic (special tabulation); 2008 CPI expenditure weights for South Africa (Statistics South Africa, 2009); Vietnam Government (2012) for Vietnam; Government of Maharashtra (2011) for India.

- NFNH to Food ratio is lower in these five countries on average by around 7% for the 40th percentile household compared with the median household, and lower by around another 7% on average for the 30th percentile household compared with the 40th percentile household.
- Differences between the NFNH to Food ratios for the 30th to 50th percentile of the expenditure distribution are almost always smaller than the difference between the NFNH to Food ratio for the median household and average (mean) expenditure.
- Differences in the NFNH to Food ratio for households at the 30th to 50th percentile of the expenditure distribution are generally not very sensitive to the level of income inequality in a country.

7.6 NFNH Costs and NFNH to Food Ratios Differ in Rural and Urban Areas

Expenditure patterns are generally quite different in rural and urban areas. Expenditures for housing, transport, recreation and communications in particular are usually higher in urban areas compared with rural areas. In addition, urban areas usually have higher incomes, which affect spending patterns. This means that the NFNH to Food ratio is almost always higher in urban areas than in rural areas.

Table 7.3 provides data on food share of household expenditure for rural and urban areas for 11 developing countries (Anker, 2011a). Even though these data indicate food share and not NFNH share, they are still useful to illustrate how different rural and urban areas are in terms of spending patterns. Food share of household expenditure is higher in rural areas in all 11 developing countries in Table 7.3. The rural-urban difference for these countries is 20.6 percentage points on average. Food share is also lower in capital cities than in other urban areas.

Since the food share of household expenditure differs between metropolitan areas, other urban areas, and rural areas, the NFNH share of household expenditure should also differ by location within countries. Table 7.4 shows how the NFNH share of household expenditure varies for rural and urban areas of Kenya and Vietnam (see data for India in Table 7.2). The NFNH to Food ratio is higher in urban areas compared with rural areas in all three of these countries, 1.25 compared with 0.48 in Kenya, 1.21 compared with 0.74 in India, and 0.92 compared with 0.77 in Vietnam.

There are several important implications of the large rural-urban differences in household expenditure patterns illustrated above.

Table 7.3 Food share of household expenditure for urban and rural areas, 11 developing countries

Country	National	Urban	Rural	Rural-urban
Bangladesh	57.1	44.5	60.5	16.0
India	52.7	42.0	54.0	12.0
Kiribati	46.0	42.0	50.0	8.0
Nepal	57.5	37.6	61.2	23.6
Oman	29.9	23.5[a]	50.3	26.8
Pakistan	58.1	35.2	68.0	32.8
Samoa	50.8	40.7[a]	53.7	13.0
Solomon Islands	52.9	34.3[a]	62.3	28.0
Tuvalu	46.3	34.5[a]	61.9	27.4
Venezuela	32.2	28.8	57.4	28.6
Vietnam	42.9	34.9	45.8	10.9
Average	47.9	36.2	56.8	20.6[b]

Notes:
[a] Food share for capital city only.
[b] Difference somewhat overstated, because food share for four countries was for the capital city, which tends to have a lower food share compared to other urban areas.

Sources: Anker (2011) based on CPI expenditure weights.

Table 7.4 Percentage distribution of household expenditure shares for food, housing and NFNH for rural and urban areas, Kenya and Vietnam

Expenditure group[a]	Kenya		Vietnam	
	Rural	Urban	Rural	Urban
Food	59.9	35.3	51.2	43.0
Housing	11.4	20.3	4.7[b]	6.4[b]
Other	28.7	44.0	42.9	53.4
NFNH to Food ratio	0.48	1.25	0.77	0.92

Notes:
[a] Expenditures adjusted for our methodology.
[b] Reported housing expenditure unrealistically low in Vietnam, because cost or value of owner-occupied housing is excluded.

Sources: KNBS (2007), Vietnam Government (2012).

- NFNH to Food ratio is almost always lower in rural areas than in urban areas in a country.
- Size of the difference in the NFNH to Food ratio between rural and urban areas varies considerably across countries.
- Household expenditure data for the area (e.g. rural, urban, or metropolitan urban) of a living wage study should be used whenever possible. Data for rural areas should be used for rural living wage estimates, and data for urban areas should be used for urban estimates.
- When only national household expenditure data are available, researchers should make every effort to obtain rural or urban data through special tabulations.

7.7 Some NFNH Expenditures Unnecessary for Decent Living Standard

It is important for a living wage to be seen as reasonable by workers, employers, governments and laypersons. For this reason, expenditures for goods or services that many people would feel are unnecessary for a living wage are sometimes excluded when estimating NFNH costs. Excluding expenses that are not needed for a decent living standard helps make it clear that a living wage estimate is frugal and reasonable.[9]

At the same time, we feel that the number of items excluded should be limited so as to avoid appearing petty, overly moralistic, or culturally insensitive.[10] As American President Franklin D. Roosevelt (1944) said, 'Liberty requires opportunity to make a living – a living decent according to the standard of the time, a living that gives man not only enough to live by, but something to live for.' We recommend limiting unnecessary expenditures to tobacco, narcotics, 'excessive' alcohol consumption, and additional cost associated with owning and operating personal motor vehicles compared with exclusive use of passenger transport when passenger transport is considered acceptable for decency.

PART III. HOW TO ESTIMATE NFNH COSTS

The preliminary estimate of NFNH costs in our methodology is based in large part on household expenditures from a recent household expenditure survey. It is not based on normative standards. This means that there is a risk that insufficient funds could be included in NFNH for decency. This is especially likely in poor countries where many and sometimes a majority of people do not have decent health care, education, etc. To help correct for this possible problem, rapid assessment post checks are done for the two NFNH expenditures that are human rights (education and health care). NFNH costs are increased when indicated as being necessary based on rapid assessment post checks. Since there is considerable variability in how countries measure and classify household expenditures and this can significantly affect NFNH estimates, our methodology requires researchers to carefully inspect and adjust the available household expenditure data as needed so that they conform to how our living wage is estimated. This improves cross-country comparability and living wage estimates. It is worth noting that other common living wage and poverty line methodologies do not consider whether or not sufficient funds are included for non-food expenses, nor do they look at how available household expenditure data are measured or classified.

7.8 Four-step Approach to Estimate NFNH Costs

A four-step approach is used to estimate NFNH costs for a living wage. The first step requires researchers to select appropriate household expenditure data from a secondary source – for rural or urban areas and percentile of the expenditure distribution that is felt to best reflect the expenditure pattern for a living wage. Step 2 adjusts the household expenditure data to be consistent with our methodology. Expenses considered to be unnecessary for a living wage are excluded and household expenditure data are adjusted to be consistent with how food, housing, and NFNH costs are estimated in our living wage methodology. Step 3 makes a preliminary estimate of NFNH costs for a living wage based on steps 1 and 2 by multiplying the adjusted NFNH to Food expenditure ratio by the cost of the living wage model diet. In step 4, rapid post checks are carried out for health care and education (and possibly transport), and adjustments are made to the preliminary NFNH estimate when necessary to ensure that sufficient funds are available for these.

7.8.1 STEP 1: Select appropriate household expenditure data

Because expenditure patterns are so different in rural and urban areas (see Section 7.7 above), data for rural areas should be used when estimating a living wage for a rural area and urban data should be used when estimating a living wage for an urban area. Every effort should be made to obtain special tabulations when data needed for a location and/or income percentile are not published.

Before using recent household expenditure data to estimate NFNH costs for a living wage, it is necessary to decide which part of the income distribution would best represent typical spending of workers who would earn a living wage. The 40th percentile is generally recommended for most developing countries. The 40th percentile household is poorer than the median (50th percentile) household and has less than average (mean) expenditure. It would be reasonable to use expenditures for the 50th percentile for countries with very high poverty rates, and the 30th percentile for some middle-income developing countries. For further discussion on this, see Section 7.5 above.

7.8.1.1 What to do when household expenditure data are not available by income level In some countries, data on household expenditure by expenditure group are available only for average (mean) household expenditures. But the pattern of household expenditure is known to differ by income, with NFNH higher for mean household expenditure (which is greatly affected by the spending of richer households because every dollar or rupee is counted equally in the calculation of mean expenditure) compared with expenditure of the median household. Analysis in Appendix 7.2 indicates that it is difficult to have hard and fast rules on how to adjust the NFNH to Food ratio when only mean expenditure data are available because there is a good deal of variation in this difference across countries. Despite this variability, making an approximate adjustment to the mean NFNH to Food ratio would be better than making no adjustment. So we suggest reducing the mean NFNH to Food ratio when necessary because of lack of data, by the following percentages: 20% for median, 25% for the 40th percentile, and 30% for the 30th percentile.

7.8.2 STEP 2: Adjusting household expenditure data to conform to Anker methodology

Other methodologies typically use household expenditure data without scrutiny. Adjustments are almost always necessary in our methodology. These adjustments are discussed in the remainder of this section. Table 7.5 is a worksheet that can be used to adjust the classification of NFNH expenditures found in secondary data so that they can be used in our methodology. Details about adjustments are discussed in subsequent sections. Table 7.6 provides an example.

7.8.2.1 Adjusting NFNH for food eaten away from home Many people eat meals away from home all around the world. Yet, our living wage methodology assumes that all meals are prepared at home, since food costs are estimated using a model diet. This means that it is necessary to take into consideration that meals away from home reduce the need for home cooked meals before using household expenditure data to estimate the NFNH to Food cost ratio. For example, if 6% of household expenditure in a country was spent for meals away from home and 50% of the cost of meals away from home was for services (such as cooking meals, washing dishes, and

Table 7.5 Worksheet for calculating NFNH to Food ratio before post checks using secondary household expenditure data

Major expenditure group	Sub-major expenditure group	% expenditure in secondary data	Adjustment explanation	% after adjustment
Food				
	Food & nonalcoholic beverages		WHEN food away is included in restaurants and hotels add part of food away here	
	Alcohol (if included here)		Put alcohol into the alcohol & tobacco major group & use 0 here	0
	Tobacco (if included here)		Exclude tobacco. Use 0 here	0
	Meals away (if included here)		Put part of meals away into restaurants & subtract that part here.[a]	
	Cooking fuel (if included here)		Put into housing & use 0 here	0
Total food				
Housing			Add cooking fuel % here WHEN cooking fuel is included in food	
Alcohol & tobacco				
	Alcohol (if included here)		(WHEN alcohol was in food group) Add alcohol here. Reduce if excessive.	
	Tobacco (if included here)		Exclude	0
Restaurants and hotels			(WHEN food away included in food group) Add part here.[a]	

Table 7.5 (continued)

Major expenditure group	Sub-major expenditure group	% expenditure in secondary data	Adjustment explanation	% after adjustment
Restaurants and hotels			(WHEN food away included here) Put part into food group & subtract that part here.[a]	
Clothing and footwear			None	
Household contents and appliances			None	
Health			None	
Education			None	
Transport				
	Private vehicle purchases		Subtract part of this when workers expected to exclusively use public transport.[b]	
	Private vehicle operation			
	Passenger transport		None	
Communication			None	
Recreation & culture			None	
Miscellaneous goods & services			None	
Total NFNH				
NFNH/food ratio = total NFNH in last column/total food in last column				

Notes:

[a] Percentage of the cost of meals away from home for the food in these meals varies across countries, especially depending on whether meals are sold in fixed establishments or on street (base assumption is 50% of cost of meals away is for the food in these meals for most developing countries, 70% for Asian type street markets, and 30% for developed countries).

[b] Additional expenses for owning and operating a private vehicle compared with exclusive use of passenger transport varies by country, especially whether motorbike or car is the norm (base assumption is 50% for developing countries).

serving), other costs (e.g. cooking fuel, electricity, rent, dishes), and profit, then 3% (i.e. 50% × 6%) of household expenditure in this example would be for the food in these meals.

National statistical offices differ in how they classify food eaten away from home in their household expenditure statistics. While a majority of countries include food eaten away from home in its own expenditure group (called restaurants and hotels in COICOP), many countries include food eaten away from home within the food expenditure group. This means that how food eaten away from home is classified in national household expenditure data needs to be taken into consideration before the NFNH to Food ratio is estimated in our methodology.

When food eaten away from home is included in its own major expenditure group as in CIOCOP, reported food expenditure should be increased by the value of the food in meals away from home and expenditure for meals away from home should be reduced by the same value. Using the above example, 3% would be added to the reported percentage for food and 3% should be subtracted from the reported percentage for NFNH.

When food eaten away from home is included in the food expenditure group (which occurs in around 22% of countries according to Anker, 2011a), value of services and profit in meals away from home should be subtracted from the reported percentage for food and added to the reported percentage for NFNH. Using the above example, 3% should be subtracted from the reported percentage for food and 3% should be added to the reported percentage for NFNH.

We have conducted ad hoc inquiries in a number of countries to estimate the percentage of the cost of meals purchased away from home that is for the food in such meals. We bought meals from vendors frequented by workers and took these meals with us. We subsequently separated out all of the food items in these meals and weighed each food item. For example, a meal might consist of 10 grams of tomato, 20 grams of chicken, 100 grams of rice, and 20 grams of greens. We then estimated the cost of the meal if it had been prepared at home by multiplying the weight of each item in the meal by its price per gram in our local food market and added 5–10% for spices/condiments and fish or chicken stock depending on what was appropriate for a country. We have found that around 50% of the cost of meals eaten away from home was for the food in these meals in the Dominican Republic, Costa Rica, and South Africa. We found that around 70% of the cost of meals was for the food in street food meals in Vietnam, Cambodia, and China. We found that around 30% of the cost of meals away from home was for the food in these meals in the United States. Researchers should use a percentage for the cost of food in meals eaten away from home that is reasonable for their location.

7.8.2.2 Adjusting for other expenditures included in food expenditure group It is common for national statistical offices to include items besides food in the food expenditure group. When this happens, it is necessary to reduce the reported percentage spent for food and increase the percentage for the appropriate expenditure group. Alcohol and tobacco are often included in the food expenditures group in household expenditure data. Cooking fuel is sometimes included in food expenditure. None of these items are included in a living wage model diet. When alcohol, tobacco or narcotics are included in the food group, this should be subtracted from food expenditure and added to NFNH expenditure. When cooking fuel is included in the food expenditure group, it should be subtracted from food expenditure and added to housing expenditure.

7.8.2.3 Adjusting for when workers expected to exclusively use passenger transport Transportation consists of three expenditure groups in COICOP: (i) purchase of personal vehicles, (ii) operation of personal vehicles, and (iii) passenger transport. When it is acceptable/decent in a location for workers earning a living wage to exclusively use passenger transportation, we recommend reducing the percentage spent for transport by the additional costs associated with owning and operating a personal vehicle compared with exclusive use of public transport. We typically assume that motorbikes/motor scooters (that are common in developing countries) are twice as expensive to own and operate as passenger transport – and we think that this is a reasonable assumption for most developing countries.[11]

The size of an adjustment for transport will be small in locations where relatively few workers own a private vehicle. This turned out to be the case in rural South Africa where households at the 30th and 40th percentile of the income distribution spend only around 1.0% for private vehicles according to secondary data. The adjustment was fairly large for the rural Dominican Republic where households in the lower half of the income distribution spend around 6% for private vehicles because many people own motorbikes.

7.8.3 STEP 3: Preliminary estimate of NFNH costs

The preliminary estimate of NFNH costs for a living wage is equal to the cost of the living wage model diet multiplied by the adjusted NFNH to Food ratio for the appropriate location and the appropriate part of the income distribution.

7.8.4 STEP 4: Post checks for health care and education (and possibly transport)

The preliminary estimate of NFNH costs for a living wage from step 3 in our methodology is subject to post checks and possible adjustments to make sure that sufficient funds are available for health care and education, because they are considered human rights around the world. Post checks are also sometimes done for transport when this is a major expense. Post checks compare the amount implicitly included in the preliminary NFNH estimate for health care and education to rapid assessment estimates of typical costs for acceptable education and health care. NFNH is then increased when a rapid assessment indicates that there is a big difference. How to do rapid post checks is discussed in the next three chapters.

7.9 Example of How to Estimate NFNH Costs: Hypothetical Example

A hypothetical example is provided below to illustrate the steps involved in estimating NFNH costs. The hypothetical distribution of household expenditure data in this example is shown in Table 7.6. In addition, we assume that the poverty rate is 35%.

7.9.1 STEP 1: Decide which part of the income distribution is appropriate to use to estimate NFNH costs

Since the poverty rate is 35%, expenditure data for households at the 40th percentile of the expenditure distribution from a recent household expenditure survey was used to estimate NFNH costs. Such households in this example spent 6.0% of household expenditure for owning and operating private vehicles, 8.0% for passenger transport, 1.7% for alcohol, 1.0% for tobacco, and 4.8% for food eaten away from home.

7.9.2 STEP 2: Adjust household expenditure data as necessary

a. Exclude unnecessary expenses

We considered tobacco unnecessary and so excluded it. We did not exclude alcohol since 1.7% of household expenditures for alcohol was not felt to be excessive. Note that the percentage for alcohol was moved from the food group into NFNH.

b. Adjust food expenditure group and restaurant expenditure group for food eaten away from home

We added half of the expenditure of the 'restaurants expenditure group' to the 'food expenditure group' (2.4%), and subtracted this same percentage (2.4%) from the restaurant expenditure group. We used half based on ad hoc inquiries we have done in developing countries that indicate that it is typical that around half of the cost of meals

Table 7.6 NFNH to Food ratio based on secondary data from household expenditure survey before and after adjustments, hypothetical example

Major expenditure group	Sub-major expenditure group	% expenditure in secondary data	Adjustments	% after adjustment
Food	**Total**	**37.6**	Alcohol and tobacco subtracted & ½ of restaurants added	**37.3**
	Food & nonalcoholic beverages	34.9		34.9
	Alcohol	1.7	Put into alcohol & tobacco major group	0
	Tobacco	1.0	Excluded	0
	Meals away from home	0	Food part of meals away added	2.4
Housing	**Total**	**16.0**		**16.0**
NFNH	**Total**	**46.4**		**42.7**
Alcohol & tobacco		0		
	Alcohol	0	Added alcohol here	1.7
	Tobacco	0	Excluded	0
Restaurants and hotels		4.8	Subtracted 2.4 (½ of 4.8 and added it to food)	4.8-2.4=2.4
Clothing and footwear		4.7	None	4.7
Household contents and appliances		5.2	None	5.2
Health		5.5	None	5.5
Education		2.4	None	2.4
Transport		14.0		11.0
	Private vehicle purchases	3.0	Subtracted 3.0 (1/2 of 6.0 as assumed private vehicles were twice as expensive as passenger transport)	1.5
	Private vehicle operation	3.0		1.5

Table 7.6 (continued)

Major expenditure group	Sub-major expenditure group	% expenditure in secondary data	Adjustments	% after adjustment
	Passenger transport	8.0	None	8.0
Communication		3.8	None	3.8
Recreation & culture		2.2	None	2.2
Miscellaneous goods & services		3.8	None	3.8
NFNH/FOOD ratio		**1.23 (46.4/37.6)**		**1.14 (42.7/37.3)**

away from home is for the food in these meals and around half is for profit and services such as food preparation, cooking, cleaning and serving.

c. **Reduce transport expenditure by additional costs associated with owning and operating a private vehicle compared with exclusive use of passenger transport**
According to the household expenditure data, 6.0% of household expenditure was for owning and operating private vehicles, while 8.0% was for passenger transport. We concluded based on discussions with workers and key informants that it was acceptable for decency for workers earning a living wage to exclusively use passenger transportation. We assumed that owning and operating a private vehicle was twice as expensive as using passenger transport. Therefore, we subtracted 3.0% (half of the 6.0% of household expense for private vehicles) from transport. We were left with a total of 11.0% for transport (i.e. 8.0% + 1/2 of 6.0%).

7.9.3 STEP 3: Calculate adjusted NFNH to Food cost ratio

The adjusted NFNH to adjusted Food ratio was 1.14 (i.e. 42.7/37.3). Note that the unadjusted ratio was 1.23 (i.e. 46.4/37.6).

7.9.4 STEP 4: Calculate post check adjustments for health care and education

a. **Calculate preliminary NFNH estimate by multiplying NFNH to Food ratio from step 3 by the cost of the living wage model diet**

The cost of the living wage model diet in this example was 9,885 per month for a reference size family of four. Therefore, the preliminary estimate of NFNH costs was 11,269 per month (i.e. 9,885 × 1.14).

b, **Compare post check estimates of costs of decent health care and education for children to amounts included for these in preliminary NFNH estimate, and increase preliminary NFNH estimate if necessary**
In this example, approximately 1,452 was included in the preliminary NFNH estimate for health care (11,269 × 5.5/42.7). The rapid health care post check found that 1,510 was needed for health care. No adjustment was made for health care, because the rapid post check amount was similar to the preliminary estimate. For education, 633 was included in the preliminary NFNH estimate (11,269 × 2.4/42.7). The rapid post check found that 950 was needed for education of children in the reference family through secondary school. For this reason, NFNH was increased by 300 per month for education. The need for additional funds for education made sense because secondary enrollment rates were low in this example, which meant that household expenditure statistics did not adequately reflect the required cost of educating all children through secondary school.

NOTES

1. Under certain circumstances a post check is also done for transportation, when this is a large expense.
2. Countries are often slow to adopt latest COICOP. Also, many countries adjust COICOP to better measure welfare and behavior rather than inflation, which is the main *raison d'être* of COICOP.
3. Anker (2011a) found that 43% of 207 countries and territories included alcohol and tobacco in their food expenditure group in their CPI expenditure weights.
4. Anker (2011a) found that 22% of 207 countries and territories included food eaten away from home in the food expenditure group in their CPI expenditure weights.
5. For developing countries, a single large 'other' expenditure group (i.e. all non-food expenses) is typically used along with food expenses to estimate living wages and poverty lines based on Engel's Law (Anker, 2011a). High-income countries such as United States, Canada and United Kingdom, with considerable secondary data series, typically use around 5 or 6 expense groups including an 'other' group with typically around 20% of all expenses.
6. 'An elasticity measures sensitivity of one variable to another. Specifically, it is a number that tells us the percentage change that will occur in one variable in response to a 1 percent increase in another variable' (Pindyck and Rubinfield, 2012). For example if income rose by 10% and the income elasticity for food was 0.60, food expenditure would increase by 6%.
7. According to Engel's law, 'The poorer is a family, the greater is the proportion of the total outgo [family expenditures] which must be used for food' (Engel quoted in Zimmerman, 1932).
8. The income elasticity of food expenditure ranges from 0.24 for high income countries to 0.78 for low income countries according to Anker (2011a).

9. This is similar to excluding cakes, candy and soda from a living wage model diet.
10. It is possible to go too far in excluding items in our opinion. For example, the Canadian Government's Market Basket Measure (MBM), which is used as a poverty line for Canada excludes alcohol, tobacco, eating out, pets, hotels, gambling, and jewelry (Human Resources Development Canada, 2003). The MIT living wage calculator for the United States excludes these items plus toys, hobbies, movies and TV (Nadeau, 2014).
11. We found that owning and operating a private vehicle is around three times more expensive than passenger transport in urban South Africa because cars predominated among private vehicles in South Africa.
12. A detailed description of COICOP is in Annex 2 of the ILO Consumer Price Index Manual (ILO et al., 2004).

APPENDIX 7.1 COICOP (CLASSIFICATION OF INDIVIDUAL CONSUMPTION ACCORDING TO PURPOSE): INTERNATIONALLY ACCEPTED CLASSIFICATION FOR HOUSEHOLD EXPENDITURES[12]

- 01 – Food and non-alcoholic beverages
  - 01.1 – Food
  - 01.2 – Non-alcoholic beverages
- 02 – Alcoholic beverages, tobacco and narcotics
  - 02.1 – Alcoholic beverages
  - 02.2 – Tobacco
  - 02.3 – Narcotics
- 03 – Clothing and footwear
  - 03.1 – Clothing
  - 03.2 – Footwear
- 04 – Housing, water, electricity, gas and other fuels
  - 04.1 – Actual rentals for housing
  - 04.2 – Imputed rentals for housing
  - 04.3 – Maintenance and repair of the dwelling
  - 04.4 – Water supply and miscellaneous services relating to the dwelling
  - 04.5 – Electricity, gas and other fuels
- 05 – Furnishings, household equipment and routine household maintenance
  - 05.1 – Furniture and furnishings, carpets and other floor coverings
  - 05.2 – Household textiles
  - 05.3 – Household appliances
  - 05.4 – Glassware, tableware and household utensils
  - 05.5 – Tools and equipment for house and garden
  - 05.6 – Goods and services for routine household maintenance
- 06 – Health
  - 06.1 – Medical products, appliances and equipment
  - 06.2 – Outpatient services
  - 06.3 – Hospital services
- 07 – Transport
  - 07.1 – Purchase of vehicles
  - 07.2 – Operation of personal transport equipment
  - 07.3 – Transport services
- 08 – Communication

  - 08.1 – Postal services
  - 08.2 – Telephone and telefax equipment
  - 08.3 – Telephone and telefax services
- 09 – Recreation and culture
  - 09.1 – Audio-visual, photographic and information processing equipment
  - 09.2 – Other major durables for recreation and culture
  - 09.3 – Other recreational items and equipment, gardens and pets
  - 09.4 – Recreational and cultural services
  - 09.5 – Newspapers, books and stationery
  - 09.6 – Package holidays
- 10 – Education
  - 10.1 – Pre-primary and primary education
  - 10.2 – Secondary education
  - 10.3 – Post-secondary non-tertiary education
  - 10.4 – Tertiary education
  - 10.5 – Education not definable by level
- 11 – Restaurants and hotels
  - 11.1 – Catering services
  - 11.2 – Accommodation services
- 12 – Miscellaneous goods and services
  - 12.1 – Personal care
  - 12.2 – Prostitution
  - 12.3 – Personal effects not elsewhere classified
  - 12.4 – Social protection
  - 12.5 – Insurance
  - 12.6 – Financial services not elsewhere classified
  - 12.7 – Other services not elsewhere classified

APPENDIX 7.2 NEED TO ADJUST NFNH TO FOOD RATIO WHEN ONLY AVERAGE (MEAN) HOUSEHOLD EXPENDITURE DATA ARE AVAILABLE

As shown and discussed in Section 7.5, the NFNH to Food ratio is higher when it is based on average household expenditure data than when it is based on expenditures of the median household or households at the 30th or 40th percentile of the household expenditure distribution. This presents a problem when the only published household expenditure data are for average household expenditures, because in this situation the NFNH to Food ratio estimated would be too high. The first thing a researcher should do in this situation is to make every effort to get a special tabulation of household expenditures by income decile or quintile. We were able to do this, for example, for rural Dominican Republic and Phnom Penh, Cambodia.

This appendix addresses the issue of what to do when after serious efforts have been made, a researcher only has data on mean household expenditure, and whether it is possible to develop guidelines for this situation. To address this, we put together data on the NFNH to Food ratio for the median household and mean household expenditure for: (i) 15 developing countries and territories from an ILO household income and expenditure survey database, and (ii) 5 developing countries where we had done living wage studies and so were able to adjust the household expenditure data to be consistent with how we estimate the NFNH to Food ratio in our methodology.

The NFNH to Food ratio was 25% lower on average (median) for the 15 developing countries and territories in the ILO database when this ratio was based on median household expenditure compared with when it was based on mean household expenditure. It was always lower for median expenditure than for mean expenditure, but there was considerable variability across countries as differences ranged from 9% to 40%.

Table 7A.1 examines the same issue of how the NFNH to Food ratio changes with household income for five developing countries where we were able to adjust the expenditure data to be consistent with our methodology. The NFNH to Food ratio was always higher when based on mean household expenditure than when based on expenditure of median household (and the NFNH share of household expenditure uniformly increased with household income in all five countries). This ratio was around 17% lower on average (median) when based on the median household expenditure compared to when the ratio was based on the mean household expenditure. As with countries in the ILO database, there was

Table 7A.1 Percentage decrease in NFNH to Food ratio when based on mean household expenditure compared with when based on expenditure of households at 50th, 40th, and 30th percentile of household expenditure distribution using Anker methodology adjustments, five developing countries

Country	Mean to median	Mean to 40th %	Mean to 30th %	Median to 40th %	40th % to 30th %
Dominican Republic (national)	25	35	43	13	12
South Africa (primary urban)	67	69	70	4	4
Vietnam (national)	11	16	20	5	4
Cambodia (Phnom Penh)	4	14	24	10	11
India (urban Maharashtra)	19	27	33	10	8
India (rural Maharashtra)	14	19	22	6	3
Total (average)	23%	30%	35%	8%	7%
Total (median)	16%	23%	29%	8%	6%

Sources: Anker, R and Anker, M (2015, unpublished) for Vietnam, Cambodia and India. Anker and Anker (2014a) for Dominican Republic. Anker and Anker (2013) for South Africa.

considerable variation in this difference across countries as it ranged from 4% to 67%. At the same time, the decrease in the NFNH to Food ratio was much smaller and much less variable as you go from the median to the 40th percentile and from the 40th to the 30th percentile of the household expenditure distribution; the ratio is around 7% lower on average between these deciles.

Implications of the above analyses are:

- When only average (mean) household expenditure data are published, every effort should be made to obtain household expenditure data by income decile or quintile including through special tabulations.
- When it is not possible to obtain these data after serious efforts, it is still necessary to adjust the mean NFNH to Food ratio downward. Although there is considerable variation across countries in how much lower the NFNH to Food ratio is for households at the 30th to 50th percentiles of the household income distribution compared to this ratio when based on mean household expenditures, an adjustment of somewhere around 20% for median household, around 25% for the 40th percentile household, and around 30% for the 30th

percentile household seem reasonable percentages to use. While it needs to be kept in mind that these percentages are very much only typical differences that may not be appropriate for specific countries, some adjustment is needed.

8. Post checks of non-food non-housing costs: Introduction

8.1 Background

One hallmark of a living wage is that a worker and her/his family should be able to afford a decent standard of living and not have to live in poverty. For this reason, the preliminary estimate of non-food non-housing (NFNH) costs, which is based largely on spending patterns from secondary data, is checked to make sure that NFNH includes sufficient funds for health care and children's education because both of these are considered human rights around the world. A check for transportation expenditures is recommended when it is a major expense and the sum of percentages of household expenditures for food, housing, education, and health care is less than 60–70% according to secondary data and so NFNH expenditures (that are not based on normative standards) are greater than 30–40% of all household expenditures. Chapter 9 discusses health care post checks and Chapter 10 discusses education post checks. Appendix 8.1 provides a brief description of how to do a transportation post check.

We call these post checks, because they are done after a preliminary NFNH cost estimate has been made. These post checks use rapid assessment methods to collect primary data to estimate amounts needed for health care and education. When the amount from a post check is substantially more than the amount included for this in the preliminary NFNH estimate, NFNH is increased to make sure that there are sufficient funds for this. Adjustments are most likely to be necessary in countries and locations where school enrollment rates are low and public health care is poor and so locations where many people are too poor at present to exercise in practice their human rights as regards health care and education.

8.2 How Post Checks Are Done

STEP 1: Calculate the amounts implicitly included in the preliminary estimate of NFNH for health care and education.

The following equations are used to calculate the amounts for health care

Table 8.1 Calculation of implicit amounts for health care and education in preliminary NFNH estimate. Used for post check

Expenditure group	% of expenditures for health care & education from household expenditure survey (1)	% of all expenditure for NFNH after adjustments discussed in chapter 7 (2)	Proportion of NFNH for health care & education (1) ÷ (2) = (3)	Amount implicitly included in preliminary NFNH estimate for health care or education (4) = (3) × Preliminary NFNH estimate
Health care				
Education				

and children's education included in the preliminary estimate of NFNH costs. Table 8.1 provides a dummy table for making these calculations.

Implicit amount for health care in preliminary NFNH estimate = Preliminary NFNH estimate × (% of expenditure for health care expenditure/total % for NFNH expenditure from secondary data after adjustments discussed in chapter 7)

Implicit amount for education in preliminary NFNH estimate = Preliminary NFNH estimate × (% of expenditure for education/total % for NFNH expenditure from secondary data after adjustments discussed in chapter 7)

STEP 2: Rapid assessment estimate of cost for decent health care and children's education through secondary school.

8.2.1 Health care

Information on typical health care needs such as frequency of illness and use of different health care providers should be based on secondary data and discussions with key informants, while information on the costs of visits to health care practitioners and pharmacies for fees, tests, and medicines for common illnesses should be based on primary data collected in the location. Rough estimates of the cost of typical health care needs of workers and families are made based on this information (see Chapter 9).

8.2.2 Education

Information on costs of educating children through secondary school is obtained from discussions with workers and key informants. Based on this information, rough estimates of the cost of education are made (see Chapter 10).

STEP 3: Compare amount from rapid assessment to amount included in preliminary NFNH estimate and adjust NFNH when needed.

In step 3, results of the rapid assessments of typical health care costs for a reference size family and typical cost of children's education are compared with the amounts implicitly included for health care and education in the preliminary estimate of NFNH. When the amount implicitly included for health care or education in the preliminary NFNH is much less than the amount found in the post checks, adjustments are made to the preliminary estimate of NFNH. Note that adjustments to the preliminary NFNH estimate should be made only when reasonably large discrepancies are found because post checks are rapid assessments and so provide only approximate estimates of typical health care and education costs.

APPENDIX 8.1 POSSIBLE RAPID POST CHECK FOR TRANSPORTATION

As discussed earlier, a rapid post check for transportation is recommended when transportation is a major expense for families, and the preliminary estimate of NFNH expenses are above 40% of all expenses.

To estimate approximate transport costs for a worker and her/his family, it is necessary to understand the transportation needs of workers and their families in terms of where they typically travel, how often they travel, and how they typically get there. Before doing this, it is necessary to decide whether workers need to own a private vehicle such as a motorbike – or it is acceptable/decent for a worker's family to rely exclusively on passenger transport. This decision should be based on the availability and cost of passenger transport, the cost of owning and operating a motorbike, and the extent of private vehicle ownership in the location. Passenger transport is usually assumed to be acceptable/decent for a living wage in developing countries.

1. Steps in Transportation Post Check

STEP 1. Gather information from socio-economic household surveys on ownership of motorbikes and typical means of transport in the area. Gather information from household expenditure surveys on expenditures for private vehicle transport and passenger transport.

STEP 2. Gather information from workers and key informants on frequency, cost, and most common means of transport to various places. Gather information from workers and key informants on what they consider to be basic travel needs for workers and families. Table 8A.1 is an example of a table that can be used as a basis for discussions with workers and key informants.

STEP 3. Set a standard as regards basic but acceptable means of transport based on steps 1 and 2. In most locations, workers earning a living wage would be expected to walk or use passenger transportation. However, in countries like Vietnam where motorbike ownership is common (87% of urban households and 76% of rural households own a motorbike), workers would expect to use a private motorbike for transportation.

STEP 4. Set a standard for how much travel a worker and his/her family needs for decency to different locations (see step 2).

STEP 5. Gather information on cost of passenger transport (and cost of owning and operating a private vehicle when necessary).

STEP 6. Calculate average monthly cost of transport for a worker and family based on steps 1–5.

STEP 7. Compare estimated cost per month for transportation from step 6 with amount included for transportation in preliminary NFNH estimate and make adjustments to NFNH estimate when necessary.

2. Discussions with Workers and Key Informants

Discussions with workers and key informants are essential to determining local transport needs, expectations, and costs. They help in deciding on appropriate transportation needs and costs for workers and their families.

Discussions should identify places where workers and their families typically travel, distances from home to each location, frequency of travel to each location, type of transport typically used, and cost of round trip for passenger transport. Table 8A.1 provides a dummy table to help record this type of information.

3. Deciding on Appropriate Type of Transport

Secondary data on ownership of motor vehicles and percentage of household expenditures for owning and operating private vehicles and passenger transport along with information from key informants and workers should provide a good sense of whether relying exclusively on passenger transport is acceptable in the local area. It is also useful to observe the type of transport workers use to go home from work at the end of the workday as well as the number of motorbikes parked at workplaces. Unless there is a strong reason to assume that it is appropriate for workers and family to use private vehicles, use of passenger transport should be assumed.

4. Calculating Transport Cost When Workers and Family Members Rely on Passenger Transport

Cost of transport per month for a worker and his/her family using passenger transport can be calculated by summing up the cost of different types of travel (i.e. commute to work, visits to town, etc.) with the cost for each type of travel calculated by multiplying number of trips per month needed by cost per trip (Table 8A.2). The cost of round trip fares to various destinations should be determined independently.

5. How to Estimate Cost of Owning and Operating a Private Vehicle

When the standard for transport set in step 3 is owning a vehicle, the cost of owning and operating a second-hand low-cost vehicle needs to

Table 8A.1 Table for recording information on typical transport needs and typical passenger transport costs – based on focus group discussions with workers and other discussions with workers and key informants

Place (nearest or most common)	Distance one way (km)	Type of transport typically used[a]	Typical frequency of adult travel per month[b]	Typical frequency of child travel per month[b]	Cost per round trip per person for passenger transport	Comments
Work (e.g. plantation, EPZ)						
Town or city						
Open air food market						
Grocery store						
Supermarket						
Primary school						
Secondary school						
Health facility						
Hospital						
Family in another 'home' location						

Notes:

[a] Indicate if most people walk, or use passenger transport (and which type such as minibus, bus, or train), or use own vehicle (and if so which type such as bicycle, motorbike, or car).

[b] Convert frequency into number of times per month when required.

Table 8A.2 Table for tabulating cost of passenger transport

Reason for travel (1)	Form of transport (2)	Number of trips per month per adult[a] (3)	Number of trips per month per child[a] (4)	Cost per round trip (5)	Total cost per month. (6) = # adults × (3) × (5) + # children × (4) × (5)
Commute to work					
Shopping and other errands					
Visits to family living elsewhere for holidays					
Visits to nearby town for recreation					
Visits to health facility					
Other typical transport needs (specify:______)					
Total	X	X	X	X	

Note: [a] For frequency of travel, values should be prorated to number of times per month. For example, if there are three visits per year to family, this should be recorded as 0.25 visits per month.

be estimated. Information should be collected from local garages, vehicle salespersons, and drivers (see Table 8A.3). Life expectancies and maintenance costs should be estimated for a second-hand vehicle in good condition.

6. Possible Adjustment to NFNH

The cost of transport needed by a worker and his/her family for a basic but decent life style based on rapid assessment should be compared to the amount for transport included in the preliminary estimate of NFNH costs. When the amount from the transport post check is much larger than amount for transport included in the preliminary NFNH estimate, NFNH should be adjusted. No increase should be made unless the difference is reasonably large, since the post check estimate of transport costs was approximate being based on a rapid assessment.

Table 8A.3 Monthly cost of owning and operating a common low-cost private vehicle

Item	Cost per event	Frequency	Estimated cost per month	Comments
Purchase price		Once	Cost/life expectancy/12	Use common acceptable inexpensive second-hand vehicle. Second-hand vehicles have lower life expectancy and higher maintenance costs than new vehicles.
Registration fees & taxes on purchase		Once	Cost/life expectancy/12	
Helmet		Once	Cost/life expectancy/12	Use basic acceptable quality
Annual insurance		Annual	Cost/12	
Checkup		Every __km	Cost × distance pm/ # km per checkup	Often free in warranty period for new vehicle
Tires, front wheels		Every __km	Cost × distance pm / # km per tire	Frequency of tire changes depends on distance driven
Tires, front wheels		Every __km	Cost × distance pm / # km per tire	Front tire often different than rear tire in # km before replacement and cost
Oil change		Every __km	Cost × distance pm / # km per oil change	More frequent for used vehicle
Brakes		Every __km	Cost × distance pm / # km for brakes	More frequent for used vehicle
Chain		Every __km	Cost × distance pm / # km for chains	More frequent for used vehicle
Springs/shock absorbers		Every __km	Cost × distance pm / # km for spring	More frequent for used vehicle
Annual fees and taxes		Annual	Cost/12	
Other (specify)				
Petrol	___ per liter[a]	___km per liter	Price per liter × distance pm / km per liter	Major expense. Use least expensive acceptable octane. Obtain average price over last 6–12 months
Total	X	X		X

Note: [a] It is best to use an average price of petrol over the past year or over the past several months, because its price is volatile in nature.

9. Health care cost rapid assessment post check

PART I. BACKGROUND AND CONCEPTUAL FRAMEWORK

Health care is considered a human right throughout the world. Therefore, it is important that a living wage includes sufficient funds for workers and their families to be able to afford adequate health care. For this reason, researchers need to do a rapid assessment of the cost of adequate health care in the study location. The preliminary estimate of NFNH cost is increased when it is found in the rapid assessment that funds included for health care in the preliminary NFNH estimate are not sufficient. Note that since this is a rapid assessment, NFNH should be increased only when there is a large difference, because rapid assessments by their very nature are only approximations.

Even in countries where government health care is free, households have out-of-pocket medical expenses. For example in many developing countries, medicines are frequently out of stock in government facilities. This requires families to purchase medicines from a private pharmacy. Furthermore, in many countries, government facilities are of poor quality and have long lines and waiting times – which can cause workers to miss work and lose pay. Getting to a government health care facility may be difficult and expensive for workers and family members. For those reasons, workers and family members in virtually all countries often go to private health care providers.

This chapter describes how to do a rapid post check for health care costs to make sure that a living wage includes sufficient funds for health care. The post check is meant to be a quick check on the cost of adequate health care for workers and their families and for this reason rapid assessment methods are used to collect information on health care costs. These include interviews and discussions with workers and key informants, and rapid inquiries of costs of services of local health providers and costs of common medicines in local pharmacies. This information is combined with secondary data on frequency of visits to various types of health care providers to get an approximate cost of adequate health care.

PART II. APPROACH TO HEALTH CARE POST CHECK

9.1 Key Aspects of Health Care in Location

Health care post checks should be based on an understanding of the situation that workers face regarding health care. This includes knowledge of: (i) common health problems and illnesses in the country and location; (ii) the mix and relative importance of different types of health care providers typically used by workers and their families; (iii) quality of care especially in government facilities; and (iv) problems that workers and families have in using public and private health care such as time and distance to each of these. These factors usually differ significantly between rural and urban areas within countries. Sources of information on health, health care, health care costs, and health care systems include the Demographic Health Survey (DHS), multi-purpose household surveys, health facility surveys, health expenditure surveys, newspaper articles, and academic journal articles. Discussions with key informants are also useful including focus group discussions with workers. Every country is different and therefore it is important to lay out the context for readers and base the health care post check on the local situation.

9.2 How to Calculate Amount Included for Health Care in Preliminary NFNH Estimate

As indicated in Chapter 8, to estimate the amount included for health care in the preliminary estimate of NFNH costs, the percentage spent on health care relative to all NFNH expenditure is multiplied by the preliminary estimate of NFNH costs. For example, if health care expenditure was 5% of all NFNH expenditure according to secondary data and the preliminary estimate of NFNH was $100, then the amount included for health care in NFNH would be $5 (i.e. 5% × $100).

9.3 Rapid Estimate of Cost of Adequate Health Care for a Worker and Family

The rapid estimation of health care costs for a family is done in four steps. Each step is described in sections 9.3.1–9.3.4.

> **STEP 1.** Determine the number of visits to different health care providers typically required per year based on secondary data.
> **STEP 2.** Determine whether it is acceptable to expect workers to use government facilities exclusively, or whether some visits to

pharmacies and private health care facilities are needed. When some visits to pharmacies and private facilities are needed (as is almost always the case), determine how many visits per year should be allotted to pharmacies, to private medical facilities, and to public facilities.
STEP 3. Estimate amount of out-of-pocket expenses associated with a typical visit to a public facility and to a private facility and the cost for common medicines at pharmacies.
STEP 4. Calculate total cost for health care for the reference family size based on steps 1–3.

Note that rapid assessment estimates are very conservative in part because they are almost always based on typical costs of outpatient care, and so implicitly assume that in-patient care is free in government facilities.

9.3.1 Number of visits to health care providers per year

Information and statistics should be gathered on how frequently people visit health care providers and which type of health care providers they visit: public facility, private providers, pharmacist, etc. The Demographic and Health Survey is an excellent source for such information. Additional information can often be found from other sources such as academic journal articles and other surveys including health expenditure surveys. Based on these statistics, the number of visits to health care providers required per year by a worker and his/her family can be estimated.

In the absence of any information on frequency of illness, we suggest using 3.5 visits per person per year. This is equivalent to one visit every 3–4 months.[1]

9.3.2 Types of providers visited

It is almost always appropriate to include funds for some visits to private providers and pharmacies, even in countries with free government facilities, as they are not always easy to access, waiting lines are often long, quality of care is often poor, and medicines are frequently out of stock. For example, in Malawi, government facilities were theoretically free, but according to workers and other key informants, government services were poor and medicines were often not available. This assessment was supported by the 2010 Malawi Demographic and Health Survey (Government of Malawi NSO and ICF Macro, 2011). For this reason, we allowed funds in our living wage estimate for workers and their families to use private health services for many of their routine visits, but not for hospitalization. In Kenya, we came to a similar conclusion and included funds for health care in private facilities for half of the required visits.

Table 9.1 Table for estimating health care costs

Type of provider	Cost per visit for typical illness (1)	Number of visits per year per person (2)	Total cost per year for family (3) = (1) × (2) × reference family size
Public provider			
Consultation fee or co-pay			
Medicine co-pay			
Medicine cost when must be purchased			
Lab test cost or co-pay			
Private medical provider			
Consultation fee			
Medicine			
Laboratory test (indicate how often private laboratory tests are required)			
Pharmacy			
Medicine			
Total			

9.3.3 Cost per visit to each type of health care provider

Cost per visit should include out-of-pocket expenses such as for medicines, laboratory tests, and consultation. This cost needs to be estimated separately for public health care providers, private health care providers and pharmacists. Information on cost of a visit to a private provider and pharmacy can be found by talking to key informants, from focus group discussions with workers, and through rapid local market surveys (i.e. visiting local health care providers and pharmacists to find out typical charges for visits and medicines for common illnesses). Table 9.1 indicates the types of cost information to collect. It should be adapted to the local situation. Note that the cost for transport to and from a health care facility, although possibly substantial, is already included in transport costs.

9.3.4 Health care cost estimate for family

An approximate estimate of the total out-of-pocket cost per year for adequate health care for a family can be estimated by multiplying the average number of visits to health care providers per year for a worker and family by the typical cost per visit (based on steps 1–3 above).

Health care cost per year
= # visits per person per year to government facility
× reference family size × cost per visit
+ # visits per person per year to private health care provider
× reference family size × cost per visit
+ # visits per person per year to pharmacy × reference family size
× cost per visit

9.4 Possible Adjustment to Preliminary NFNH Estimate for Health Care Costs

The amount implicitly included for health care in the preliminary estimate of NFNH costs should be compared with the amount estimated to be needed for adequate health care in the rapid assessment. When the rapid assessment estimate of the cost of adequate health care for a worker and family is substantially greater than the amount included for health care in the preliminary NFNH estimate, NFNH should be increased. No adjustment should be made when the difference is relatively small or negative, because the rapid assessment of health care costs provides only an approximation of health care costs.

PART III. EXAMPLE: RURAL MALAWI HEALTH CARE POST CHECK[2]

9.5 Amount Included for Health Care in Preliminary NFNH

The preliminary estimate of NFNH costs for living wage for rural Malawi was K13,365 per month. Since household expenditure statistics indicated that 6% of rural NFNH expenditure was for health care, this meant that approximately K800 per family per month (i.e. 6% of K13,365), was included for health care in the preliminary estimate of NFNH.

9.6 Rapid Estimate of Health Care Costs for Reference Family in Rural Malawi

9.6.1 Number of episodes of illness per year

In Malawi, 18.4% of rural respondents reported being ill in the past two weeks according to the latest integrated household survey (IHS3). This implied approximately 4.8 episodes of illness per person per year (i.e.

.184 × 26 two-week periods), or 24 illness episodes per year for the reference size family which has 5 members.

9.6.2 Types of illness

Of persons who reported being ill in IHS3 (Republic of Malawi, 2012), 41.9% reported having fever and malaria, 11.0% diarrhea, 7.6% respiratory infection, 12.6% sore throat and flu, 6.6% headache, and 20.4% other. These data indicated that malaria, fever, and diarrhea were the most common illnesses.

9.6.3 Types of health care providers visited

Of those who reported being ill in IHS3, the vast majority sought treatment as only 6.9% did nothing, probably because the illness was not felt to be important. Of those who sought treatment, a government facility was used 54.4 % of the time, while a local pharmacy and private medical facility were each used around 25% of the time (despite the fact that government facilities were free). This implied that visits to private health care providers were common, and so including funds in a living wage for such visits was reasonable and necessary.

9.6.4 Use of private clinics and pharmacies

Given the serious problems in accessing public health care reported by the vast majority of respondents in the 2010 Demographic and Health Survey (Government of Malawi NSO and ICF Macro, 2011) and all of the people we spoke to in Malawi, it was clearly necessary for decency for families to be able to use private clinics and pharmacies some of the time.

9.6.5 Cost of typical health care visits and medicines

Visits to private clinics and pharmacies in the local area and information from key informants both indicated that the consultation fee for a visit to a private clinic cost K200–300 per visit, common medicine for a bout of malaria (most common illness) cost around K1,200, and common medicine for dysentery (another common illness) cost around K700. Laboratory tests were commonly used during antenatal care, and for malaria, TB and HIV. Lab tests typically cost around K4,000 per test and we assumed that a lab test was required every four visits.

9.6.6 Rapid estimate of cost of adequate health care for a worker and family

Our rapid assessment of health care costs for a reference size family is indicated in Table 9.2. Total cost added up to around K24,600 per year for a family of five, and so to around K2,000 per month. We assumed that

Table 9.2 Estimated health care costs example

Type of provider	Cost per visit for typical illness (1)	Number of visits per year per person (2)	Total cost per year for family (3) = (1) × (2) × reference family size
Public provider			
Consultation fee	No cost	2.4	0
Medicine when provided	No cost	1.2	0
Medicine when must be purchased privately	K950	1.2 (assume medicine available half the time)	K5,700
Lab test (every four visits)	No cost		
Private clinic/doctor			
Consultation fee	K250	1.2	K1,500
Medicine	K950	1.2	K5,700
Laboratory test (every four visits)	K4,000	0.3	K6,000
Pharmacy			
Medicine	K950	1.2	K5,700
Total			K24,600

serious illnesses and injuries were treated in government hospitals, and that 2.4 visits per person per year were to a private health care provider.

9.7 Comparing Health Care Costs Found in Post Check with Amount Included for Health Care in Preliminary Estimate of NFNH and Adjustment

In light of the above rapid assessment estimates of health care costs, we added K1,200 per month to our preliminary estimate of NFNH costs (i.e. approximately K2,000 needed minus approximately K800 included in preliminary NFNH estimate).

NOTES

1. According to OECD statistics (OECD/WHO, 2012), the average number of consultations per year with doctors in OECD countries is 6.4, which implies a visit approximately every two months (the range was from 3 to 14.6). According to CDC (Schappert and Rechsteiner, 2008), there are nearly four visits per person per year in the United States to physician offices and hospital outpatient and emergency departments, which implies a visit around every three months on average.
2. Although this example is based mainly on results of a living wage report for rural southern Malawi, assumptions and amounts have been changed for purposes of exposition.

10. Education cost rapid assessment post check

PART I. BACKGROUND AND CONCEPTUAL FRAMEWORK

Education is considered to be a human right in the world today. The right to education is part of the 1948 United Nations Declaration of Human Rights, the 1959 Declaration of the Rights of the Child, and the 1966 International Covenant on Economic, Social and Cultural Rights. Because of this, a post check is done to make sure that sufficient funds are included in non-food non-housing costs (NFNH), and therefore in the living wage, to enable workers to send their children to school.

This chapter describes how to do a rapid post check to make sure that a living wage includes sufficient funds for children's education. When the amount included in NFNH is substantially less than the cost of education for children according to a rapid assessment, the preliminary estimate of NFNH is increased. Note that since this is a rapid assessment, an increase should be made only when there is a large difference, because rapid assessments by their very nature are only approximate.

Education post check adjustments are generally particularly important in countries where school attendance is low. This is because household expenditure data from household surveys reflect actual expenditure rather than household needs. When many children do not go to school, household survey expenditure data would indicate low expenditures by households for education.

PART II. APPROACH TO EDUCATION COST POST CHECK

Part II describes how to do an education rapid assessment cost post check. Determining the amount implicitly included in NFNH for education is more complex than for health care, because most government statistical offices classify educational expenditures differently from the way that laypersons think of education costs. The cost of school books and supplies is generally included in the cultural expenditure group rather than in the education expenditure group; and cost of school uniforms is generally included in the clothing and footwear expenditure group.

10.1 Primary and Secondary Education for Children of Workers Assumed Necessary for Decency

For decency, we feel that a living wage should be sufficient to enable children of workers to attend primary and secondary school. Achieving primary education is an United Nations Millennium Development Goal. While attending secondary school is not a Millennium Development Goal, secondary school attendance is the norm in most countries. The net secondary school enrollment rate was 66% worldwide in 2013, ranging from 33.7% in Sub-Saharan Africa to 77.1% in East Asia and the Pacific developing countries (World Bank, 2016).

10.2 Usually Assume Children Attend Public School

It is almost always appropriate to assume that children attend state/public school and that attendance at private school is not required for basic decency (unless public school is not available). Data are generally available from household surveys and the World Bank World Development Indicators database on the percentage of school children who attend private school. At the same time, it is necessary to keep in mind that the line between public and private education is not as clear as the dichotomy implies, because many 'private schools' receive public funding, and many 'public schools' expect contributions from households.

10.3 Key Aspects of Education System

Key features of the education system in the country should be succinctly indicated in a living wage report. This is especially important for international readers. Number of standards and official ages for primary school and secondary school help set the stage for understanding the education system. This is usually common knowledge and is available on the UNESCO website.

Information on net primary school and net secondary school enrollment rates in the country[1] should be disaggregated when possible by gender, rural and urban areas, and income quintile, because there are often large differences (especially for secondary education) by location, gender and income. These differences tend to be greater, the farther away a country is from the target of universal education. Information on enrollment rates is very useful for understanding the extent to which current household expenditures for education in national statistics reflect needs. When the secondary school enrollment rate is low, the amount spent on education according to household surveys will be much lower than the amount needed to educate children through secondary school.

For primary education according to UNICEF (2015): 'more than half of countries and areas worldwide have achieved or nearly achieved universal primary education – that is, they have a net enrolment rate or net attendance rate of more than 95 per cent. In about 20 countries, however, net enrolment or attendance is less than 80 per cent. These countries are concentrated mainly in West and Central Africa and in South Asia, and many of them are affected by conflict.' For secondary education, the UNICEF (2015) website contains relevant information by gender, location, and income for most countries. Academic journal articles can also provide useful information.

In addition to reporting rural and urban school enrollment rates, it is useful but not required for a living wage report to discuss common problems with public schools such as high repeater rates and low continuation rates as well as other indicators of the quality of education such as class sizes, student-teacher ratios, availability of textbooks, and availability of basic services in schools such as electricity, potable water, and adequate sanitation. This type of information can be found on the World Bank, UNESCO and UNICEF websites as well as from journal articles and DHS reports. The UNESCO website has a special data set for Sub-Saharan Africa that includes indicators of educational quality.

10.4 How to Calculate Amount Included for Education in Preliminary Estimate of NFNH Costs

The amount implicitly included for education in the preliminary estimate of NFNH costs is determined using secondary household survey data. The percentage spent on education relative to all NFNH expenditure is multiplied by the preliminary estimate of NFNH costs. For example, if education expenditure is 5% of all NFNH expenditure according to household expenditure data and the preliminary estimate of NFNH costs is 100, then the preliminary estimate of funds included for education in the preliminary estimate of NFNH would be 50 (5% × 100).

10.5 How Education Expenditures Are Classified in Household Expenditure Statistics

10.5.1 Classification of Individual Consumption according to Purpose (COICOP)

Most countries use Classification of Individual Consumption according to Purpose (COICOP) to classify household expenditures. In this classification, education (expenditure group 10) only includes expenditures for educational services (such as school fees and teacher tutoring). 'It [COICOP] does not include expenditures on educational materials such as books (09.5.1) and stationary (09.5.4), or educational support services such as health care services (06), transportation services (07.3), catering services (11.1.2), and accommodation services (11.2.0)' (ILO et al., 2004, p. 479). Nor are school uniforms, jackets and bags considered to be education expenditure in COICOP as they are included in the clothing expenditure group. This means that a considerable part of what households spend for children's schooling does not appear as educational expenditures in CIOCOP and therefore expenditure statistics for most countries understate the amount that households actually spend on education because of how COICOP is structured.[2] Rural Dominican Republic and rural Malawi provide examples of this, as according to household expenditure survey data only 1.0% is spent on education in rural Dominican Republic and only 1.5% is spent on education in rural Malawi despite the considerable educational expenses for households in these countries as we found in living wage studies for these countries.

10.5.2 Other national classifications of household expenditures

Some countries deviate from COICOP and use a more comprehensive education expenditure group. This is done in order to better measure household well-being. When this happens, a more realistic percentage of household expenditures for education is found. In Kenya and Vietnam, for example, 5.9% of reported household expenditures are for education.[3] Detailed information for Vietnam on the percentage distribution of education expenditures is informative: textbooks (6.8%), uniforms (5.2%), study tools (5.7%), school fees (33.1%), school fund (8.2%), extra classes (11.1%), and other costs that include tutoring (28.4%). These data show that education services and fees (that are included in education in COICOP) comprise around 80% of education costs for households in Vietnam.

10.5.3 Implications of different household expenditure classifications for measuring education expenditures

The implication of the above discussion on classifications used for education expenditures is that reported percentages of household expenditures for education across countries differ partly because of the classification used for household expenditures. A classification can be fairly comprehensive and yield realistic estimates of education spending by households (e.g. Kenya and Vietnam), or a classification can be narrow and yield unrealistically low estimates of education expenditure (e.g. Malawi and the Dominican Republic, which follow COICOP). This means that care is required when deciding whether additional funds should be added for education to the preliminary estimate of NFNH costs.

In order for the comparison between education costs from a rapid education post check and the estimate of education funds included in the preliminary estimate of NFNH costs to be comparable, the types of educational expenditures included in a rapid post check should be as similar as possible to the types of educational expenditures included in the classification used to measure education expenditures in secondary household expenditure data.

10.6 Estimating Education Costs

Most governments theoretically provide free primary and secondary education. However, there are often significant education costs for households even when education is theoretically free. Households pay for different fees and services in different countries so that a list of education costs needs to be country-specific. Education costs often include some or all of the following expenses:

1. School fees each semester and one-time registration fees. School fees are often especially important for secondary school.
2. Uniforms and equipment. It is common for schools to require students to wear school uniforms and for students to need a school bag to carry books to and from school.
3. Learning materials such as textbooks, exercise books, and other stationary supplies including pens and pencils.
4. Supplementary tutoring. In some countries, school children (especially in secondary school) require supplementary tutoring in order to advance properly in their studies. This functions as a shadow system to help support teacher salaries (Bray, 2007). Supplementary tutoring is often required for students – even good students – to advance. We found these costs to be considerable in living wage studies for Kenya,

Vietnam, and Mauritius. Bray and Bunley (2005) found this for Cambodia.
5. Tests and examinations. Fees for examinations are common in many countries. We found such fees even in kindergarten in Kenya.
6. Transport. Costs for transport to and from school are common, especially for secondary school.
7. Other expenses. There are often various other expenses associated with public education such as PTA contributions, teacher motivation fees, personal gifts to teachers, and fees associated with school cleaning, heating, and maintenance.

The cost of public education for households varies enormously by country. According to an article published by UNESCO: 'In some settings all in-school costs are met by the government, and the out-of-school costs, uniforms, transport, etc. are so small that they are not thought by analysts to deserve much attention. . . . In other settings, household and community expenses are so large that they comprise over half the total, even in public systems of education. Cambodia is one country in this category.' (Bray, 1999). Other countries cited in the same publication where more than half of total primary public education expenditure was paid for by households included Myanmar, Togo, Uganda, and Vietnam.

Unfortunately, there are no international databases that indicate costs to households for public education. Nor is this well-researched, even though expenses associated with school attendance are especially high for poor parents in many countries. Therefore, to determine education cost to parents, it is necessary to draw up a list of typical education costs by level, and then find out how much workers typically pay for each type of expense from key informants, focus group discussions, and discussions with workers, and possibly from discussions or written questionnaires filled out by parents and/or school officials such as principals, teachers and administrators.

10.6.1 Gathering information on costs of children's education

Table 10.1 is a dummy table to record typical household education expenses for children in public schools and to calculate the annual cost of education per child and per reference size family. This table should be adapted to reflect the types of local school costs paid by households. Since this table records annual costs, expenses per month or per semester should be converted into annual costs.

The last column of Table 10.1 indicates whether or not an expense is classified under the education expenditure group in national household expenditure statistics. National statistical offices almost always publish a

Table 10.1 Table of typical annual household costs for school per student by level (list of expenses should be country-specific)

Type of expense	Pre-primary (when common)	Primary	Lower secondary	Upper secondary	Classified under education in national expenditure statistics? (Yes or No)
Registration fees					
School fees					
School funds such as building fund					
Fees for typical extra activities and materials (e.g. art supplies, physical education equipment)					
Supplemental tutoring (when customary)					
Teacher appreciation/ gifts					
School maintenance (e.g. cleaning, utilities, furniture)					
Examination fees					
Uniforms					
School bag					
Learning materials (e.g. books)					
School supplies (e.g. notebooks, pencils)					
Other expenses specify: ________					
Total of above expenses when Yes in last column (1)					

Table 10.1 (continued)

Type of expense	Pre-primary (when common)	Primary	Lower secondary	Upper secondary	Classified under education in national expenditure statistics? (Yes or No)
Number of years in each level (2)					
Total cost × number of years in each level (3) = (1) × (2)					∑ across rows
Average cost per child per year (4) = (3) ÷ 18					∑ across rows
Average cost for reference family per month (5) = (4) × number of children in reference family ÷ 12	X	X	X	X	

statistical glossary for their national classification of household expenditures. When summing up school cost in Table 10.1 only those costs that are classified as an educational expense in national statistics should be included, so that comparisons can be made to the educational expenses implicitly included in the preliminary NFNH estimate.

10.6.2 Possibility that pre-primary school and/or nursery school is common and required for decency

In some countries, it is customary for children to attend pre-primary school and/or nursery school. A judgment needs to be made as to how common it is for children to attend nursery/pre-primary school and so whether or not attendance at nursery/pre-primary school is necessary for decency. When attendance in pre-primary school is considered to be necessary for decency in a country, then the column for pre-primary education should be filled in Tables 10.1 and 10.2.

Table 10.2 provides a hypothetical example of how to calculate education cost for a family with two children using results from Table 10.1.

Table 10.2 Hypothetical example of how to calculate average education cost per month for a family with two children

Type of expense	Nursery/ pre-primary (when common)	Primary	Lower secondary	Upper secondary	Total
Total annual cost per student (1)	100	200	300	400	
Number of years in each level (2)	4	6	3	3	
Total annual cost per student × number of years in level (3) = (1) × (2)	4 × 100 = 400	6 × 200 = 1200	3 × 300 = 900	3 × 400 = 1200	400 + 1200 + 900 + 1200 = 3700
Average cost per year per child (4) = (3) ÷ 18					3700 ÷ 18 = 206
Average cost for reference family per month (5) = (4) × Number of children ÷ 12					206 × 2 ÷ 12 = 34

10.7 Comparing Cost of Education with the Amount Included for Education in Preliminary Estimate of NFNH Costs

Education costs from the rapid assessment should be compared with the amount included in NFNH costs for education. If costs from the rapid assessment are much greater than the amount included for education in the preliminary estimate of NFNH, then NFNH should be increased accordingly. To be practical and conservative, small differences should be ignored, in part because the post check is based on a rapid assessment that provides an approximate estimate of education costs and in part because a small adjustment could possibly be controversial and would be in any case inconsequential.

10.8 Summary of Steps in Education Cost Post Check

STEP 1. Gather background information on the education system in the country from local sources and secondary sources such as UNESCO, UNICEF, DHS, and academic journal articles.
STEP 2. List education expenses of families and indicate whether each education expense is included in the education expenditure group in the national classification of household expenditures. The national statistical office should have a glossary that indicates which expenditures are included in the education expenditure group in its classification of household expenditures.
STEP 3. Calculate amount implicitly included for education in the preliminary estimate of NFNH costs.
STEP 4. Gather information from workers and key informants about costs to families of sending children to school. The idea is to do a rapid assessment to approximate the cost of education to families. Since not all schools charge the same amount, information should be obtained from several sources. Exclude outliers when calculating average costs.
STEP 5. Calculate average education costs through secondary school for a reference size family based on information gathered in step 4.
STEP 6. Compare amount included for education in the preliminary NFNH estimate to the rapid assessment estimate of education costs for the reference size family, and increase the preliminary NFNH cost estimate when a large difference is found.

PART III. EXAMPLES OF EDUCATION RAPID ASSESSMENT POST CHECKS

10.9 Example of Education Post Check Loosely Based on Rural Malawi

10.9.1 Background information on Malawi education system

The educational system in Malawi has eight years of primary school (beginning at age 6) and four years of secondary school. Very few children attend private school. The net attendance rate for primary school was 84.6% with 89% of primary school students attending a government school. However, classes were generally extremely large. The student to teacher ratio in primary school was 83 and there was a high rate of teacher absenteeism.

Secondary school attendance rates were low. Only 8.8% of 14–17-year-olds attended secondary school (National Statistical Office (NSO) and ICF Macro, 2011).

Pre-primary school was not common. Although some children went to nursery school, working parents generally rely on extended family members to care for their pre-primary age children.

10.9.2 Cost of education to households in rural Malawi

Despite the fact that government primary schools are theoretically free, families are expected to contribute towards running school. Focus group discussions with workers indicated the following costs of school per month for primary and secondary schools (Table 10.3). Teachers at local schools felt that these costs provided a reasonably accurate account of educational costs to parents.

10.9.3 Comparing cost of education with amount included for education in preliminary estimate of NFNH costs

Based on the above cost figures, we estimated that school expenses for a family with three children (the reference size family for rural Malawi) for children through secondary school would be around K1,212 per month (for expenses classified under education expenditure group in Malawi household expenditure statistics). This was K404 more than the K808 per month included for education in the preliminary estimate of NFNH costs. Finding a large difference was expected, since average education expenditures of households in Malawi are low because so few children go to secondary school.

In light of the above, K400 per month was added to our preliminary estimate of NFNH costs to ensure that sufficient funds are available to workers to cover children's educational expenses through secondary school at government schools.

10.10 Example of Education Post Check Loosely Based on Lake Naivasha, Kenya Area

10.10.1 Background information on the Kenyan education system

Desire for education is very strong in Kenya. Parents very much want their children to go to school in order to help prepare them for a better life. This desire was clearly reflected in discussions we had with workers and others. This is also reflected by fact that 17.2% of government budget and 6.7%

Table 10.3 Typical annual household costs per public school student by school level for Malawi

Type of expense	Primary	Lower secondary	Upper secondary	Whether classified as education in national statistics (Yes or No)
School fees	Free	12,000	14,000	Yes
School funds such as building fund/general purpose fund	600	1,000	1,000	Yes
Uniforms	0	200	250	No
School bag	25	25	25	No
Learning materials (e.g. books)	1,350	2,000	2,500	Yes
School supplies (e.g. notebooks, pencils)	120	150	200	Yes
Examination fees		1,000	1,500	Yes
Other expenses specify:	None	0	0	N/A
Total costs classified under education in national statistics (Yes in last column)	2,070	16,150	19,200	
Number of years in each level	8	2	2	
Total costs × number of years	16,560	32,300	38,400	87,260
Average cost per child per year assuming parents responsible for children until age 18				4,848
Average cost per family per month for reference family with three children				4,848 × 3 ÷ 12 = 1,212

of GDP is spent on education in Kenya (World Bank, World Development Indicators, 2015a).

Kenya's educational system has eight years of primary school (beginning at age 6) and four years of secondary school. Primary school enrollment rates are high in Kenya. Almost all children attend primary school. Primary school net enrollment rate was 82% in 2009 and the primary school completion rate was 91% in 2006 (World Bank, World Development Indicators, 2016b). Secondary school net enrollment rate was lower but still reasonably high at 50% in 2009 (World Bank, World Development Indicators, 2016b).

In order to satisfy the grassroots demand for education, government abolished user fees for public primary school in 2003. While quickly increasing enrollment in primary school from 6,000,000 to approximately 7,200,000 just in the first year (Riddell, 2003), quality of education deteriorated. The average student to teacher ratio in primary school went from 32 in 1999 to 47 in 2010. In addition to large class sizes, UNICEF (2014) reported that school facilities often lacked desks and have inadequate latrines and insufficient water.

10.10.2 Cost of education in Kenya

Almost all students in Kenya go to a public school.[4] It is therefore reasonable to expect children of workers earning a living wage to attend public school and not private school. Many workers sent their children to nursery school. Therefore, we included two years of pre-primary school in our calculations.

During focus group discussions, workers expressed that school costs are of great concern. Workers mentioned having to pay sometimes or always for: school uniforms, sweaters, socks and shoes; exercise books and textbooks; exam fees; activity fees; teacher motivation fees; district education fee; one-time admission fee. Newspaper articles mention that parents are paying fees for secondary school, even though secondary school fees were formally abolished in 2009 (Howden, 2014).

Information on school costs indicated by workers in focus group discussions ranged from around KSh3,000 to KSh7,500 per year for primary school per year and from around KSh10,000 to KSh24,000 per year for secondary school. Although these were only a few approximate estimates, they were consistent with amounts mentioned in recent newspaper articles. They indicated costs of roughly KSh5,000 per year for pre-primary and primary school and around KSh14,500 per year for secondary school – around KS6,000 per child per year when averaged over 18 years of childhood.

10.10.3 Comparing costs for education with amount included for education in preliminary estimate of NFNH costs

Our preliminary estimate of NFNH costs included KSh1,466 per month for education. This was similar enough to the rapid assessment estimate of education costs of KSh1,509 that we did not make any adjustment.

Table 10.4 Typical annual household costs per student for public school by level for Lake Naivasha area of Kenya

Type of expense	Pre-primary	Primary	Secondary	Classified as education in national statistics?
District education fee		1,000		Yes
One-time admission fee (prorated to cost per year)		100		
School fees	4,000	0	8,000	Yes
School funds		500		Yes
Uniforms	750	750	750	Yes
School bag		100	100	Yes
Books		700	1,500	Yes
Exercise books		800	2,000	Yes
Fees for compulsory extra activities		100	400	Yes
Teacher motivation		500	500	Yes
Examination fees	600	450	1,250	Yes
Total costs classified under education in national statistics (Yes in last column)	5,350	5,000	14,500	
Number of years in each level	2	8	4	
Total cost x years	10,700	40,000	58,000	108,700
Average cost per child per year assuming parents responsible for children for 18 years				108,700 ÷ 18 = 6,039
Average cost per month for reference family with 3 children				6,039 × 3 ÷ 12 = 1,509

NOTES

1. According to the World Bank (2016), the net primary school enrollment ratio is the 'ratio of children of the official primary school age who are enrolled in primary school to the total population of the official primary school age.' Net secondary enrollment ratio is the 'ratio of children of the official secondary school age who are enrolled in secondary school to the population of the official secondary school age.' The gross enrollment rate is the 'ratio of all children attending primary school to the number of children of primary school age.' In places where many students repeat grades, the gross enrollment rate can be misleading, and therefore the net enrollment rate is preferred.
2. The reason why education expenditures are classified as they are in COICOP is that COICOP is mainly concerned with measuring inflation, and it is felt that inflation for school uniforms is likely to be similar to inflation for other types of clothing, inflation for school transport is likely to be similar to inflation for other types of transport, and so on.
3. In addition to tuition fees, Kenya includes the following in education expenditures: 'books & other materials, uniform, boarding fees, transport, contribution for school building or maintenance, extra tuition fees, examination fees, PTA & other related fees, pocket money & shopping, other expenses' (KNBS, 2007, p. 38). Vietnam includes uniforms, textbooks, study tools, school fund, extra classes, and tutoring (Vietnam Government, 2012).
4. Only 10.6% of primary school students attend a private school and only 12.7% of secondary school children attend a private school according to World Bank's World Development Indicators.

11. Provision for unexpected events and sustainability

PART I. BACKGROUND AND CONCEPTUAL FRAMEWORK

Unforeseen events and expenses can quickly throw workers living at a basic life style into poverty and debt from which it is often difficult to recover. Possibilities of such events are numerous, such as accidents, illnesses, and death/funerals. For this reason, it is common when estimating a living wage to add a small margin above the cost of the basic quality life allowed for by a living wage (Anker, 2011). This added margin helps workers to ride out costly unforeseen events. Without a margin, a living wage is not sustainable. It must not be forgotten that the living standard afforded on a living wage is basic and without frills and without a built-in cushion. It also must not be forgotten that 'Savings is not only about accumulation. It is about smoothing consumption in the face of volatile and unpredictable income, and helping to ensure the living standards of poor people whose lives are difficult and uncertain' (Deaton, 1989, p. 61).

PART II. APPROACH TO DETERMINE AMOUNT FOR SUSTAINABILITY

It is common for definitions and descriptions of living wage in corporate codes of conduct of multinational companies and NGOs to mention the need for some funds for 'savings' or 'discretionary income' or 'emergencies' (e.g. Adidas, Debenhams, John Lewis, Gap, Sainsbury, and Social Accountability International, see Anker (2011)). A 'provision for unexpected events' is included the definition of living wage agreed upon by the Global Living Wage Coalition (see Chapter 1).

There is no generally agreed margin for unexpected events to use for a living wage to help ensure sustainability. The Anker (2011) review of living wage methodologies provides some information on this. Social Accountability International as well as ourselves in earlier work used 10%. Ad hoc living wage estimates for factories in Asia with mostly young single women workers used 15% and 25% (Anker, 2011). London's living wage includes 15% 'to protect against unforeseen events' (GLA Economics, 2015). The first minimum wage law for Massachusetts in 1914 included a 2.6% 'reserve for emergencies.'

To be conservative, we recommend including 5% above the cost of the basic living style afforded by a living wage to allow for unforeseen events to help ensure sustainability. This percentage is a judgment call given the lack of consensus. We feel that 5% is consistent with the fact that our methodology uses decency standards and is fairly comprehensive in the goods and services covered. At the same time, 5% is conservative enough that it should not lead to criticism of living wage estimates as being unreasonably high.

To calculate an amount for the provision for unexpected events and sustainability, food cost, housing cost, and all other cost should be summed to get total living cost. This total living cost should then be multiplied by the 5% margin to get the amount for unexpected events and sustainability. This should be added to the living cost.

12. Family size for a living wage

PART I. BACKGROUND

There is a broad consensus that 'living wage is a family concept. A worker should be able to support a family on a living wage' (Anker, 2011, p. 49). This consensus is incorporated in typical living wage definitions such as the Global Living Wage Coalition (GLWC) definition indicated in Chapter 1. The larger the reference family size, the higher the living wage estimate.

This chapter discusses how to determine an appropriate family size to use to estimate a living wage for a particular country and location – called the reference family size. Determining an appropriate reference family size for a living wage is not a simple arithmetic calculation. It requires judgment and should be based on different types of information, since each type has advantages and disadvantages/biases.

Section 12.1 discusses the type of family that a living wage should be able to support, and Section 12.2 discusses how to determine an appropriate reference size family for a living wage. Section 12.3 discusses why it is sometimes a good idea to add additional funds so that workers are able to help parents and relatives since many workers in developing countries have a social/cultural obligation to provide such support. Sections 12.4–12.6 provide examples.

PART II. CONCEPTUAL FRAMEWORK

12.1 Definition of Family

While a living wage needs to support a worker and his or her family, there are different definitions of family. We use the immediate family of a worker consisting of a worker, spouse or partner, and children – and do not include a worker's parents or extended family members – although in countries and societies where cultural norms as regards financial assistance to parents and/or extended family members are very strong, including some funds for this is warranted (see Section 12.3).

12.1.1 Difference between family and household

Household and family are related but different concepts. In addition, the definition of household varies from survey to survey (e.g. sleep under same roof, or eat from a common pot, or share livelihoods, or some combination of these). This means that 'household' and 'family' are not interchangeable even though they are often used in this way.[1]

> The terms household and family are not always used consistently in the literature. A household is usually defined as a group of persons (or one person) who make common provision for food, shelter, and other essentials for living, but practices [on how household is measured] vary significantly among countries. As a consequence, measures of household size and composition obtained from censuses or other sources in different countries are sometimes not directly comparable. The term family is used even less consistently. In the social science literature and in common usage 'family' refers to a group of kin – persons related by blood, marriage or adoption. (Bongaarts, 2001)

Therefore, average household size observed in a particular household survey does not necessarily provide a good measure of an appropriate reference family size for a living wage. For example, when a spouse migrates to a city for work, this reduces observed average household size in both rural and urban areas. It typically creates a new one-person household in the city and reduces average household size in rural areas – even though there is no change in the size of the family economic unit.

12.1.2 For decency, workers should be able to afford to live with their family in the location where they work

A common phenomenon in developing countries is for migrant workers to live without their families in cities or on/near farms mainly because they cannot afford to have their family live with them at a minimal level of decency on their current wages. We believe that for decency, a living wage should be sufficient for a worker to be able to afford to have their spouse/partner and children live with them in the locality where they work. Long periods of living apart create many health, safety, and psychological problems. Male workers living alone are especially prone to injuries and illnesses, including sexually transmitted diseases. Women workers living alone are especially vulnerable to violence and sexual assault. All workers living alone have added stress from separation from family. Children of migrant workers who are left behind are deprived of being brought up by parents.

For these reasons, our methodology assumes that a living wage needs to be high enough for workers to be able to afford to live with their family in the area where they work. It is not that workers must live with their family or that it is unacceptable when workers choose to live separately – it is rather that the decency concept of a living wage implies, in our opinion, that workers should have the financial means to be able to afford to have their family live with them. We do not believe that many people in the world would consider it decent for workers to have no choice but to live separately from their spouse and children because wages are too low to allow for them to live together.

Yet in many countries, it is common for workers to have no alternative but to live separately from their family for long periods of time because of low wages. This is especially common for workers who move to work in a city or on a plantation. Many migrant workers live without their family in slums. It is also common for migrant workers to live with unrelated workers in small dorm rooms.

The requirement that workers be able to afford to live with their immediate family if they so choose means that a living wage needs to be based on living standards and living costs in the location where workers are employed. It also means that it is not appropriate to estimate a separate living wage for migrants. This includes international migrants such as Haitians in Dominican Republic, or Mexicans in the United States. If a living wage was estimated based on living costs for families of international migrants in their country of origin, as has often been suggested to us, the living wage would be too low for a decent standard of living for nationals in their own country. More generally, having lower wages for migrant workers compared with non-migrant workers would likely lead to employers discriminating against the local population.

PART III. APPROACH TO DETERMINING APPROPRIATE FAMILY SIZE FOR ESTIMATING A LIVING WAGE

12.2 How to Determine Appropriate Family Size for Estimating Living Wage

Three approaches have been used to determine family size for estimating a living wage: (i) number of children born per women, (ii) average household size, and (iii) a typical family size – often four (Anker, 2011). While all three approaches provide valuable information, each approach can be misleading regarding the appropriate reference family size for estimating a living wage. It is therefore important to look at several measures of family size and use judgment to decide on the reference family size for estimating a living wage. Appendix 12.1 provides a table to record and organize relevant secondary data.

12.2.1 Family size of four persons a common assumption

Past living wage studies have often used four persons as the reference family size.[2] There are several advantages to this assumption. First, family size of four is:

> a relatively easy and uncontroversial assumption to use . . . This assumption is widely used; it roughly represents population replacement; and it is reasonably consistent with fertility rates found in many developing countries. Use of a household size below four would imply that a living wage would not be sufficient to ensure survival of countries over the long run [without international migration], and this seems contrary to the idea of a living wage. (Anker, 2011, p. 45)

Our view is that four persons should generally be the minimum reference family size for estimating a living wage, although it is worth noting that researchers carrying out six living wage studies in China using our methodology felt that 3.5 persons was appropriate in light of China's one-child policy for many years, albeit with important exceptions.

A reference family size of four is, however, too small for many countries and locations where women have significantly more than two children. This is especially common in Sub-Saharan Africa where around 70% of countries have a total fertility rate of at least four. Furthermore, fertility rates are generally higher in rural than in urban areas (e.g. total fertility rate is 5.9 in rural Kenya compared with 4.6 in urban Kenya, see example below). All of this means that a living wage reference family size of four is too small for most of Sub-Saharan Africa and the Middle East and some other parts of the world such as Pakistan, and for many rural areas in developing countries.

12.2.2 Average household size

Average household size is a useful statistic for determining a living wage reference family size, but it needs to be adjusted before it is used for this purpose. It might seem common sense to use average household size to estimate a living wage, as average household size would seem to represent typical family responsibilities. Indeed, it is common for other methodologies to use average household size to estimate living wages (Anker, 2011)[3] and poverty lines in developing countries (Tabatabai, 1996).

There are, however, several problems with using average household size from surveys and censuses as the living wage reference family size. First, household and family are different concepts as explained above. Second, average household size observed in surveys and censuses, is affected by the definition of household used. Third, average urban household size is significantly reduced by migration whereas average family size for a living wage should not be affected by this. Fourth, average household size is reduced by the proportion of households without children (such as single-person households) even though such households are not relevant for estimating a living wage which is a family concept. Fifth, average household size is affected by the frequency of extended family households which include two or more nuclear families and so possibly more than two adult workers, despite the fact that our methodology is concerned with nuclear families with at most two workers.

The first two points above imply that average household size from a specific survey or census is not always a reliable measure of average family size – and so that several data sources should be used. The third, fourth, and fifth points above imply that average household size from surveys might provide an underestimate or overestimate of an appropriate living wage reference family size and so need to be adjusted.

12.2.2.1 Exclude single-person households when measuring average household size Before using data on household size, single-person households (which definitely do not include children) should be excluded, since they are not relevant for estimating a living wage which is a family concept. This can be important for urban areas in developing countries where many people move without their family in search of employment; this can also be important in higher income countries where many young adults support themselves.

12.2.2.2 Exclude especially large households when measuring average household size Before using data on household size, very large households (that almost always include multiple nuclear families) should be excluded, since living wage in our methodology is concerned with the wage required by a nuclear family with at most two full-time earners. This can be an important adjustment for countries where extended families are common. Pakistan provides a good example of this. Average urban household size is 6.6 but 5.7 when single person households and very large households are excluded. A reasonable way of identifying households that are likely to include more than one nuclear family is to exclude households with more than the sum of the total fertility rate plus 5, thereby allowing for three additional children to represent households with unusually high fertility plus two parents. For example, if the total fertility rate was 2, households with eight or more members would be excluded when calculating average household size. If the total fertility rate was 3, households with nine or more members would be excluded.

12.2.3 Number of children born and surviving per woman

12.2.3.1 Number of children born per woman (total fertility rate) Total fertility rate (TFR) indicates the number of children women typically have over their lifetime.[4] This is an important determinant of typical family size, since this can be thought to equal the total fertility rate plus two adults. For example, typical family size could be considered to be four when total fertility rate is 2 (i.e. two children and two adults), although in countries and locations with very high fertility rates or high mortality rates, the total fertility rate overestimates the number of children in a family at any point in time.

12.2.3.2 Taking child mortality into consideration A sizable number of children die in some countries. For example in rural Malawi where infant mortality rate is 7.3%, mortality rate for ages 1–4 is 6.1% (National Statistical Office and ICF Macro, 2011), and total fertility rate is 5.5 (World Bank, 2016), approximately 0.75 births die by age 5 for a typical woman. This means that the total fertility rate overstates the number of children needing to be supported in countries with high child mortality. For this reason, the total fertility rate needs to be adjusted for child mortality to estimate the typical number of surviving children per woman. In countries with low child mortality rates, the total fertility rate does not overstate the number of children surviving by much. For example, only around 0.02 births would die by age 5 on average in Mauritius, which has a total fertility rate of 1.76 births and a child mortality rate of 1.4%.

The following equation can be used to calculate the average number of surviving children per woman:

> *Average number of surviving children* = *TFR* x (1 − *child mortality rate per* 100 *births*)

12.2.3.3 Number of children less than age 18 per woman changes over time especially in high fertility countries The number of children that couples are responsible for starts at zero, increases as children are born, and decreases with child mortality and when children reach majority and move away to start their own life. This means that the number of children less than age 18 in a family is often lower than the number of children that are born and survive. This difference is especially large in countries with high fertility where children are necessarily born over a longer period of time.

To get an idea of how many children under age 18 that women have at different points in time in high fertility countries, we estimated this for non-metropolitan urban areas of Kenya using the following reasonable assumptions: (i) child-rearing period is 30 years; (ii) total fertility rate is 4; (iii) child mortality rate is 7.3%; and (iv) average birth interval is three years. We found in this example that even though the total fertility rate is four, women have on average:

- Between 3 and 4 children under age 18 (3.7 on average) for 9 years (30% of the time)
- Between 2 and 3 children under age 18 (2.8 children on average) for 6 years (20% of the time), and
- Less than 2 children under age 18 for 15 years (50% of the time)

This exercise shows that despite a total fertility rate of 4, women have between three and four children who are less than age 18 only around 30% of the time and approximately three children who are less than age 18 only around 20% of the time. From this exercise, it is clear that a family size of six (based on a total fertility rate of four plus two parents) significantly overstates what would be a reasonable living wage reference family size. We felt that five persons was reasonable in this case, because women have between three to four children under age 18 for around 15 years. It is worth noting that a family size of five was consistent with statistics on adjusted average household size for this area of Kenya.

12.2.4 Important to consider rural-urban differences in family size

Family size is often quite different in rural and urban areas in developing countries. For this reason, *separate reference family sizes for rural and urban areas in a country are often warranted for estimating a living wage*. According to Demographic and Health Surveys from around 2000, average household size was 5.4 in rural Asia compared with 4.9 in urban Asia; 5.0 in rural Latin America compared with 4.6 in urban Latin America; 6.1 in rural Near East/Middle East compared with 5.4 in urban Near East/Middle East; and 5.3 in rural Sub-Sahara Africa compared with 5.1 in urban Sub-Sahara Africa (Bongaarts, 2001).

12.2.5 Drawing it all together to determine a living wage reference family size

Judgment is required to decide on an appropriate family size to use to estimate a living wage for a particular country and location – although it is worth noting that an appropriate reference family size for most locations is generally uncontroversial. Three ways of determining an appropriate reference family size were discussed above along with possible problems and biases. We recommend using information from all three approaches to help decide on an appropriate reference family size, since all three approaches provide insights – while keeping in mind their advantages and biases. In summary we recommend that:

- The minimum family size used to estimate a living wage should be 4 persons, because smaller family sizes would not allow for population reproduction and so eventual survival of a country; 3.5 persons could be used in exceptional circumstances such as in urban China that has had a one child policy for decades.
- The maximum reference family size used to estimate a living wage in locations with very high fertility should be 6 persons.
- Family size should be expressed in half persons (i.e. 3.5, 4, 4.5, 5. 5.5, 6) in recognition of the fact that judgment is required to determine an appropriate reference family size.

Four persons is likely to be the most common family size for urban areas of developing countries outside Sub-Sahara Africa and the Middle East. A family size of 4.5 or 5 persons is likely to be common for rural areas around the world and for urban areas of Sub-Sahara Africa. A family size of 5.5 or 6 is likely to be restricted mostly to rural Sub-Saharan Africa and parts of the Middle East and Asia.

12.3 Possible Need to Include Additional Funds to Assist Parents and Relatives Outside Nuclear Family

Workers in many countries, even married workers, are expected to help support their parents. In addition, cultural norms in many developing countries require workers to help other relatives and share resources. Such a cultural norm is very strong in Sub-Sahara Africa where anyone with money is expected to share with relatives, and requests for money from relatives cannot be rejected. This means that many workers are more or less required to help parents and other relatives – if these workers are to remain part of their society.

In locations where there are very strong social/cultural norms of helping parents or other relatives more generally, we feel that it is reasonable and appropriate to include a small separate expense category for this. Without some additional funds for helping parents and other relatives in many developing countries, workers would not have sufficient income on a living wage to be able to afford a decent living standard for their own immediate family. It is preferable to include some funds for this compared with increasing the family size needing to be supported by a living wage because extended families are amorphous, and it is neither reasonable nor realistic in our opinion to expect companies to support an open-ended number of extended family members.

We feel that 5% or the value of one workday per month at a living wage represents a reasonable and conservative amount for this. Such an amount is much lower than the tithe given to religious organizations by many people around the world. Also, including a modest sum for assistance to relatives helps justify any decision to use a conservative family size as well as any decision not to include parents or other relatives in the reference family size. Regardless, it is important to justify including some funds for helping parents and other relatives in a living wage report to convince possible skeptics.

PART IV. EXAMPLES

To get an idea of how to decide on reference family size for a living wage, three examples are provided. One example has high fertility and high child mortality (non-metropolitan urban Kenya), one example has a total fertility rate just above 2 and low child mortality (rural Dominican Republic), and one example has low fertility and low child mortality (urban Vietnam).

12.4 Example 1: Reference Family Size for Urban Townships Surrounding Lake Naivasha, Kenya (High Fertility and High Child Mortality)

A major challenge to determining a reference family size for this location was that statistics for urban Kenya are highly influenced by the situation in large metropolitan cities such as Mombasa and Nairobi where fertility rates are lower than in non-metropolitan urban areas such as the townships surrounding Lake Naivasha. We used a combination of urban and rural demographic measures to help determine reference family size because the study area was demographically speaking between rural areas and large cities.

12.4.1 Adjusted average household size

Average household size in Kenya differs greatly in rural and urban areas and between sources. According to the 2005/06 HIES (Kenyan National Bureau of Statistics, 2007), average household size for families with two or more persons was 4.6 in urban areas and 5.9 in rural areas (around 5.3 on average). Average family size excluding single-person households according to the 2008/09 DHS was substantially lower at 3.8 for urban areas and 5.0 for rural areas (around 4.4 on average).[5] Averaging values from these two surveys implied slightly less than 5 person reference family size for the area near Lake Naivasha flower farms.

12.4.2 Number of surviving children under age 18

Total fertility rate (TFR) in Kenya was 2.9 in urban areas, and 5.2 in rural areas (KNBS 2010) – with TFR falling over time. Since the townships surrounding Lake Naivasha consisted mainly of migrants from rural areas, and since the total fertility rate of migrants is typically between the rate in the originating area (5.2) and the rate in the destination area (2.9), we concluded that the TFR in this area was around four, which implied a family size of around six persons assuming no mortality (two parents + four children).

Since close to 0.3 out of every 4 births die on average before age 5 (as child mortality rate for Kenya was 7.3% according to World Bank World Development Indicators), this implied 3.7 surviving children per family (and so implied a family size of 5.7) after adjusting for child mortality. However, since this many children are necessarily born over a long period of time, there were typically around three children below age 18 on average per family in this area, which implied a reference family size of around 5.

12.4.3 Reference family size for non-metropolitan urban Kenya

In summary, since there were no estimates of family size or fertility for non-metropolitan urban Kenya, and since townships surrounding Lake Naivasha were demographically speaking between rural areas and large cities, we used a combination of urban and rural statistics to determine the reference family size. Both the adjusted average household size for households with two or more members, and the average number of surviving children under age 18 typically at home indicated a reference family size of around five persons.

12.5 Example 2: Reference Family Size for Rural Dominican Republic (Total Fertility Rate Above Two and Low Mortality)

12.5.1 Adjusted total fertility rate

Total fertility rate (TFR) in the Dominican Republic was 2.4 births and higher in rural areas than in urban areas by about 0.5 births according to the 2007 DHS (Centro de Estudios Sociales y Demográficos (CESDEM) and Macro International Inc., 2008). TFR had, however, been falling in recent years and so was probably somewhere around 2.5 births in rural Dominican Republic when the living wage study was undertaken. Child mortality in the Dominican Republic was 2.7%, which reduced the estimated number of surviving children slightly from 2.5 to 2.43.

12.5.2 Adjusted average household size

Average adjusted household size was slightly less than 4 persons (3.9) for rural households excluding single-person households and households with 8 or more persons according to data from the 2007 DHS (Centro de Estudios Sociales y Demográficos (CESDEM) and Macro International Inc., 2008) and 2010 Household Census (Oficina Nacional de Estadistica and Ministero de Economia, Planificacion y Desarrollo, 2012).

12.5.3 Reference family size for rural Dominican Republic

In summary, both the adjusted average household size and the mortality adjusted total fertility rate were relatively consistent. Adjusted average household size (3.9) and adjusted total fertility rate (2.4) for rural areas taken together implied a reference family size of around four.

12.6 Example 3: Reference Family Size for Urban Vietnam (Low Fertility and Low Mortality)

12.6.1 Adjusted average household size

The average household size in urban Vietnam was 3.83 according to the 2012 Vietnam Household Living Standards Measurement Survey (Vietnam Government, General Statistics Office, 2012). The average household size excluding single-person households was 3.93, since around 3% of urban households were single-person households.[6]

12.6.2 Adjusted total fertility rate

The total fertility rate for urban Vietnam was 1.80 (2.05 for country and 2.20 for rural areas) according to the Vietnam Government General Statistics Office (2012). Since the child mortality rate was low (2.4% according to World Bank (2015b), the number of surviving children in urban areas (1.76) and the number of children born (1.80) were almost the same. These data implied an average family size of 3.76 for urban Vietnam.

12.6.3 Reference family size for urban Vietnam

In summary, average adjusted household size in urban areas (3.93) as well as mortality adjusted total fertility in urban areas (3.76) both implied a reference family size of slightly less than 4 persons. It was clear that a living wage reference family size of 4 persons was appropriate for urban Vietnam.

NOTES

1. Indian censuses provide an example of how 'family' and 'household' have been used interchangeably. 'Household' was used in 1872, 1881 and 1951 to the present while 'family' was used between 1891 and 1941.
2. Four of the 11 methodologies review in Anker (2011) used a family size of four. The typical family size for living wage estimates in United States in the early twentieth century was five persons (see Ryan, 1906).
3. Five of 11 living wage methodologies for developing countries reviewed in Anker (2011) used average household size.
4. Total fertility rate is 'a basic indicator of the level of fertility, calculated by summing age-specific birth rates over all reproductive ages. It may be interpreted as the expected number of children a woman who survives to the end of the reproductive age span will have during her lifetime if she experiences the given age-specific rates' (United Nations Statistics Division, 2016).
5. It was not possible to exclude especially large households from this calculation for Kenya as the largest household size reported was 7+ for the DHS and 9+ in the HIES.
6. It was not possible to exclude especially large households from the calculation for Vietnam as the largest household size reported was 6+.

APPENDIX 12.1 RECORDING SECONDARY DATA ON REFERENCE FAMILY SIZE

Table 12A.1 is a form for recording information needed to decide on the appropriate reference size family for a living wage. It is a good idea to collect information from several secondary data sources for household size, because reported household size is sensitive to definition and measurement. Note that for sources that indicate only average household size and not the distribution of households by number of members, only the average household size should be filled in with an indication that the distribution of households by number of members was not available. There may also be several sources available for TFR and U5MR. It is useful to list all available sources with an indication of which sources are the most relevant and reliable.

Table 12A.1 Table for recording total fertility rate, under 5 mortality rate, and household size distribution by number of household members

1. Total fertility rate (TFR)			
Source and year of data	Rural	Urban	Location-specific (specify)
Conclusion and explanation of best TFR			
2. Under 5 mortality rate (U5MR)			
Source and year of data	Rural	Urban	Location-specific (specify)
Conclusion and explanation of best U5MR			
3. Calculate mortality adjusted total fertility rate using 1 and 2 above			
Mortality adjusted TFR			

Table 12A.1 (continued)

4. Household size (use additional sheets for other sources or years)			
Source and year: ______			
# persons in household	% of households		
	Rural	Urban	Location-specific (specify)
1			
2			
3			
4			
5			
6			
7			
8			
9			
10			
11			
12+			
Average household size			
Average household size excluding 1 person households and especially large households (with more than adjusted TFR + 5 persons)			

SECTION II

Estimating a living wage

13. Number of workers per family

PART I. BACKGROUND AND CONCEPTUAL FRAMEWORK

13.1 More Than One Worker per Family

Living wage is a family concept. It is therefore appropriate to expect more than one adult in a family to work and provide financial support for the family. For this reason, the cost of a decent living standard for a reference size family is assumed to be defrayed over the number of full-time equivalent workers in a family. The larger the number of full-time equivalent workers in the family, the smaller the living wage. The issue is not whether more than one person in a family should be expected to work, but how to determine the number of workers in a reference family. This chapter describes how to estimate the number of full-time equivalent workers in a reference family to use to estimate a living wage.

The 2011 ILO review of living wage methodologies (Anker, 2011) found that one worker per couple and two workers per couple have been the most common assumptions used in previous methodologies to estimate living wages. Neither of these assumptions is realistic or reasonable in today's world. The one worker (usually male) breadwinner model of the household which might have been the norm 50 to 100 years ago in Western countries is not relevant in many places in the world today. The other common assumption – that all adults work full-time – is equally unrealistic. In all countries, many adults who wish to work are unemployed or unable to find full-time work throughout the year. In addition, many adults work part-time because they have family care responsibilities. In our methodology, the number of full-time workers per family is always between one and two full-time equivalent workers. We have found that the range for the number of full-time equivalent workers per couple in our methodology tends to be between around 1.5 to around 1.9 (see Section 13.6.4).

13.2 Number of Workers per Family Needs to be Country- and Location-Specific

There is large variation around the world in the extent to which women are in the labor force (with much less variation for men). Unemployment rates and the extent to which male and female workers are able to find full-time equivalent work throughout the year also vary around the world. Because of these variations, the number of full-time workers per family that can be expected to provide support needs to be country-specific, should usually differ between rural and urban areas in a country, and should be region-specific in large countries.

PART II. APPROACH TO DETERMINE THE NUMBER OF FULL-TIME EQUIVALENT WORKERS PER FAMILY

This section describes how to estimate the number of full-time equivalent workers per couple who provide support. Estimates are based on three different statistics namely:

(i) labor force participation rate (LFPR),
(ii) unemployment rate (U), and
(iii) part-time employment rate and/or hours of work (PT).

Definitions, sources of information, and variation by important factors such as sex, age, and location, as well as possible pitfalls in the use of these data, are discussed in Sections 13.3 to 13.5. Equations used to estimate the number of full-time equivalent workers per family are presented in Section 13.6. Appendix 13.1 provides dummy tables to record secondary data for LFPR, U and PT.

13.3 Labor Force Participation Rate (Probability of Being Economically Active)

13.3.1 Definition and measurement of labor force participation rate

Labor force is the sum of the number of persons employed and the number of persons unemployed. The labor force participation rate is the ratio of the labor force to the working age population, expressed as a percentage (ILO, 1982). Thus, labor force participation rate provides an estimate of the probability that someone is either working/economically active or unemployed/looking for work.

Before discussing variations in labor force participation rates by age, sex and region of the world, it is important to point out that labor force data are often subject to significant bias and error and so caution is needed when using data on labor force participation rates. It has been shown that measurement of labor force activity on surveys is very sensitive to how survey questions are asked and labor force is defined (Anker et al., 1987). There are important biases in the internationally accepted definition of work as regards unpaid family work. Typical work performed by women in or near home is often poorly measured in practice in surveys. For example, housework, care work, caring for small animals, firewood collection and water collection that are typically done by women are not usually considered as labor force activity in practice (Anker et al., 1987).

13.3.2 Labor force participation rates differ by age

Age-specific labor force participation rates typically display an inverted U shape. Rates increase from age 15 as youth leave school and join the labor force; rates are typically fairly stable from age 25, especially for men, until later ages when rates decline as workers retire and leave the labor force. This means that labor force participation rates are much lower for youth (ages 15–24) than for adults ages 25+. For the world, the youth labor force participation rate (ages 15–24) is 48.5% compared with 68.8% for adults ages 25+. A large difference between youth and adult labor force participation rates is found in every region of the world (see Table 13.1). For this reason, we use labor force participation rates for persons 25–59 to estimate the number of full-time equivalent workers per couple. Ages 25–59 are prime working ages with family responsibilities. In contrast, many of those ages 15–24 have not yet joined the labor force because they are still in school, while many of those above age 60 have retired and left the labor force. Inclusion of those less than age 25 and those above age 60 would inappropriately reduce the estimated labor force participation rate used to estimate a living wage.

For this reason, in our methodology *labor force participation rates are estimated for ages 25–59, data permitting.*

13.3.3 Labor force participation rates differ by gender

Labor force participation rates (LFPR) are lower for women than for men throughout the world, because some or many women are out of the labor force in part because women are responsible for child care and care for the elderly throughout the world (Table 13.1). This is not only true for the world as a whole (LFPR is 83.7% for men ages 25+ compared with 54.2% for women ages 25+), but it is also true for every region in the world.

Table 13.1 Labor force participation rates by age, sex and region, 2012

Region	Male			Female			Total		
	Adult	Youth	Total	Adult	Youth	Total	Adult	Youth	Total
World	83.7	56.1	77.1	54.2	40.5	51.1	68.8	48.5	64.1
Middle East	84.7	46.5	74.3	21.0	13.2	18.7	55.0	30.3	48.1
North Africa	85.1	46.8	74.3	26.1	19.7	24.4	55.1	33.4	49.1
South Asia	90.7	57.3	81.3	35.0	23.4	31.8	63.4	41.0	57.1
Latin America and Caribbean	85.3	62.1	79.5	57.0	42.7	53.6	70.7	52.5	66.3
South-East Asia and Pacific	89.5	59.2	81.8	63.0	45.1	58.8	76.0	52.3	70.1
Sub-Sahara Africa	87.4	55.9	76.3	71.5	51.4	64.6	70.4	53.6	70.4
East Asia	84.7	58.8	79.4	67.7	61.1	66.4	76.3	59.8	73.1
Central & South-East Europe	76.2	49.6	70.7	53.6	34.1	50.2	63.9	42.0	59.8
Developed Economies & Europe	70.9	49.2	67.5	54.0	45.3	52.8	62.2	47.3	60.0

Notes: Youth is defined as ages 15–24 and adults as ages 25+. Labor force participation rates for ages 25–59 are higher than for ages 25+ because participation rates are lower at ages 60+.

Source: ILO KILM, 2013a.

It is for this reason in our methodology that *labor force participation rates for men and women are averaged to determine a participation rate for couples and families.*

13.3.4 Female labor force participation rates affected by cultural norms

Labor force participation rates for adult males are fairly similar around the world, although they are lower for developed countries and Europe.[1] In contrast, female labor force participation rates vary greatly by region along with cultural norms and acceptability of women working outside the home and family farm (Table 13.1). Regional adult female participation rates range from a low of around 20% to a high of around 70% – going from 20–25% in Middle East and North Africa; to around 35% in South Asia; to around 63–68% in South-East and East Asia and around 72% in Sub-Saharan Africa.

For this reason, in our methodology, it is *important to use country-specific data on labor force participation and region-specific data in large and diverse countries* such as India where there are large regional differences in female labor force participation.

13.3.5 Labor force participation rates differ in rural and urban areas

Labor force participation rates are generally higher in rural areas than in urban areas in developing countries mainly because many women in rural areas work on a family farm or care for family-owned animals. This is why *it is important to use rural and urban specific data on labor force participation.*

13.3.6 Child labor should be ignored

Children often work and make important contributions to family income in developing countries. This possibility should not be considered when estimating a living wage, because child labor is not consistent with decency in the twenty-first century. This is another reason why labor force participation rates for young persons are not used to determine the number of workers per family in our methodology.

13.3.7 Sources of data on labor force participation rates

ILO LABORSTAT and ILO KILM online websites provide data on labor force participation rates by age and sex for almost every country in the world. The main problem with these data for estimating a living wage is that they are national rates and not the rural and urban rates required. For this reason, researchers should try to find rural and urban rates from national sources such as censuses, labor force surveys, demographic surveys, and household surveys. Note that researchers always need to keep in mind that judgment is necessary when multiple data sources are available because labor force participation rates often differ between surveys for various reasons such as ones discussed above.

13.4 Unemployment Rate (Absence of Work)

13.4.1 Definition of unemployment rate

Unemployment rate is calculated by dividing the number of unemployed persons by the number of persons in the labor force (that includes unemployed persons). For a person to be considered unemployed according to the international definition of unemployment, s/he needs to be: above a specified age, without any work in the reference period (even 1 hour of work in the past week is considered as being employed), available for work in the reference period, and actively seeking work in the reference period (ILO, 1982).

Unemployment rates are necessarily sensitive to how questions are asked on labor force surveys and household surveys, since the definition of unemployment is partly subjective. It is not clear, for example, what constitutes actively looking for work (or its meaning) in locations where few if any jobs are available. Indeed, many people without work do not actively look for work in locations with few if any job opportunities, since there is no reason to actively look for work in such locations. As a result, such people are considered to be outside of the labor force and not unemployed.

13.4.2 Unemployment rates usually lower in rural areas than in urban areas in developing countries

Unemployment rates are generally lower in rural areas than in urban areas in developing countries. One reason is that many people in rural areas who are without work do not actively look for work (one criterion in the definition of unemployment) because it would be fruitless to look for work when very few jobs are available. Another reason why unemployment rates are generally lower in rural areas compared with urban areas in developing countries is that many people in rural areas work on a family farm or with family animals and so are considered to be labor force participants even when this work is done for only an hour or two each day.

In light of the above discussion, *it is important to identify and use separate unemployment rates for rural and urban areas whenever possible.*

13.4.3 Unemployment rates higher for youth

Youth unemployment rates are much higher than adult unemployment rates throughout the world (Table 13.2). Youth unemployment rate is 2.8 times the adult unemployment rate for the world as a whole and is higher than the adult unemployment rate in all regions of the world. The ratio of youth unemployment rate to adult unemployment rate ranges from around 2 in Sub-Sahara Africa; to around 5 in South-East Asia and Pacific. Youths are in a better position than adults to be able to 'afford' to be unemployed, in part because they can continue to live with their parents. Educated youth unemployment is especially high, because many educated youths come from wealthier families.

Unemployment rate to estimate a living wage should be based on ages 25–59 when possible. It is important to exclude youths (ages 15–24) when estimating unemployment rates for a living wage.

13.4.4 Sources of data on unemployment rates

It is usually advisable to find several unemployment rate estimates including estimates by age and for rural and urban areas. First, unemployment rates often differ by survey and source partly because of the subjectivity of how unemployment is defined and measured and partly because unemployment rates reported by governments are sometimes influenced by political considerations. Second, rural and urban unemployment rates always differ, and only national unemployment rates are available from international sources. Third, available unemployment rates are not always

Table 13.2 Youth and adult unemployment rates by region of the world, 2012

Region	Youth unemployment rate (ages 15–24)	Adult unemployment rate (ages 25+)	Ratio youth/adult unemployment rates
World	12.6	4.5	2.8
Developed Economies & Europe	17.9	7.3	2.4
Central & South-East Europe	17.1	6.9	2.5
East Asia	9.5	3.5	2.7
South-East Asia & Pacific	13.0	2.5	5.2
South Asia	9.8	2.3	4.2
Latin America & Caribbean	13.5	4.9	2.7
Middle East	28.1	7.5	3.8
North Africa	23.8	7.1	3.3
Sub-Sahara Africa	11.9	6.2	2.0

Notes: Youth defined as ages 15–24 and adults as ages 25+ in source.

Source: ILO KILM, 2013a.

recent and unemployment rates are sensitive to economic conditions that change year by year and month by month. It is also advisable to use national sources whenever possible because they are more likely to be up-to-date than international sources.[2]

Because unemployment rates differ by source, geographic coverage, age group, and year, judgment is often required before using them to estimate a living wage. For example, in the Dominican Republic while we found a recent national unemployment rate, we were unable to find recent rural and urban unemployment rates. But since we found rural and urban unemployment rates for an earlier year, we applied the ratio of rural to urban unemployment rates from this earlier year to the recent national unemployment rate to estimate recent rural and urban rates. In Kenya, judgment was required because there were no official government unemployment rates and the unemployment rates we found ranged from 17–40% and came from 1999 to 2010. This meant that we needed to consider the credibility of each source and how recent it was. In China, official unemployment rates are based on a registration system that is known to understate unemployment. The official urban unemployment rate was 4.1% for 2014. A national household survey found that the unemployment rate averaged 10.9% between 2002 and 2009 (Feng et al., 2015). Chinese researchers decided to use this unemployment rate of 10.9% for their living wage estimate as they judged it to be more realistic.

13.5 Part-time Employment and Less than Full-time Work over the Year

The internationally accepted definition of labor force participation is binary. People are either in the labor force or out of the labor force without any consideration of how many hours they work. Someone who works one hour per week is counted the same as someone who works 50 hours per week. And depending on when a labor force survey is conducted, someone who works only in peak seasons is counted the same as someone who works year-round. This creates problems for estimating a living wage, since we are interested in the number of full-time equivalent workers per family over the year. It is for this reason that it is necessary to take part-time employment into consideration.

There is no internationally accepted definition of part-time employment, which makes it problematic to use data on part-time employment rates without careful thought. Preferable are data on the distribution of hours worked, because these data allow researchers to calculate the percentage of workers who work less than a specific cut-off such as 20 or 30 hours per week.

13.5.1 Sources of data on part-time employment and hours of work

It is worth looking to see if data are available from government websites and publications and from academic publications. National data on part-time employment or the distribution of number of hours worked are often available.[3] But, unfortunately, when data on part-time employment are available, they are often only available for the entire country – yet part-time employment rates differ greatly for rural and urban areas within countries as well as for men and women. This means that for many countries, it is necessary to rely partly on discussions with workers and key informants about the extensiveness of part-time work for rural and urban areas and for male and female workers. In such discussions, it is important to keep in mind that there are two distinct types of less than full-time work over the year – work that is always part-time (e.g. urban part-time job or caring for family-owned animals) and full-time work that is done only in certain seasons (e.g. peak season farm work). Our experience is that part-time wage jobs are often uncommon in developing countries but that work in rural areas is often part-time and often seasonal. When data are not available on part-time employment or hours of work and discussions with workers and key informants indicate that there is not much part-time employment, we suggest using a 5% part-time employment rate for urban settings as a practical and reasonable assumption.

13.6 Equations to Estimate Number of Full-time Equivalent Workers per Family

Estimating the number of full-time equivalent workers per family begins with two assumptions.

1. One member of the family is assumed to be a full-time worker year-round. This assumption is used because a living wage is concerned with a situation in which at least one adult worker in the reference family is working.
2. Part-time work is assumed to be half-time work. This assumption is made for reasons of practicality when data on hours of work are not available.

Two equations are used to estimate the number of full-time equivalent workers per family to help estimate a living wage. Equation 1 estimates the typical proportion of full-time equivalent work per working age adult in the general population. Equation 2 estimates the number of full-time equivalent workers per reference family.

13.6.1 Equation 1: Proportion of full-time equivalent work per working age adult in the general population

Proportion of full-time equivalent work per working age adult = Average adult LFPR × (1 − unemployment rate) × (1 − [part-time employment rate÷2])

Where:

LFPR (labor force participation rate) measures the probability that an adult age 25–59 is economically active.
1 − unemployment rate for ages 25–59 measures probability that someone in the labor force is able to find work.
1 − [part-time employment rate ÷ 2] measures extent to which someone with work is working full-time using simplifying assumption that part-time employment is half-time.

13.6.2 Equation 2: Number of full-time equivalent workers per family

Number of full-time equivalent workers per family = 1+ proportion of full-time work per working age adult calculated in equation 1

These equations are based on the assumption that one adult in the family has full-time work year-round, and that the amount of work done by the second adult is the proportion of full-time work of adults aged 25–59 in the general population. The reason for assuming one full-time worker in a family is that most companies, governments, NGOs, unions and laypersons are concerned with workers who are employed full-time and year-round.

13.6.3 Implication of the assumption that one family member is a full-time worker year-round

There are several important implications of assuming one full-time worker in the reference family. First, it implies that living wage estimates are not relevant for part-time workers, and it is not appropriate to convert a monthly living wage into an hourly or daily living wage for part-time workers. The lack of equivalency between living wage per hour or per day and living wage per month comes about because part-time workers do not work a sufficient number of hours to enable them to earn enough to support their family at a decent living standard. Minimum wage laws for Shenzhen and Chengdu, China, provide examples of this lack of equivalency for hourly (CNY18.5 and CNY14.6) and monthly minimum wages (CNY2,030 and CNY1,500) as the hourly minimum wage is 58% and 69% higher respectively than the hourly value of the monthly minimum wage in these two cities. Second, this assumption means that when permanent workers are not provided full-time work throughout the year, it is necessary to adjust for this. We saw this situation in rural Malawi where permanent tea plantations workers were offered 23 days of work per month on average over the year rather than 26 days of full-time work because of low yields of tea bushes during the slack season. Not offering full-time work throughout the year to permanent workers is also common in factories where demand is seasonal such as being high say around Christmas and low during the summer.

13.6.4 Likely range for number of full-time equivalent workers per family

Table 13.3 provides results on how the number of full-time equivalent workers per couple was estimated in five living wage studies carried out for Global Living Wage Coalition members. The range of values is fairly small for these five studies, only ranging from 1.58 to 1.78, despite very different labor market conditions in these five countries. Rural Malawi has a very high labor force participation rate (96% for ages 25–59). But rural Malawi has a very high rate of part-time employment over the year due to the importance of a rain-fed small farm sector, which pulls down the estimated number of full-time equivalent workers for rural Malawi. South Africa Cape Winelands and rural Dominican Republic have lower labor force participation rates (78% and 77% respectively) and Bangladesh has

Table 13.3 Calculation of number of full-time workers per family in five countries

Factors	Malawi (rural)	Bangladesh (urban)	South Africa (Cape Winelands)	Dominican Republic (rural)	China (Shenzhen)
Labor force participation rate ages 25–59	96.0%	66.0%	77.5%	76.8%	89.2%
Unemployment rate ages 25–59	3.0%	4.7%	17.0%	8.6%	10.8%
Part-time employment rate	63% full-time hours	18.2%	4.6%	5.3%	5.0%
Number of full-time equivalent workers per family	1.59	1.58	1.63	1.67	1.78

Source: Anker and Anker, 2014a, 2013, and 2013a and unpublished living wage reports for Bangladesh and China.

a much lower labor force participation rate (66%) than rural Malawi, but they also have lower part-time employment rates compared with Malawi. China (Shenzhen) has the highest estimated number of full-time workers per couple of the countries included in Table 13.3, because it has very high labor force participation rates for both women and men and low part-time employment rates, although it has a somewhat high urban unemployment rate of 10.9% according to national survey data. If the 4.1% official unemployment rate for Shenzhen had been used, which is based on an unemployment registration system that is known to undercount unemployment, there would have been 1.83 full-time workers per couple, which would represent a situation where labor force participation rates are very high for both women and men, and unemployment rates and part-time employment rates are both very low.

PART III. EXAMPLE

13.7 Number of Workers per Family: A Hypothetical Example

13.7.1 Labor force participation rate (LFPR)

Labor force participation rate for ages 25–59 is around 80%, according to recent household surveys.

13.7.2 Unemployment rate (U)

Open unemployment is not common in the area. For persons ages 25–59, it was 1.9% according to a recent population census and around 4% according to a recent household survey. It is not unusual to find different unemployment rates from different sources, and it is necessary to evaluate the credibility of the sources and the year in which they were executed. In this case, both sources were considered credible, and their unemployment rates were not very far apart. We split the difference and used 3%.

13.7.3 Part-time employment (PT)

Part-time employment rate is 15%, 5% for men and 25% for women.

13.7.4 Calculation of number of full-time equivalent workers per family

Based on the below discussion, we substituted the following values in equations 1 and 2 below to get the number of full-time equivalent workers per family:

- Labor force participation rate = .80
- Unemployment rate = .03
- Proportion of full-time work = .15

Equation 1:

Proportion of full-time work per adult = $(.80\ LFPR) \times (1 - .03U) \times (1 - .15PT \div 2) = 0.72$

Equation 2:

Number of full-time equivalent workers per family = 1 worker + 0.72 = 1.72 full-time equivalent workers per couple

NOTES

1. Male labor force participation rates for ages 25+ are approximately 84% for the world. Rates are lower for Developed Economies and Europe (71%) and Central and Eastern Europe (76%) where school attendance often extends beyond age 25, social assistance facilitates withdrawal from the labor force, and retirement benefits allow early retirement.
2. ILO KILM and ILO LABORSTAT websites indicate national unemployment rates by age based on information provided to ILO by national authorities. ILO KILM tabulates and presents unemployment rates for ages 15–24 and ages 25+. The main problem with ILO unemployment rate data for estimating a living wage is that they are national values – but separate rural and urban values should be used to estimate a living wage.
3. ILO LABORSTAT and ILO KILM provide data on hours of work for some countries. Most of these are drawn from an OECD database and usually only cover formal sector employment.

APPENDIX 13.1 SECONDARY DATA ON LABOR FORCE PARTICIPATION, UNEMPLOYMENT AND PART-TIME EMPLOYMENT USED TO DETERMINE THE NUMBER OF FULL-TIME EQUIVALENT WORKERS PER FAMILY

Our living wage methodology assumes that more than one family member works and provides financial support for the family. To estimate a typical number of full-time equivalent workers per couple, secondary data are required on labor force participation rates, unemployment rates, and part-time employment rates for persons aged 25–59.

The available secondary data for the location of interest (e.g. rural or urban) should be indicated in the tables below. Since values for these variables are sensitive to how they are defined and measured and how recently they were measured, it is useful to collect information on these from several sources and years.

1. Labor Force Participation Rate from Secondary Data Sources

Information on labor force participation rates by five-year age groups, sex and location of interest should be recorded in Table 13A.1. With this information, it is possible to calculate the average labor force participation rate for ages 25–59. Separate copies of Table 13A.1 should be used for additional data sources and/or years.

2. Unemployment Rate from Secondary Data Sources

Information on unemployment rates by five-year age groups, sex and location of interest (e.g. rural/urban/national) should be recorded in Table 13A.2. With this information, it is possible to calculate the average labor force participation rate for ages 25–59. Note that separate copies of Table 13A.2 should be used for additional data sources and/or years.

3. Part-time Employment Rate from Secondary Sources

The part-time employment rate is the proportion of workers who work part-time – often defined as % of workers who work less than 20 or 30 hours per week.

Table 13A.1 Labor force participation rates (LFPRs) by age, sex and location

Source and year	Rural			Urban			National		
Age group	M	F	All	M	F	All	M	F	All
15–19									
20–24									
25–29									
30–34									
35–39									
40–44									
45–49									
50–54									
55–59									
Calculate average 25–59[a]									

Note: [a] It is easiest to estimate this by summing age specific labor force participation rates for ages 25–59 and dividing this sum by 7. This creates a synthetic measure of labor force participation rate for ages 25–59. Alternatively, when data on population and number of workers for ages 25–59 are available, a labor force participation rate for ages 25–59 can be estimated by dividing the number of labor force participants ages 25–59 by the population age 25–59.

Table 13A.2 Unemployment rates by age and location

Source and year	Rural			Urban			National		
Age group	M	F	All	M	F	All	M	F	All
15–19									
20–24									
25–29									
30–34									
35–39									
40–44									
45–49									
50–54									
55–59									
Calculate average 25–59									

Table 13A.3 Part-time employment rate by location

Source	Year	Rural	Urban	National	Definition used by source

Table 13A.4 Summary table for labor force variables

<table>
<tr><td colspan="7">LFPR</td></tr>
<tr><td>Source</td><td>Year</td><td>Age group</td><td>Rural</td><td>Urban</td><td>National</td><td>Comments</td></tr>
<tr><td></td><td></td><td></td><td></td><td></td><td></td><td></td></tr>
<tr><td></td><td></td><td></td><td></td><td></td><td></td><td></td></tr>
<tr><td>Conclusion for LFPR</td><td colspan="6"></td></tr>
<tr><td>Justification for conclusion</td><td colspan="6"></td></tr>
<tr><td colspan="7">Unemployment rate</td></tr>
<tr><td>Source</td><td>Year</td><td>Age group</td><td>Rural</td><td>Urban</td><td>National</td><td>Comments</td></tr>
<tr><td></td><td></td><td></td><td></td><td></td><td></td><td></td></tr>
<tr><td></td><td></td><td></td><td></td><td></td><td></td><td></td></tr>
<tr><td>Conclusion for unemployment rate</td><td colspan="6"></td></tr>
<tr><td>Justification for conclusion</td><td colspan="6"></td></tr>
<tr><td colspan="7">Part-time employment rate</td></tr>
<tr><td>Source</td><td>Year</td><td>Rural</td><td>Urban</td><td>National</td><td>Definition used</td><td>Comments</td></tr>
<tr><td></td><td></td><td></td><td></td><td></td><td></td><td></td></tr>
<tr><td></td><td></td><td></td><td></td><td></td><td></td><td></td></tr>
<tr><td>Conclusion for part-time employment rate</td><td colspan="6"></td></tr>
<tr><td>Justification for conclusion</td><td colspan="6"></td></tr>
</table>

4. Table for Summarizing Data and Decisions on Labor Force Participation Rate, Unemployment Rate and Part-time Employment Rate

Table 13A.4 provides a dummy table for summarizing results and decisions from Tables 13A.1 to 13A.3. Space is provided to record conclusions and justifications about which rates are most suitable for estimating number of full-time equivalent workers per reference family.

14. Take home pay required and taking statutory deductions into account

PART I. BACKGROUND AND CONCEPTUAL FRAMEWORK

Up to this point, this manual has been concerned with the income that workers need to be able to afford a basic but decent life for themselves and their family. Thus, so far, this manual has been concerned with determining take home pay required.

However, statutory deductions from pay (such as income taxes, social security taxes, and union fees) reduce take home pay and money available for day-to-day expenses. This means that two living wage estimates are needed – net living wage, which is the take home pay/disposable income required for decency, and the gross living wage, which is the gross pay required to ensure sufficient net take home pay for decency. This is shown in Figure 14.1. The difference between net and gross living wages is statutory payroll deductions and possibly income taxes.

Statutory deductions from pay are different from voluntary deductions. Voluntary deductions (such as for personal savings accounts, Christmas fund, or voluntary provident fund contribution) are similar in a sense to household expenditures. Statutory deductions are different, because they reduce disposable income available to workers to support a basic but decent life style without reducing expenses in any way. This chapter discusses how to take statutory deductions from pay into consideration to estimate a gross living wage.

Figure 14.1 From net living wage to gross living wage

PART II. APPROACH TO CALCULATING TAKE HOME PAY NEEDED FOR A LIVING WAGE

Previous chapters in this manual covered how to calculate the income that a worker and her/his family need for decency. This chapter discusses how much gross pay is needed for workers to have sufficient net pay/disposable income to be able to afford this basic but decent living standard.

14.1 Statutory Deductions from Pay

Almost all countries have statutory deductions from pay. These deductions are required by law. The types of statutory deductions differ across countries, but typical deductions include income tax, social security tax, contributions to government funds/schemes for health insurance, unemployment insurance and pension/provident funds, and mandatory union fees. Statutory deductions reduce workers' take home pay and consequently money available to support a decent life. Therefore, it is necessary to include statutory deductions in living wage estimates.

14.1.1 Income tax

Almost all countries impose an income tax. But in most countries, income tax is not imposed until earnings surpass a minimum income threshold (that may or may not include the value of in kind benefits). Since the minimum threshold for paying income tax in some countries is above a living wage, it is not always necessary to adjust a living wage for income tax.

14.1.2 Other typical statutory deductions from pay

Most countries have other statutory deductions from pay besides income tax. They come in different forms, and have different names. Whatever they are called, they reduce workers' disposable income. And they can be quite large. For example, social security taxes are 12% of pay in Vietnam. Workers in Shenzhen and Zhengzhou, China, have statutory payroll deductions of 11% for pension, unemployment insurance and medical insurance. Workers in Brazil pay 8% in social security taxes plus often mandatory union fees of more than 1%. Workers in Ethiopia, a very poor country, pay around 6% for social security tax, plus often 2% for union fees, and would pay around another 15% in income tax at a living wage for the small city of Ziway. Examples of statutory deductions we have found in previous living wage studies include:

- Social security/social insurance
- Pension

- Disability insurance
- Provident fund
- Unemployment insurance
- Government medical insurance
- Union dues

14.2 Person-specific Statutory Deductions from Pay

There are statutory and court ordered deductions from pay that are person-specific such as repayment of loans, child support, and alimony. A living wage does not need to be adjusted for such deductions.

14.3 Voluntary Deductions from Pay

There are various deductions from pay that are voluntary, since workers have a choice. We consider these deductions as similar to expenditures and so in a sense spent from disposable income. Therefore, the living wage does not need to be adjusted for voluntary deductions. Typical examples of voluntary deductions from pay that we have encountered include:

- Personal savings accounts
- Christmas savings fund
- Funeral fund
- Voluntary health insurance contribution
- Voluntary pension or provident fund contribution

14.4 How to Take Statutory Deductions from Pay into Account

To begin with, it is always useful to list all statutory payroll deductions and how they are calculated. This information is available from government sources and local enterprises. The following equation relates gross living wage to the amount of disposable income required by a worker and his/her family to be able to afford a decent living standard (net living wage).

Gross living wage = Disposable income needed for decency (net living wage) + Statutory deductions from pay

Calculations of statutory deductions from pay are based on taxable income. Countries differ in how they calculate taxable income, the types of income taxed, and tax deductions and exemptions. Since taxes are normally applied to gross taxable pay, the net living wage needs to be 'grossed up' to account for taxes and other statutory deductions. Local enterprises and local representatives of certification companies are in a good position to provide information on tax laws and often to help do tax calculations.

Gross living wage can be calculated from the net living wage in three steps:

> **STEP 1:** Subtract income exempt from taxes (e.g. possibly value of in kind benefits) from the net living wage.
> **STEP 2:** Calculate *gross living wage (excluding tax exempt income)* by dividing net taxable income (from step 1) by (1 – tax rate). The tax rate to use is the sum of the rates for all statutory deductions.
> **STEP 3:** Calculate *gross living wage* by adding tax exempt income to the result from Step 2.

PART III. EXAMPLE

This section contains a hypothetical example of how to take statutory deductions into consideration.

14.5 Hypothetical Country Example from a Country with Relatively Simple Tax Codes

Assume that country X has four statutory deductions from pay. Taken together, they represent 12% of pay.

- Social insurance for pension (8%)
- Unemployment insurance (1%)
- Medical insurance (2%)
- Union fees (1%)

Further, assume that the net living wage is 5,000 per month, in kind benefits are valued at 500 per month and exempt from tax, and income up to 500 is exempt from tax. Therefore, the gross living wage can be calculated as follows:

> STEP 1: Net taxable income = 4,000 (net living wage 5,000 – in kind benefits 500 (not subject to tax) – tax exempt income 500).
> STEP 2: Gross living wage excluding tax exempt income = 4,545 (taxable income 4,000 divided by 0.88 (which is 1−.12)).
> STEP 3: Gross living wage = 5,545 (4,545 from step 2 + 500 in kind benefits + 500 income exempt from tax)

SECTION III

Prevailing wages and gaps to a living wage

15. Measuring prevailing wages to compare to a living wage

PART I. BACKGROUND

15.1 Introduction

Determining the gap between prevailing wages and a living wage is an important part of most living wage studies. This is essential information for the public, workers, employers and others in the value chain (e.g. producers, retailers, brands, and buyers); standard setting organizations with a living wage clause in their codes of practice; governments setting minimum wages and developing policies to reduce poverty; trade unions for collective bargaining and public awareness raising campaigns; and NGOs and international organizations concerned with poverty and worker rights. This makes it necessary to measure wages received by workers. However, this is not as straightforward as it might seem, because remuneration comes in many forms. This chapter discusses which forms of remuneration are appropriate to include in wages to compare them with a living wage. Although most forms of remuneration should be included when comparing workers' wages with a living wage, some forms of remuneration should be excluded, such as deferred benefits and overtime pay. Incentive pay and in kind benefits should be treated with caution.

There are two distinct ways to measure prevailing wages for comparison to a living wage. One way is based on wages paid in a particular industry and/or in particular establishments. This approach is used when a living wage study focuses on particular establishments or a particular industry because the study is funded by a company, NGO, or standard setting organization that wants to know whether an industry or establishment pays a living wage to workers. It involves collection and analysis of primary data and often requires access to payroll data or collective bargaining agreements (CBAs).

A second way uses average wages for relevant occupations and industries according to published secondary data. These wages are included in a wage ladder.

The remainder of this chapter focuses on the first approach in part because for the second approach there is no choice but to use published average wage data as reported – although the following discussion is still useful for the second approach because it indicates how published average wages differ from the wages that conform to our guidelines for measuring prevailing wages for comparison to a living wage.

15.2 What are Wages and Remuneration?

According to ILO Convention 95 (Protection of Wages Convention) (1949), '***wages*** means remuneration or earnings, however designated or calculated, capable of being expressed in money terms.' According to ILO Convention 100 (Equal Remuneration Convention) (1951), '***remuneration*** includes the ordinary, basic or minimum wage or salary and any additional emoluments whatsoever payable directly or indirectly, whether in cash or in kind, by the employer to the worker and arising out of the worker's employment.'

This means that remuneration is complex and paid in a variety of forms such as:

- Basic wage including cost of living adjustment
- Cash allowances and bonuses
- In kind benefits
- Productivity bonuses
- Overtime pay
- Pay premiums for holidays, weekends, night work
- Fringe benefits
- Employer contributions to pensions and provident funds
- Deferred payments such as severance pay and pension.

How to treat each of the above to determine if an establishment pays a living wage and if a worker receives a living wage is discussed below. More detailed discussion is provided on in kind benefits in Chapter 16. Note that it is important to indicate in a transparent way in a living wage report how current wages are determined for comparison to a living wage. The following formula is used:

Prevailing wage for comparison to a living wage = Basic wage with cost of living adjustment + most cash allowances + some fringe benefits + some productivity cash bonuses + some in kind benefits

PART II. DETERMINING IF WORKERS RECEIVE A LIVING WAGE

15.3 Principles for Deciding Forms of Remuneration to Include in Prevailing Wages for Comparison to a Living Wage

As indicated above, remuneration is received in various forms. The remainder of this chapter discusses how different forms of compensation should be treated to determine if workers receive a living wage. The following general principles are used to decide which forms of remuneration should be included in current wages to determine gaps between current wages and a living wage.

- **Receipt assured**
  Workers need to be able to count on receiving a wage, allowance, bonus, or benefit so that they are able to pay for ongoing expenses. Wages, benefits, and bonuses that are at the whim or discretion of the employer are too uncertain to ensure that workers can afford to maintain a decent life each and every month. This criterion means that bonuses that are not more or less guaranteed should not be counted for comparison to living wage. This includes when employers, at their own discretion, give workers a bonus at the end of a profitable year.

- **Received within one year**
  Workers have limited capacity to smooth out their spending over time without having to borrow and run the considerable risk of getting into perpetual debt. We assume that workers are able to smooth out expenditures for up to one year. This criterion means that guaranteed cash allowances such as for national holidays and a 13th month cash bonus would qualify for inclusion in wages for comparison to a living wage. On the other hand, this criterion would exclude deferred payments such as pensions, provident fund, and severance pay, because they are received well in the future (in addition to being far from guaranteed in many countries).

- **Earned during standard working hours working at a normal pace**
  The definition of a living wage (see Chapter 1) indicates that it must be earned in standard working hours. This means that overtime pay and pay premiums for holidays, weekends and night work are not appropriate to include in remuneration for comparing prevailing wages to a living wage. This also means that incentive pay bonuses

that require working overtime should not be included – this occurs when incentive payments are based on targets that are so high that many workers are not able to reach the target during standard working hours.[1]

- **Received in cash (except for in kind benefits and medical insurance)** Remuneration needs to be available for ongoing expenses (i.e. paid in cash) or reduce such expenses (such as some in kind benefits). This implies that fringe benefits such as unpaid vacations, maternity leave and employer contributions to government social security programs should not be counted since they do not increase take home pay over what full-time workers earn. On the other hand, the value of in kind benefits and private medical insurance should be included because they reduce the cash wage required to pay for a decent standard of living. To avoid possible abuse, however, special rules are used to determine the monetary value of in kind benefits (see Chapter 16).

15.4 Common Forms of Remuneration and Whether They Should be Included in Wages for Comparison to Living Wage

This section discusses how to treat common forms of compensation for the purposes of comparing current wages with a living wage based on the above principles. Appendix 15.1 provides a compilation of different forms of remuneration that employers have indicated to us as worthy of inclusion in wages for comparison to a living wage – many of which are not appropriate for this purpose.

15.4.1 Basic wage and cost of living adjustment

Basic wage and cost of living adjustment *should be included* in wages for comparison to living wage.

15.4.2 Overtime pay and pay supplements for holidays, weekends, and night work

Overtime pay *should not be included* in wages for comparison to living wage. A living wage should be earned in a standard workweek (see definition of living wage in Chapter 1). Pay supplements for night work, weekends and holidays should also be excluded when they are in addition to pay for standard working hours.

15.4.3 Production incentive bonuses

Production bonuses are an important form of wage payment for many workers in developing countries. Many factories and farms in developing countries emphasize incentive payments such as production bonuses whereby workers receive higher wages when they produce more than a preset minimum output. For example, tea pluckers in Malawi received a basic minimum wage for 44 kilos of plucked tea in a day in 2014, and additional pay for each additional kilo of plucked tea in the day. Similarly, sewers of shirts might receive x rupees for sewing, say, 100 shirts during a day, and x/100 rupees for each additional shirt sewn during the day.

While production bonuses add to the disposable income of workers and so logically should be included in wages for comparison to a living wage, production bonuses are uncertain, often earned by only some workers, and often require overtime. This means that production bonuses need to be carefully scrutinized. Production bonuses received by most workers, and not associated with an especially fast work pace or overtime could be included for comparison to a living wage. This means that it is necessary to know how much most workers can produce during standard working hours at normal speed and skill. For example, say that workers receive a basic wage for 100 shirts sewn, plus a bonus for each additional shirt. If a typical worker is able to sew 120 shirts working at normal speed during standard working hours, then it would be appropriate to include in the prevailing wage the production bonus for an extra 20 shirts. If, on the other hand, typical workers are only able to sew 90 shirts working at normal speed during normal work hours, production bonuses should not be included in prevailing wages for comparison with a living wage because typical workers would not be able to achieve the bonus during normal working hours.

15.4.4 Cash allowances and benefits

Cash allowances differ from production incentive bonuses in that they are not linked to performance or productivity. Cash allowances and benefits should be included in wages for comparison with a living wage, because they increase the disposable income of workers when the general principles indicated above are met. Cash allowances can be an important part of wages in developing countries and are often included in CBAs.[2]

When cash allowances are paid once a year (e.g. year-end Tet bonus in Vietnam) or twice a year (e.g. twice yearly Eid bonus in Bangladesh), they should be pro-rated to represent a monthly value. For example, if all workers received a cash bonus on national Independence Day, this amount should be divided by 12 and added to the monthly salary. If all workers received a monthly salary of 2,400 plus a '13th month' payment of 2,400, the 13th month bonus would be worth 200 per month (2400/12). A 13th month payment is legally binding in many countries. According to Wozniak (2015), workers receive a 13th month bonus in 16 Latin American countries.

Examples of typical cash allowances include:

- 13th month pay
- Transportation cash allowance
- Housing cash allowance
- National holiday cash bonuses
- Birthday cash bonus

15.4.5 In kind benefits

Some types of in kind benefits should be included as partial payment of a living wage. Which in kind benefits are acceptable and how these in kind benefits should be valued for comparison to a living wage is discussed in detail in Chapter 16.

15.4.6 Fringe benefits

Most fringe benefits do not qualify for inclusion in wages for comparison to living wage.[3] This includes unpaid vacation days and public holidays, sick leave and maternity leave, and employer payments required by law such as contributions to social security. Private medical insurance paid for by an employer is included in wages.

15.5 Allowances and Benefits Not to Include in Remuneration for Comparison to a Living Wage

The following allowances and benefits should not be included in wages for comparison with a living wage, because they do not meet all of the principles indicated in Section 15.3.

- Overtime pay should not be included because living wage needs to be earned during standard working hours.
- Time off for holidays, annual leave, and sick leave should not be included because they do not add to disposable income of workers above what they normally earn.
- Maternity and paternity leave should not be included because they do not add to disposable income of workers above what they normally earn.
- Employer contributions required by law, such as for social security programs, unemployment insurance, and workers' compensation/injury insurance should not be included because they do not add to disposable income of workers within one year.
- Pension, provident fund, and severance payment should not be included because they are not received within one year.

15.6 Types of Workers to Use to Determine Whether Establishments or Industries Pay a Living Wage

To determine whether an establishment or industry pays a living wage, it is necessary to decide on the type or types of workers to use to measure prevailing wages, since establishments employ different types of workers each with its own range of wages. For example, garment factories have various types of production workers (e.g. machine operators, folders, cutters, and iron men), support staff (e.g. mechanics, cleaners, loaders, security guards, and drivers), and management. Within occupations there are various sub-categories. For example, in garment factories there might be several sub-categories of machine operators such as assistant machine operators, junior machine operators, machine operators, and senior machine operators. It would be possible to use the wages of (i) all workers, or (ii) all production workers, or (iii) certain type or types of workers, or (iv) workers with certain grades, or (v) occupations with the largest numbers of workers.

To determine if an establishment or industry pays a living wage, we recommend using:

- Occupations or grades with the largest numbers of production workers. The proportion of all workers in each occupation or grade should be indicated.
- Categories of workers should be large enough so that the selected categories include the majority of workers. Our recommendation is in keeping with the practice of the Fair Labor Association (FLA, 2016) with whom we collaborated, which collects compensation data for the four largest occupations in each establishment.

We do not recommend using wages of all workers in an establishment, because this would include management who have higher pay and apprentices who have lower pay. Nor do we recommend using wages of all production workers, because this would mix higher and lower paid activities and occupations.

NOTES

1. How paid public holidays, paid vacation days, and paid sick leave should be treated depends on how workers are paid and the type of contract they have. Pay for public holidays, sick days, and vacation days should be added to wages per month and per year when workers are employed on a daily basis, because they increase take home pay. Paid public holidays, vacation days and sick days should not be added to wages when they do

not affect take home pay per month or per year – which usually happens with monthly or yearly contracts.

2. We have found that workers receive a variety of cash allowances in living wage studies. For example, we found that cash allowances represented around 20% of wages for new hires on Kenya fresh cut flower farms. A survey of 68 enterprises covering 46,121 employees in Vietnam by the Vietnam General Confederation of Labor (2013) found that 95% of employees received an end of year cash bonus, 25% received cash meals allowance, 17% received cash housing allowance, and 25% received cash responsibility allowance. We found that factory workers in Vietnam also received cash bonuses for some of the following: Birthday, Children's Day, Company Day, Solar New Year Day, National Day, Victory Day, birth, marriage, and death in the family.
3. According to the Davis-Bacon Act of the Federal Government of the United States, 'fringe benefit examples are: life insurance, health insurance, pension, vacation, holidays, sick leave, other "bona fide" fringe benefits. However, payments required by federal, state or local law are **not** fringe benefit contributions. Such payments required to fund Social Security, unemployment compensation and workers' compensation programs, as required by law, do not count as fringe benefits' (United States Department of Labor, Wage and Hour Division, undated).

APPENDIX 15.1 VARIOUS FORMS OF REMUNERATION CLAIMED BY EMPLOYERS IN OUR EXPERIENCE AND WHETHER THEY SHOULD BE INCLUDED IN PREVAILING WAGE FOR COMPARISON TO A LIVING WAGE

Table 15A.1 Various forms of remuneration claimed by employers

Forms of remuneration	Whether to include in wages for comparison to a living wage
Cash wages, allowances, and bonuses	
Basic wage	Include.
Housing allowance	Include.
Transport allowance	Include.
Non-production bonuses paid once or several times during year	Include. Pro-rate to get monthly amount. Examples: 13th month, Eid allowances, birthday bonus, bonuses for holidays.
Retention bonus	Include. For industry use average amount per worker.
Allowance to visit 'home'	Include. For industry use average cost or value per worker when amount varies with distance and/or family size.
Attendance allowance	Include. For industry use average amount per worker; or adjust for % receiving.
Child allowance	Include. For industry use average amount per worker.
Production/incentive bonus	Include when earned during standard working hours at normal working pace. Exclude if need to work overtime to meet minimum target.
Overtime	Exclude. Not earned in normal work hours.
Night shift, weekend, and holiday pay premiums	Exclude. Not earned in normal working hours.

Table 15A.1 (continued)

Forms of remuneration	Whether to include in wages for comparison to a living wage
Cash bonus when profits are good	Exclude as uncertain, unless assured in advance such as when based on last year's business results and given to most workers.
Responsibility allowance/Technical skill allowance	Exclude. Few workers receive these and usually for only higher paid workers.
In kind benefits (limits set on amounts)	
Housing and utilities such as water or electricity for home	Include when decent. Deduct co-pay. Maximum 15% of wages. Exclude housing for seasonal workers as they still need year around housing.
Meals	Include. Deduct co-pay.
Food rations or food commodities given for free or sold at concession rates	Include. Deduct co-pay.
Transport to work and from work (and to town on weekends from agricultural estates)	Include when safe.
Child care/crèche	Include. For industry use average value over all workers.
School for workers' children	Include. For industry use average value over all workers.
Meals in crèche or school	Include if paid for by employer. For industry use average over all workers
Medical services not required by law and not related to work injuries and illnesses	Include. Need to determine cost per worker to employer.
Private medical insurance	Include. Deduct co-pay.
Medical expenses paid for treatment in other clinics and hospitals	Include. Need to determine cost per worker to employer.
Transport to hospital/other health services	Include when for other than work-related problems. Need to determine cost per worker to employer.

Medical services related to work injuries and illnesses	Exclude. Work-related.
Schools or hospitals on estate, in factory, or in industrial zone supported by government or Fairtrade	Exclude. Not paid for by employer and so no cost to employer.
Security guard for company housing	Exclude. Protects company property.
Christmas meal or food basket	Exclude. Small value and similar to charity.
Drinking water at work	Exclude. Work-related expense.
Right to collect firewood for free	Exclude. Difficult to value as takes worker or spouse time. No cost to employer.
Transport within workplace	Exclude. Work-related.
Educational assistance for children, scholarships, etc.	Exclude. Unless many workers' children receive this.
Land to build house on	Exclude. Land not owned by worker & cannot be sold.
Land to grow vegetables	Exclude. Difficult to value as takes worker or spouse time. Little or no cost to employer.
Animal husbandry facilities	Exclude. Difficult to value as takes worker or spouse time. Small cost to employer.
Recreation facilities and activities	Exclude. Benefits employer to improve worker morale. Often small cost. For company football team, only some men participate.
Flowers for weddings or funerals	Exclude. Infrequent and small value.
Condolence allowance for death of relative	Exclude. Infrequent and small value.
Fringe benefits and other benefits	
Paid time off for sickness or holidays	Exclude unless employed on daily basis.
Unpaid time off for sick leave, holidays, maternity leave	Exclude. Does not increase monthly pay.
Gratuity/severance pay	Exclude. Not received within year.
Funeral costs for worker who dies	Usually exclude. Not received within year. Can be included if considered as an insurance.
Support for night classes	Exclude. Does not affect living expenses or immediately add to wages.
HIV/AIDS or reproductive health classes	Exclude. Does not affect current wage.

Table 15A.1 (continued)

Forms of remuneration	Whether to include in wages for comparison to a living wage
Occupational health and safety programs	Exclude. Work-related.
Protective clothing, and work-related equipment and supplies	Exclude. Work-related.
Finish work at 1:30 so can do other work	Exclude. Similar to overtime.
Pension	Exclude. Does not increase current income.
Care for retirees	Exclude. Does not increase current income.
Loans and advances	Exclude. Does not increase current income.
Fairtrade premium or similar scheme	Exclude. Not paid by employer.
Community projects such as building schools or other facilities in community	Exclude. Not mainly for workers but for community. Not part of remuneration – it is not in return for work performed.
Job security	Exclude. Does not reduce living cost.
Visa or work permit	Exclude. Work-related.
Employers legally mandated contributions to Social Security or National Health Services	Exclude. Does not increase current income.

16. In kind benefits as partial payment of a living wage

Since in kind benefits can be an important component of remuneration, it is important to determine their monetary value. How to value in kind benefits is controversial. Workers, trade unions, and governments are concerned about potential abuse, even though they recognize that in kind benefits can be of personal value to workers. Employers think that in kind benefits should be considered as partial payment of wages as a matter of fairness – in part because in kind benefits are often an important business expense and in part because in kind benefits benefit workers.

Given the controversial backdrop and the importance of in kind benefits, an analysis of how in kind benefits are treated as partial payment of wages in national laws of 162 countries was undertaken by one of the authors (Anker and Anker, 2015). ILO Conventions and Recommendations were also reviewed. This report is, as far as we know, the most comprehensive analysis to date of in kind benefits as partial payment of wages. This chapter draws on that analysis to develop guidelines and principles on how to value in kind benefits as partial payment of a living wage that would be considered fair and reasonable by workers and employers.

Part I provides background information on what in kind benefits are, their history of abuse, and how national laws around the world and ILO Conventions and Recommendations treat in kind benefits as partial payment of wages. Part II discusses principles, approaches and recommended guidelines for valuing in kind benefits as partial payment of a living wage. This discussion draws on Part I as well as living wage studies conducted for the Global Living Wage Coalition. Part III provides examples.

PART I. BACKGROUND

16.1 What Are In Kind Benefits?

16.1.1 Definition of in kind benefits

According to the OECD glossary of statistical terms (2002):

> Payments in kind are goods and services furnished to employees free of charge or at markedly reduced cost that are clearly and primarily of benefit to the employee as consumers. They comprise food, drink, fuel and other payments in kind; and cost, other than capital cost, of workers' housing borne by employers (cost for employer owned dwellings, cost of dwellings not employer owned, other housing costs).

16.1.2 Why in kind benefits are considered as partial payment of living wage

In kind benefits reduce the cash wage that workers require for living expenses. When workers receive essential goods and services such as free meals, free housing, or free transport to work, their need for cash income to support a basic but decent living standard is reduced. This means that it is appropriate to include a fair and reasonable monetary value for in kind benefits when determining if an employer pays a living wage and a worker receives a living wage.

In kind benefits can be an important part of remuneration and of considerable value to workers (as well as a major expense for employers). For example, we estimated that the value of in kind benefits equaled approximately 25% of wages of newly hired workers for flower farms near Lake Naivasha, Kenya (Anker and Anker, 2014). In contrast, in kind benefits were found to be unimportant in factories in China (Wang et al., 2016) and Bangladesh (Khan et al., 2016).

16.1.3 Wide variety of in kind benefits

Workers receive a variety of in kind benefits around the world with the most important being food, housing, and transport. In kind benefits are especially important and prevalent in certain industries (e.g. agriculture and restaurants), occupations (e.g. domestics and servers), and countries. A list of common in kind benefits is provided in Section 16.6. See Appendix 15.1 and endnotes in Section 16.6 for an indication of some of the many types of in kind benefits mentioned by employers.

16.2 Historical Background of Abuse by Employers in Providing and Valuing In Kind Benefits

The history surrounding in kind benefits is associated with many examples of abuse. According to a report for the International Labor Conference (ILO, 2003, p. 52), 'Historically, the payment of wages in kind has led to abuses. The method of payment known as the "truck system", or barter, as practiced by employers who exploited the wretchedness of those workers, kept the workers in a state of dependency bordering on slavery.'

ILO reports prepared by Committees of Experts for discussion in International Labor Conferences are strewn with examples of concern about the use of in kind benefits as partial payment of minimum wages for well over half a century. In 1951, discussions for Convention 99, Minimum wage fixing machinery (Agriculture), stated 'The Workers' group expressed its intention of establishing a provision prohibiting this [in kind] form of payment of minimum wage' (ILO, 1992, p. 126). This prohibition was not included in the Convention. In 1967, 'When this matter was discussed by the Meeting of Experts in 1967, the view was expressed that the ideal situation would be to prohibit the partial payment of minimum wages in kind' (ILO, 1992, p. 126). Discussions in 1971 prior to adoption of Convention 131, Minimum Wage Fixing, indicated that, 'Once again during the Conference this point [prohibiting in kind benefits as partial payment of minimum wages] was the subject of long discussions' (ILO, 1992, p. 126).

> The question of whether to include a provision in Convention No. 131 [1971] regarding the partial payment of the minimum wage in kind was submitted to member States in the questionnaire prepared by the Office for the first Conference discussion. It emerged from the responses that the ratification of a new Convention would run into difficulties if it did not include a provision authorizing the partial payment of minimum wages in kind. However, many governments felt that this practice, while it might be necessary in certain circumstances, should be discouraged. (ILO, 2014, p. 26)

16.2.1 Consensus of cautious acceptance of in kind benefits with caveats

The general consensus that has emerged over the years from discussions between ILO's tripartite stakeholders is that in kind benefits are a fact of life and an accepted form of wage payment around the world. At the same time, there is a consensus that it is important to set restrictions and be cautious on how in kind benefits are treated as partial payment of minimum wages in order to reduce and hopefully avoid abuse. As a 2014 ILO Committee of Experts report strongly suggested by putting the following quote in bold:

> Encourage the tripartite constituents to endeavor to limit the [in kind] items included in the minimum wage to what appears to them strictly necessary in view of the situation in the country. The Committee therefore considers that caution is required in taking into account benefits in kind. (ILO, 2014, p. 27)

16.3 Practices in National Laws

16.3.1 National laws allow in kind benefits as partial payment of wages in almost all countries

Table 16.1 presents a summary of how in kind benefits are treated in the national laws of 162 countries (Anker and Anker, 2015). It indicates that almost all countries in the world allow in kind benefits as partial payment of wages.

16.3.2 National laws often restrict when in kind benefits can be partial payment of wages

We found that only around 10% of countries do not allow in kind benefits as partial payment of wages. However, most countries place restrictions on when in kind benefits can be considered as partial payment of wages. The following restrictions were found in our review of national laws (Table 16.1).

- **Allowed only when worker agrees**
  More than 40% of countries allow wages to be reduced for in kind benefits only when workers agree to this (and usually only when workers agree in writing or in a CBA). At least 70% of European countries require agreement from workers before in kind benefits can be considered as partial payment of their wages. We also found a consensus for the federal government and all five states in the United States that we looked at – employee agreement is required before an in kind benefit can be considered as partial payment of wages.[1]

- **Allowed only in special circumstances**
  At least 7% of countries allow in kind benefits as partial payment of wages only when workers are transferred away from home or when work is in a remote area. This restriction occurs mainly in Arab States and Africa (that includes Egypt and Libya).

- **Allowed only in certain occupations, industries and locations**
  At least 12% of countries allow in kind benefits as partial payment of wages only in occupations, industries and locations where it is customary.

- **Not allowed as partial payment of minimum wage**
  At least 12% of countries do not allow in kind benefits to reduce cash wage received to less than minimum wage.

Table 16.1 Summary of how in kind benefits are treated as partial payment of wages, 162 countries

Can in kind benefits be considered as partial payment of wages?	Africa (N=50)	Arab States (N=10)	Americas (N=34)	Asia (N=28)	Europe (N=40)	Total (N=162)
No (no apparent qualifiers)	8%	30%	3%	29%	3%	10%
Yes (but only for workers in special situations such as transfer of workplace or work in remote area)	18%	20%	3%	0%	0%	7%
Yes (but only when customary in an occupation or industry such as agriculture, domestic, and restaurant)[a, b]	16%	0%	15%	11%	10%	12%
Yes (only when employee agrees)[c]	18%	0%	15%	21%	25%	19%
Yes (only when written agreement or CBA)	10%	10%	18%	21%	45%	22%
Yes (but cannot reduce cash wage to less than cash minimum wage)	4%	10%	18%	7%	20%	12%
Yes (no apparent qualifiers)[c, d]	34%	30%	32%	14%	15%	25%

Notes: Column totals can sum to more than 100% because countries can be in more than one category.

[a] Four countries that allow in kind benefits as partial payment of wages in government decrees or regulations were placed in this category because they were generally concerned with industries and occupations where in kind benefits are customary (Benin, Mali, Myanmar, and Netherlands).

[b] Four countries that allow in kind benefits as partial payment of wages in only certain occupations or industries without indicating if this is customary were included in this category (El Salvador, domestics; Honduras, rural; Nicaragua, agriculture and domestics; Serbia, domestics).

[c] Two countries that allowed in kind benefits as partial payment of wages but excluded a specific industry or occupation were included in this category (Morocco, agriculture; Bolivia, domestics).

[d] Three countries allow deductions for in kind benefits for only housing. They are included in yes (no apparent qualifiers) (Bahrein, the United Kingdom) and yes employee agreement required (Bangladesh).

Table 16.1 (continued)

[e] When both agreement and written agreement/CBA are indicated for a country, this country is included in yes when the employee agrees (Djibouti, Eritrea, Ethiopia, Zambia, Romania).

Sources: Anker and Anker (2015).

16.3.3 National laws often limit amount that can be deducted from pay for in kind benefits

We found that at least 44 countries (at least 30% of countries) limit the amount or percentage of pay that can be deducted for in kind benefits. Limits are obviously set to avoid possible abuse and provide workers with sufficient agency over how they spend their earnings. The average (mean) maximum percentage of wages that can be paid in kind is 35.5% in these 44 countries, with a median of 30% (Table 16.2). Common percentages are 20%, 25%, 30%, and 50%. This percentage was lower than 20% in only two countries and higher than 50% in only two countries.

In addition, a number of other countries limit the amount of in kind benefits that can be considered as partial payment of wages in other ways. Statutes in at least 10 countries set specific values allowed for different in kind benefits. At least 12% of countries do not allow cash wage received to fall below minimum wage.

16.3.4 National laws sometimes require in kind benefits to meet minimum standards

Some countries require food and housing in kind benefits to meet minimum standards. Cameroon and Niger require lodging to correspond with an employee's family situation. Cameroon, Niger and Benin specify that the quality of lodging must be 'sufficient and decent' or 'adequate and decent.' Egypt specifies that food and housing be 'suitable,' and Yemen requires housing and food to be 'adequate.' Comoros requires housing to be 'hygienic.'

To be counted as partial payment of wages, in kind housing is required to meet minimum standards in South Africa, Mali and New York State. Housing in Mali must have 'durable structure; roof and exterior walls; windows for adequate ventilation and light; lit at night as customary in region; equipped kitchen; habitable condition; 14 cubic meters air space; hygienic toilet and 20 liters of water per day per person with potable drinking water'.[2] Agricultural housing in South Africa must have 'durable waterproof roof; glass windows that open; electricity if available on farm; safe water; flush or pit toilet; at least 30 square meters of space'.[3] Lodging

Table 16.2 Maximum percentage allowed for in kind benefits as partial payment of wage, 44 countries with an identified maximum percentage (also see notes to table for 10 additional countries that restrict amount by setting specific values for in kind benefits)

Country	Maximum % allowed	Notes
Africa		
Angola	50%	Cannot exceed market value. Food, clothing & accommodation mentioned.
Botswana	40%	
Cape Verde	50%	
Chad	38% (see comment)	2 MW hours for daily rations & 1 MW hour for meal. Implies 3/8 of MW for one meal & rations for 8-hour workday.
Equatorial Guinea	50%	
Eritrea	20%	
Guinea Bissau	50%	
Mali	38% (see comment)	2.5 MW hours for food & 0.5 MW hour for lodging. Implies 3/8 of MW for 8-hour workday.
Mozambique	25%	
Sao Tome and Principe	50%	
Senegal	38% (see comment)	2 MW hours for daily rations & 1 MW hour per meal. Implies 3/8 for one meal & rations for 8-hour workday.
South Africa	20% (agriculture)	10% for food; 10% for accommodation. For agricultural workers.
Tanzania	68% (domestics)	For domestic workers
Average (N=13)	*41% (40% median)*	
Arab States		
Bahrein	25%	For housing. Only housing allowed.
Average (N=1)	*25%*	

Table 16.2 (continued)

Country	Maximum % allowed	Notes
Americas		
Argentina	20%	
Brazil	70% (of MW)	Percentage overstated for most employees since based on minimum wage
Canada (Manitoba)	20% (see comment)	Meal valued at $1; lodging valued at $7 per week. 20% assumes lodging & 1 meal per day. MW was C$10 then.
Chile	50%	
Colombia	30% (of MW)	Food, clothing and lodging mentioned for all workers. Fuel, crops also mentioned for agricultural workers.
Costa Rica	33%	Food, clothing and housing mentioned
Dominican Republic	50%	
Ecuador	25%	
Guatemala	30%	Not more than cost to employer. Food mentioned.
Honduras	30%	Not more than cost to employer. Food & housing mentioned.
Mexico	50% (domestics)	
Nicaragua	50%	
Panama	20%	
Paraguay	30%	Also 60% for domestics
Average (N=14)	36% *(30% median)*	
Asia		
Cambodia	20% (see comment)	Varies with distance from MW: 0% if MW or less; 20% for 1–3 MW; 30% for 3–10 MW; 50% for >10 MW. Health care not allowed.
Fiji	15%	5% for housing; 5% for food; 15% for board, fuel, light and accommodation.
Indonesia	25%	

Table 16.2 (continued)

Country	Maximum % allowed	Notes
New Zealand	20%	15% board; 5% lodging. Not more than cost to employer.
Papua New Guinea	50%	
Average (N=5)	*26% (20% median)*	
Europe		
Azerbaijan	50%	
Belgium	40%	
Greece	10-15%	
Hungary	20%	
Netherlands	30% (domestics)	
Portugal	50%	Not more than market value
Romania	30%	
Serbia	50% (domestics)	
Spain	30%	
Russian Federation	20%	
Ukraine	30%	
Average (N=11)	*33% (30% median)*	
World (N=44)	*35.5% mean* *30.0% median*	Only 2 countries <20% Only 2 countries >50% (and were for domestics; or relative to minimum wage)

Notes: MW indicates minimum wage.
In addition, 16 countries (approximately 10% of countries for which we had information) do not allow in kind benefits to reduce wage received in cash to below MW. This has the effect of limiting the amount wages paid in in kind benefits for many workers.
In addition, specific monetary values for in kind benefits were indicated in statutes in some countries (e.g. Burkina Faso, Comoros, Mali, Cameroon, Canada (Manitoba), United States (California, Connecticut, New York), Pakistan, Seychelles, Netherlands, United Kingdom). Setting specific amounts for different in kind benefits limits the total value of in kind benefits. For example, in Connecticut, full meals were valued at $0.85 and light meals are valued at $0.55; in California, breakfast was valued at $3.26, lunch at $4.47, and dinner at $6.01.

Source: Anker and Anker (2015).

in New York 'must meet generally accepted standards for protection against fire, and all structural, sanitation and similar standards in State or local laws, codes, regulations and ordinances'.[4]

For meals/food provided as an in kind benefit, Comoros sets types and amounts of food required. Libya requires that food consist of three meals a day in order to qualify for in kind benefit status. Mali and some states in the United States (e.g. Connecticut and New York) require that meals include a food item from three or four different food groups.

16.3.5 National laws use a variety of methods to determine monetary value of in kind benefits as partial payment of wages

There is no consensus on the appropriate method to use to value in kind benefits as partial payment of wages. Countries use a variety of methods and approaches. Table 16.3 indicates different methods we identified in national laws and regulations in our global review of national laws.

The most common approach relies on the general principle of 'fair and reasonable value' or similar words – which is the terminology in ILO wages conventions. This approach is used in at least Botswana, Gambia, Guinea, Swaziland, Tanzania, Uganda, Zimbabwe, Belize, Granada, the United States (federal law), Iran, Japan, Philippines, Vanuatu, and Cyprus. While 'fair and reasonable' is an excellent guiding principle, it is too vague on its own to be used in practice to determine monetary values for in kind benefits.

We found three valuation methods in national laws and codes that embody the principle of fair and reasonable.

- **Monetary amounts specified**
  At least 10 countries indicate specific monetary amounts allowed in their labor laws – Burkina Faso, Comoros, Mali, Cameroon, Canada (Manitoba), the United States (California, Connecticut, and New York), Pakistan, Seychelles, Netherlands, and the United Kingdom. In addition, three African countries express monetary amounts for meals, food rations, and lodging in terms of the hourly minimum wage rate (Chad, Mali, and Senegal).[5] Cambodia allows the percentage limit for in kind benefits to increase along with a worker's wage. It is 0% at or below the minimum wage, 20% for 1–3 times minimum wage, 30% for 3–10 times minimum wage, and 50% for more than 10 times minimum wage. ILO Convention 189 (ILO, 2011) mentions the possibility of valuing in kind benefits at 'prices fixed by public authorities'.

- **Market rates**
  At least 10 countries use market rates to value in kind benefits in their laws. This includes Angola, Mozambique, Afghanistan, Fiji,

Table 16.3 Valuation methods used in national laws and regulations to determine monetary value of in kind benefits

Valuation method	Number of countries identified	Countries
Amount set in law	10	Burkina Faso, Comoros, Mali, Cameroon, Canada (Manitoba), United States (California, Connecticut, New York), Pakistan, Seychelles, Netherlands, United Kingdom
At or below market rate	10	Angola, Mozambique, Afghanistan, Fiji, India, Czech Republic, Portugal, Israel, Slovakia, United States (Maryland)
At or below cost to employer	5	Seychelles, Guatemala, Honduras, New Zealand, Ukraine
Amount equal to x hours at minimum wage rate	3	Chad, Mali, Senegal
Amount increases with wage	1	Cambodia
As indicated by employer	1	Luxembourg
Set by judge when parties do not agree	1	Ecuador
Set by experts	1	Colombia
Fair and reasonable value	15	Botswana, Gambia, Guinea, Swaziland, Tanzania, Uganda, Zimbabwe, Belize, Granada, United States, Iran, Japan, Philippines, Vanuatu, Cyprus
ILO Conventions		
'Fair and reasonable'		ILO Convention 95 (Protection of Wages, 1957) and several other ILO Conventions
'Objective criteria such as market value, cost price, or prices fixed by public authorities, as appropriate'		ILO Convention 189 (Domestic Workers, 2011) Article 12 (2) (b)

Sources: Anker and Anker (2015) and ILO Conventions 95 and 189.

India, Czech Republic, Israel, Portugal, Slovakia, and United States (Maryland). ILO Convention 189 (ILO, 2011) mentions the possibility of valuing in kind benefits at 'market value'.

- **Value of in kind benefits cannot exceed cost to employer**
  This is used in at least five countries to prevent employers from profiting when providing in kind benefits. This includes Seychelles, Guatemala, Honduras, New Zealand, and Ukraine. ILO Convention 189 (ILO, 2011) mentions the possibility of valuing in kind benefits at 'cost price'.

- **Other methods**
  Colombia requires unspecified experts to value in kind benefits. Luxembourg uses values indicated by the employer. Ecuador uses values set by a judge when parties do not agree.

16.3.6 Employers in United States required to keep records and inform workers on how much is deducted from pay for in kind benefits

Although we did not investigate this issue in our global legal review of national labor laws from 162 countries, we did look at this for five states and the Federal Government of the United States. We found that employers in all five states (New York, Texas, California, Connecticut and Maryland) are required to keep records of their costs for in kind benefits and provide workers with statements of how much they deducted from their pay for in kind benefits. This transparency provides workers with an opportunity to understand and challenge deductions that they feel are unfair.

16.4 ILO Conventions and Recommendations and In Kind Benefits

A number of ILO Conventions and Recommendations address issues related to in kind payment of wages.[6] Their main features are described below.

16.4.1 Three main conditions for authorizing in kind benefits as partial payment of wages

Three main conditions are mentioned for authorizing in kind benefits as partial payment of wages in ILO Conventions and Recommendations. These are included in the ILO Protection of Wages Convention 95 (1949) Article 4 (1)[7] and repeated in other ILO Conventions and Recommendations. In kind benefits need to be:

- Customary or desirable for industry or occupation.
- Appropriate for personal use and benefit of workers.
- Monetary value attributed is fair and reasonable.

16.4.2 Monetary value of in kind benefits should be limited (one ILO Convention and one ILO Recommendation)

ILO Convention 189 (Domestic Workers) Article 12(2) states that the monetary value of in kind benefits should be limited: 'May provide for the payment of a limited proportion of the remuneration of domestic workers in the form of payments in kind.' ILO Recommendation 201 (Domestic Workers) Article 14 elaborates further:

> When provision is made for the payment in kind of a limited proportion of remuneration, Members should consider: (a) establishing an overall limit on the proportion of the remuneration that may be paid in kind so as not to diminish unduly the remuneration necessary for the maintenance of domestic workers and their families.

16.4.3 Minimum standards for in kind benefits required (one ILO Convention and one ILO Recommendation)

According to Plantations Convention 110 (ILO, 1958) Article 27(3) and Social Policy (Basic Aims and Standards) Convention 117 (ILO, 1962): 'Where food, housing, clothing and other essential supplies and services form part of remuneration, all practicable steps should be taken to ensure that they are adequate and their cash value properly assessed.' Article 86(2) provides detailed specifications for adequate housing: 'Minimum standards shall include specifications concerning – (a) the construction materials to be used; (b) the minimum size of accommodation, its layout, ventilation, and floor and air space; (c) verandah space, cooking, washing, storage, water supply and sanitary facilities.' Workers Housing Recommendation 115 (ILO, 1961) Articles 7 and 8 provide detailed specifications for housing standards. The Tripartite Declaration of Principles Concerning Multinational Enterprises and Social Policy (ILO, 2006) Article 34 states that 'Where they [multinational enterprises] provided workers with basic amenities such as housing, medical care or food, these amenities should be of a good standard.'

16.4.4 Employers should be required to inform workers when in kind benefits are deducted from pay (several ILO Conventions)

Several ILO Conventions indicate that workers should be informed of all deductions from pay including for in kind benefits. For example, ILO Convention 95 (Protection of Wages, ILO, 1949) Article 8(2) indicates that 'Workers shall be informed, in the manner deemed most appropriate by the competent authority, of the conditions under which and the extent to which such deductions may be made.'

16.4.5 Worker agreement required (one ILO Convention)
Domestics Workers Convention 189 (ILO, 2011) Article 12(2) states that measures should be 'taken to ensure such payments in kind are agreed to by workers'.

PART II. PRINCIPLES AND APPROACH USED FOR VALUING IN KIND BENEFITS AS PARTIAL PAYMENT OF A LIVING WAGE

In this section, the general approach and principles to be used for valuing in kind benefits as partial payment of living wage are discussed and guidelines are provided. These principles and guidelines are based in large part on our review of labor laws in 162 countries and ILO Conventions and Recommendations (see above and Anker and Anker, 2015). They are also based on general principles of a living wage.

16.5 General Approach and Principles

The approach we use to estimate the value of in kind benefits as partial payment of living wage has three steps.

- STEP 1: Decide whether an in kind benefit should be considered as partial payment of a living wage.
- STEP 2: Estimate monetary value for each acceptable in kind benefit.
- STEP 3: Ensure that the total estimated monetary value for all in kind benefits is less than maximum percentage(s) limit(s) allowed for in kind benefits.

16.6 STEP 1: Guidelines for Determining which In Kind Benefits to Consider as Partial Payment of a Living Wage

To be considered as partial payment of a living wage, in kind benefits need to meet the following criteria.

- **Considered of benefit and value to workers or their families and for personal use**
  This requirement is included in national laws in many countries as well as in ILO Conventions and Recommendations. In kind benefits

that meet this criterion reduce the cash income workers require to afford a decent standard of living. This excludes clothing and equipment for work and other in kind benefits that are not for personal use.

- **Meets minimum standard**
  This requirement is included to ensure that provision of in kind benefits is consistent with the decency concept of a living wage. This criterion is included in laws in a number of countries as well as in the ILO Plantations Convention. This implies, for example, that housing would need to meet a minimum healthy housing standard (see chapters on housing) and that transportation would need to be safe. This could also imply that meals should be reasonably nutritious and so generally include at least three food groups: (1) food high in carbohydrates such as rice, wheat, maize, potato, cassava, or plantains; (2) protein-rich food such as beans, pulses, meats, fish, or dairy; and (3) fruits or vegetables. Despite this, we feel that researchers need to be flexible with regard to meals and housing as even poorly balanced meals, or housing that is not quite up to the local healthy housing standard can be valuable to workers.[8]

- **Customary for an industry when estimating typical prevailing wages in an industry**
  This requirement is included in national laws in many countries as well as in ILO Conventions. It limits the types of in kind benefits that can be considered as partial payment of wages for an industry. This is important protection for workers.

- **Received within one year**
  In kind benefits should be received within a year so as to be available for ongoing living expenses.

- **Guaranteed – not at discretion of employer**
  In kind benefits should not be at the discretion or whim of the employer. Otherwise, workers would not be able to count on receiving the benefit.

- **Included on following allowed list of common and desirable in kind benefits**
  A restricted list of common in kind benefits for the personal use of workers and their families is used in our methodology. Using this restricted list is practical, since it simplifies the work of researchers

and auditors by not requiring them to look at all in kind benefits claimed by employers and so possibly spend considerable time valuing dubious and/or relatively inconsequential in kind benefits in terms of monetary value. This approach also helps to ensure that valuing in kind benefits as partial payment of living wage is not abused by employers who might inappropriately claim various in kind benefits.[9] At the same time, the list of allowed in kind benefits includes the most important in kind benefits found around the world and the vast majority of the value of in kind benefits. This means that researchers and auditors would only need to value in kind benefits as partial payment of wages that are on the allowed list unless a *very good case* can be made for including other in kind benefits as partial payment of living wage.

16.6.1 List of acceptable in kind benefits as partial payment of living wage

a. Meals at work
b. Food rations or food commodities given for free or sold at concession rates
c. Housing (including electricity, water, and fuel)
d. Transport to and from work (and to town on weekends from agricultural estates)
e. Child care
f. School for children of workers
g. Medical clinic and medical care not required by law and not for work-related matters
h. Medical insurance not required by law

16.6.2 List of common in kind benefits that should not be considered as partial payment of a living wage (see Appendix 15.1 and endnotes for other in kind benefits sometimes claimed by employers)

a. Visas or work permits for migrant workers
b. Clothing, equipment, and supplies for work
c. Dormitories or shared housing for seasonal workers[10]
d. Drinking water provided to workers at work
e. Land for kitchen garden
f. Charitable contributions to the community that do not go exclusively to workers
g. Employers' contributions to Social Security or National Health Service required by law

h. Time off work for vacation, sick leave, maternity leave, or public holiday

16.7 STEP 2: Guidelines for Determining Fair and Reasonable Value for In Kind Benefits

The following guidelines are used to estimate the value of acceptable in kind benefits as partial payment of a living wage. They are intended to be fair and reasonable to both workers and employers. They are also intended to be cautious in how in kind benefits are valued – in keeping with the views and experiences worldwide of workers, employers and governments.

- **Value of an in kind benefit should not exceed its cost to employer.** This criterion prevents employers from 'profiting' on providing in kind benefits. This criterion – which is included in a number of national laws (see Table 16.3) – would be considered fair and reasonable by workers and is especially important in situations where workers have not agreed in writing or CBA to any particular valuation. Most employers would also consider this criterion fair and reasonable. After all, employers are in the business of producing shirts or bananas or whatever, and not in the business of providing lunches, transport, etc. to workers. Therefore, they would not expect to profit from the provision of in kind benefits. It also should not be forgotten that most in kind benefits help employers to run their businesses better. For example, providing a nutritious free lunch ensures that workers have sufficient nutrition to perform their work at a high level and do not faint on the job; it ensures that workers are on time for work in the afternoon; and it reduces security risks by reducing the number of times workers enter and exit the workplace. Providing free transport to a worker may be the only way to ensure a sufficient supply of workers when establishments are located in industrial zones on the outskirts of a city. Free transport to work ensures that workers are on time to work, which is especially important in locations where public transport is unreliable. In kind benefits are therefore often very advantageous to employers. As they help employers to run their business better, most employers would be unwilling to offer their workers the option of the equivalent amount in cash in place of the in kind benefits they provide. When employers are asked to indicate how much various in kind benefits cost them, they should also indicate how they estimated their costs to make sure that their values reasonably reflect their cost to employers. For example, the cost of a lunch to an employer might be the sum of the amounts they pay for food, kitchen staff and cooking fuel. Or, the cost of a lunch to the employer might be the amount they pay a contractor to provide lunch. Cost of transport for a worker might be the sum of the costs for petrol, driver, and depreciation, maintenance and repair of vehicle (provided that vehicle and driver are used exclusively for transport of workers to and from work; if not, a reasonable proportion of these costs should be used). Or, cost used for transport might be the cost of an outside transit company used by the establishment. Cost of housing might consist of costs for repairs and maintenance, plus depreciation and utilities. The total cost to the employer of in kind benefits should be divided by the number of employees to get the cost per employee. The reason why it is important to ask employers to indicate how they estimated their costs is to enable researchers to evaluate how realistic these estimated costs are, since in our experience many employers do not have a good idea of their costs and some exaggerate costs. Depending on responses from employers, researchers may need to make their own estimate of the cost of in kind benefits to employers, especially for important in kind benefits such as meals, housing, and transport.

- **Value of an in kind benefit should not exceed its replacement cost to workers if they purchased it on the market**. This criterion is included in a number of national laws (see Table 16.3), although different words are used to express this such as: 'market price', 'market value', 'market rate', 'fair market price', 'ordinary market value', 'fair price offered for sale', 'prevailing market rate', 'lowest price at which employer would sell items or provisions at retail to the public', and 'regional prices'. All of these phrases refer to what in kind benefits cost in the market place with an emphasis on this being 'fair', or 'ordinary.' This criterion would be considered fair and reasonable by workers and employers.
- **Value of free meal should not exceed cost of replacing equivalent meal prepared at home**. This is a criterion specific to the valuation of free meals. The reason for including this criterion is that the most relevant replacement cost of free meals to most workers is the cost of meals prepared at home that would be brought to work and not the cost of meals sold in the market.[11] Note that the cost of a meal prepared at home will almost always be lower than the market price and employer cost, because meals prepared at home do not include labor costs or various overhead costs. In addition, employers sometimes provide meals that are more expensive (even at market price or at cost) than workers can afford or would choose on a daily basis. An Ethiopian farm, for example, indicated to Ergon (2012) that the free

lunch they provide on workdays was worth around 20% of a typical wage. If the value of such meals were considered as partial payment of wages, the cash wage received by workers would not even be enough to buy sufficient nutritious food for a worker's family.

- **Value of in kind benefit cannot be lower than an alternative cash allowance option offered to workers when such an option is available.** Some CBAs and companies offer workers a choice between a cash allowance and a free good or service. For example, workers in the latest Kenya flower farm CBA are given a cash housing allowance when they do not have free on-farm housing. In such a situation, it is fair to consider the value of free housing to be worth at a minimum the value of the housing cash allowance option.
- **When an in kind benefit is not free**, such as a subsidized lunch or medical care or housing cost, for which workers have a co-pay, the cost to workers needs to be subtracted, thereby reducing the value of the in kind benefit to workers.

In summary, in our methodology, the value of acceptable in kind benefits should be estimated in several different ways. The researcher would then need to choose one of these values taking into consideration the various guidelines and points indicated above. Value used should usually be the lowest of the valuations (cost to employer, market replacement value), and subject to consideration of any co-payment by workers and maximum limit restriction (see Section 16.8).

16.8 STEP 3: Rules for Maximum Limit(s) for Value of In Kind Benefits

It is important from the point of view of human rights, that workers have self-determination in how to use their earnings. Also, many national laws place a maximum limit on the value of in kind benefits (see discussion on this in Part I). With this as background, the following maximum limits are used for in kind benefits as partial payment of living wage.

- **Maximum value of 30% of wage for all acceptable in kind benefits allowed.** 30% is the median limit for all in kind benefits as partial payment of wages found for 44 countries from around the world in our global legal review (Table 16.2). Thirty percent is high enough to amply 'reward' employers who provide decent quality in kind benefits while allowing workers agency and self-determination over how they spend most of their earnings.
- **Maximum limit of 15% of wage allowed for housing and 10% for any other in kind benefits such as food or transport.** Setting maximum

allowed percentages for individual in kind benefits is common in national law to help prevent possible abuse.

- **Exception of 50% limit allowed in special situations**. We feel that it is appropriate to include the possibility of a 50% maximum limit in situations where employers are obliged to provide workers and their families with all or almost all basic needs by law or by circumstances (e.g. remote location). Laws in a number of countries use a 50% maximum limit for in kind benefits (see Table 16.2).
- **Maximum value for all in kind benefits as partial payment of wage should not bring cash wage below minimum wage when this restriction is stipulated in law**. In locations where laws do not allow in kind benefits to reduce cash wage below minimum wage, this restriction should be honored. These countries include at least Argentina, Chile, Panama, Canada (Manitoba), Mexico in the Americas; Armenia, Czech Republic, Israel, Malta, Romania, San Marino, Slovakia, and Spain in the European region of ILO; and Iran, Cambodia, China, Mauritius, Seychelles, and Tunisia in Africa and Asia. After researchers have estimated values for each in kind benefit, it is necessary to check that the total for all in kind benefits does not exceed the 30% allowed.
- **Value of an in kind benefit should not exceed amount included in living wage for the item**. The reason for this criterion is that it is possible for the value of an in kind benefit based on the above guidelines to exceed the amount included for this item in NFNH costs. If this value were used uncritically, it would mean that the cash living wage (i.e. living wage minus value of in kind benefits) would not be sufficient and this is reflected in expenditure statistics. This situation is most likely to occur when a free in kind benefit is so common in a location that families in that location necessarily do not spend much on this item. Free transport to work is an example of this in locations where most workers commute to work on a company bus or walk.[12] For example, if a living wage was \$100 with \$10 included in living costs for transport and the estimated value of free transport to work of \$20 was used as partial payment of the living wage, the resulting cash living wage of \$80 would not be sufficient to support a decent living standard, because more would be taken out of the wage for transport than was allotted to transport in the living wage estimate.

16.9 Difference between How to Value In Kind Benefits for Discussion with an Industry Value Chain and for Auditing Establishments

It is necessary to distinguish between the value of in kind benefits provided by typical establishments in an industry used for discussions about an industry value chain and the value of in kind benefits for audits of particular establishments to determine if they pay a living wage. Since each establishment may provide different in kind benefits, this means that each establishment has its own monetary value for in kind benefits. This also means that estimating the value of in kind benefits for an industry is only possible for expositional purposes using typical values for the industry. For example, in an industry where most establishments provide free lunch and free transport but nothing else and these are worth around 20% of basic pay, the prevailing wage could be said to be 1.2 times basic pay for expositional purposes. This estimate of prevailing wage for the industry could then be compared with the living wage to determine the typical gap between living wage and prevailing wages in the industry. Knowledge of the typical gap in an industry is important for discussions with employers, unions, government, standard setting organizations, and the value chain about wages and the possible need to develop an action plan to increase wages.

When auditing a particular establishment to see whether it pays a living wage, however, it is not appropriate to use the typical value of in kind benefits in an industry. Rather, it is necessary to determine the monetary value of in kind benefits provided by each establishment being audited to determine whether or not it is paying a living wage.

The overall approach used to determine the value of in kind benefits for an industry or an establishment is the same. The only difference is that average values of typical in kind benefits are estimated for an industry whereas values of the in kind benefits actually provided by the establishment are determined for auditing.

PART III. EXAMPLE OF ESTIMATING THE VALUE OF MULTIPLE IN KIND BENEFITS

A hypothetical example is provided in Table 16.4 to illustrate how in kind benefits should be valued as partial payment of wages for comparison to a living wage. In this example, a range of in kind benefits is provided for illustrative purposes. The cost to the employer and market replacement value are shown for each benefit in Table 16.4 (in a living wage study these values would need to be determined). The base wage plus allowed cash

Table 16.4 Hypothetic example of in kind benefits and their value for estimating prevailing wage (table is based on the assumption that basic wage + cash allowances + cash bonuses = $200)

In kind benefit	Whether allowed as partial payment of wages for comparison to living wage	Cost to employer	Cost in market or replacement cost	Value to use to calculate wages for comparison with living wage pending check on maximum % allowed	Maximum amount allowed pma	Amount used (minimum of (5) and (6))
(1)	(2)	(3)	(4)	(5)	(6)	(7)
Lunch (24 meals pm)	Yes	$0.90 per meal	$0.70 per meal outside. $0.50 per home meal	$12 pm (24 meals at $0.50 replacement cost)	$25.4 pm ($200 × 12.7%)	$12 pm
House (and utilities) for worker & family	Yes, if decent	$50 pm	$55 pm	$50 pm (cost to employer)	$39 pm ($200 × 19.5%)	$39 pm
Transport to work	Yes, if safe	$10 pm	$15 pm	$10 pm (cost to employer)	$25.4 pm ($200 × 12.7%)	$10 pm
Food sold at concession prices	Yes	$20 pm (worker pays $14). Therefore, value $6 pm	$22 pm	$6 pm ($20 cost to employer less $14 worker co-pay)	$25.4 pm ($200 × 12.7%)	$6 pm

School for workers' children	Yes	$36 py ($3 pm) per student.2/3 of workers have one child in school. Therefore $2 pm per worker.	$54 py ($4.50 pm) per student.2/3 of workers have one child in school. Therefore $3 pm per worker.	$2 pm per worker (cost to establishment)	$25.4 pm ($200 × 12.7%)	$2 pm
Recreational facilities	No	$2 pm	$2 pm	0	0	0
Christmas basket	No	$5 py	$4 py	0	0	0
Land to grow food	No	$2 py	$5 py	0	0	0
Private medical insurance	Yes	$6 pm (worker pays $3 pm)	$6 pm	$3 pm ($6 cost to employer less $3 worker co-pay)	$25.4 pm ($200 × 12.7%)	$3 pm
Clinic for work-related problems	No	$3 pm	$3 pm	0	0	0
Protective clothing & equipment	No	$20 pm	$20 pm	0	0	0
Maximum total allowed						$85.8 pm (42.9% of cash wage)
Total used						$72 pm (OK as 36% of cash wage)

Note: [a] When there is more than one in kind benefit, 12.7% of cash wage is the maximum amount allowed for each benefit, except that 19.5% of cash wage is the maximum allowed for housing. pm indicates per month; py indicates per year.

allowances and cash bonuses is assumed to be $200 per month in this example.

The first step is to consider whether each in kind benefit should be included in wages for comparison with a living wage. In this example, Christmas basket, land to grow food, clinic for work-related problems, and protective clothing and equipment are excluded and therefore valued at zero (column 5). The cost of protective clothing to the employer is set relatively high in this example to show that even when a work-related benefit such as protective clothing has a high cost and value, it should be excluded because it is not for personal use.

The second step is to estimate the value of each in kind benefit in several ways – its cost to the employer, its market cost, and its replacement cost to the worker. These values are shown in columns 3 and 4. In estimating these values, the following should be kept in mind:

1. All values should be for the same time period. For example, the value of school was converted from annual cost to monthly cost to be consistent with the rest of the table.
2. Worker co-payments should be deducted from values as shown in this example for food sold at concession prices and private medical insurance.
3. For benefits that do not affect all workers, such as school and transport – the average value over all workers should be used. Thus the example shows that if school costs the employer $3 per student per month, and 2/3 of workers have one child in school, the cost of this benefit to the employer is $2 per worker per month.

The lowest of these values for each in kind benefit in columns 3 and 4 should be selected at this point and indicated in column 5.

The third step is to estimate the maximum value allowed for each in kind benefit and the maximum value allowed for all in kind benefits together based on the rules indicated in Section 16.8 – 15% of wage for housing, 10% for each other benefit, and 30% in total for all in kind benefits (column 6). Estimating maximum value for each in kind benefit is not as simple as it might seem because rules on maximum percentage allowed refer to the total wage received, which includes the value of in kind benefits. For example, if the wage was $100 and it consisted of $70 cash and $30 in kind benefits, in kind benefits would represent 30% of the total wage and 42.9% of the cash wage. Most national laws indicate the percentage of a total wage that can be deducted for in kind benefits and so start from total wage and not cash wage, which is where we start. This means that 11.1% (1/.90−1) of cash wage is the maximum allowed when there is only one in kind benefit and 17.6% (1/.85−1) is allowed for housing when housing is the only in kind benefit. When there are two or more acceptable in kind benefits, an iterative process is needed where the total value of all in kind benefits is compared to the 42.9% (1/.7−1) maximum of cash wages allowed with the lower of these chosen, and then go back and recalculate the maximum of each benefit allowed using this new total wage (cash wage plus new total in kind). Given the difficulty involved in using such an iterative process, we recommend using the following simplified guidelines that approximate the iterative process:

1. Use 11.1% (1/.9−1) of cash wages for each allowed in kind benefit besides housing (and 17.6% for housing) when there is only one acceptable in kind benefit.
2. Use 12.7% of cash wages for each allowed in kind benefit besides housing when there are two or more acceptable in kind benefits (i.e. average of 11.1% allowed when one in kind benefit and maximum of 14.3% allowed when the total value of all in kind benefits equals or exceeds the 30% of wages limit), and 19.5% (average of 17.6% and 21.3%) of cash wage for housing.
3. Apply a final check to steps 1 and 2 by adding up the values of all in kind benefits and reduce this total to a maximum of 42.9% of cash wages when the total exceeds 42.9% of cash wages.

NOTES

1. Written authorization is required in California, Maryland, New York and Texas. Connecticut requires employees to agree at time of hiring, and Federal law requires voluntary and uncoerced acceptance of benefits by employees. Federal law (voluntary uncoerced acceptance of benefits by employee required) is weak in practice as 'courts have [generally] held that when an employee accepts a job voluntarily and without coercion, such acceptance automatically includes the in kind benefits the employer may bestow upon the employed' (Luers, 1998, pp. 215–16).
2. Labour Code §L.96(2)(3); Decree n. 96–178/P-RM, 13 June 1996, on the application of the Labour Code. §D.86–10, D.86–12.
3. South Africa Basic Conditions of Employment Act 1997 as amended 2002 Section 7.
4. New York: New York State Department of Labor, Part 142, Minimum Wage Order for Miscellaneous Industries and Occupations Part 142 of Title 12 of the Official Compilation of Codes, Rules, and Regulations of the State of New York (Part 142–2.20).
5. A meal in Chad and Senegal is valued at one hour at the minimum wage. Daily food rations are valued at one hour at minimum wage in Chad and two hours in Senegal. Food rations in Mali are valued at 2.5 hours of minimum wage and accommodation at 0.5 hour of minimum wage.
6. This includes Convention 95 and Recommendation 95 (Protection of Wages, 1949); Convention 99 and Recommendation 89 (Minimum wage fixing machinery (Agriculture), 1951); Convention 110 and Recommendation 110 (Plantations, 1958);

Recommendation 115 (Workers' Housing, 1961); Convention 117 (Social Policy Basic Aims and Standards, 1962); and Convention 189 and Recommendation 201 (Domestic Workers, 2011). There is also the ILO Tripartite Declaration of Principles Concerning Multinational Enterprises and Social Policy (2006).

7. '1. National laws or regulations, collective agreements or arbitration awards may authorize the partial payment of wages in the form of allowances in kind in [indentation and numbering added for clarity]:

    (1) industries or occupations in which payment in the form of such allowances is customary or desirable because of the nature of the industry or occupation concerned;
    (2) the payment of wages in the form of liquor of high alcoholic content or of noxious drugs shall not be permitted in any circumstances.

    2. In cases in which partial payment of wages in the form of allowances in kind is authorized, appropriate measures shall be taken to ensure that –

    (a) such allowances are appropriate for the personal use and benefit of the worker and his family; and
    (b) the value attributed to such allowances is fair and reasonable.' (ILO Wages Convention 95)

8. For example, although tea estates in Malawi served lunches that included only beans and rice, we concluded that it would be appropriate to include the value of this lunch as partial payment of a living wage – even though it included only two food groups because Malawi is such a poor country and lunch provided needed calories and proteins.
9. In Malawi, the employers' tea estates organization (TAML) indicated to us that tea estates provided the following list of in kind benefits (with average cost per worker per day in 2013 in kwacha indicated in brackets): meals/drinks (57.5), housing (43.6), water to house (6.5), security for housing compounds (6.2), medical clinic (12.8), school/crèche (17.2), football team (10.7), funerals for workers who die (20.2), leave grants (18.2), gratuity/severance pay (17.8), and protective clothing (35.4). All together, the value of these in kind benefits summed to 58% of the basic wage of K560. Many in kind benefits claimed are not considered as partial payment of wages in our methodology. This includes protective clothing (as for work and not for personal use), gratuity (as received when worker leaves employment sometime in future), leave grants (as uncertain and mainly for management), security for housing compounds (as protects tea estate housing assets), and football team (as only for some men).
10. The reason why dormitory accommodation for seasonal workers is not considered to be partial payment of a living wage is because it does not reduce the need for a permanent home for the worker's family.
11. We developed an Excel spreadsheet to calculate the cost of meals prepared at home. See Chapter 3.
12. We have encountered this situation in living wage studies for Mauritius and Sialkot Pakistan. Mauritius labor law requires employers to provide free transport when a worker lives more than 3 kilometers from work (or give cash for public transport). As a result, most workers in Mauritius commute to work in a company bus, and so a considerable portion of transport costs in Mauritius shows up as a business expense and not as a household expenditure in expenditure statistics. Therefore, it is not appropriate to consider free transport to work as partial payment of the living wage in Mauritius because there are relatively few funds for transport included in estimated NFNH costs.

17. Living wage in context: Wage ladder and wage trends

PART I. BACKGROUND AND CONCEPTUAL FRAMEWORK

It is important to put living wage estimates into context by comparing them with other wage and economic indicators and so observe how far prevailing wages, minimum wages, and poverty line wages are from a living wage. Recent trends in real wages are also important, because they help put current wages into an historical context. This is especially relevant for countries and industries where real wages have fallen in recent years and therefore workers are facing increased pressure.

PART II. APPROACHES

This chapter describes two approaches that should be used in a living wage report to provide a contextual backdrop for a living wage estimate. One approach graphically illustrates in a 'wage ladder' the size of gaps between a living wage estimate, prevailing wages, and other wage indicators. A second approach uses graphs of recent trends in real wages of workers and wage costs to employers. Note that this chapter has a different format than other chapters because examples are provided throughout the chapter.

17.1 Wage Ladder

17.1.1 What is a wage ladder?

A wage ladder is a tool for illustrating how a living wage compares with other wages and economic benchmarks for a country. The wage ladder was first developed by Rut Tufts for the Jo-In project in Turkey (Lally, 2011), and has been further developed since. Its purpose is to illustrate gaps between a living wage and other wages and economic benchmarks in a simple visual format. Wage ladders typically include wage and economic benchmarks that are commonly used and understood by the public, such as legal minimum wage, collectively bargained wages, average wages, poverty line wages, and wages required for decency according to politicians, trade unions, NGOs, researchers, and others. The idea is to include a variety of reference points in a wage ladder in order to put the living wage into perspective and illustrate where the living wage is in comparison with other commonly understood wage indicators. 'When charted together these figures [a wage ladder] provide a backdrop against which to consider the wages paid by factories in the region or country' (Lally, 2011).

17.2 Wage Ladder Tool

We developed an Excel program to graphically display a wage ladder. It provides for the living wage and prevailing wages of up to four different types of workers for a particular industry or establishment to be displayed on the chart with components of prevailing wages shown in staked columns (sum of basic wages, cash allowances, in kind benefits, and taxes). Overtime pay can be shown as the highest stack in a prevailing wage column, so that it can be viewed as an addition to prevailing wages without overtime. Similarly, the living wage can be displayed as the sum of basic wage, cash allowances, in kind benefits, and taxes. This Excel program is available on request from the authors.

The wage ladder tool allows for up to seven horizontal reference points to be displayed on the wage ladder such as average wages, poverty line wages, and minimum wage. These reference points are represented by horizontal lines on the chart as the so-called 'rungs of the ladder'.

17.2.1 Displaying the living wage and prevailing wages in an establishment or an industry in a wage ladder

- **Living wage**
  The living wage is displayed as a stacked bar in the wage ladder tool – so that various components of the living wage can be displayed. The highest stack on the living wage column should be statutory deductions from pay so both gross and net living wage are shown in the same column.

- **Prevailing wages in industry or establishment**
  When a living wage study and estimate focuses on a particular industry or establishment, wages of typical workers in that industry or establishment should be included in a wage ladder to illustrate the gap between current wages and a living wage. Because wages differ by occupation, seniority, grade and type of contract, there are

almost always several prevailing wages for an industry or establishment. Estimates for important types of workers should usually be included in a wage ladder. This helps facilitate discussion between workers and employers as well as with the value chain about improving wages.

17.2.2 Typical reference points to include in a wage ladder

To construct a meaningful wage ladder, reference points should be comparable to the living wage to the extent possible in terms of year, whether expressed per hour, per day or per month, and forms of remuneration included. When it is not possible to make reference points fully comparable, notes to the wage ladder should clearly indicate differences such as different years, and inclusion or exclusion of taxes, overtime pay, in kind benefits, cash allowances, various bonuses, etc. Note that average wage data generally indicate gross wages (before taxes), include overtime pay and exclude the value of in kind benefits. Poverty line wages measure how much after tax wages are needed to avoid poverty.

Typical reference points charted on a wage ladder (usually displayed as horizontal lines) include the following possibilities. Note that all of the following would not be included in a wage ladder for a particular country or location.

- **Average wages by occupation and industry**
  Data on average wages in different industries and occupations are very relevant and almost always available from government statistical office websites and from ILO LABORSTAT. The coverage (e.g. urban formal sector registered establishments), sources, and wage components included (e.g. whether or not overtime and in kind benefits are included) should be indicated. We have also found it effective to include the wage of the lowest paid government worker in wage ladders.

- **Minimum wages**
  Most countries have a statutory minimum wage. This represents a floor wage below which employers are not legally allowed to pay. In many countries, there are several legal minimum wages that might differ by occupation, sector, region, and/or city. Minimum wages can be per hour, day, or month. This means that it may be necessary to adjust minimum wages so that they are for the same reference period and for a similar sector and geographical area as the living wage. Minimum wages are *gross wages* without overtime since they are before taxes.

- **National poverty line wage**
  Most countries have poverty lines, and many countries have separate rural and urban poverty lines. Poverty lines are usually stated per person per day and so need to be multiplied by the living wage reference family size and divided by the living wage number of full-time earners per family to determine a poverty line wage for comparison with a living wage. For example, if a national poverty line was 30 pesos per person per day, the reference family size was 4 persons and the number of full-time workers per family was 1.5, then the national poverty line wage would be 2,433 pesos per month (i.e. 30 × (365/12) × 4/1.5). Poverty line wages indicate *net take home wage* – they do not take payroll taxes or income taxes into consideration. Whenever possible, a rural poverty line or an urban poverty line should be used depending on the location of the living wage study, because rural and urban poverty lines are usually quite different. When a country has different poverty lines for different family sizes, the poverty line for the living wage reference family size should be used.

- **World Bank international poverty line wages**
  Two World Bank international poverty lines are commonly used:
  $1.80 PPP per person per day extreme poverty line, and
  $3.10 PPP per person per day poverty line.[1]
  In October 2015, these poverty lines replaced $1.25 PPP and $2 PPP a day poverty lines previously used by the World Bank. What happened was that the World Bank re-estimated PPPs in 2011 and found that the purchasing power of national currencies relative to the United States was different than they previously thought in 2005. This helps explain why the World Bank extreme poverty line went from $1.25 PPP to $1.80 PPP, and the poverty line went from $2 PPP to $3.10 PPP, since the new poverty lines are measured in the new 2011 PPPs whereas the old poverty lines were measured in 2005 PPPs.

  Additional – higher – poverty lines are suggested by the World Bank for some regions. We suggest using these higher poverty lines for Latin America and the Caribbean, Eastern Europe and Central Asia, and upper middle income countries since they are more realistic.

  > In more developed regions, higher international poverty lines [than $2 a day in 2005 PPP] are more appropriate. When comparing poverty rates across countries within Latin America and the Caribbean (LAC) region, the $4 a day [in 2005 PPP] poverty line provides a more meaningful standard. For Eastern Europe and Central Asia (ECA) region, the $5 [in 2005 PPP] a day poverty line is often used.[2] (World Bank, 2015)

Note that since these values are expressed in 2005 PPP they imply somewhere around \$6.2 PPP and \$7.75 PPP in 2011 PPP.

International poverty lines expressed in PPP are meant to be understandable to the public. A \$3.10 PPP poverty line is meant to be the local equivalent to what \$3.10 would buy in the United States. This means that in order to calculate World Bank poverty lines in local currency, it is necessary to multiply a country's PPP for private consumption in the current year (expressed in 2011 PPP) by \$3.10. The World Bank World Development Indicators database includes 2011 PPP values by year for each country. Since a PPP value is not reported by the World Bank for the current year, it is necessary to estimate the current PPP value by multiplying the 2011 PPP value for the latest available year by the ratio of cumulative inflation in the country in subsequent years and months and dividing by cumulative inflation for the same period of time in the United States, the comparator country for PPP.

To translate World Bank poverty lines into poverty line wages it is necessary to follow the same procedures described above for national poverty line wages (i.e. multiply by days per month and living wage reference family size and divide by the living wage number of full-time equivalent workers per family). As with national poverty line wages, the World Bank poverty line wages represent *net take home wages*.

- **Collective bargaining agreement wages**
  Wages in collective bargaining agreements (CBAs) are useful benchmarks, because they have been agreed to by workers and employers. When CBAs specify cash allowances and in kind benefits, the value of these benefits should be included in the CBA wage used in the wage ladder to the extent feasible so that the CBA wage is comparable to the living wage. Overtime pay should be excluded from a CBA wage, because a living wage should be earned in standard working hours. Note that CBA wages are *gross wages*, since they are before taxes.

- **Trade union estimates of living wage**
  It is common for trade unions and trade union officials to indicate how much they believe that workers need to earn for decency. They often, but not always, refer to this as a living wage. It is useful to include this estimate in a wage ladder as a reference point.

- **Living wage estimates from NGOs and researchers**
  It is not unusual for NGOs and researchers to estimate a living wage. It is useful to include these on a wage ladder as reference points

when they exist. For example, we found that the Worker Rights Consortium (2010) estimated a living wage for the Dominican Republic and Center for Social Concern (2016) estimates each month for major cities in Malawi how much it costs for a basic needs basket of goods and services for a family. The Asia Floor Wage (2015) is available for 12 Asian countries.

- **Living/decent wage estimates of politicians and others**
  It is common for politicians and others to indicate how much they feel that workers need to earn for decency. For example, the President of the Dominican Republic, referred to 10,000 pesos per month as a 'misery wage' around the time we were doing a living wage study (Dominican Today, 2013). We included this wage in a wage ladder for the Dominican Republic. It was very effective, because our living wage estimate was not much above the President's 'misery wage,' even though it was well above what many workers were earning in the banana sector that was the focus of our living wage study in the Dominican Republic.

17.3 Example of Wage Ladder for Fresh Cut Flower Farms in Lake Naivasha, Kenya

Figure 17.1 is a wage ladder for Kenya with focus on fresh cut flower farms in the area around Lake Naivasha. It indicates, in stacked columns, our living wage estimate and prevailing wages for greenhouse workers (most common type of flower farm worker) who began working on their farm at different times between 1997 and 2014 since pay is based on seniority. Horizontal cross lines/reference points in Figure 17.1 include statutory minimum wage for agriculture, World Bank poverty line wages, the national urban poverty line wage for Kenya (since Lake Naivasha flower farm workers live in urban areas), the average wage for urban formal sector employees, a low income employee according to Kenyan income tax law, and a trade union estimated living wage.

17.3.1 Interpretation of the Kenya wage ladder

The wage ladder for Kenya provided information about how the living wage compared with other wage indicators and with prevailing wages of greenhouse workers in the flower farm industry. Some insights follow:

1. Comparing living wage to other benchmarks
   a. All flower farm workers earned well above the minimum wage for agriculture. However, only flower farm workers with more than 10

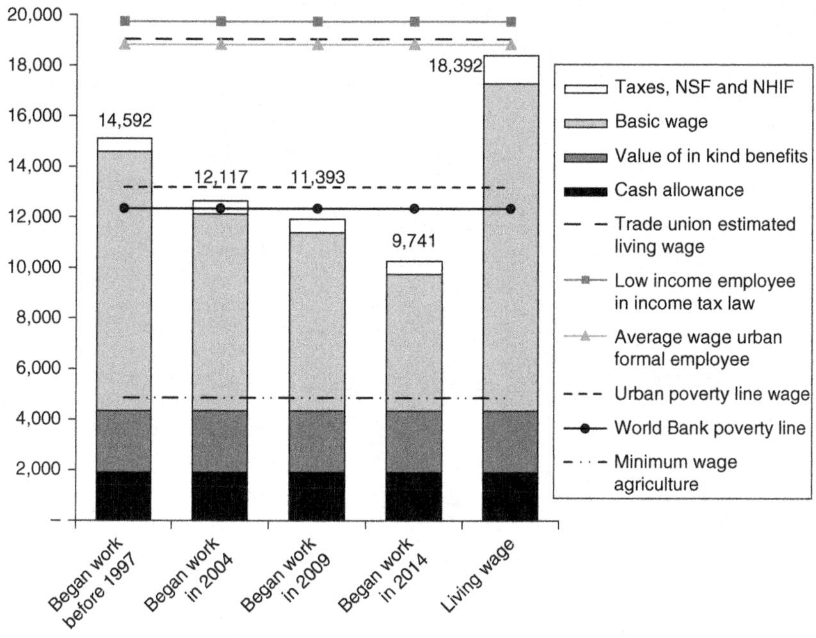

Figure 17.1 Example of wage ladder for flower farm workers in the area around Lake Naivasha, Kenya (in Kenyan shillings per month)

years of seniority earned more than the World Bank poverty line wage and the government urban poverty line wage.

b. Our living wage was similar to the living wage according to the trade union representing flower farm workers.

c. Statutory deductions and taxes were important. There were deductions from pay for social security, national health insurance schemes, and union fees. Workers would also pay income tax if they earned a living wage.

2. Comparison between the living wage and prevailing wages in the fresh flower farm industry
   a. There is a considerable gap between what workers earn and a living wage. This gap is greater for workers with less seniority.
   b. The gap between prevailing wage and living wage is significantly increased by statutory taxes workers have to pay.

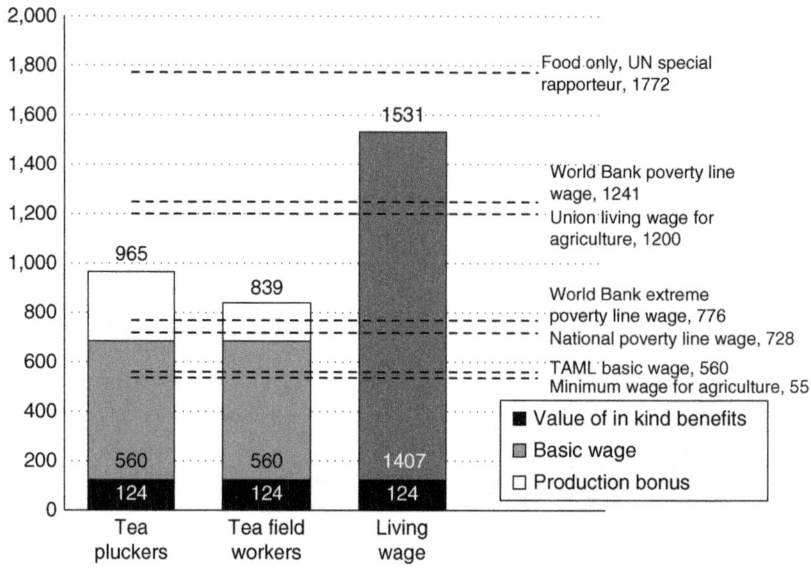

Figure 17.2 *Example of wage ladder for tea estate workers in southern Malawi (in Malawi kwacha per day)*

3. Information about prevailing wages
   a. Cash allowances and in kind benefits are important parts of the pay of flower farm workers.
   b. There are large differences in worker pay by seniority.

17.4 Example of Wage Ladder for Tea Estates in Southern Malawi

Figure 17.2 is an example of a wage ladder for tea estates in southern Malawi. Average wages for tea field workers and tea pluckers are shown because together they comprise a high percentage of tea estate workers. Their wages are compared with our living wage estimate as well as with a variety of reference points.

17.4.1 Interpretation of the wage ladder for southern Malawi

The wage ladder helps illustrate the following:

1. Comparing living wage to other benchmarks
   a. Our living wage is above the World Bank poverty line wages, union living wage for agriculture and the national poverty line

wage. It is also well above the minimum wage for agriculture and the Tea Association of Malawi (TAML) basic wage. But our living wage is well below what the UN Special Rapporteur estimated to be the cost of food only.
    b. The minimum wage and the Tea Association of Malawi basic wage are even lower than the World Bank extreme poverty line wage.
2. Comparison of prevailing wages on tea estates and the living wage
    a. There is a large gap between what tea estate workers earn and a living wage.
3. Information about prevailing wages
    a. Wages of tea estate workers are very low. Tea field workers earn even less than the World Bank poverty line wage.
    b. In kind benefits and production bonuses are an important part of compensation for tea estate workers.

17.5 Recent Trends and Changes in Wage

To understand the context of current wages and assist a meaningful dialogue between government, stakeholders and the value chain, figures showing changes in real wages (i.e. wages adjusted for inflation) in recent years are very useful. Graphs of wage trends expressed in USD are useful for export industries that sell all or almost all of their output in foreign currency. The past 10 years is usually a reasonable reference period to use, as it is long enough for trends and changes to become apparent without being too far in the past. The context of a large gap between current wages and a living wage is quite different in countries and industries where real wages have been falling over time compared with countries and industries where real wages have been rising over time. Which wage trends to graph should be determined by what is important in the location and/or industry.

17.5.1 Need to adjust for inflation to maintain purchasing power of wages

Wages should be adjusted for inflation before graphing them over time, so that real wages are shown rather than nominal wages. This is done by dividing nominal wage in year x by inflation since the initial year in the wage series to year x.

17.5.2 Usefulness of indexing real wages to a base year

It is informative to illustrate wage trends over time by indexing real wages to a particular initial or base year so that graphs illustrate percentage change. For example, real wages for 2005–2015 would be divided by the

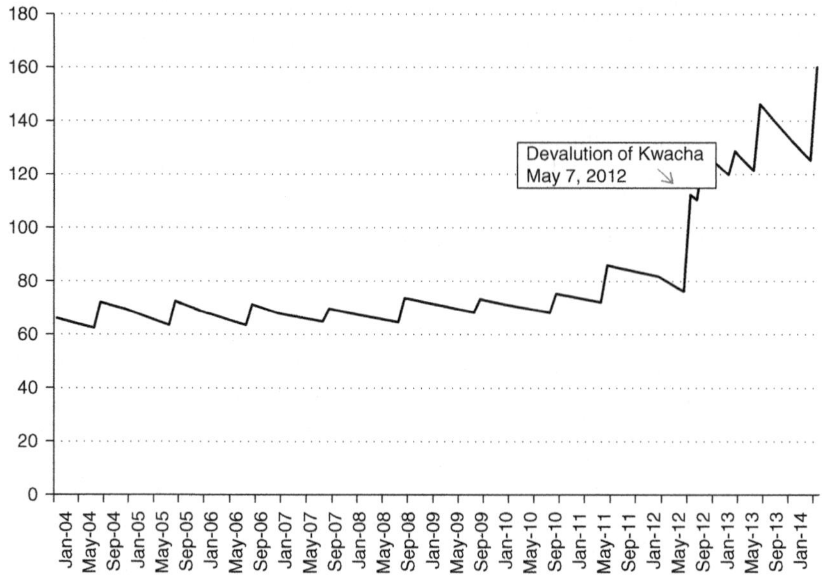

Figure 17.3 Real basic wage per day of tea estate workers (in real 2004 kwacha), Malawi, 2004–2014

2005 value. Wages in 2005 would be 1.0. Wages in subsequent years would indicate the percentage increase or decrease in real wages since 2005.

17.5.3 Examples of graphs that illustrate recent changes in real wages

17.5.3.1 Example 1: Malawi: Case of almost no change in real wages for years followed by rapid increase in real wages Figure 17.3 for Malawi clearly shows that real wages of tea estate workers increased dramatically following the devaluation of the kwacha in 2012 – but this occurred after many of years with very little change in real wages. Notice the sawtooth pattern between 2004 and 2012 when real wages repeatedly fell and rose. This reflected a fixed nominal wage, which was depreciated by inflation until wages were raised to keep up with inflation.

17.5.3.2 Example 2: Kenya: Case of decreasing real wages Figure 17.4 shows that real wages on fresh cut flower farms in Kenya fell between 2004 and 2014. This fall in real wages was especially steep for new hires compared with workers with 10 years of seniority and came about because of the terms in CBAs. This figure also shows how real wages were related to real minimum wages. See example 4 in Section 17.5.4 for a discussion.

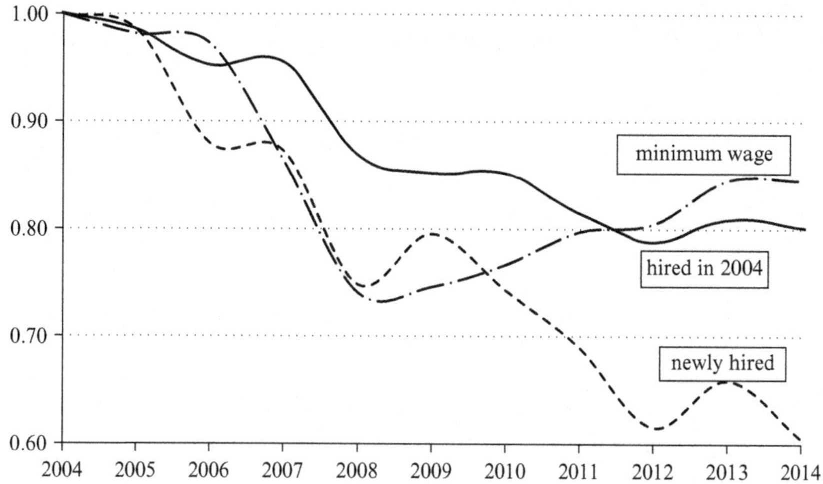

Figure 17.4 *Change in real flower farm CBA wage (basic wage plus cash allowances) and statutory minimum wage for agriculture, indexed to 2004, Kenya 2004–2014*

17.5.4 Graphs that compare prevailing wages and minimum wage in recent years

It is interesting for readers to see graphically how prevailing wages in an industry have changed in recent years compared with the statutory minimum wage. This can be shown in a figure that includes statutory minimum wage and prevailing wage.

17.5.4.1 Example 3: Malawi: Case where prevailing wage tracks statutory minimum wage but tends to be slightly higher Figure 17.5 for Malawi shows how the basic wage for tea workers in Malawi closely tracks the statutory minimum wage. Figure 17.5 also shows that the wage for tea workers is adjusted more frequently than the statutory minimum wage and is usually slightly higher than the statutory minimum wage.

17.5.4.2 Example 4: Kenya: Case where decrease in real value of prevailing wages was greater than decrease in real value of minimum wage Figure 17.4 for Kenya illustrates that the purchasing power or real value of both the statutory minimum wages and the wages of flower farm workers fell between 2004 and 2014. The fall in real wages of flower farm workers was fairly continuous. In contrast, the real value of the statutory minimum wage bottomed out in 2008 at the time of the world financial crisis and

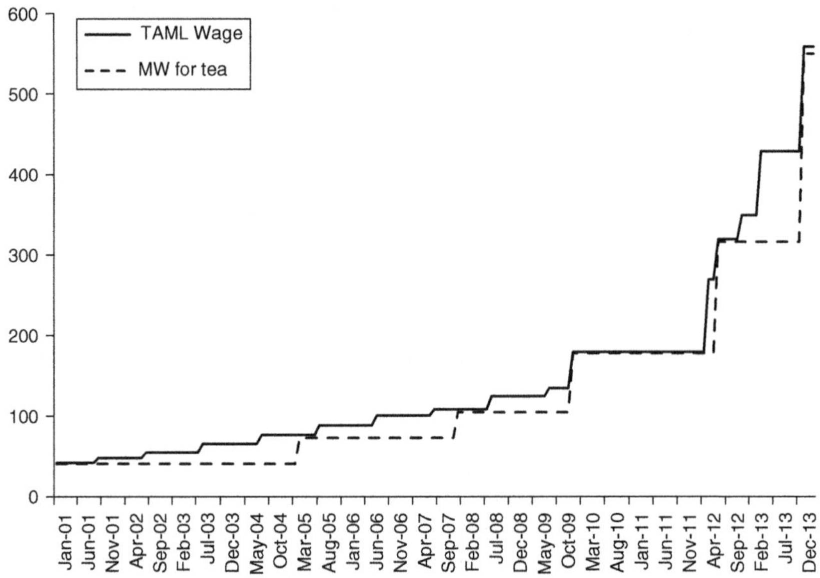

Figure 17.5 Basic daily wage of tea estate workers (TAML wage) and statutory minimum wage (MW), Malawi 2001–2014 (in Malawi Kwacha)

increased after this. As a result, the purchasing power of the minimum wage fell less than the purchasing power of flower farm wages.

17.5.4.3 Example 5: Chengdu, China: Case where real average wages increased rapidly and at a faster pace than real minimum wage Figure 17.6 for Chengdu, China, shows a large increase in both real average wages and real minimum wage between 2006 and 2014. Real wages increased by 125% and real minimum wages increased by 85%.

17.5.5 Graphs that illustrate recent changes in wages expressed in US dollars

An important metric for employers in export industries is wage costs in dollars, because their revenues are in foreign currency. For this reason, it is often useful to graph how prevailing wages in dollars changed in recent years.

17.5.5.1 Example 6: Increasing wages in dollars for Kenyan flower farms Figure 17.7 indicates large continuous increases in prevailing wages in US dollars over the past 10 years for fresh cut flower farms in

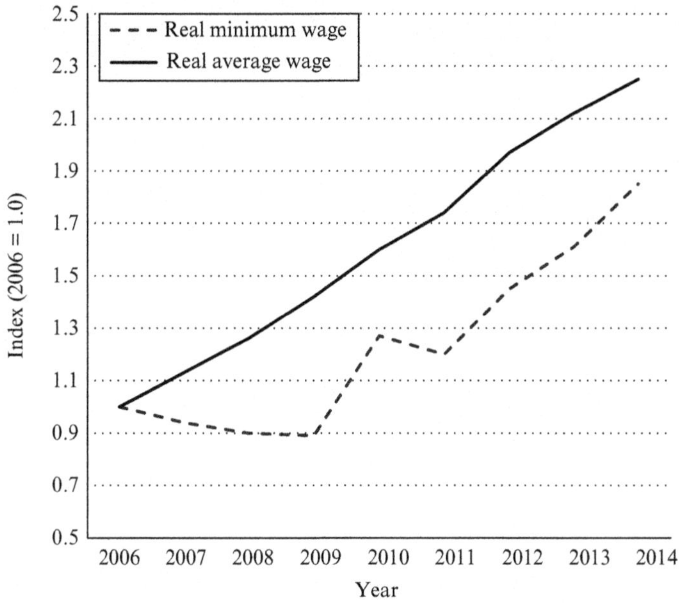

Figure 17.6 Real minimum wage and real average wages indexed to 2006 urban Chengdu, China, 2006–2014

Kenya. This means that these employers experienced increasing cost pressure unless export prices and/or productivity substantially increased.

17.5.6 Graphs that compare wage trends to other economic indicators

Depending on the situation, it can be effective to include in a living wage report a figure that compares wages and other economic indicators. This can help provide a context for stakeholder discussion. Sometimes this can be done using a figure from another report or publication. We did this in our Dominican Republic living wage report where we included a figure from an ILO report (Figure 17.8).

17.5.6.1 Example 7: Graph comparing changes in real wages and real labor productivity: Case of a disconnect between labor productivity and wages Figure 17.8 compares real wages and real labor productivity in the Dominican Republic between 2000 and 2010. It clearly shows that real wages decreased and then plateaued despite a large increase in labor productivity, which indicated that the expected link between labor productivity and wages broke down in the Dominican Republic.

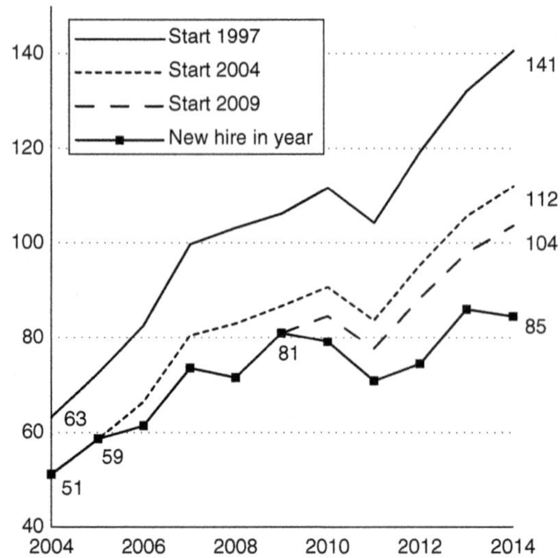

Figure 17.7 *Flower farm basic wage plus cash allowances per month in US dollars, Kenya 2004–2014*

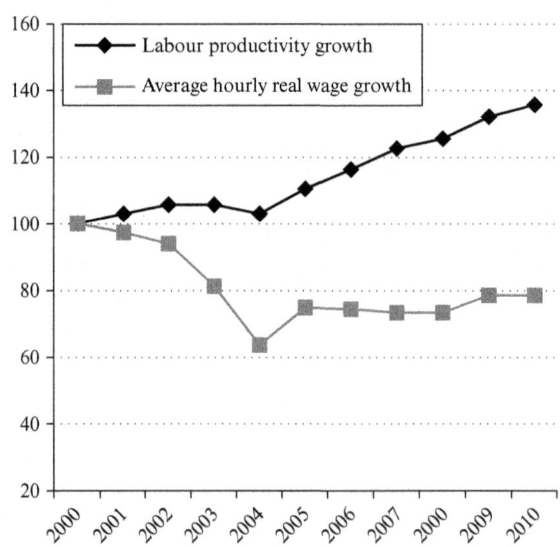

Source: ILO (2013).

Figure 17.8 *Real average hourly wage and labor productivity, 2000–2010, for the Dominican Republic (index 2000=100)*

NOTES

1. According to the World Bank, 'Purchasing Power Parity conversion factor is the number of units of a country's currency required to buy the same amounts of goods and services in the domestic market as U.S. dollar would buy in the United States' (World Bank, 2016). PPPs in developing countries typically indicate that the purchasing power of local currencies is two to three times greater than their equivalent amount in UDS. This difference, however, varies greatly across developing countries. It is greater than three in India and Pakistan (3.3), less than two in China (1.7), and fairly close to 1 in Brazil (1.2).
2. Other World Bank sources also mention the $4 per day (in 2005 PPP) poverty line measure in Latin America and the Caribbean (World Bank, 2015) and Eastern Europe and Central Asia (World Bank, 2014).

SECTION IV

Typical living wage report and updating a living wage estimate

18. Suggested outline of a living wage report

We recommend that living wage reports use a similar outline to the extent possible. In this way, they can be more easily compared. This chapter provides our suggestions for a typical report with explanations of what should be in each section and why.

1. Background

This section should be relatively short consisting of one or two paragraphs. It should indicate: (i) area the living wage estimate is estimated for (e.g. rural, urban, city x), including whether it focused on areas near a particular industry (e.g. coffee, tea) or industrial zones; (ii) short description of Anker methodology, its credentials, its past use, and a listing of its main principles in bullet points (e.g. transparency, normative basis, time and place-specific nature, international comparability, practical and modest cost, and consideration of all relevant forms of remuneration); and (iii) organization or organizations that supported the study.

2. Living Wage Estimate

This section should indicate the living wage estimate and the month and year of the study so that readers do not have to search through the report to find it. Gross and net living wage should be indicated. A brief indication of the size of gap to prevailing wages or other relevant wage comparators should be provided.

It is useful to indicate in a second paragraph how much effort was put into estimating the living wage such as collection of new information on local costs and use of a range of secondary information, as well as that conservative assumptions were used to estimate the living wage. Such discussion helps give credibility to a living wage report. It is useful to include an Appendix to the report listing sources of information.

3. Context

This section should highlight noteworthy aspects in a country, region, and/or industry that are important to understanding the living wage estimate and so help put it in context. Examples of context discussions in previous living wage reports include the following topics. For the Dominican Republic: the importance of immigrant Haitian workers and the need to earn enough to support a family based on costs in the Dominican Republic and not in Haiti; the importance of small holder farmers. For Malawi: high level of poverty; recent very high inflation rate and currency devaluation; few job opportunities in rural areas and importance of tea estate employment. For Kenya: the fact that flower farm workers live in urban slums surrounding flower farms and not in a rural area; existence of collective bargaining agreement and consequently better working conditions than typical for agriculture; decreasing real wages for workers and increasing cost pressures for flower farms in past decade. For South Africa: recent large increase in legal minimum wage; right to adequate food, water, housing and health care included in South African Constitution; recent living wage campaign by main trade union.

4. Concept and Definition of a Living Wage

This section should provide a brief introduction to living wages. It should: (i) cover the concept and idea behind a living wage, (ii) provide the Global Living Wage Coalition (GLWC) definition of a living wage, and (iii) provide historical background and context to living wages. The latter could include quotes such as from human rights conventions, ILO Constitution, historical figures, etc. in the text or in an Appendix. See Chapter 1 in this manual and Anker (2011) for useful quotations.

5. How a Living Wage is Estimated

This section should describe the Anker methodology used to estimate the living wage and include Figures 2.1–2.3 for clarity.

SECTION I. COST OF A BASIC BUT DECENT LIFE FOR A WORKER AND HIS OR HER FAMILY

6. Food Costs

A short introductory paragraph should describe how food costs were estimated using a model diet that is nutritious in more than only calories, low in cost for a nutritious diet, consistent with local food preferences, and based on food prices found in a local market survey. It should then indicate estimated food costs per person per day and per family per month. This paragraph should also indicate that there are three sections concerned with: (i) principles used to develop the model diet, (ii) description of the model diet, and (iii) food prices used to estimate cost of the model diet.

6.1 General principles of living wage model diet

This section should indicate the general principles used to establish the model diet (WHO/FAO recommendations as regards calories, proteins, fats, carbohydrates, and fruits and vegetables); consistent with local food preferences; relatively low in cost for a nutritious diet; consistent with development level of country and location; and when possible quantities are expressed in number of portions.

6.2 Living wage model diet

This section should describe the living wage model diet including reference to the Excel calorie requirement and model diet programs available on the Edward Elgar website. Discussion should start by indicating how the model diet meets WHO/FAO nutritional standards. This section should also indicate why (and by how much) the cost of the model diet is increased to take into account the need for: variety in the diet, minimal spoilage, and salt/spices/sauces/condiments to make the diet palatable.

Next, the model diet should be described in bullet points using quantities easily understood by laypersons to the extent possible (e.g. two slices of bread, three meat meals per week, one cup of milk per day for children, etc.). Use of bullet points here, helps improve presentation. This should be followed by an indication of noteworthy aspects of the model diet in bullet points. The purpose of this discussion is to make readers aware that food costs for a living wage are as low as possible while meeting nutritional requirements and being consistent with local conditions and local food habits and preferences. The model diet itself should be presented in a table at the end of this section including a comments column with interesting features of the model diet.

Finally, for countries where other model diets and/or food consumption data are available, it is useful to include a short discussion that compares the living wage model diet with other model diets and/or to food consumption according to secondary data. There could also be discussion comparing the percentage distribution of food expenditure by major food group in the living wage model diet to the percentage distribution of food expenditures according to household survey data. The purpose of such discussions is to indicate that the living wage model diet is reasonable. Therefore, explanations should be provided for major differences.

6.3 Local food prices

This section should describe how the food prices used to estimate the cost of the living wage model diet were obtained. Discussion should start by describing how food prices were collected in a local market survey and then go on to indicate in bullet points noteworthy aspects of the selection of food items used to represent major food groups in the living wage model diet. The purpose of this discussion is to indicate that food items were selected in a way to reduce food costs and so help ensure that the cost of the model diet is kept as low as possible for a nutritious diet. There should also be a short discussion about seasonality in food price and any possible adjustments to the food prices collected. Note that including photos of local food markets where workers typically shop is strongly encouraged, because it helps situate readers, especially international readers.

7. Housing Costs

An introductory paragraph should indicate that housing costs are estimated by summing up separate estimates of the costs of rent for an acceptable dwelling (or rental equivalent value when owner-occupied dwellings are used because there is little or no rental market), utility costs, and possibly minor repairs and maintenance – and then indicate the estimate of housing costs (rent and utilities) in the location. The introductory paragraph should also discuss how the Anker methodology differs from the usual methodology to measure living wages and poverty lines for developing countries, where all non-food costs (including housing costs) are estimated in one go and why the Anker methodology yields better estimates of the cost of acceptable housing especially in countries where housing conditions are generally poor, as well as in countries where the cost/value of owner-occupied housing is assumed to be zero in the household expenditure statistics. This paragraph should indicate that this chapter includes sections concerned with: (i) local standard for basic acceptable housing, (ii) rent or user cost of acceptable housing, and (iii) utilities and other costs.

7.1 Standard for basic acceptable local housing

This section should indicate the housing standard for the location and how it was arrived at based on international minimum standards and current local housing conditions. The discussion should start with a description or table that indicates local housing conditions according to recent secondary data (for example, percentage of houses with different types of floors, walls, roof, toilet, water source, electricity, etc.). This discussion should be followed by a listing in bullet points in the text of the local housing standard and how this standard differs from current housing conditions. Discussion should point out how the housing standard is basic and far from being extravagant. Readers should be given a vivid picture of how workers currently live and how basic housing would be even for workers earning a living wage. Including photos in the text of local housing is strongly encouraged – photos of both current housing of workers and basic acceptable housing.

7.2 Rent or user cost for basic acceptable housing

This section should indicate how many houses researchers visited, the condition and rent of these houses, and how the researcher estimated the rental cost of local housing using this information. It is important to describe very clearly houses that workers currently live in, rent for these houses, and rent for housing at the local housing standard. Researchers should include a table with information collected such as size (number of rooms and number of square meters), rent, amenities (such as toilet and water source), and comments that describe aspects of each house visited that make it unacceptable or acceptable. Note that for locations where there are few if any rental housing units (such as in many rural areas), it is necessary to estimate the user cost of owned housing that meets the local basic acceptable housing standard by estimating the cost of building and maintaining such a dwelling.

7.3 Utilities and other housing costs

This section should indicate how utility costs and other costs such as taxes, fees, and routine maintenance and repairs were estimated. Discussion in this section should also indicate current conditions regarding use of electricity, water, and cooking fuel and if these would differ for workers earning a living wage.

8. Non-food and Non-housing (NFNH) Costs

This section should begin with a brief description of the Anker methodology used to estimate non-food non-housing costs (NFNH). The second paragraph should indicate the amount estimated for NFNH along with the types of expenditures it covers. The remainder of this section should describe how the NFNH to Food ratio is estimated by taking into consideration: (i) unnecessary expenditures, and (ii) peculiarities of available household expenditure data. A preliminary estimate of NFNH costs is made by multiplying the NFNH to Food ratio by cost of the model diet and then possibly adjusting NFNH based on rapid adjustment post checks. Although not required, it is useful to indicate how the NFNH to Food ratio for the location compares to NFNH to Food ratios for other countries and locations to see how typical or unusual it is.

9. Post Checks of Non-food and Non-housing Costs

This section should begin with a brief discussion of how a blind and uncritical use of an extrapolation method to estimate NFNH costs runs the risk of underestimating amounts required for NFNH needs. This section should then indicate that for this reason the costs of acceptable health care and education of children are estimated using rapid assessment methods in order to determine if the amounts for these two human rights included in the preliminary estimate of NFNH costs (from the previous section) are sufficient. The amounts for education and health care are increased when this is necessary according to the post checks discussed in the next two sections.

9.1 Health care post check

This subsection should start with a brief description of major health care challenges in the country and location. This should include a discussion of the quality, availability and challenges of government provided health care. This discussion should also indicate the extent to which people use private health care and why. The purpose of this discussion is to establish the extent to which workers would reasonably need money to pay for private health care (and public health care when there are expenses for this). This should be followed by discussion of how frequently people visit public and private health care providers based on secondary data. Rough estimates of cost per visit to each type of provider should be made, based on primary data collected in the location from visits to pharmacies and private clinics and discussion with workers and key informants. Based on this secondary data and primary information, cost of visits to different health care providers (pharmacies, private care, public care) should be estimated and described. The sum of these estimates of likely health care costs should be compared with the amount included for health care in the preliminary NFNH estimate, with an adjustment made to this amount when required.

9.2 Education post check

This section should start with a brief description of the education system in the country and location. This should include an indication of enrollment rates and the availability, quality and challenges of public schooling. This discussion should also indicate the extent to which people use private schools and if by chance this is required for decency. Since education is considered a human right internationally, there should then be a short paragraph indicating that one assumption of the Anker methodology is that children of workers earning a living wage should be able to complete secondary school. This should be followed by discussion about different expenses parents have for school and how much they cost based on discussions with workers and key informants in the location and relevant research papers or other sources of information. The estimated amount needed to educate children through secondary school should be compared with the amount included for education in the preliminary estimate of NFNH costs with an adjustment made to this amount when required. Note that since the amount included for education in the preliminary estimate of NFNH costs is sensitive to how household expenditures for education are classified in national household expenditure statistics, the expenditure classification used for education should be indicated.

9.3 Possible transportation post check

This post check should be included in reports when transport is a major expense for families and the sum of percentages of household expenditures for food, housing, education and health care is less than around 60%. This section should start with an indication of amount included for transport in the preliminary estimate of NFNH costs. Discussion should then indicate the proportion of households in the location that own a motorbike or motor vehicle according to household survey data, as well as the distribution of transport expenditures for private vehicles compared to public passenger transport according to household expenditure statistics and CPI expenditure weights. Based on this information and discussions with workers and key informants, it should be explained why it is felt to be reasonable to expect workers earning a living wage to rely exclusively on public passenger transport or to own a private vehicle such as a motorbike. A quick approximate estimate of the cost of transport needs per month for the reference family should then be made by adding up likely costs for common transport costs such as commuting to work, shopping, errands, children's school, doctors, and recreation as well as for visiting extended families once or a few times per year. Note that if ownership of a motorbike is felt to be a local norm, it is necessary to estimate costs of owning and operating a motorbike given the number of kilometers of travel expected. The rapid estimate of the cost of transport should then be compared to the amount included for transport in the preliminary estimate of NFNH costs with this increased when required.

10. Provision for Unexpected Events to Ensure Sustainability

This section should be short. A brief explanation should be provided of why a small margin is provide for unforeseen events – to help ensure sustainability and help workers avoid getting into a downward debt cycle. The percentage used to calculate this (5%) should be indicated along with the amount in local currency. In countries where extended family obligations are especially strong and a researcher feels it is warranted to include additional funds for these obligations (usually 5%), this should be indicated and justified in the text.

SECTION II. LIVING WAGE FOR WORKERS

11. Family Size Needing to be Supported by Living Wage

This section should indicate that living wage is a family concept and therefore that it is necessary to determine an appropriate reference family size for the location. This section should indicate the reference family size and how it was determined, and why it is a reasonable family size for estimating a living wage for the country/location. Note that it is useful to include information on average household size from several sources because average household size from surveys and censuses is sensitive to how households are defined and measured.

12. Number of Full-time Equivalent Workers in Family Providing Support

This section should start by indicating that since living wage is a family concept, there is more than one full-time worker in the reference size family, but less than two full-time workers because of voluntary inactivity, unemployment and part-time work. Discussion should then describe how the number of full-time workers per couple used to estimate the living wage was estimated using labor force participation rates, unemployment rates, and part-time employment rates for the location and appropriate age group. This discussion should include information on each of these factors from several data sources when possible along with a critical appraisal of these data to explain and justify how the number of full-time workers per couple was determined.

13. Take Home Pay Required and Taking Taxes and Statutory Deductions from Pay into Account

Up to this point, a living wage report would have been concerned with how much take home pay a worker needs to be able to afford a basic but decent standard of living for his/her family. This section should start by indicating that it is necessary to take into consideration income tax and statutory deductions from pay to ensure sufficient take home pay and sufficient disposable income for workers to be able to afford a decent standard of living for themselves and their family. This discussion should indicate all statutory payroll deductions along with their percentages or amounts, whichever applies.

SECTION III. ESTIMATING GAPS BETWEEN LIVING WAGE AND PREVAILING WAGES

14. Prevailing Wages (for Industry or Establishment when Living Wage Study is Done for Company or Certifying Organization)

One important reason for estimating a living wage is to determine if workers receive a living wage and if employers pay a living wage. This section should indicate prevailing wages in a country for different occupations and industries. Prevailing wages should also be indicated for an industry or establishment of interest when a living wage study is funded by a company or certifying/standards organization. Discussion should start with an indication of: (i) the types/major groups of workers being considered, and (ii) the general principles used to determine which forms of remuneration (e.g. base pay, overtime, production bonuses, cash allowances, in kind benefits, and fringe benefits) should be included in current wages for purposes of comparing them to a living wage and thereby determining the gap between current wages and a living wage.

14.1 Basic wage, cash allowances and bonuses, and overtime pay

Common forms and amounts of remuneration in the industry or establishment of interest should be listed along with an indication of whether or not each is appropriate for inclusion in wages for comparison to a living wage. This naturally leads to an estimate of remuneration in the industry or establishment of interest that is appropriate to compare with living wage. This discussion and results should be provided for major types of workers in the industry or establishment of interest (e.g. tea plucker, fieldworker, and factory worker for tea plantations; grades 4–7 for garment workers in Bangladesh).

14.2 In kind benefits as partial payment of living wage

Since in kind benefits provided by employers can reduce the amount of cash wage required to ensure that workers earn a living wage, this section should estimate fair and reasonable monetary values for in kind benefits when a living wage study focuses on a particular industry or establishment. In this way, a more complete picture of prevailing wages in an industry or establishment is provided and therefore more realistic estimates of gaps between prevailing wages and a living wage. Note that this section can sometimes be fairly long because of the controversy often surrounding in kind benefits. Discussion should start with a brief explanation of why in kind benefits can be valuable to workers along with a list of typical in kind benefits provided in the industry or establishment of focus. This should be followed by discussion of the general principles and guidelines used to determine which in kind benefits are appropriate to include as partial payment of a living wage as well as how to estimate fair and reasonable values for them. Next, in a series of subsections each in kind benefit provided should be described and valued in a critical and transparent manner using the already indicated principles and guidelines. Finally, a short subsection should draw together results for all of the individual in kind benefits.

15. Living Wage in Context and Compared with Other Wages

15.1 Wage ladder

It is important to put a living wage estimate into context by comparing it with other wage indicators – so that gaps between the living wage and other wages can be determined such as to minimum wage, poverty line wages, and various prevailing wages. This should be done in a wage ladder where the living wage estimate and other wage indicators are displayed visually next to each other. Observed wage gaps should be discussed in the text based on this wage ladder figure.

15.2 Recent wage trends

When possible, it is informative to include figures and discussion on recent trends in wages, labor costs and labor productivity, because this provides an important context for understanding pressures on workers and employers. A situation where real wages have fallen in recent years represents quite a different context and pressure for workers compared with a situation where real wages have risen substantially in recent years, regardless of the current gap between prevailing wages and living wage.

16. Conclusions

This section should provide a summary as well as indicate important conclusions. It is important for the conclusions section to be well written and convincing, because many readers only look at a conclusions section. This section should start by indicating the estimated net and gross living wages, so that readers can immediately know the living wage. This section should include summary tables that indicate how the living wage was estimated (see Chapter 19). Discussion should indicate gaps between prevailing wages and the living wage. This discussion should provide additional information on these gaps when a living wage study focused on a particular industry. Next, discussion should emphasize and illustrate how the living wage is a conservative estimate of how much is needed for decency. Such discussion is important so that readers are not left with the impression that the living wage is an exaggerated and utopian estimate of needs. This should be done using examples of some of the conservative assumptions that were used to estimate the living wage and therefore the basic level of living that is affordable on the living wage estimate. It is also often useful to point out interesting aspects of local living conditions, recent wage trends and possibly increased pressure on workers, and the extent to which employers and actors higher up the value chain may be in a position to help raise wages and so move wages toward a living wage. It is often useful to end by indicating how much effort was put into estimating the living wage so that readers are aware of how seriously estimation of a living wage was taken.

17. References

A complete list of references should be included at the end of the text.

19. Summary tables to include in a living wage report

Summary tables Tables 19.1 and 19.2 are important parts of a living wage report because they indicate in an easy to see way how a living wage was estimated. This increases transparency. This chapter includes and describes these summary tables. Note that whenever possible a living wage should be expressed in a way that is familiar to stakeholders such as a daily wage or a monthly wage.

Table 19.1 has three parts. Part I indicates costs for a basic but decent standard of living for the reference size family. This information can also be used in living income reports and estimates that are concerned with livelihoods of small farmers and businesses. Part II indicates the gross living wage and net take home pay living wage. Part III indicates basic *cash* living wages (gross and net) that workers would need assuming that they receive typical cash allowances and in kind benefits in an industry or establishment of interest.

Table 19.2 indicates some key values and assumptions used to estimate the living wage.

Table 19.1 Summary table to calculate a living wage (to include in a living wage report)

PART I. FAMILY EXPENSES	**Local currency**	**USD**
Food cost per month for reference family (1)		
Food cost per person per day		
Housing costs per month (2)		
Rent per month for acceptable housing[a]		
Utility costs and minor repairs per month		
Non-food non-housing (NFNH) costs per month taking into consideration post checks (3)		
Preliminary estimate of NFNH costs		
Health care post check adjustment		

Table 19.1 (continued)

Education post check adjustment		
Other possible post check adjustments (if any)		
Additional amount (5%) for sustainability and emergencies (4A)		
Possible additional amount (usually 5%) for extended family support (4B)		
Total costs per month for basic but decent living standard for reference family (5) [5 = 1+2+3+4A+4B]		
PART II. LIVING WAGE PER MONTH		
Net living wage per month (6) [6 = 5/# full-time workers]		
Statutory deductions from pay (7) (list these in notes to table)[b]		
Gross living wage per month (8) [8 = 6+7]		
WHEN LIVING WAGE STUDY HAS AN INDUSTRY OR ESTABLISHMENT FOCUS		
PART III: CASH (BASIC) LIVING WAGE ASSUMING WORKERS RECEIVE TYPICAL IN-KIND BENEFITS, AND TYPICAL CASH ALLOWANCES AND TYPICAL BONUSES AND BENEFITS IN AN INDUSTRY OR ESTABLISHMENT		
Value per month of common in-kind benefits in industry or establishment (9A) (indicate in notes to table)[c]		
Value per month of common cash allowances and bonuses and benefits in an industry or establishment (9B) (indicate in notes to table)[d]		
Net cash (basic) living wage assuming workers receive typical in-kind benefits, cash allowances, bonuses, and benefits in an industry or establishment (10) [10 = 6 - 9A - 9B]		
Gross cash (basic) living wage assuming workers receive typical in-kind benefits, cash allowances, bonuses, and benefits in an industry or establishment (11) [11 = 8 - 9A - 9B]		

Notes:

[a] In locations with little or no rental housing market, indicate user cost for acceptable owner-occupied house.

[b] Statutory deductions from pay include the following items and percentages:

[c] Common in kind benefits include the following items and values:

[d] Common cash allowances and bonuses include the following items and amounts:

Table 19.2 Key values and assumptions used to estimate living wage (to include in a living wage report)

Key values and assumptions	
Location (industry or establishment if relevant)	
Exchange rate of local currency to USD	
Number of full-time workdays per month	
Number of hours in normal workweek	
Number of full-time workers per couple	
Reference family size	
Number of children in reference family	
Preliminary ratio of NFNH costs to FOOD costs	

20. Updating a living wage estimate

PART I. BACKGROUND

It is necessary to update a living wage for inflation so that it retains its purchasing power and remains sufficient to support a basic but decent living standard. It is also necessary to periodically update a living wage for improvements in living standards and expectations that accompany economic development. For example, decency standards in China today are higher than they were 30 or even 10 years ago.

The issues addressed in this chapter are: (i) how to update a living wage estimate for inflation, and (ii) how often a new living wage study and new living wage estimate should be done.

PART II. HOW TO UPDATE A LIVING WAGE ESTIMATE

20.1 Updating a Living Wage Estimate for Inflation to Ensure it Retains its Purchasing Power

We recommend using the consumer price index (CPI) to update a living wage estimate. This should be done at least every year (and more frequently than once a year in high inflation countries, see Section 20.2). CPI is easy to use, widely accepted, and available for virtually all countries in the world.[1] The usual way of measuring inflation for any period of time is to divide the CPI index for the month of interest (say July) by the CPI index for an origin month (say December). For example, if a CPI index was 216.2 in July and 210.0 in the previous December, inflation in the December to July period was 2.95% (i.e. 216.2/210.0 - 1).[2]

We recommend first updating a living wage estimate for inflation to the end of the living wage study year. For example, if a living wage study was done in March, it would be updated for inflation to December in the same year. Then this new end of year living wage would be updated in subsequent years by further inflation. Up-to-date monthly and annual CPI inflation rates are available on most government statistical office websites.

Table 20.1 Updating living wage estimates for inflation for four living wage studies (in local currency)

Country	Study date	Original gross living wage per month	Gross living wage, December 2014	Gross living wage, December 2015	Comment
Dominican Republic	Oct. 2013	14,956[a]	15,258 (+2.0%)	15,616 (+4.4%)	National CPI used
Kenya	March 2014	17,578	18,285 (+4.0%)	19,749 (+12.4%)	Urban CPI used
Malawi	Jan. 2014	35,222	39,185 (+11.3%)	50,580 (+43.6%)	Rural CPI used
South Africa	May 2013	3,153[a]	3,431 (+8.8%)	3,616 (+14.7%)	Western Cape Province CPI used

Notes: Changes in taxes were not considered in this table.
[a] Dominican Republic and South Africa original living wage estimates were adjusted to be consistent with the approach used in this manual to calculate gross living wage.

Sources: Inflation rates from: Malawi National Statistics Office; Statistics South Africa; ILO LABORSTA and IMF for Kenya and Dominican Republic.

Government statistical websites also indicate the geographic area for which inflation was estimated and often report separate urban and rural inflation rates. Whenever possible, the CPI for the same geographic area (e.g. rural or urban) for which a living wage was estimated should be used to update a living wage for inflation. For example, we updated our living wage estimate for Western Cape Province using inflation rates for Western Cape Province and we updated our living wage estimate for rural Malawi using rural inflation rates for Malawi.[3]

Table 20.1 indicates how living wages for four living wage studies we have done for the Global Living Wage Coalition would be updated for inflation without considering possible changes in taxes.

20.2 More Frequent Updates Needed for High Inflation Countries

Waiting one year before updating a living wage in very high inflation countries would put workers in a very difficult position. In such situations, a living wage should be increased more frequently. Although there cannot be a hard and fast rule, it seems reasonable to increase a living wage more frequently than every year when inflation is more than 10% annually. Rural

Malawi provides an example of a location where a living wage should be updated more often than annually, since its annual inflation rate has been more than 20% for several years.

20.3 Taking Changes in Taxes and Other Mandatory Deductions into Consideration when Updating a Living Wage for Inflation

It is necessary to take into consideration possible changes in taxes and other mandatory payroll deductions when updating a gross living wage in order to maintain the real value of take home pay. This is likely to be especially important in countries with high inflation rates, progressive tax rates, and low tax thresholds as well as in countries which changed their tax laws. It is possible, for example, for an inflation adjusted living wage to push workers earning living wage into a higher tax bracket. This means that relevant tax laws and payroll deduction rules should be reviewed and taken into consideration when adjusting a living wage for inflation.

20.4 Updating a Living Wage for Economic Development and Improvements in Living Standards and Norms

As countries develop, what people consider as decent improves. For this reason, a living wage is higher in China and Vietnam today than it was one, two, or three decades ago. The issue here is how often a new living wage study should be done so that the living wage represents current decency standards.

We recommend that a new living wage study be done every 5–10 years, depending on how rapidly a country is developing and living standards are improving. We recommend that a new living wage study be done at the earliest five years after an original living wage study and at the latest 10 years after an original study. This recommendation is consistent with recommendations of International Conferences of Labor Statisticians (ICLS) for how frequently to update expenditure weights used to estimate CPI.[4] We do not recommend doing a new living wage study every several years partly because people's expectations and norms change slowly, partly because it is difficult to measure small changes in living conditions and standards, and partly because secondary data used to help estimate a living wage such as 'household expenditure surveys may be conducted only once every five or ten years, or even at longer intervals' (ILO et al., 2004, p. 23).

We recommend that the decision of how soon to do a new living wage study in a country within the 5–10 year recommended period be based on how much real GDP per capita (i.e. GDP per capita adjusted for inflation) increased in a country. We recommend doing a new living wage study when inflation adjusted GDP per capita increases by 50% (or in 10 years at the latest).[5] Data on real GDP per capita are available for virtually all countries from the World Bank and others; a 50% rule is easy to understand and monitor; and a 50% increase in real GDP per capita is large enough for living conditions and norms to improve for most people. To get an idea of how a 50% rule would work in practice, we looked at this for the past 10 years (2005–2015) for the 187 countries in the IMF database.[6] We found that a new living wage benchmark would have been needed before 10 years for 24 (13%) of the 187 countries (e.g. China in six years and India in eight years).[7]

NOTES

1. An alternative approach to using CPI would be to calculate and use a living wage-specific inflation rate for countries that report separate inflation rates for food and housing (using living wage-specific expenditure weights for food, housing, and other). We do not generally recommend this approach despite its advantage conceptually partly because it is more complicated, partly because such an inflation rate would not be as widely recognized or accepted as CPI, and partly because many countries do not publish separate food and housing inflation rates. However, we do suggest calculating and using a living wage-specific inflation rate in years when there is a spike in food costs in order to ensure that the real value of the living wage is maintained in such difficult years for workers.
2. It is worth noting that in locations with very large seasonal or month-to-month differences in inflation rates perhaps because of the importance of seasonal commodities, the standard approach to measuring inflation can be misleading for periods of less than one year (e.g. December to July). A way of dealing with this situation 'is to change the focus from short-term month-to-month price indices and instead focus on making year-over-year price comparisons for each month of the year' (ILO et al., 2004, p. 396), since these 'can be viewed as a seasonally adjusted annual consumer price index' (ILO et al., 2004, p. 403). Rural Malawi presents such a situation as from 2007 to 2015, the annual inflation rate for September to February averaged 59.2% whereas it was -28.1% for March to August. For this reason, when we updated a living wage to October from previous December, we used 10/12ths of the reported year-over-year inflation rate for October.
3. IMF reports December to December inflation rates for almost all countries ('Inflation, end of period consumer prices, percentage change') on http://www.imf.org/external/pubs/ft/weo/2015/01/weodata/index.aspx.
4. The 1987 ICLS recommended that expenditure 'weights should be updated periodically, and at least once every ten years' (ILO et al., 2004, p. 65) while the 2003 ICLS recommended that CPI weights be updated 'at least once every five years' (ILO et al., 2004, p. 485).
5. It is also worth considering doing a new living wage study/estimate sooner than 10 years in countries with very high inflation because high inflation disrupts lives and distorts consumer behavior as well as the economy and the job market.
6. We used a three-year average of real GDP per capita (e.g. 2005 used 2003–2005 and 2015 used 2013–2015). This smoothed out annual variations and implicitly assumed a small lag in expectations.
7. Since the 50% rule might be too stringent as it identified only 13% of countries before 10 years, we also looked at a less stringent 42.33% rule (i.e. 4% compound annual growth rate for 9 years). This less stringent rule did not make much difference as only 9 additional countries were picked up as candidates for a new benchmark before 10 years. One reason why the 50% rule did not identify more countries was the 2008/09 financial crisis.

Bibliography

Anker, M. 1991. Epidemiological and statistical methods for rapid health assessment. *World Health Statistics Quarterly*. (44), 94–7.

Anker, R. 2005. A new methodology for estimating internationally comparable poverty lines and living wage rates. Working paper no. 72. Policy Integration Department, Statistical Development and Analysis Group. Geneva: ILO.

Anker, R. 2006. Living wages around the world: A new methodology and internationally comparable estimates. *International Labour Review*. 145(4), 309–38.

Anker, R. 2006a. Poverty lines around the world: A new methodology and internationally comparable estimates. *International Labour Review*. 145(4), 279–307.

Anker, R. 2011. *Estimating a living wage: A methodological review*. Conditions of Work and Employment Series No. 29. Geneva: ILO.

Anker, R. 2011a. Engel's law around the world 150 years later. *Political Economy Research Institute (PERI) working paper 247*. Amherst, Massachusetts: University of Massachusetts.

Anker, R. and Anker, M. 1989. Measuring the female labour force in Egypt. *International Labour Review*. 128(4), 511–20.

Anker, R. and Anker, M. 2013. *A shared approach to estimating living wages: A short description of the shared methodology*. London: ISEAL Alliance. Available at www.isealalliance.org/sites/default/files/Descripton%20of%20Living%20Wage%20Methodology%2020131124.pdf [Accessed 14 December 2014].

Anker, R. and Anker, M. 2013a. *Living wage for rural Dominican Republic with focus on banana growing area of the North*. Fairtrade International, Social Accountability International. Available at www.isealalliance.org/sites/default/files/LivingWageReportEnglish_DomRep.pdf [Accessed 5 January 2016].

Anker, R. and Anker, M. 2013b. *Living wage for rural South Africa with focus on wine grape growing area in Western Cape Province*. Fairtrade International. Available at www.isealalliance.org/sites/default/files/LivingWageReport_SouthAfrica.pdf [Accessed 5 January 2016].

Anker, R. and Anker, M. 2013c. *Living wage for Nagpur India*. Unpublished report.

Anker, R. and Anker, M. 2014. *Living wage for Kenya with focus on fresh flower farm area near Lake Naivasha*. Fairtrade International, Sustainable Agriculture Network/Rainforest Alliance and UTZ. Available at www.isealalliance.org/sites/default/files/LivingWageReport_Kenya.pdf [Accessed 5 January 2016].

Anker, R. and Anker, M. 2014a. *Living wage for rural Malawi with focus on tea growing area of southern Malawi*. Fairtrade International, Sustainable Agriculture Network/Rainforest Alliance and UTZ. Available at www.isealalliance.org/sites/default/files/LivingWageReport_Malawi.pdf [Accessed 5 January 2016].

Anker, R. and Anker, M. 2015. *In kind benefits as partial payment of wages: A review of laws around the world*. Unpublished.

Anker, R., Khan, M. E., and Gupta, R. B. 1987. Biases in measuring the labour force: Results of a methods test in Uttar Pradesh, India. *International Labour Review*. 126, 151–67.

Asia Floor Wage. 2015. *What is the Asia Floor wage?* Available at www.asia.floorwage.org/what [Accessed 23 January 2016].

Australian Bureau of Statistics. 2010. *Appendix 4. Owner-occupied housing. Outcome of the 16th Series Australian Consumer Price Index Review, Dec 2010*. Available at www.abs.gov.au/ausstats/abs@.nsf/Latestproducts/6469.0Appendix4Dec%202010?opendocument&tabname=Notes&prodno=6469.0&issue=Dec%202010&num=&view= [Accessed 8 February 2016].

Australian Bureau of Statistics. 2011. *Position paper ABS review of counting homeless methodology*. Available at http:/www.abs.gov.au/ausstats/abs@.nsf/Latestproducts/D27107E6A3B6EAF3CA2578E20019328F?opendocument [Accessed 5 January 2016].

Banco Central de la Republica Dominicana. 2011. *Metodologia indice de precios al consumidor (IPC) base diciembre 2010*. Santo Domingo. Available at www.bancentral.gov.do/publicaciones_economicas/otros/metodologia_IPC_base_diciembre_2010.pdf.

Bangladesh National Nutrition Council. (2013). *Food composition tables for Bangladesh*. BNNC Dhaka.

Barbosa, A., Barbosa e Silva, M., Veiga, J., and Zacareli, M. 2016. *Living wage report rural Brazil Minas Gerais South/Southwestern region coffee growing industry*. Unpublished. Available at www.isealalliance.org/sites/default/files/Living_Wage_Benchmark_Report_Brazil.pdf [Accessed 12 August 2016].

BBC News. 2010. *Bangladesh increases garment worker minimum wage*. Available at www.bbc.com/news/world-south-asia-10779270.

Beals, R. K. 2012. Look at maintenance costs before leaping into homeownership. *US News and World Report* (29 May).

Bender, A. 1992. Meat and meat products in human nutrition in developing countries. *FAO food and nutrition paper 53*. Rome: FAO.

Bilsborrow, R. E., DeGraff, D., and Anker, R. 1998. *Poverty monitoring and rapid assessment surveys*. Geneva: ILO.

Blades, D. 2010. *Owner occupied housing: Housing in ICP 2011 issues to be resolved: Second technical advisory group meeting (February 17–19, 2010)* Page 13. World Bank. Available at http://documents.worldbank.org/curated/en/700381468149399250/pdf/904480WP001-05010Box0385317B0PUBLIC.pdf [Accessed 8 June 2016].

Blake, K. S., Kellerson, R. L. and Simic, A. 2007. *Measuring overcrowding in housing*. Washington DC: US Department of Housing and Urban Development. Available at www.huduser.gov/publications/pdf/measuring_overcrowding_in_hsg.pdf [Accessed 6 February 2016].

Bongaarts, J. 2001. Household size and composition in the developing world. *Population Council working paper 2001 No. 144*. New York: Population Council. Available at www.popcouncil.org/uploads/pdfs/wp/144.pdf [Accessed 24 December 2014].

Bray, M. 1999. *Private costs of public schooling: Household and community financing of public primary education in Cambodia*. Paris: UNESCO. Available at www.datatopics.worldbank.org/hnp/files/edstats/KHMpub99.pdf [Accessed 20 January 2016].

Bray, M. 2007. *The shadow education system: Private tutoring and its implications for planners (2nd edition)*. Paris: UNESCO.

Bray, M. and Bunley, S. 2005. *Balancing the books: Household financing of basic education in Cambodia*. Washington DC: World Bank.

Bureau of Indian Standards. 2002. *Method of measurement of plinth, carpet and rentable areas of buildings* (2nd revision). New Delhi: BIS.

Butte, N. and King, J. C. 2002. *Energy requirements during pregnancy and lactation*. Energy background paper prepared for the joint FAO/WHO/UNU Consultation on Energy in Human Nutrition.

CABE. 2010. *Mapping standards for the home*. Available at http://webarchive.nationalarchives.gov.uk/20110118095356/http:/www.cabe.org.uk/publications/housing-standards [Accessed 8 March 2016].

Cambodia National Institute of Statistics. 2009 (special tabulation, unpublished). *Cambodia socio-economic survey 2009*.

Carlson, A., Lino, M., Juan, W-Y., Hanson, K., and Basiotis, P. P. 2007. *Thrifty food plan, 2006*. (CNPP-19). US Department of Agriculture, Center for Nutrition Policy and Promotion.

CDC. 2006. *Healthy housing reference manual*. Available at www.cdc.gov/nceh/publications/books/housing/cha02.htm [Accessed 5 January 2016].

CDC. 2013. *State indicator report on fruits and vegetables 2013*. National Center for Chronic Disease Prevention and Health Promotion. Available

at www.cdc.gov/nutrition/downloads/State-Indicator-Report-Fruits-Vegetables-2013.pdf [Accessed 5 January 2016].
CDC. 2013a. *Nutrition for everyone: Basics protein*. Available at www.comenius.susqu.edu/biol/010/tobin-janzen/nutrition%20for%20everyone_%20basics_%20protein%20_%20dnpao%20_%20cdc.pdf [Accessed 5 January 2015].
Center for Social Concern. 2016. *The basic needs basket surveys*. Available at www.cfscmalawi.org/bnb.html [Accessed 23 January 2016].
Center on Wisconsin Strategy. 2013. *Living wage ordinances: Experiences, evidence and best practice*. Available at http://www.cows.org/_data/documents/1556.pdf [Accessed 1 January 2016].
Centre for Affordable Housing Finance in Africa. 2015. *2015 Yearbook*. Parkview, South Africa: Centre for Affordable Housing Finance in Africa.
Centro de Estudios Sociales y Demográficos (CESDEM) y Macro International Inc. 2008. *Encuesta Demográfica y de Salud 2007*. Santo Domingo, República Dominicana: CESDEM y Macro International Inc. Spanish document. Available at http://dhsprogram.com/pubs/pdf/FR205/FR205.pdf [Accessed 19 November 2016].
Chastre, C., Duffield, A., Kindness, H., LeJeune, S., and Taylor, A. 2007. *The minimum cost of a healthy diet: Findings from piloting a new methodology in four study locations*. Save the Children. June. Available at www.savethechildren.org.uk/sites/default/files/docs/The_Minimum_Cost_of_a_Healthy_Diet_Final_1.pdf [Accessed 19 November 2016].
China CDC, Institute of Nutrition and Food Safety. 2009. *China Food Composition*. Beijing, China CDC.
Clugston, G. A. undated. *Food and nutritional needs in emergencies*. WHO. Available at www.who.int/nutrition/publications/en/nut_needs_emergencies_text.pdf [Accessed December 2014].
Committee for Population, Family and Children, Hanoi and ORC Macro. 2003. *Vietnam Demographic and Health Survey 2002*. Calverton, Maryland, USA: ICF Macro.
Connecticut Department of Labor, Minimum Wage Regulations, Sec. 31-60-3. Deductions and allowances for reasonable value of board and lodging. Available at https://www.ctdol.state.ct.us/wgwkstnd/laws-regs/adminregs.htm#31-60-3 [Accessed 19 November 2016].
COSATU. 2009. *10th National Congress Declaration*. Johannesburg. Available at www.cosatu.org.za/ [Accessed 1 March 2010].
Cox, A. 2008. Innovative ways sought to house Alex residents. *The Star Newspaper*. 28 April, p. 6.
Deaton, A. 1989. Savings in developing countries: Theory and review. *Proceedings of the World Bank annual conference on development economics*, pp. 61–96.

Diewert, E. 2010. *Notes on the treatment of housing in the national accounts and the ICP*. Washington DC: International Comparison Program.

Dominican Today. 2013. *Dominican Republic president admits wages of misery*. 1 August. Available at www.dominicantoday.com/dr/poverty/2013/8/1/48489/Dominican-Republic-president-admits-wages-of-misery [Accessed 23 January 2016].

Economic Policy Institute (EPI). 2008. *Basic family budget calculator*. Available at www.epi.org. [Accessed 16 January 2016].

Ecuador Ministry of Labor. 2015. *The living wage in Ecuador and other wage policies*.

Ergon Associates. 2012. *Wage ladders introduction and overview*. Presentation to World Banana Forum, Guayaquil, February 2012. Available at www.fao.org/fileadmin/templates/banana/documents/WGs_outputs/WG02/WBF_WG02_Wages_Overview_Ergon__1_.pdf [Accessed 19 August 2016].

Ethical Tea Partnership (ETP). 2015. *Malawi 2020 tea revitalisation programme*. Available at www.ethicalteapartnership.org/wp-content/uploads/Malawi-2020-Factsheet_final3.pdf [Accessed 16 April 2016].

Ethical Tea Partnership and Oxfam. 2013. *Understanding wages in the tea industry*. Available at http://policy-practice.oxfam.org.uk/publications/understanding-wage-issues-in-the-tea-industry-287930 [Accessed 19 August 2016].

ETU. 2014. *Housing subsidies and support services*. Available at www.etu.org.za/toolbox/docs/government/housing.html [Accessed 27 February 2016].

EUFIC (European Food Information Council). 2012. Fruit and vegetable consumption in Europe – do Europeans get enough? *EUFIC REVIEW 01/2012*. Available at www.eufic.org/article/en/expid/Fruit-vegetable-consumption-Europe/ [Accessed 24 July 2014].

EUROSTAT. July 2014. *Housing conditions*. Available at www.ec.europa.eu/eurostat/statistics-explained/index.php/Housing_conditions [Accessed 27 February 2016].

Fair Labor Association (FLA). 2016. *Guide for collection of compensation data*. Unpublished.

Fairtrade International. *Fairtrade standard for hired labour. Version: 15.01.2014_v1.0*. Available at http://www.fairtrade.net/fileadmin/user_upload/content/2009/standards/documents/generic-standards/2015-01-19_HL_EN.pdf [Accessed 19 November 2016].

FAO. 2012. *FAO/INFOODS Databases: Analytical food composition database version 1.0 data base AnFooD1.0*. Available at www.fao.org/infoods/infoods/tables-and-databases/faoinfoods-databases/en/ [Accessed 20 January 2016].

FAO. 2013. Dietary protein quality evaluation in human nutrition. *FAO food and nutrition paper 92*. Rome: FAO.

FAO. 2014. *Definition and classification of commodities*. Available at www.fao.org/waicent/faoinfo/economic/faodef/faodefe.htm [Accessed 10 November 2014].

FAO. 2014a. *Milk and dairy products in human nutrition: Questions and answers*. Available at www.fao.org/fileadmin/user_upload/newsroom/docs/Milk%20and%20Dairy%20Q&A.pdf [Accessed 6 August 2014].

FAO/INFOODS. 2014. *Online food composition database*. Available at www.fao.org/infoods/infoods/tables-and-databases/international-databases/en/ [Accessed 5 January 2016].

Feng, S., Hu, Y., and Moffitt, R. 2015. *Long run trends in unemployment and labor force participation in China*. Cambridge: National Bureau of Economic Research.

GLA Economics. 2015. *A fairer London: The 2015 living wage in London*. London: Greater London Authority.

Glickman, L. 1997. *A living wage: American workers and the making of consumer society*. Ithaca, NY: Cornell University Press.

Global Living Wage Coalition (GLWC). 2016. Available at www.isealalliance.org/sites/default/files/GLWC_who_we_are.pdf [Accessed 21 September 2016].

Goldschmidt-Clermont, L. 1982. *Unpaid work in the household: A review of economic evaluation methods*. Geneva: ILO.

Goldschmidt-Clermont, L. 1987. *Economic evaluations of unpaid household work: Africa, Asia, Latin America and Oceana*. Geneva: ILO.

GoodWeave International. 2014. *Generic international standard for rug producers. Draft version 2.5.1 May 2014*. Available at www.goodweave.org/uploads/GoodWeave-Standard-First-Stage-v-2-5-1-May-2014.pdf [Accessed 27 February 2016].

Government of India, Ministry of Home Affairs. 2010–2011. *Census terms*. Available at www.censusindia.gov.in/Data_Products/Library/Indian_perceptive_link/Census_Terms_link/censusterms.html [Accessed 3 February 2016].

Government of India, Ministry of Housing and Urban Poverty Alleviation. 2012. Press release 2012. *Income criteria for EWS & LIG revised upwards for defining beneficiaries under government schemes for housing*. Available at www.pib.nic.in/newsite/erelease.aspx?relid=89039 [Accessed 27 February 2016].

Government of India, Ministry of Housing and Urban Poverty Alleviation. 2013. *Affordable housing in partnership: Scheme guidelines*. Available at www.mhupa.gov.in/writereaddata/AHP-Guidelines.pdf [Accessed 27 February 2016].

Government of India, Ministry of Housing and Urban Poverty Alleviation (JNNUM Directorate). 2013a. *Prototype interactive public questions and answers*. Available at www.mhupa.gov.in/writereaddata/nbo.pdf [Accessed 27 February 2016].

Government of India, National Institute of Nutrition. 2010. *Dietary guidelines for Indians: A manual*. Hyderabad, India: National Institute of Nutrition. Indian Council of Medical Research. Available at http://ninindia.org/dietaryguidelinesforninwebsite.pdf [Accessed 23 September 2016].

Government of Maharashtra, Directorate of Economics and Statistics, Planning Department. 2011. *A report on household consumption expenditure based on data collected in state sample of 63rd round of national sample survey (July, 2006–June, 2007)*. Mumbai: Directorate of Economics and Statistics, Planning Department, Government of Maharashtra, Mumbai.

Government of Maharashtra. undated. *A report on "housing condition" based on data collected in state sample of 65th round of national sample survey (July, 2008–June, 2009) Vol 1*. Mumbai: Directorate of Economics and Statistics, Planning Department, Government of Maharashtra.

Government of Malawi, National Statistical Office (NSO) and ICF Macro. 2011. *Malawi demographic and health survey 2010*. Zomba, Malawi and Calverton, Maryland, USA: NSO and ICF Macro.

Government of Sri Lanka, Department of Census and Statistics, Ministry of Policy Planning Economic Affairs, Child Youth and Cultural Affairs. 2015. *Household income and expenditure survey 2012/13 final report*. Available at www.statistics.gov.lk/HIES/HIES2012_13FinalReport.pdf [Accessed 23 September 2016].

Government of Vietnam, National Institute of Nutrition. 2014. *Minimum living subsistence for common areas 2013–2020*. In Vietnamese. Unpublished.

Gyourko, J. and Tracy, J. 2005. *Using home maintenance and repairs to smooth variable earnings*. Federal Reserve Bank of New York. Available at www.newyorkfed.org/medialibrary/media/research/economists/tracy/home_maintenance.pdf [Accessed 8 February 2016].

Habitat for Humanity, Africa and Middle East Office. 2008. *A right to a decent home: Mapping poverty housing in the Africa & Middle East Region*. Pretoria. Available at www.downloads.habitatforhumanity.org.uk/MappingPovertyHousingInAME.pdf [Accessed 23 September 2016].

Hadi, A. N. B. A. 2014. *Housing policy and housing program in Malaysia*. Gelugor, Penang: Universiti Sains Malaysia.

Hall, J., Moore, S., Harper, S. and Lynch, J. 2009. Global variability in fruit and vegetable consumption. *Am J Prev Med*. 36(5), 402–9.

Heston, A. 2013. Chapter 12 Dwelling services. In: *Measuring the real size of the world economy.* Washington DC: World Bank, pp. 319–42.

House of Commons Library. 2011. *Housing: Overcrowding*. SN/SP/1013.

Howden, D. 2014. Kenyan parents sue ministers over illegal school fees. *The Guardian*. 24 January.

Human Resources Development Canada (HRDC). 2003. *Understanding the 2000 low income statistics based on market basket measure*. Ottawa: Government of Canada.

ILO. 1919. Constitution, Geneva. Available at www.ilo.org/ilolex [Accessed 16 December 2010].

ILO. 1928. *Methods of compiling housing statistics. Studies and reports. Series N (Statistics). No. 13.* Geneva: ILO. Available at http://staging.ilo.org/public/libdoc/ilo/ILO-SR/ILO-SR_N13_engl.pdf [Accessed 15 January 2016].

ILO. 1935. Resolution of the committee of statistical experts of the International Labour Office, Second session, Geneva, 16–18 December 1935, in International Labour Office, *The International Standardization of Labour Statistics. A review of the statistical work of the International Labour Office and various international statistical conferences* Studies and Reports, Series N (Statistics) No. 25. (Revision of No. 19).

ILO. 1944. *Declaration concerning the aims and purposes of the International Labour Organisation (Declaration of Philadelphia)*. Available at www.ilo.org/ilolex [Accessed 16 December 2010].

ILO. 1949. *Protection of Wages Convention, No. 95*. Available at www.ilo.org/dyn/normlex/en/f?p=NORMLEXPUB:12100:0::NO::P12100_INSTRUMENT_ID:312240 [Accessed 22 January 2016].

ILO. 1951. *Equal Remuneration Convention No. 100*. Available at www.ilo.org/dyn/normlex/en/f?p=NORMLEXPUB:12100:0::NO::P12100_ILO_CODE:C100 [Accessed 21 January 2016].

ILO. 1958. *Plantations Convention, No. 110*. Available at www.ilo.org/dyn/normlex/en/f?p=NORMLEXPUB:12100:0::NO::P12100_ILO_CODE:C110 [Accessed 15 August 2016].

ILO. 1961. *Recommendation No. 115 Concerning Worker's Housing*. Available at http://www.ilo.org/dyn/normlex/en/f?p=NORMLEXPUB:12100:0::NO::P12100_INSTRUMENT_ID:312453 [Accessed 15 August 2016].

ILO. 1962. *Social Policy (Basic Aims and Standards) Convention. No 117*. Available at www.ilo.org/dyn/normlex/en/f?p=NORMLEXPUB:12100:0::NO:12100:P12100_INSTRUMENT_ID:312262:NO [Accessed 15 August 2016].

ILO. 1970. *Minimum Wage Fixing Convention No. 131*. Available at www.ilo.org/ilolex [Accessed 16 December 2010].

ILO. 1982. *13th International Conference of Labour Statisticians*. Geneva: ILO.

ILO. 1992. *Minimum wages: Wage fixing machinery, application and supervision. Report III (Part 4B) for International Labor Conference 79th Session*. Geneva: ILO.

ILO. 2003. *Protection of wages. Report for International Labor Conference 91st Session*. Geneva: ILO.

ILO. 2006. *Tripartite declaration of principles concerning multinational enterprises and social policy (MNE declaration)*. Available at www.ilo.org/empent/Publications/WCMS_211136/lang--en/index [Accessed August 2016].

ILO. 2008. *Declaration on social justice for fair globalization*. Available at www.ilo.org/ilolex [Accessed 16 December 2010].

ILO. 2008a. *Global wage report 2008/09*. Geneva: ILO.

ILO. 2011. *C189 – Domestic Workers Convention, 2011 (No. 189)*. Available at www.ilo.org/dyn/normlex/en/f?p=NORMLEXPUB:12100:0::NO::P12100_ILO_CODE:C189 [Accessed 31 January 2016].

ILO. 2013. Growth, employment and social cohesion in the Dominican Republic. *ILO background paper for ILO-IMF tripartite consultation on job-rich and inclusive growth in the Dominican Republic*. Santo Domingo. 30 January.

ILO. 2013a. *Key indicators of the labour market (KILM)*. Geneva: ILO. Available at www.ilo.org/empelm/what/WCMS_114240/lang--en/index.htm [Accessed December 2014].

ILO. 2014. *General survey on minimum wage systems 2014. International Labor Conference 103rd session*. Geneva: ILO.

ILO. 2014a. *Viet Nam wage policy in the context of market economy and economic integration*. Hanoi: ILO. Available at www.ilo.org/wcmsp5/groups/public/---asia/---ro-bangkok/---ilo-hanoi/documents/publication/wcms_322656.pdf [Accessed 23 September 2016].

ILO/IMF/OECD/UNECE/Eurostat/The World Bank. 2004. *Consumer price manual*. Geneva: ILO.

ILO, LABORSTA, HIES. undated. *Household income and expenditure survey database*. Available at http://laborsta.ilo.org/STP/guest [Accessed 14 January 2016].

IMF. undated. *World economic outlook database*. Available at www.imf.org/external/pubs/ft/weo/2015/01/weodata/index.aspx [Accessed 29 February 2016].

International Code Council. 2009. *International Residential Code R304 for one and two family dwellings. Minimum room area*. Available at https://law.resource.org/pub/us/code/ibr/icc.irc.2009.html [Accessed 23 September 2016].

International Textile, Garment and Leather Workers' Federation. 2008. *Bargaining for a living wage: A trade union guide*. Available at www.cleanclothes.org/resources/recommended-reading/bargaining-for-a-living-wage-a-trade-union-guide [Accessed 12 April 2016].

Ireland, Office of the Attorney General. 1966. *Housing Act 1966. Part IV, Section 63. Overcrowded and unfit houses*.

Kenya Revenue Authority, Domestic Taxes Department. 2009. *Employers guide to pay as you earn in Kenya, revised edition, form P.7*. Available at www.revenue.go.ke/incometax/pdf/PAYRuide2009.pdf.

Khan, M. E., Anker, R., Anker, M. and Barge, S. 2016. *Living wage report, Dhaka, Bangladesh and satellite cities: Context the garment industry*. Available at http://www.isealalliance.org/sites/default/files/Dhaka_Living_Wage_Benchmark_Report.pdf [Accessed 17 September 2016].

KNBS (Kenya National Bureau of Statistics). 2007. *Basic report on well-being in Kenya based on Kenya Integrated Household Budget Survey 2005/06)*. Nairobi: Kenya National Bureau of Statistics.

KNBS (Kenya National Bureau of Statistics). 2015. *Consumer price indices, CPI and inflation rates, Table 3: National Average Prices of Selected Commodities*. Available at www.knbs.or.ke/index.php?option=com_phocadownload&view=category&id=14:cpi-and-inflation-rates-2013&Itemid=599 [Accessed 20 January 2016].

KNBS (Kenya National Bureau of Statistics) and MEASURES DHS. 2010. *Kenya demographic and health survey 2008–09*. Calverton, Maryland, USA: ICF Macro.

Labowitz, S. and Bauman-Pauly, D. 2015. *Beyond the tip of the iceberg: Bangladesh's forgotten apparel workers*. New York: New York University, Stern Center for Business and Human Rights. Available at http://people.stern.nyu.edu/twadhwa/bangladesh/maps.html [Accessed 10 February 2016].

Lally, A. 2011. *Wage ladder background study. Fair Wear Foundation*. Available at www.fairwear.org/ul/cms/fck-uploaded/documents/fwfpublications_reports/wageladderbackgroundstudy.pdf [Accessed 23 January 2016].

Living Wage Foundation. *Living wage employers*. Available at www.livingwage.org.uk/employers [Accessed 5 March 2016].

Luce, S. 2004. *Fighting for a living wage*. Ithaca: ILR Press.

Luers, W. M., 1998. Workfare wages under the Fair Labor Standards Act. *Fordham Law Review*. 67 (1), 203–38.

Maharashtra Housing and Area Development Authority (MHADHA). 2014. *Affordable housing in joint partnership with private land owners/developers*. Available at https://mhada.maharashtra.gov.in/?q=affordable housing [Accessed 10 September 2014].

Mathenge, M. and Tschirley, D. 2006. *Seasonal analysis of selected fresh fruit and vegetable prices at wholesale level in key urban markets of Kenya, Working paper 22*. Tegemeo Institute/Egerton University and the Department of Agricultural Economics at Michigan State University. Available at http://fsg.afre.msu.edu/kenya/WPS22.pdf [Accessed 9 January 2016].

McMullen, A. and Maher, S. 2011. *Let's clean up fashion 2009: The state of pay behind the high street*. Labour Behind the Label. Available at www.women-ww.org/documents/LBL-LCUF2011.pdf [Accessed 5 January 2016].

McMullen, A., Luginbühl, C., Nolan, K., Crabbé, C. and Ajaltouni, N. 2014. *Tailored wages: Are the big brands paying the people who make our clothes enough to live on?* Labour Behind the Label. Available at www.cleanclothes.org/livingwage/tailoredwages/tailored-wage-report-pdf [Accessed 5 January 2016].

Millward, D. J. 2013. The use of protein: Energy ratios for defining protein requirements, allowances and dietary protein contents. *Public Health Nutrition*. 16(5), 763–8.

Moolla, R., Kotze, N. and Block, L. 2011. Housing satisfaction and quality of life in RDP houses in Braamfischerville, Soweto: A South African case study. *Ubaani izziv*. 22(1), 138–43.

Muehlhoff, E., Bennett, A. and McMahon, E., 2013. *Milk and dairy products in human nutrition*. Rome: FAO.

Nadeau, C. A. with Schultheis, E., prepared for Glasmeier, A. K. 2014 update. *Living wage calculator: User's guide/technical notes*. Cambridge: Department of Urban Studies and Planning. Massachusetts Institute of Technology.

National Statistical Office (NSO) and ICF Macro. 2011. *Malawi demographic and health survey 2010*. Zomba Malawi and Calverton, Maryland, USA: NSO and ICF Macro. Available at http://dhsprogram.com/pubs/pdf/FR247/FR247.pdf [Accessed 23 September 2016].

NICUS (Nutrition Information Center University of Stellenbosch, South Africa). 2007. *How to eat correctly*. Available at www.sun.ac.za/english/faculty/healthsciences/nicus/how-to-eat-correctly/nutrients/dri [Accessed 23 September 2016].

OECD. 2002. *Glossary of statistical terms, payments in kind*. Available at http://stats.oecd.org/glossary/detail.asp?ID=2026 [Accessed 31 January 2016].

OECD and Statistics Norway. 2010. *User cost for rents of dwellings in the West Balkan Countries*. Washington DC: International Comparison Program.

OECD/WHO. 2012. *Health at a glance: Asia/Pacific 2012*. Paris: OECD Publishing. DOI: http://dx.doi.org/10.1787/9789264183902-en.

Office of the High Commissioner for Human Rights. 1991. *Sixth session, General Comment 4. The Right to Adequate Housing (Article 11 (1) of the Covenant Document E/1991/23.*

Oficina Nacional de Estadistica. (Special tabulation unpublished) 2007. *Encuesta nacional de Ingresos y gastos de los hogares: Resultados generals 2007*. Santo Domingo.

Oficina Nacional de Estadistica and Ministero de Economia, Planificacion y Desarrollo. 2012. *IX Censo nacional de poblacion y vivienda 2010. Characteristicas de la vivienda y del hogar volumen II*. October 2012. Santo Domingo: Oficina Nacional de Estadistica and Ministero de Economia, Planificacion y Desarrollo.

Pindyck, R. S. and Rubinfield, D. L. 2012. *Micro Economics, 8th edition*. Upper Saddle River, New Jersey: Prentice Hall.

Pope Leo XIII. 1891. *Rerum Novarum: Encyclical on human work on capital and labour*. Available at http://w2.vatican.va/content/leo-xiii/en/encyclicals/documents/hf_l-xiii_enc_15051891_rerum-novarum.html [Accessed 5 January 2016].

Pottie, D. 2003. Housing the nation: The politics of low-cost housing policy in South Africa since 1994. *Politeia*. 22(1), 119–43.

Prentice, A. M. and Prentice, A. 1988. Energy costs of lactation. *Ann. Rev. Nutr*. 8, 63–79.

Ravaillon, M. 1998. Poverty lines in theory and practice. *Living standards measurement study working paper No. 133*. Washington DC: World Bank.

Republic of Kenya, Ministry of Housing. 2004. *Sessional paper No. 3 of 2004 on national housing policy for Kenya*. Nairobi.

Republic of Kenya, National Building and Planning Authority. 2009. *Planning and Building Regulations 2009*. Volume A. Republic of Kenya, National Building and Planning Authority. Nairobi. Available at https://law.resource.org/pub/ke/ibr/ke.building.2009.html.

Republic of Malawi. 2005. *Integrated Household Survey 2004–2005*. Zomba: National Statistical Office.

Republic of Malawi, National Statistical Office. 2010b. *Population and housing census 2008. Analytical report: Volume 10. Economic activity*. December 2010. Zomba, Malawi: Republic of Malawi, National Statistical Office.

Republic of Malawi. 2012. *Third Integrated Household Survey (IHS-3) 2010–2011. Household socio-economic characteristics report*. Zomba: National Statistical Office.

Republic of Mauritius, Ministry of Housing and Lands. undated. Available at http://housing.govmu.org/English/Pages/default.aspx [Accessed 8 March 2016].

Republic of South Africa. 1997. *South African Basic Conditions of Employment Act No. 75 of 1997 for Farm Worker Section*. Capetown

Republic of South Africa. 1998. *Government Gazette, Housing Consumer Protection Act No. 95 1998*. Capetown.

Riddell, A. 2003. *The introduction of free primary education in sub-Saharan Africa*. UNESCO. Available at http://unesdoc.unesco.org/images/0014/001469/146914e.pdf [Accessed 20 January 2016].

Rockefeller, J. D. 1921. Co-operation in industry. *International Labour Review*, 2(1).

Roosevelt, F. D. 1944. *State of the Union message to Congress*. Available at www.presidency.uscb.edu/ws/index.php?pid-16518 [Accessed 31 March 2010].

Ruel, M., Minot, N. and Smith, L. 2005. *Patterns and determinants of fruit and vegetable consumption in sub-Saharan Africa: A multi-country comparison*. Geneva: WHO. Available at www.who.int/dietphysicalactivity/publications/f&v_africa_economics.pdf?ua=1 [Accessed 24 July 2014].

Ryan, J. 1906. *A living wage: Its ethical and economic impacts*. New York: Macmillan Co.

Seale, J. L. and Regmi, A. 2006. Modeling international consumption patterns. *Review of Income and Wealth*. 52(4), 603–24.

Schappert, S. and Rechsteiner, E. 2008. Ambulatory medical care utilization estimates for 2006. *NHSR Number 8*. CDC.

Schoenfeldt, H. C. and Hall, N. G. 2012. Dietary protein quality and malnutrition in Africa. *British Journal of Nutrition*. 108, Supplement S2, S69–S76.

Schwartz, M. and Wilson, E. undated. *Who can afford to live in a home? A look at data from the 2006 American Community Survey*. US Census Bureau. Available at www.census.gov/housing/census/publications/who-can-afford.pdf [Accessed 8 April 2016].

Shaheen, N., Rahim, A. T., Banu, M., Bari, L., Tukun, A. B., Mannan, M. A., Bhattacharjee, L., and Stadlmayr, B. 2013. *Food composition tables for Bangladesh*. Institute of Nutrition and Food Science, Centre for Advanced Research in Sciences, University of Dhaka, Dhaka, Bangladesh.

Smith, A. 1776 (1982 edition). *The wealth of nations*. London: Penguin Books.

Social Accountability International (SAI), personal communication. 2014. *Codes of practice*.

State Bank of Mauritius. *Loan calculator*. Available at www.sbmgroup.mu/loan_calculator.php?lang=en [Accessed 30 March 2016].

Statistics Mauritius. Ministry of Finance and Economic Development. 2015. *Household budget survey 2012. Analytical report*. Port Louis.

Statistics South Africa. 2008. Housing in the Consumer Price Index. Pretoria, p. 3. Available at www.statssa.gov.za/cpi/documents/Housing%20in%20the%20SA%20CPI%201%20July%2008%20final.pdf [Accessed 12 August 2016].

Statistics South Africa. 2009. *Consumer Price Index (CPI) 2008 weights* (primary urban areas) Statistical release P0141.5. Pretoria.

Sustainable Agricultural Network/Rainforest Alliance. 2005. *Sustainable Agriculture Standard.* Available at www.rainforest-alliance.org/business/agriculture/documents/standards_indicators_2005.pdf [Accessed 4 March 2016].

Tabatabai, H. 1996. *Statistics on poverty and income distribution: An ILO compendium*. Geneva: ILO.

Tariq, F. undated. *Facilitating community development with housing microfinance: Appraising housing solutions for Pakistan after disasters.* Available at http://web.mit.edu/incrementalhousing/articlesPhotographs/pdfs/TARIQ-COMMUNITY=PAKISTAN.pdf [Accessed 29 February 2016].

Thale, T. 2001. *New plan for better housing, City of Johannesburg.* 16 November. Available at www.joburgnews.co.za/november/housing.stm [Accessed 10 August 2008].

The Economist. 2014. Education in Kenya, classroom divisions: Paid-for private schools are better value for money than the "free" sort. *The Economist*. 22 February. Available at www.economist.com/news/middle-east-and-africa/21596981-paid-private-schools-are-better-value-money-free-sort-classroom [Accessed 12 January 2016].

Theobald, H. E. 2005. Dietary calcium and health. *Nutrition Bulletin*. 30(3), 237–77.

Thibbotuwawa, M. 2016. Personal communication.

Thiele, B. 2002. The human right to adequate housing: A tool for promoting and protecting individual and community health. *American Journal of Public Health*. 92(5), 712–15.

Thom, K. 2013. Escom tariff hike. . . Malawi to become highest in the region. *BNL Times*. 12 December.

Thorpe, V. 2007. *Executive summary of the final report of the Jo-In project in Turkey*. Available at http://www.jo-in.org/english/resimler/080623_JO-IN_Final_Report.pdf [Accessed 4 October 2014].

United Kingdom Housing Act. 1985. *Housing Act 1985: Part X – Definition of Overcrowding*.

UN-Habitat. 2003. *The challenge of slums*. Nairobi: UN-Habitat.

UN-Habitat. 2003a. *Slums of the world: The face of urban poverty in the new millennium?* Nairobi: UN-Habitat.

UN-Habitat. 2006. *State of the world's cities report 2006/07*. Nairobi: UN-Habitat.

UN-Habitat. 2009. *Urban indicators guidelines*. Nairobi: UN-Habitat.

UN-Habitat. 2013. *State of the world's cities 2012/13*. Nairobi: UN-Habitat.

United Nations. 1948. *Universal Declaration of Human Rights*. Available at www.un.org/en/universal-declaration-human-rights/ [Accessed 5 January 2016].

United Nations. 1957. *Standard Minimum Rules for the Treatment of Prisoners, Economic and Social Council Resolution 663 C I (XXIV) and 2076 (LXII)*. New York: United Nations. Available at www.unodc.org/pdf/criminal_justice/UN_Standard_Minimum_Rules_for_the_Treatment_of_Prisoners.pdf [Accessed 15 January 2016].

United Nations. 1959. *Declaration of the Rights of the Child: General Assembly Resolution 1386(XIV)*. New York: United Nations.

United Nations. 1966. *International Covenant on Economic, Social and Cultural Rights: General Assembly Resolution 2200A (XXI)*. New York: United Nations.

United Nations. 1998. *Principles and recommendations for population and housing censuses. Rev 1*. New York: United Nations. Available at http://unstats.un.org/unsd/demographic/sconcerns/housing/housingmethods.htm [Accessed 4 February 2016].

United Nations. 2015. *2030 Agenda for sustainable development*. Available at www.un.org/sustainabledevelopment/sustainable-development-goals/ [Accessed 5 January 2016].

United Nations. 2016. *UNDATA glossary*. Available at http://data.un.org/Glossary.aspx?q=total+fertility+rate [Accessed 3 February 2016].

United Nations, Department of Economic and Social Affairs, Statistical Division. 2008. Principle and recommendations for population and housing censuses, Revision 2. *Statistical papers. Series M No.67/Rev.2*. New York: United Nations.

United Nations, Population Division. 2000. *Charting the Progress of Populations. Chapter XII: Floor area per person*. ST/ESA/SER.R/151.

United Nations Statistics Division. 1999. *Classification of Individual Consumption according to Purpose (COICOP)*. Available at http://unstats.un.org/unsd/cr/registry/regcst.asp?Cl=5 [Accessed 1 February 2014].

United Nations Statistics Division. 2016. *UNdata*. Available at http://data.un.org/Glossary.aspx?q=Total+fertility+rate+(TFR) [Accessed 15 August 2016].

United Nations. undated. *Official list of MDG indicators*. Available at http://mdgs.un.org/unsd/mdg/host.aspx?Content=indicators/officiallist.htm [Accessed 5 January 2016].

UNESCO. 2014. Data Centre. *Regional and country profiles*. Available at http://www.uis.unesco.org/DataCentre/Pages/regions.aspx [Accessed 20 January 2016].

UNHCR. 2007. *Handbook for emergencies, 3rd edition*. Geneva: UNHCR.

UNICEF. 2014. *The Children: Primary School Years*. Available at http://www.unicef.org/kenya/children_3795.html [Accessed 20 January 2016].

UNICEF. 2015. *Current status + progress: Rapid acceleration of progress is needed to achieve universal primary education by 2015*. Available at http://data.unicef.org/education/primary [Accessed 12 January 2016].

United States Department of Housing and Urban Development. 2007. *Measuring overcrowding in housing, 2007*. Washington DC.

United States Department of Labor, Wage and Hour Division (WHD). undated. *Davis-Bacon and related acts.* Available at http://www.dol.gov/whd/programs/dbra/faqs/fringes.htm [Accessed 22 January 2016].

United States Federal Government. 1938. Wage payments under the Fair Labor Standards Act of 1938 (29 C.F.R. 531) §531.30 "Furnished" to the employee.

United States Institute of Medicine. 1991. *Nutrition during lactation*. Washington, DC: National Academy Press.

USDA. 2007. *The low-cost, moderate-cost, and liberal food plans*. Center for Nutrition Policy and Promotion. CNPP-20. Washington DC.

USDA NAL (National Agricultural Library). 2014. *National nutrient database for standard reference release 27*. Available at http://ndb.nal.usda.gov/ [Accessed 14 December 2014].

Uttar Pradesh Housing and Development Board (UPAVP), Architectural and Planning Section. 2014. *Plans and development for affordable housing: Designs for EWS houses*. Lucknow.

UTZ, personal communication. 2014. *Code of conduct*.

Van der Hoeven, R. and Anker R. (eds.). 1994. *Poverty monitoring: An international concern*. New York: St Martins Press.

Vietnam General Confederation of Labor, Institute of Workers and Trade Unions. 2013. *Report on minimum living needs of employees in enterprises in 2013*. Hanoi. Unpublished.

Vietnam Government. 2005. *Housing Law 2005; Section 4 Social housing development article 47 (2)*. Hanoi.

Vietnam Government, General Statistics Office. 2012. *Data result of the Viet Nam household living standards survey 2010*. Hanoi.

Vietnam National Wage Council Technical Division. 2014. *Report: Identifying minimum living needs of workers*. Hanoi. Unpublished.

Wang, S., Wang, Y., Gu, F., and Lu, D. 2016. *Living wage for Shenzhen with focus on manufacturing industrial parks*.

Weaver, C. M, Proulx, W. R. and Heaney, R. 1999. Choices for achieving adequate dietary calcium with a vegetarian diet. *The American Journal of Clinical Nutrition*. 70 (3 Suppl), 543S–548S.

WHO. 1985. *Energy and protein requirements: Report of a joint FAO/WHO/UNU expert consultation*. WHO Technical Report Series No. 724. Geneva: WHO.

WHO. 1989. *Health principles of housing*. Geneva: WHO.

WHO. 2003. *Joint WHO/FAO expert consultation on diet, nutrition and the prevention of chronic diseases*. Geneva: WHO.

WHO. 2004. *Human energy requirements: Report of a joint FAO/WHO/UNU expert consultation*, Rome, Italy, 17–24 October 2001. Available at http://www.who.int/nutrition/publications/nutrientrequirements/9251052123/en/ [Accessed 6 September 2016].

WHO. 2013. *Technical notes on drinking-water, sanitation and hygiene in emergencies: How much water is needed in emergencies?* Geneva: WHO.

WHO. 2015. *Guideline: Sugars intake for adults and children*. WHO, Geneva.

WHO. undated. Website on nutrition. Available at http://www.who.int/nutrition/topics/5_population_nutrient/en/index1.html [Accessed 7 August 2016].

WHO/FAO. 2003. *Diet, nutrition and the prevention of chronic disease: Report of a Joint WHO/FAO Expert Consultation*. WHO technical report series 916. Geneva: WHO. Available at http://www.who.int/dietphysicalactivity/publications/trs916/en/gsfao_introduction.pdf?ua=1 [Accessed 19 November 2016].

WHO/FAO/UNU. 2007. *Protein and amino acid requirements in human nutrition: Report of a WHO/FAO/UNU expert consultation*. WHO Technical Report Series 935. Geneva: WHO.

Wikipedia *Average height around the world*. Available at http://en.wikipedia.org/wiki/Template:Average_height_around_the_world [Accessed 14 December 2014].

Williams, F. M., Steibling H. K., Swisher, I. G., and Weiss, G. S. 1937. *Family living in Knott County, Ky. U.S. Department of Agriculture Technical Bulletin No. 576*. Department of Agriculture. Washington DC.

Wodon, Q. and Beegle, K. 2006. Labor shortages despite underemployment? Seasonality in time use in Malawi, in Blackden, M. and Wodon, Q. (eds.). *Gender, time use and poverty in Sub-Saharan Africa*. Working paper 73. Washington DC: World Bank.

Woetzel, J., Ram, S., Mishke, J., Garemo, N., and Sankhe, S. 2014. *A blueprint for addressing the global affordable housing challenge*. McKinsey Global Institute.

Worker Rights Consortium. 2010. *Living wage analysis for the Dominican Republic*. Washington DC: Worker Rights Consortium. Available at http://ciee.typepad.com/files/wrc-living-wage-analysis-for-the-dominican-republic-2.pdf [Accessed 15 August 2016].

World Bank. 2007. *Malawi poverty and vulnerability assessment: Investing in our future, synthesis report*. Washington DC: World Bank. Available at https://openknowledge.worldbank.org/handle/10986/7557. License: CC BY 3.0 Unreported.

World Bank. 2014. *The face of poverty in Europe and Central Asia*. Available at http://www.worldbank.org/en/news/feature/2014/02/10/face-of-poverty-in-europe-and-central-asia [Accessed 23 January 2016].

World Bank. 2015. *Latin America's poverty gains due more to higher wages than better job*. Available at http://www.worldbank.org/en/news/press-release/2015/06/03/latin-america-poverty-gains-higher-wages-better-jobs [Accessed 23 January 2016].

World Bank. 2015a. *GINI index (World Bank estimates)*. Available at http://data.worldbank.org/indicator/SI.POV.GINI [Accessed 29 January 2016].

World Bank. 2015b. *Millennium development goals*. Available at http://data.worldbank.org/data-catalog/millennium-development-indicators [Accessed 12 January 2016].

World Bank. 2016. *Net enrollment rate, secondary, both sexes (%)*. Available at http://data.worldbank.org/indicator/SE.SEC.NENR/countries/1W-ZF-4E-8S?display=graph [Accessed 20 January 2016].

World Bank. 2016a. *PPP conversion factor, private consumption (LCU per international $)*. Available at http://data.worldbank.org/indicator/PA.NUS.PPP [Accessed 23 January 2016].

World Bank. 2016b. *World Development Indicators*. Available at http://data.worldbank.org/indicator [Accessed 3 February 2016].

World Bank. undated. *Poverty and equity data FAQs*. Available at http://data.worldbank.org/indicator [Accessed 7 September 2015].

Wozniak, L. 2015. *Taking stock of 13th month and 14th month bonus requirements in Latin America, Europe, and Asia*. Available at https://www.radford.com/home/insights/articles/2015/taking_stock_of_13th_14th_month_bonuses_in_latam_europe_asia.asp [Accessed 4 March 2016].

Zhou, Z., Tian, W., Wang, J., Liu, H. and Cao, L. 2012. *Food consumption trends in China. Report for the Australian Government Department of Agriculture, Fisheries and Forestry*.

Zimmerman, C. 1932. Ernst Engel's law of expenditures for food. *The Quarterly Journal of Economics*. 47(1), 78–101.

Index